A House Where All Belong

Redesigning Education Abroad for Inclusive Excellence

About the Series

Standards in Action (2022–) is a book series that seeks to bridge big ideas and foundational principles in education abroad to the creative approaches and practical tactics that can turn those concepts into reality. As our field seeks to face down hard challenges and reinvent itself for the future, these books provide the inspiration and the guidance needed to usher in the new era. The series is curated by Amelia J. Dietrich, Senior Director for Research and Publications at The Forum on Education Abroad.

Other titles in this series:

The Half Yet to Be Told: Study Abroad and HBCUs
Voices from the South: Decolonial Perspectives in International Education
Sustainable Education Abroad: Striving for Change

ISSN: 2833-0595
For more information, visit: https://www.forumea.org/standards-in-action

Standards in Action Series

A House Where All Belong

Redesigning Education Abroad for Inclusive Excellence

Nick J. Gozik and Heather Barclay Hamir
Editors

The *Standards in Action* series is published by The Forum on Education Abroad, the standards development organization (SDO) for the field of Education abroad as recognized by the U.S. Department of Justice and the Federal Trade Commission. For more information, visit www.forumea.org

ISBN: 978-1-952376-21-4 (paperback)

ISBN: 978-1-952376-23-8 (ebook)

doi.org/10.36366/SIA.1.978-1-952376-21-4

Library of Congress Control Number: 2022944115

Printed on demand to reduce waste.

First printing, 2022.

The Forum on Education Abroad
PO Box 1773
Carlisle, PA, USA 17013

The Forum on Education Abroad is hosted by Dickinson College.

www.forumea.org

Acknowledgments

My deep gratitude goes to the many people who made this project possible, including my co-editor, Dr. Heather Barclay Hamir, and our more than fifty authors and reviewers, who live in five world regions and have origins in six continents. My thanks also to The Forum, and especially Dr. Amelia Dietrich, who guided us through this project, as well as colleagues at the university where I started this project, Boston College, and at my current institution, Elon University, for their support. – *NJG*

This project is immeasurably stronger thanks to the 50+ authors and peer reviewers who contributed their insights, experience, and critical eye to this volume. I owe special thanks to Amelia Dietrich at The Forum on Education Abroad for her incredible support over the two years of this project, and to Margaret McCullers for key insights at a critical moment. As always, I am grateful to my supportive husband, Zubair, and tolerant children, Zain and Tennyson, who put up with long hours and late dinners without complaint. – *HBH*

Contents

The Time for Waiting Is Over

Dawn Michele Whitehead

At such a challenging time in the United States and in the world, where we are still in the midst of a global health pandemic, a global reckoning for racial justice, and a climate crisis, we find that people of color and people with lower incomes continue to be impacted disproportionately by these realities. Elected officials and community leaders around the globe are responding and reacting in different ways to meet these global challenges in their local contexts. Higher education has also been called upon to make changes as these issues have exacerbated existing disparities, and institutions have verbally committed to become more equitable and inclusive to respond appropriately to this moment. While education abroad is a part of higher education, as a field, we haven't always brought the knowledge and research from colleagues outside education abroad into our own work in a systemic way. However, the current climate has pushed many of us in the field to think more critically about how we do business, who is included, and who is being left behind.

While the issue of engaging more diverse students in education abroad [illegible] new one, it is part of a continuous conversation that has occurred [illegible]ents, on campuses, and at national conferences and meetings [illegible] However, today's climate has brought a sense of urgency [illegible]. But many are still asking, when are we going to stop [illegible]g? Where is the change? Why are we still having these [illegible]e reached a point for action. The conversation [illegible]ions where individuals lament the lack of participation by key groups of students to a critical dialogue where the finger is pointing back at us, leaders and practitioners in the field.

A House Where All Belong is the right book at the right time to challenge education abroad professionals to push our field forward to become the field that is designed for today's diverse learners who could and should participate in education abroad, not the students who studied abroad almost 100 years ago when the University of Delaware sent their first group of students abroad to France. Higher education has evolved, and education abroad must also evolve. As the editors of this book argue, that evolution starts with us. With introspection, self-reflection, acknowledgment, and change, we can move to real action to transform education abroad.

The editors also carefully identified all aspects of the education abroad process (program design, curriculum, learning outcomes, effective assessment, student development, advising, staffing, hiring, outreach, messaging, marketing, and the application) and brought together a talented group of authors who could eloquently and intellectually speak to the importance of equity mindedness and inclusive excellence for the different dimensions of the process. These authors also provide practical strategies that an administrator, program leader, advisor, HR professional, and/or any campus colleague could use to begin the process of institutional-level change in education abroad. If we truly take an equity-minded approach, we must rethink, reimagine, and change our processes and practices at the institutional level. Equity-minded institutions focused on the institutional actions to meet the needs of the students they have, which means there must be collaboration across the units and departments. Many of the authors in this book articulate clear ways to collaborate in the name of reinventing study abroad processes to ensure equity is at the center.

It is truly exciting to hear so many voices remind us of our legacy as a field while also challenging us to be the change we want and need to be for today's education abroad. In the musical *Suffs,* Ida B. Wells, the journalist and anti-lynching crusader is portrayed, and she sings a song called *Wait My Turn.* She sings, "deeds not words say the words on your jacket. So sick of rhetoric with no action to back it." Many in our field echo these words and have been working independently or in groups to advance equity minded education abroad. They are also tired of the rhetoric of being more inclusive without any real action, and they have waited their turn. *A House Where All Belong* provides the inspiration and the strategy for education abroad professionals and friends to take action to meet this moment.

1

Unpacking Education Abroad's Invisible Knapsack in the Pursuit of Inclusive Excellence

Nick J. Gozik and Heather Barclay Hamir

When we started working on this book, following the publication of *Promoting Inclusion in Education Abroad: A Handbook of Research and Practice* (Barclay Hamir & Gozik, 2018b), the world was a different place. Over the course of writing, in the U.S. alone, we have experienced a global health pandemic, a highly charged political divide in the run up to the 2020 elections, and the expansion of the Black Lives Matter movement catalyzed by the death of Ahmaud Arbery, George Floyd, and Breonna Taylor at the hands of police. Ongoing discussions and debates have likewise continued to evolve around topics such as gender, sexual orientation, and disabilities, with diverging views informed by various factors including politics, age, faith, and socioeconomic status. Rather than remaining lodged in one moment, this volume has evolved in lockstep with the world around us, and our sincere hope is that it will serve as a guide for those working to affect change in one area within a much broader landscape, that of education abroad.

Study abroad in the U.S. as we know it today emerged in the 1920s largely as an elite endeavor. In recent decades, overseas programming has become much more diverse, with participation of students from various backgrounds and academic interests; a much wider array of destinations; and a greater mix of activities abroad (e.g., study, research, community-based learning, internships), hence the term "education abroad" in place of "study abroad." *Promoting Inclusion in Education Abroad* explored strategies to expand participation among underserved groups, including first-generation students, students with disabilities, community college students, students of color, STEM majors/minors, and male-identifying students,[1] among others. At the same time, education abroad remains limited, with less than 3% of U.S. college students going abroad each year (Kim & Lawrence, 2021) and approximately 1 out of 10 who graduate with some sort of study abroad credit (Institute of International Education, 2020b). While few students study abroad overall, even fewer are students of color, as education abroad persistently enrolls a majority of White female students despite efforts toward greater inclusion.

Among the many inequities in the U.S. and other countries, why should we focus on this one? The answer to this question largely depends on how one understands the value of higher education (Barclay Hamir & Gozik, 2018b). When viewed as a public good (even for private institutions), much has to do with providing access to all members of a society, with notable benefits to both the society as a whole and individuals, for example, longer life spans, better access to health care, better dietary and health practices, greater economic stability and security, and more stable employment and greater job satisfaction (United Nations, n.d.). It also means that, once students are admitted, they have access to all programming and services available on a campus. If two students graduate with the same diploma, yet only one is able to participate in activities that enrich learning outside the classroom, technically both have the same degree, yet one is much better positioned for the workforce and civic life. This point is reaffirmed by Kuh's research on student gains through high-impact practices (HIPs) including education abroad (Kuh, 2008; Kuh et al., 2017).

Equally important to the previous question is an appreciation of what steps need to be taken to address inequities that exist within higher education. Among U.S. scholars, there is a general consensus that change cannot take place without systematic and structural modifications; to simply amend

---

[1]Our preference is to use "male-identifying" and "female-identifying," with an understanding that gender is fluid and culturally constructed, with some individuals, for example, who may not identify with the gender that they were assigned at birth. For the sake of readability, we use "male" and "female" here. In subsequent chapters, data collection methods and gender response options vary, but are most likely based on self-reporting; accordingly, any time the terms "male" or "female" are used, it assumes male-identifying or female-identifying unless otherwise stated. If authors refer to gender in another way—e.g., when citing specific survey data with known methods—that will be explicitly referenced, e.g., assigned male at birth.

a policy or add a program may only offer a limited solution and not get at the root of the problem. In fact, this book stems from a deep concern that, as a profession, *education abroad has continued to operate largely without challenging the cultural core of who we are and what we do.* This is not because scholars and practitioners do not care. Many are genuinely committed to widening access, and as noted earlier, there has been real success. At the same time, we continue to operate with a dominant narrative written by White (and largely female) participants and a predominantly White profession. The question we must ask ourselves now is: *If education abroad had been originally designed for and by people of color or other minoritized communities, what assumptions would inform programming and how might programming differ from what we know today?*

This book accordingly is intended to move the field ahead, drawing on the momentum and heightened imperative for social change. If our first volume (Barclay Hamir & Gozik, 2018c) examined strategies for increasing participation, this book looks at the *education abroad process*, from the time that students arrive on campus and begin considering going abroad, to when they go overseas, and upon their reentry. By taking a systematic approach, chapter authors critically examine our field's assumptions, policies and procedures, and types of programming to reconsider and reinterpret what the field offers.

This approach aligns with The Forum on Education Abroad's (The Forum) latest version of the *Standards of Good Practice for Education Abroad* (The Forum on Education Abroad, 2020), which includes a Guiding Principle on equity, diversity, and inclusion (EDI). While the focus is largely on U.S. institutions and practices, it is written for anyone—including overseas resident staff and colleagues at global institutions—who works with students from U.S. universities and colleges engaged in education abroad. It also comes with an understanding that many of the themes explored here go well beyond U.S. borders and deal more generally with the universal question of how students from all backgrounds can best be supported.

Equity, Diversity, and Inclusion

Amid a sea of terminology, it may seem that the words we use in talking about differences and how to negotiate them are unimportant. In fact, this could not be further from the truth. Words do matter and especially those we explore in this volume related to EDI. Here, we use terminology as developed by the Association of American Colleges and Universities (AAC&U), which has been adopted by a number of institutions, including The Forum. Falling within the broader initiative of "Making Excellence Inclusive," the AAC&U has defined these three terms, each of which stands on its own, while also coming together to form a whole:

> **Diversity:** Individual differences (e.g., personality, prior knowledge, and life experiences) and group/social differences (e.g., race/ethnicity, class, gender, sexual orientation, country of origin, and ability as well as cultural, political, religious, or other affiliations).
>
> **Inclusion:** The active, intentional, and ongoing engagement with diversity—in the curriculum, in the co-curriculum, and in communities (intellectual, social, cultural, geographical) with which individuals might connect—in ways that increase awareness, content knowledge, cognitive sophistication, and empathic understanding of the complex ways individuals interact within systems and institutions.
>
> **Equity:** The creation of opportunities for historically underserved populations to have equal access to and participate in educational programs that are capable of closing the achievement gaps in student success and completion. (Association of American Colleges & Universities, n.d.)

A simple way of understanding this terminology comes from the chief diversity officer at the University of Michigan, Robert Sellers, who uses the metaphor of a dance to explain that: "diversity is where everyone is invited to the party; equity means that everyone gets to contribute the playlist; and inclusion means that everyone has the opportunity to dance" (University of Michigan, n.d.). Within higher education, it becomes clear that one cannot have inclusion or equity without also making sure that there are diverse faculty, staff, and students. At the same time, it is not sufficient to only hire diverse recruits or admit a diverse group of students; students need support and opportunities for inclusion once they are on campus, and campus or organizational culture must foster a sense of belonging for faculty and staff as well.

Among the three terms, equity is likely the most elusive and difficult to achieve. It is not necessarily the result of a simple equation, that is, "Diversity + Inclusion ≠ Equity" (Joyce, 2020). In addition, some specialists have expressed concern with the merging of "equity, diversity, and inclusion" within the "EDI" acronym, as it is easy to focus more on diversity and inclusion and overlook equity. To achieve equity, organizations must begin with an understanding that the very structures with which they operate are not equitable by nature and that, "it is necessary to move beyond just having people in the room" (YW Boston, 2019). It also means questioning and making changes to core values and policies, including around hiring, the assignment of tasks, evaluation, and promotion. Advocates of gender parity, for example, note that women are often penalized for taking time off for maternity leave or in aligning their work schedules around childcare needs (*The New York Times*, 2019). In this case, retooling for equity requires a readjustment in the assumptions around what constitutes attributes such as "loyalty," "hard work," and "dedication," while also making it easier for parents to establish a work–life balance.

Equity may be more difficult precisely because it suggests a need for some members of an organization to acknowledge and cede the privileges that they enjoy—a seemingly tall task, even for faculty and staff who in principle are supportive of diversity and inclusion initiatives. Those who have been successful may balk at the idea of giving up what they feel they have rightly achieved and earned. At the same time, it behooves leaders to create inclusive environments where members of an organization feel welcomed and do not see a need to leave, thus taking away valuable skills, creativity, and expertise. As President and CEO of Living Cities Ben Hecht notes, "organizations cannot afford *not* to do this work, but they also can't enter into it lightly, under the misconception that a training or workshop checks the box" (Hecht, 2020). This sort of change does not happen overnight and requires a long-term strategy and buy-in at all levels, starting at the top.

When combined as a joint concept, the order of the three terms explored thus far—equity, diversity, and inclusion—varies in use, with "DEI" and "EDI" being most prevalent. We believe that it is important to have all three included and not to truncate the terminology to "diversity and inclusion," for instance. At the same time, we have intentionally chosen to use "EDI" in this publication, following the lead of The Forum and other organizations, with a belief that if equity is not placed in front, it is easy to omit. Much of this volume is precisely dedicated to strategies and activities designed to achieve equity and so this ordering aligns well.

As noted earlier, EDI falls under the umbrella of the AAC&U's "Making Excellence Inclusive" initiative, leading to the widespread use of "inclusive excellence." Begun in the mid-2000s, inclusive excellence was conceived in the wake of legal challenges to affirmative action (Milem et al., 2005), specifically the use of race in admissions decisions, as a way to strengthen the integration of diversity efforts within the larger assessment and improvement structures of institutions. This project has changed the landscape of higher education by offering a framework that positions educational excellence and diversity as intertwined and mutually reinforcing facets of campus activity for the first time. The original definition by the AAC&U (Milem et al., 2005) applies a strength-based perspective, with the goal that inclusive excellence addresses the social inequities that exist both for the benefit of those who have been marginalized and—critically—for *all* students. If students are to be prepared for an increasingly diverse world, it is imperative that those with limited exposure to difference—or a low societal imperative to adapt to others' cultural preferences, as with majority culture individuals—learn to understand and communicate effectively with people who are different from themselves. Education abroad can play a vital role in exposing students to new cultures and peoples, though here too we contend that such programming must be undertaken with EDI in mind (Barclay Hamir & Gozik, 2018b).

Along with EDI has been the inclusion of a "J" for justice, often as part of "social justice" and/or "racial justice." The language around social and racial justice has been long present in the U.S., though has been connected more recently with international education in *Social Justice and International Education: Research, Practice, and Perspectives* (2020) edited by LaNitra Berger. In Berger's edited volume, social justice is defined differently by individual contributors, yet together they provide a framework that addresses three essential themes:

> (1) identifying and challenging institutional structures that perpetuate social inequality using a critical theoretical lens; (2) embracing a "bottom up" approach to thinking about how specific marginalized groups are affected by their relationships to power and privilege; and (3) developing processes and exercises that seek to analyze and interrogate individual and group biases. (p. 3)

The additive value of justice to EDI work emphasizes the need to rethink all aspects of the educational experience and environment taking into consideration that these environments were not originally designed for marginalized groups. Several of the chapters in this volume directly apply a social justice approach (e.g., Chapter 8 on inclusive application design, Chapter 9 on decolonizing education abroad, and Chapter 12 on Fulbright Noir) and all are informed on some level by the social justice work that has taken place over decades. While "justice" is not explicitly named in a number of chapters, the premise of this volume aligns with the intent of this construct: We must redesign education abroad by engaging communities who were not originally part of the creation and expansion of these opportunities, thereby creating room for different perspectives and priorities than tradition may suggest. Global educators must move beyond past efforts that merely attempt to reframe the same programs and services to appeal to a more diverse audience, particularly where this work occurs in the absence of input from the groups we intend to serve. Only through our willingness to reconsider every aspect of the education abroad journey will we uncover the design flaws in our "house" that have prevented greater equity of participation and lived experience abroad.

Lastly, we recognize that the terminology outlined here is U.S. centric, given our intended audience of those working with U.S. students, domestically or abroad (Gozik, 2018). Given the genesis of inclusive excellence, research and writing on this topic often focuses on EDI related to marginalized racial and ethnic identities in the U.S. context. Whereas race is especially salient in the U.S., other categories, for example, religion, ethnicity, gender, and disability, may be more prevalent in discourse and action in another setting. The definitions here allow for a shared language for the authors of this volume to employ, if also with a recognition that they are socially constructed and have a different meaning in other contexts.

EDI and Education Abroad

Advancing EDI in education abroad begins by taking stock of our current state. As we noted in 2018, the disparity between who is enrolled in postsecondary education and who goes abroad remains noticeable. As an example, racial and ethnic minority participation in study abroad increased almost 3% since 2018, reaching 31.3% in the 2020 *Open Doors* report (Institute of International Education, 2020a). However, participation still lags well behind overall trends in higher education, where racial and ethnic minority students represented 44% of postsecondary enrollments in 2017 with continuous growth projected through 2028 as the U.S. population becomes increasingly diverse (Snyder et al., 2019, p. 257). A similar pattern exists with respect to students with disabilities, whose participation in education abroad increased 2% over the same period to 10.5%, yet 19.1% of undergraduates reported disabilities in 2015–2016, the most recent reporting year (Snyder et al., 2019, p. 268).

The story these data tell over the three years since publication of *Promoting Inclusion in Education Abroad* does not fully represent the challenges that we face in our EDI efforts. As Figure 1.1 illustrates, over the past 20 years, the progress in diversifying education abroad participation is not closing the gap with respect to overall demographic change in higher education enrollment.

In the past decade, the field has indeed made progress, closing the gap in participation to 12.8%, yet that improvement merely returned participation rates of racial/ethnic minority students to levels already seen in the prior decade. With the magnitude of disruption in the U.S. and globally due to economic fallout and social and political instability, there are significant concerns that these same students will be the hardest hit, and we will once again lose ground in our collective efforts to promote inclusion in education abroad participation.

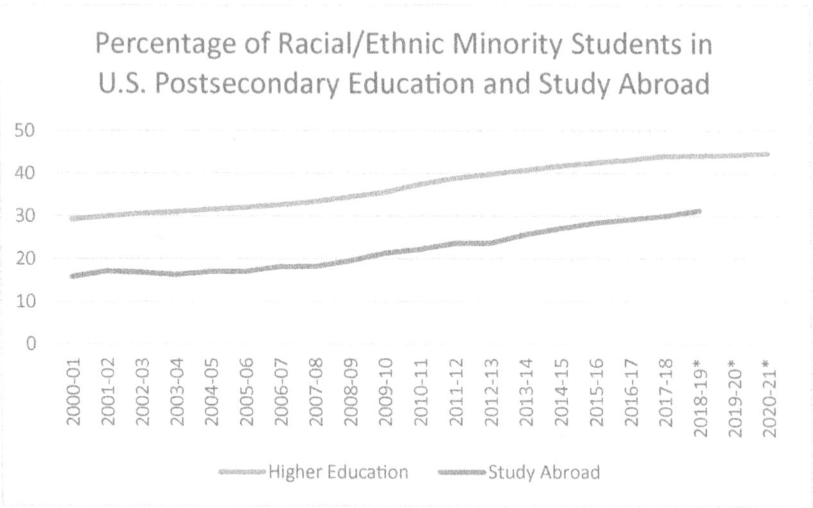

Fig. 1.1 Source: Chart by authors, using data from the Institute of International Education (2020a) and the Digest of Education Statistics (Snyder et al., 2019).

The larger trend of educational disparity remains the backdrop for any discussion of who does or does not participate in education abroad. Rather than being discouraged by these trends, we see them as a sobering wakeup call regarding our assumptions about how to advance EDI within education abroad, a microcosm of the same concerns within the college-going experience. As with higher education itself, education abroad metrics tend to over-rely on representational data as a measure of success. We previously noted that significant attention has been paid to those who have access to the experience of education abroad—what we think of as opening the door to these opportunities. Yet, greater attention must be focused on inclusion beyond mere access, "applying this lens to inform pre-departure preparation, program design, and training for faculty and staff" (Barclay Hamir & Gozik, 2018a, p. 203). Representation does matter, but it is not the entire story, and the failure to look beyond it may be part of the reason participation rates are not changing faster.

Creating more equitable access to education abroad participation—opening the door—is only the beginning of EDI work in this space. Students' experiences and well-being are affected by what happens when they go *through* the door, meaning their experiences prearrival, on-site, and upon return. The metaphorical "house" of education abroad emerged out of a long history of work with groups of students, destinations, and program models that informed and then formed the principal structures of our work, from application processes to reentry. As the world changes, and more importantly the students within our educational system change, the assumptions embedded within all aspects of our work must also keep up. In this sense, we must redesign the metaphorical education abroad "house" we collectively inhabit to ensure that it is ready for and welcoming of the students we actually intend to serve; that it is, in fact, a house where all belong. This entails more than just cosmetic changes that are the equivalent of putting up new wallpaper and buying new furniture. Instead, we must be open to examining the very foundation and frame, to rebuild and reimagine its structure (e.g., walls, windows, openings) and systems (e.g., plumbing, electrical, and HVAC) as we seek to welcome and authentically engage all students.

Efforts to create educational equity within higher education have typically started without a parallel examination of the assumptions and biases embedded in higher education itself. That failure to support the whole student ultimately leads to inequities of experience, as higher education attrition and degree completion trends continue to demonstrate (National Center for Education Statistics, 2019). Beyond the numbers, the experience of past participants informs the decisions of future students, with the potential to create counternarratives if those who participated found that staff throughout the process were not prepared to answer their specific questions or create an environment where students with different backgrounds and experiences all felt a sense of belonging.

To achieve different outcomes requires us first to review critically the role we play in the enrollment patterns we see, which sounds easier than it is. As noted earlier, the history and norms of education abroad have been largely shaped by predominantly White and often female students and practitioners. Given that international experience is often required or strongly preferred to be hired into education abroad positions, there is a natural pathway for social reproduction à la Bourdieu (1986): The experience of the student participant becomes the "normal" for new practitioners, reinforcing assumptions that are often unexamined. These assumptions can be surfaced through engagement with invested colleagues on campus who themselves are committed to EDI, or by changing hiring norms to include more individuals who represent underserved identities and those who are passionate about EDI, bringing new perspectives to office policies and practices. Yet ultimately, rethinking our roles in the inequities we see requires systematically rethinking policies, practices, and the underlying assumptions and biases that form them, from our beliefs about what constitutes a "good" education abroad candidate to our understanding of the needs and interests of students who are abroad.

Education Abroad's Invisible Knapsack

When we are in the midst of the norms we have created, it can be challenging to untangle the assumptions and unconscious biases that may contribute to differential outcomes for our students, whether in terms of who goes abroad or how they experience their time abroad. That process of identifying, defining, and naming cultural phenomena underpins every effort to unmake the influence of power, privilege, and marginalization in society, from White privilege to heteronormativity to critical race theory. To progress, we must also name the norms and assumptions that lead to recurring enrollment patterns in education abroad and then we must work actively to undo them.

For those of us who are White, including both editors of this volume, White privilege as a construct serves as a useful lens through which to begin this discussion, particularly given the cultural influences that shape U.S. education and education abroad as we know it. In the late 1980s, Peggy McIntosh translated her research on male privilege to the idea that White individuals in the U.S. enjoy similar types of privileges compared to those who identify as Black, Indigenous, People of Color (BIPOC). In her seminal essay, "White privilege: Unpacking the invisible Knapsack" (1989), she describes the unearned advantages enjoyed by White people in the U.S. due to the color of their skin, advantages received in nearly every aspect of their lives and of which they are largely unaware. In describing why this phenomenon is invisible and pervasive, McIntosh states:

> As a white person, I realized I had been taught about racism as something which puts others at a disadvantage, but had been taught not to see one of its corollary aspects, white privilege, which puts me at an advantage. (p. 10)

It is disturbing to realize the continued, critical relevance of the concept and the specific examples provided in the essay. As this volume is being published, more than three decades after McIntosh's article first came out, most of the advantages described remain true for White individuals, ranging from assumptions that a White person will not be followed in a store, to continuing representations of White people as the driving force behind "civilization" and the history of the U.S. (p. 10). For all the discourse at national and local levels, the fundamental structures of White privilege remain largely undisturbed, which cannot help but ripple through our work as international educators if left undisrupted.

Not all individuals will experience White privilege the same way. In a *Washington Post* opinion piece, for example, Steve Majors (Majors, 2020) explains that, within the same family, having lighter or darker skin can significantly impact how one navigates the world. As a Black man who passes for White, he does not have the same fear of interacting with police as do his brothers with darker skin. Similarly, he recognizes the favors that he likely received from White faculty who treated him differently from fellow Students of Color. So, White privilege is not just about a self-defined racial identity; it is just as much about the perception of others. Moreover, it may be that the concept of White privilege feels less applicable to some, even if there is an agreement that discrimination and racism are real and endemic.

Dialogue on how to promote EDI in education abroad has expanded significantly over the past decade, with substantially more complex exploration of this topic at conferences and a broad range of professional development opportunities to help practitioners advance in their work. It is common now to find EDI highlighted in office resources and mission statements, all of which takes us in a positive direction. To McIntosh's point though, educators need to focus on identifying the corollary assumptions embedded in our policies, practices, and beliefs as a foundational step to understanding how to make meaningful progress in our EDI efforts. Given its endemic nature within U.S. culture, it follows that White privilege must also be ingrained in our collective practices, beliefs, and policies within higher education and, therefore, within education abroad. Viewed from this perspective, it is not difficult to unpack elements of education abroad's invisible knapsack of advantages for White students.

As an illustration, here are a few examples of White privilege that we have observed relative to White students studying in the top three study abroad destinations for U.S. students—the United Kingdom, Italy, and Spain—which collectively enrolled nearly one-third of all participants in 2018–2019 (Institute of International Education, 2020a). As a White student,

- I will commonly see people with my skin color in promotional materials, individually and in groups.
- People in my host country are unlikely to be surprised when they learn that I am U.S. American.
- People in my host country are also unlikely to assume that stereotypical media or entertainment portrayals of people who look like me may be true of me.
- I am likely to find that most information shared to prepare me for my program answers my main questions about how I may experience the culture of my host country.
- Resident staff are probably prepared to answer most of my questions and understand my experience in the local context based on their history with other students like me.

The last three statements apply equally well to students in other marginalized groups. Similarly, other examples illustrate further embedded assumptions that may affect LGBTQ+ students or students who have a visible or invisible disability:

- I know that my sexual preferences and practices are generally legal and accepted by members of the community where I am studying abroad.
- I do not fear being asked questions, receiving ridicule or criticism, or being the victim of violence based on how I present my gender identity in a classroom or while walking down the street.
- When I apply to study abroad, faculty and administrators guiding me through the process generally understand my abilities and can offer advice and support catered to my needs.

It was disturbingly easy to create these lists, and many other privileges inherent to White, heteronormative participants without visible or hidden disability could just as easily be listed here. So, why is this exercise not a common practice in our field? Why have we not unpacked and remade our knapsack to make education abroad truly inclusive?

The answer to these questions stems in part from the fact that education abroad as a profession and an educational activity has been structured around certain forms of privilege, certainly including race and ethnicity as we have thus explored, yet also around socioeconomic status, students' areas of study, sexual orientation/gender identity, and parents' educational status, among others. If the first education abroad program developed in the U.S. at the University of Delaware in 1923 (n.d.) was designed for and composed solely of males, helping them to develop greater business acumen, over time, it evolved into the demographic trends the field has experienced for decades, where roughly two-thirds of participants are female, and a significant majority of participants are White. The evolution of study abroad from that first business-focused program included shifting toward an emphasis on language and centers of Western culture; such programs made sense in the locations that continue to remain popular in education abroad, including Italy, France, the United Kingdom, and Spain. Although much has changed, many of the suppositions around where students should go and who is deemed a good fit are deeply embedded within an intersection of privileged identities that cannot be boiled down to just one, that is, race or gender or socioeconomic class. Identity is far more complicated and nuanced, as is education abroad's "invisible knapsack" of today. However, complexity is not an excuse for inaction; if we do not interrogate our assumptions and privileges, it will be impossible to truly (re)design a house where all belong, as we advocate for in this volume.

The traditions of the profession continue to create implicit advantages and disadvantages based on how similar or dissimilar one is from assumed norms. To move forward, it is necessary to deconstruct the privileges and advantages embedded in our practice; our failure to do so is in part why we struggle to move the needle regarding who we serve and how we serve them. To paraphrase Kendi (2019), there is no neutral, there is only racist or antiracist, a construct that can be extrapolated to all the -isms, for example, sexism, heterosexism, and ableism. If we are not deliberately evaluating "neutral" policies and practices, then we are most certainly perpetuating inequities in access to education abroad, advising, and the in-country experience.

Our Own Positionality

As editors and authors, we come with our own perspectives and assumptions. While both editors have experienced some aspect of underrepresentation, for example, first-generation status, gender, and sexual orientation, the reality is that we also enjoy considerable privilege as individuals who are White, cis-gendered, educated, and upper-middle class by birth or upward social mobility. Some of our identities that might mark us as different are invisible, allowing us to blend easily, revealing only what and when we want to share. So, despite years of work on EDI issues, we have also come to acknowledge our own "invisible knapsacks."

With these limitations in mind, we have intentionally sought out authors and peer reviewers with a wide range of identities. More than 50 authors and peer reviewers who have contributed to this volume currently live in five world regions and have origins in six continents. The authors work in different types of institutions and organizations, from nonprofit and for-profit entities (including program providers and funding organizations), government agencies, and private and public colleges and universities. Many grew up speaking languages other than English at home, ascribe to varying faiths and beliefs, and have lived and studied overseas. They are faculty, practitioners, and scholar-practitioners, including those not in education abroad, who can offer new ideas from outside the field.

Of course, we have wanted to stay clear of tokenism; instead, from the beginning of the project, the goal has been to draw from a rich and diverse community of colleagues, to make sure that we represent the profession to the greatest extent possible. This latter point squares with the vision and mission of The Forum.

Moving the Needle: Reenvisioning the Education Abroad Process

If it is necessary to recognize the privilege and assumptions embedded in education abroad, it is just as critical that we apply that lens to interrogate and overhaul existing practices and policies. This involves moving beyond the strategies employed to date, which have often been done piecemeal, tackling one stage of the overall education abroad process at a time rather than taking a holistic and systematic approach. Many offices, for example, have done a good job of making marketing more inclusive through images and testimonials of diverse students on their websites and in publications. This has not rested at what one might call the "Benetton approach," as simply a marketing ploy that embraces the full spectrum of skin color (Giroux, 1993); there has been a genuine desire to ensure that a wide range of students see themselves authentically represented in marketing materials.

What often misses the mark, however, are the other stages of the process through which students learn about, apply for, and ultimately engage in education abroad. What happens when the male, first-generation, Mexican American, engineering student walks in the door? How do advisors engage him to uncover and address his questions or concerns? Is the application process so long and cumbersome that it inadvertently serves as a barrier, or overtly serves to screen students out? What does funding look like, and how is it explained? Are the specific needs of this student and others addressed in predeparture and on-site orientations? Are on-site staff prepared to address any microaggressions or identity-based concerns that may occur within the program and the host society? Does the student feel fully supported upon reentry? The fact that many have addressed just one aspect of the education abroad process and not all of the others is cause for optimism that meaningful change is possible.

Within each of the stages of the education abroad process, there is an opportunity and need to question one's assumptions. Coming back to the terminology around EDI, here we seek to focus on not just getting students "in the door" of the education abroad house we are living in, our intention is to ensure that everyone may contribute fully—something that, in turn, pushes us to question notions of "fairness" and what is "right." Taking the application process, for instance, we still speak about GPA minimums for education abroad as a fact, when in reality, they are a construct developed by individuals who were trying to create a structure to exchange students and needed some markers to set the parameters for comfort on each side. If good academic standing is acceptable to receive a degree from a U.S. institution, why is it not the default for education abroad, instead of lower GPA requirements requiring justification? What elements of the education abroad application are the most useful in evaluating students, and why? Do those assumptions bear out in the experience or behavior of students abroad?

With any phase of the education abroad process, we might ask a set of simple questions: If we invented study abroad today within the cultural context and values we espouse, what would that look like? Would it be the same as or different than what we see as the "ideal"? And, to get to this ideal, it may help to ask: If education abroad as we know it in the U.S. had been developed by minoritized groups in the first place, what would it look like and how would it operate? It is hard to imagine that the program models, procedures, and policies would be exactly the same. The aim of this book is precisely to reexamine each stage of the education abroad process, with the goal of systematically and holistically shifting how we work with students.

Overview of Subsequent Chapters

Subsequent chapters expand upon the themes that we have raised here and allow for a more in-depth analysis of the context and process of education abroad, with the goal of creating a more holistic and systematic set of changes for promoting inclusive excellence. The volume is organized into three parts: Framing the Discussion, Lessons Learned, and Next Steps.

In the first section, the authors provide additional context for work on EDI in education abroad. In Chapter 2, "Advancing Inclusive Excellence in Education Abroad," Alma Clayton-Pedersen, Thandi Dinani, Kevin Hovland, and Nick J. Gozik return to the original concept of AAC&U's "Inclusive Excellence," of which Clayton-Pedersen was a chief architect. Noting areas where more work needs to be done, particularly in terms of intercultural and global learning, they offer a model by which leaders and practitioners can move forward in meaningful and sustainable ways. Chapter 3, "The Promise of Equity-Minded Practice: Lessons Learned From Higher Education for Education Abroad," by Eduardo Contreras, Asabe Poloma, and Ana M. Martínez Alemán, continues where Clayton-Pedersen et al. leave off by exploring the history of EDI efforts in U.S. higher education over the past several decades, while drawing on concrete examples from other fields that can be applied to education abroad.

The second and largest section reviews the phases of the education abroad process and organizational factors that shape it. Before students even step foot on campus, the authors of Chapters 4 and 5 make the argument that much is necessary to ensure that staff and programs, respectively, are adequately prepared. Chapter 4 "Inclusive Excellence Begins With Us: Developing Inclusive Organizational Cultures and Hiring Practices," by Heather Barclay Hamir, Aileen Bumphus, Patricia Izek, and Betty Jeanne Taylor, draws on literature and best practices from the fields of human resources and leadership studies to demonstrate the need for more diverse staffing, as well as the ways in which institutions and organizations can retool their practices around recruitment, hiring, onboarding, and retaining staff. For their part, Malaika Serrano, David Wick, and Devin Walker in Chapter 5, "Equity-Minded Program Design for Inclusive Excellence," apply backward design to lay out methods for developing more inclusive programming, beginning with learning objectives and including all program components.

Once students arrive on campus, Brett Berquist, Shelley Jessee, and Jennifer Calvert Hall in Chapter 6, "Passing the Mic: The Role of Outreach, Messaging, and Marketing in Building Inclusive Excellence in Education Abroad," offer illustrations from the U.S. and New Zealand for how best to reach out to historically underrepresented students and encourage participation. As is the case in other chapters (e.g., 12, 13), they recommend collaborating with returning students, understanding that word of mouth and student-to-student communication is often far more powerful than any single marketing campaign. Chapter 7, "Advancing Inclusive Practices Through Appreciative Advising in Education Abroad" by Nikki Bruckmann, Opal Leeman Bartzis, and Chris Van Velzer, describes the power of appreciative advising, an asset-based approach that focuses on students' strengths and realization of their self-identified goals. The authors of Chapter 8 "Dismantling Exclusive Practices: Applications as Tools for Inclusion," Taylor Woodman, Jeremy Gombin-Sperling, and Qimmah Najeeullah, similarly point out that it is equally important to reduce barriers to entry, including around the selection of students. This includes understanding how such practices are often guided by a skewed understanding of "fairness," missing the mark entirely on equity.

Chapters 9 and 10 look more closely at students' academic experiences. Chapter 9, "Decolonizing Education Abroad: Grounding Theory in Practice" by Santiago Castiello-Gutiérrez and Nick J. Gozik, explores education abroad through the prism of decolonization, borrowing from approaches introduced in South Africa and stemming from a history of postcolonial thinking and activism. Similarly, Neriko Musha Doerr and Yuri Kumagai present case studies in Chapter 10, "Flickers of Difference: Living and Learning With Others Through Inclusive Classroom Projects," which offer collaborative learning projects that can be applied on the home campus or abroad, helping students understand others' viewpoints through dialogue, examine their own assumptions, and learn to relate to diverse individuals.

Chapters 11 and 12 focus on the program abroad, where on-the-ground staff play a key role in students' experiences. Chapter 11, "Training "American" Identity: Engaging On-Site Staff in Equity, Diversity, and Inclusion Work," by Martha Johnson, Bradley Titus, and Mariarosa Mettifogo, illustrates a training program developed for resident staff on diversity and the historical context of "American" identity(ies). The modules are adaptable to different country sites, demonstrating the need to modify content based on varying cultural and linguistic factors. In Chapter 12, "Fulbright Noir: Race, Identity, and Empowerment in the Fulbright U.S. Student Program," LaNitra Berger, Lee Rivers, Erica Lutes, and Marie-Aimee Ntawukulityayo offer the perspective of overseas staff, responding to the needs of diverse U.S. students through Fulbright programming in Europe and globally.

Chapters 13 and 14 follow the return of students back to the U.S. Chapter 13, "Reentry Strategies to Apply Lessons Learned From Abroad," by Maraina Montgomery, Neal McKinney, Jane Nzomo, Angela Manginelli and Lily López-McGee provides case studies from four institutions that have been successful in developing reentry programs tailored to the needs of diverse students, helping the latter to reintegrate on campus, while also encouraging peers to engage in overseas experiences. Closing out the education abroad process and bringing us back to the beginning of the planning cycle, Katherine Yngve and Elizabeth Brewer explore innovative outcomes assessment efforts in Chapter 14, "Alignment, Belongingness, and Social Justice: Using Assessment to Advance Inclusive Excellence in Education Abroad," with the goal of instilling a sense of belongingness in all students, and especially those who have historically been underrepresented.

Lastly, in Conclusion, "Acting With Courage: Charting a Path Forward for Education Abroad," we return with a synthesis of key themes and recommendations to guide efforts in redesigning education abroad to advance inclusive excellence. Given the need for strong models with proven success in this area, organizations outside education abroad serve to illustrate how goals related to EDI are served within the larger educational space, suggesting strategies for practitioners and institutions to consider. Taken as a whole, the range of chapters outlines concrete strategies that can be applied across an array of institutions and organizations, in the U.S. and abroad. Rather than simply addressing one stage of the education abroad process, we advocate for a holistic and systematic approach, which can move the needle to realize goals around inclusive excellence.

Variations in Terminology and Capitalization

As we have noted, words matter and particularly in discussing politically and emotionally charged topics like EDI. In this and the concluding chapter, we have made a conscious decision, for example, to capitalize "White" in referring to race and ethnicity, along with other racial descriptors such as Black, Brown, and Indigenous, in accordance with the *Publication Manual of the American Psychological Association* (American Psychological Association, 2020) and the guidance of the National Association of Black Journalists (2020). Doing so ensures that each of these identities—including those that have been historically marginalized—is fully recognized. It also acknowledges the ways in which Whiteness functions in institutions and communities, while not permitting those who identify as White to sit out of conversations related to race (Mack & Palfrey, 2020), with an assumption that they are exempt. At the same time, other authors have not chosen to capitalize, and as editors, we support the individual decisions of all author teams to express these complex topics in accordance with their own views and values.

Similarly, readers will note that in some chapters authors have employed terminology such as BIPOC, going beyond the earlier term "People of Color," which has existed since colonial times, to something that is more inclusive (Garcia, 2020). Adding "Black" and "Indigenous" can also be a way of recognizing that not all people of color face equal levels of injustice (Clarke, 2020). Others take issue with this term, feeling that they do not want to be lumped in with other groups or that they do not agree with the formation of the group. Accordingly, within this volume, some authors instead have employed "People of Color" or referred to individual groups, rather than a broader amalgamation.

Rather than impose one style guide for this terminology and capitalization, we have encouraged individual authors to determine what is most appropriate for their respective chapters, based in many instances on individual subjects and case studies. The one exception is that we have asked all to refer to "EDI" as in "equity, diversity, and inclusion" rather than "DEI," per the discussion earlier, with a goal of foregrounding equity within this book. Such nomenclature also aligns with the stylistic choice of The Forum.

Concluding Thoughts

In the usual course of our lives, if we intend to redesign something—whether it is a house, a process, an office, or an organization—we would first ensure that we had thought through the plan for that redesign to make sure the end result served the intended purpose. However, we often have ideas in mind of what we hope to accomplish, and that makes the design process easier. With respect to EDI work in education abroad, or even in higher education, our vision of a redesigned system suffers from the lack of clear models of practice to follow. The piecemeal approach so often implemented in the profession contributes to the hazy sense of what holistic good practices looks like, and in the United States, this is further compounded by the widespread and ongoing struggle for equity and justice across multiple marginalized communities. This intersection of societal, institutional, and individual factors means that in our efforts to redesign education abroad, we perhaps need to think less in terms of incremental change and more in terms of truly rethinking what it is we do and why we do it. Given that we are not, in fact, dealing with a physical structure, where errors could be costly and potentially render a house unlivable, we encourage readers to view the advice and practical examples provided throughout this book as permission to explore, dream, and be bold in how we rethink our work. If we do so with inclusive excellence as our guiding principle, with a self-reflective and self-aware mindset focused on what is best for all students, we cannot help but improve from where we are now. We hope that readers will find inspiration, insights, and practical steps throughout this volume to inform their work in education abroad, and that as a collective, we will learn even more through iterative improvement across the field.

Acknowledgments

We are deeply thankful for the thoughtful feedback of Eduardo Contreras, Amelia Dietrich, and Christina Yao on earlier drafts of this chapter.

References

American Psychological Association. (2020). *Publication Manual of the American Psychological Association* (7th ed.). American Psychological Association.

Barclay Hamir, H., & Gozik, N. J. (2018a). Expanding the reach of education abroad: Recommendations for research, policy, and practice. In H. Barclay Hamir & N. J. Gozik (Eds.), *Promoting inclusion in education abroad: A handbook of research and practice* (pp. 197–212). Stylus.

Barclay Hamir, H., & Gozik, N. J. (Eds.). (2018b). *Promoting inclusion in education abroad: A handbook of research and practice.* Stylus.

Bourdieu, P. (1986). The forms of capital. In J. Richardson (Ed.), *Handbook of theory and research for the sociology of education* (pp. 241–258). Greenwood.

Clarke, C. (2020, July 2). BIPOC: What does it mean and where does it come from? *CBS News.* https://www.cbsnews.com/news/bipoc-meaning-where-does-it-come-from-2020-04-02/

Garcia, S. E. (2020, June 17). Where did BIPOC come from? *The New York Times.* https://www.nytimes.com/article/what-is-bipoc.html

Giroux, H. A. (1993). Consuming social change: The "United Colors of Benetton." *Cultural Critique, 26*(Winter (1993–1994)), 5–32. https://doi.org/10.2307/1354454

Gozik, N. J. (2018). Diversity in an age of nationalism: Education abroad and the role of terminology. *The Global Impact Exchange, 201*(Winter), 13–15. https://www.diversitynetwork.org/page/GlobalImpactExchange

Hecht, B. (2020). Moving beyond diversity toward racial equity. *Harvard Business Review.* https://hbr.org/2020/06/moving-beyond-diversity-toward-racial-equity

Institute of International Education. (2020a). *Open Doors.*

Institute of International Education. (2020b). *Open Doors 2020 fast facts.*

Joyce, J. (2020, January 24). Diversity and inclusion must be about equity, not buzzwords or an image. *Triad Business Journal.* https://www.bizjournals.com/triad/news/2020/01/24/diversity-and-inclusion-must-be-about-equity-not.html

Kendi, I. X. (2019). *How to be an antiracist.* One World.

Kim, H. S., & Lawrence, J. H. (2021). Who studies abroad? Understanding the impact of intent on participation. In *Research in Higher Education* (issue 0123456789). Springer Netherlands. https://doi.org/10.1007/s11162-021-09629-9

Kuh, G. (2008). *High-impact educational practices: What they are, who has access to them, and why they matter.* AAC&U.

Kuh, G., O'Donnell, K., & Schneider, C. G. (2017). HIPs at ten. *Change: The Magazine of Higher Learning, 49*(5), 8–16. https://doi.org/10.1080/00091383.2017.1366805

Mack, K., & Palfrey, J. (2020, August). *Capitalizing black and white: Grammatical justice and equity.* MacArthur Foundation Perspectives. https://www.macfound.org/press/perspectives/capitalizing-black-and-white-grammatical-justice-and-equity

Majors, S. (2020, June 11). I'm a black man with white privilege. I see how it distorts America. *The Washington Post.* https://www.washingtonpost.com/outlook/black-white-privilege/2020/06/11/e9da09b8-ab78-11ea-a9d9-a81c1a491c52_story.html

McIntosh, P. (1989). White privilege: Unpacking the invisible Knapsack. *Peace and Freedom, July/August,* 10–12. https://doi.org/10.4324/9781351133791-3

Milem, J. F., Chang, M. J., & Antonio, A. L. (2005). *Making diversity work on campus: A research-based perspective.* https://www.aacu.org/sites/default/files/files/mei/MakingDiversityWork.pdf

National Association of Black Journalists. (2020). *NABJ statement on capitalizing black and other racial identifiers.* NABJ Style Guide. https://www.nabj.org/page/styleguide

National Center for Education Statistics. (2019). *Table 326.10: Graduation rate from first institution attended for first-time, full-time bachelor's degree-seeking students at 4-year postsecondary institutions, by race/ethnicity, time to completion, sex, control of institution, and percentage of applications accepted: Selected cohort entry years, 1996 through 2012.* https://nces.ed.gov/programs/digest/d19/tables/dt19_326.10.asp

Snyder, T. D., de Brey, C., & Dillow, S. A. (2019). *Digest of education statistics 2018, 54th edition.* https://files.eric.ed.gov/fulltext/ED601992.pdf

The Forum on Education Abroad. (2020). *Standards of good practice for education abroad* (6th ed.). https://doi.org/10.36366/S.978-1-952376-04-7

United Nations. (n.d.). *Higher education.* Retrieved October 14, 2020, from https://www.un.org/en/academic-impact/higher-education

University of Delaware. (n.d.). *Our history.* https://www.udel.edu/academics/global/study-abroad/history

University of Michigan. (n.d.). *Defining diversity, equity and inclusion.* Retrieved October 14, 2020, from https://diversity.umich.edu/about/defining-dei/

YW Boston. (2019). *Beyond the DE&I acronym: What are diversity, equity, and inclusion?* https://www.ywboston.org/2019/03/beyond-the-acronym-dei/

Framing the Discussion

2

Advancing Inclusive Excellence in Education Abroad

Alma Clayton-Pedersen, Thandi Dinani, Kevin Hovland and Nick J. Gozik

The persistent underrepresentation of students of color, first-generation students, and other marginalized groups in education abroad programs represents a failure of higher education to engage the full educational benefits of its diverse campus communities. It is not only that these students continue to miss out on a potentially life-changing learning experience. Education abroad experiences themselves—their goals, designs, content, pedagogies, and locations—are diminished because participants are missing the contributions and perspectives of broadly diverse cohorts. These missing elements are critical to understand the cultural similarities and differences that education abroad is designed to explore.

Similarly, when education abroad professionals do not design their programs so that participants are exploring questions of race, class, power, and privilege intentionally and vigorously—the very issues that have historically shaped participation in education abroad—they fail to prepare students for an interconnected, interdependent, and just global future. Consequently, the case for the relevance of education abroad programs to the widest range of students is often lost. In addition, one of the most compelling arguments for recruitment to education abroad programs and other paths to global learning is blunted.

The good news is that colleges and universities are making progress in this area, and good intentions are evident. The Forum on Education Abroad, for example, includes Equity, Diversity, and Inclusion (EDI) as one of four Guiding Principles in its *Standards of Good Practice for Education Abroad* (2020a). To build on such progress, institutional leaders need to continue to situate their inclusion efforts within the context of broad questions of educational quality and definitions of excellence. As Clayton-Pedersen and Musil argue, "diversity is not typically a focus at any level of 'quality improvement' efforts. As a result, education leaders routinely work on diversity initiatives within one committee on campus and work on strengthening the quality of the educational experience within another" (2005, vii). By insisting that the demands for inclusion and quality are coupled, those who translate their institutional goals into practice can gain important insights into the systemic obstacles that need to be removed. In this way, they may also develop new, creative approaches to their work.

This chapter provides an overview of the concepts of Inclusive Excellence along with several closely related educational reform efforts. In addition to illuminating an important theoretical foundation, the chapter also offers practical strategies for applying the Inclusive Excellence framework to the ongoing critical challenge of improving equity in education abroad, through the implementation of what is referred to as the "RIBS" model.

The practical recommendations are designed to stimulate conversation and collaboration in all functional areas of education abroad. Inclusive Excellence ideals are not nurtured in a siloed environment. Excellence and inclusion are not two separate goals for education abroad. They must be pursued together, each furthering the other. Success requires insights, collaboration, and resources from across the campus and up and down the organization.

What Is Inclusive Excellence?

Before continuing further, it is necessary to define what we mean by "Inclusive Excellence"—a term that has been used widely though not always sustaining its original definition and purpose. Inclusive Excellence is a framework that many colleges and universities have used to strengthen and coordinate their efforts in four areas critical to mission: diversity, inclusion, equity, and educational quality. The framework has emerged from decades of practice at a wide range of campuses, where institutions have observed that while their student bodies were becoming more diverse, institutional structures and metrics of quality and equity were not keeping pace with change.

The James Irvine Foundation provided initial funding to Claremont Graduate University and the American Association of Colleges and Universities (AAC&U) to establish the Campus Diversity Initiative (CDI). The CDI engaged a group of 28 California colleges and universities over a period from 2000 to 2005. The CDI informed and assessed an array of campus diversity and inclusion efforts. The Inclusive Excellence framework emerged early during this process and informed the professional development opportunities designed over the course of the 5-year project. In 2003, AAC&U received additional funding from the Ford Foundation to continue to develop and refine Inclusive Excellence and share it with a national audience.

AAC&U was a logical choice to take national leadership on this work as its member institutions have always been deeply engaged in efforts to reform undergraduate education. These efforts included foregrounding questions of diversity and democracy in the curriculum and mission; developing well-articulated learning outcomes for all students; inventing and refining assessment tools needed to measure those outcomes; building capacity to utilize data that are produced by those assessment tools; improving pedagogies linked to student learning outcomes; and helping faculty members, administrators, and professional staff acquire the skills needed for all of the above. Additional information can be obtained from *Diversity Digest* (2003) and four AAC&U publications, including a monograph and three briefing papers developed as a *Making Excellence Inclusive* series (AAC&U, 2005–2007).

AAC&U enjoyed the further advantage of close relationships with valuable partners. The University of Southern California, Center for Urban Education (CUE), National Survey of Student Engagement, Indiana University Bloomington (NSSE), The National Institute for Learning Outcomes Assessment (NILOA), and others made critical contributions to the work of Inclusive Excellence. Other AAC&U initiatives provided insights and tools: VALUE (Valid Assessment of Learning in Undergraduate Education), LEAP (Liberal Education and America's Promise), and Shared Futures: Global Learning and Social Responsibility, primary among them. As this list suggests, there is an extensive literature related to both the theory of Inclusive Excellence and the data that support it.

The current definition of Inclusive Excellence emerged through these collaborative efforts that were intended to be flexible enough to evolve through practice and be adapted to individual campus realities, while also incorporating four primary elements:

1. A focus on student intellectual and social development. Academically, it means offering the best possible course of study for the context in which the education is offered.

2. A purposeful development and utilization of organizational resources to enhance student learning. Organizationally, it means establishing an environment that challenges each student to achieve academically at high levels and each member of the campus to contribute to learning and knowledge development.
3. Attention to the cultural differences that learners bring to the educational experience and that enhance the enterprise.
4. A welcoming community that engages all of its diversity in the service of student and organizational learning (Milem et al., 2005, p. vi).

In this chapter, we focus on the *practices* that help advance Inclusive Excellence. "The action of making excellence inclusive," according to AAC&U's website, "requires that we uncover inequities in student success, identify effective educational practices, and build such practices organically for sustained institutional change" (2020). We examine each of these actions in turn later, providing additional theoretical context as needed and explicitly linking them to education abroad when possible.

Uncovering Inequities in Student Success

As Williams, Berger, and McClendon argue, "To create a 'culture of inclusive excellence,' higher education leaders must consider how their campus environments can adapt to meet the needs of today's highly diverse entering students, rather than beginning with the assumption that diverse students must assimilate into existing environments with relatively narrow measures of quality" (2005, p. 9). Key to such an undertaking is developing appropriate metrics for success, collecting data on those metrics, and disaggregating those data to illuminate disparate outcomes.

Such practices reflect the development *of equity-mindedness,* which refers to a demonstrated awareness of and willingness to:

- address equity issues among institutional leaders, faculty, staff, and students;
- take stock of the contradictions between the ideals of democratic education and the social, institutional, and individual practices, as well as policies, expectations, and unspoken rules, that contribute to persistent inequalities in outcomes among different groups; and
- acknowledge the sociohistorical context of exclusionary practices, racism, and the effect of power asymmetries on opportunities and outcomes for

those who are underserved, underrepresented or have been marginalized. (Bensimon et al., 2016; Witham et al., 2015)

Equity-mindedness in education abroad means that diverse perspectives and cultures are represented among those engaged in the process of setting program priorities. All stakeholders need to be confident that their inclusion is not solely dependent upon them having been previously overlooked or excluded. For example, most education abroad opportunities are an added expense for students. Few institutions include such costs as part of tuition and not all provide for full aid transferability as part of their financial aid packages. When not all costs associated with the program (travel, food, housing, etc.) are included in tuition and ineligible for institutional aid, it makes it difficult for low-income students to participate, regardless of background. For other students, the challenge may be fear or lack of knowledge about the power of an education abroad experience. Often, even middle-income students of all races and ethnicities must work while attending college, making it difficult for them to have an education abroad experience. Together, stakeholder groups can identify and address the structural barriers reflected in current education abroad designs and supports.

Institutions can begin by assessing the degree to which *all* students view education abroad as a desirable learning experience. How do these viewpoints look when they are disaggregated by race, ethnicity, class, gender, and other diversity dimensions? What if leaders considered education abroad similarly to the majors that require more institutional resources than others? For example, science, technology, engineering, and mathematics (STEM) majors require work in laboratory and/or field settings, which necessitate added expenses. Leaders should consider education abroad or campus-based global learning a necessary endeavor for students who envision future careers that require global understanding and/or engagement. The cost of the laboratory expenses is included as part of STEM students' tuition; the means of broadening participation in education abroad could be addressed similarly.

Identify Effective Educational Practices

In recent years, there has been an explosion of work related to establishing and assessing student learning outcomes. At the most basic level, well-defined and well-articulated student learning outcomes are required before any determination of educational effectiveness can be made. This is true for a course, a major, general education, and education abroad. The AAC&U VALUE project has taken the lead in creating assessment tools to measure the effectiveness of 16 educational practices vis-à-vis learning outcomes. This process included the creation of rubrics derived from commonly used outcomes developed by teams of faculty experts representing colleges and universities across the U.S. For example, the Global Learning Rubric defines[1] and identifies the following outcome areas: Global Self-Awareness, Perspective Taking, Cultural Diversity, Personal and Social Responsibility, Understanding Global Systems, and Applying Knowledge to Contemporary Global Contexts. Each outcome area corresponds to a description of the evidence of what the outcome would look like (AAC&U, n.d.).

Ultimately, using the Global Learning Rubric or a similar process should enable practitioners to assess the effectiveness of their programs. If students are not demonstrating the expected evidence of global learning, the learning practice will likely need to be reexamined. In addition, if some students are reaching expected outcomes and others are not, an equity-minded approach and disaggregated data are needed to access the program elements.

Advancing Inclusive Excellence requires global and study away educational experiences to enhance participants' ability to understand the dynamics of the global challenges humanity faces, while examining an array of worldviews. These include the recent COVID-19 pandemic, fair trade across country boundaries, fair wages for workers, and the varied human conditions created by poverty. It also includes different worldviews among various population groups within their own country. Inclusive Excellence strategies seek to ensure that students complete their education abroad and study away with a worldview that goes beyond the place where they have the experience. Instead, a goal should be to assist students in putting the challenges and perspectives of other countries in relationship to their own to understand both better. The goal of global learning should be to develop students' understanding of the important role everyone has in maintaining the safety of humanity equitably, as well as the sustainability of our globe.

While some programs may accomplish this goal, too often learning outcomes from education abroad mainly reflect students' individual growth and

[1] AAC&U Value Rubric definition of Global Learning: Global learning is a critical analysis of and an engagement with complex, interdependent global systems and legacies (such as natural, physical, social, cultural, economic, and political) and their implications for people's lives and the earth's sustainability. Through global learning, students should (1) become informed, open minded, and responsible people who are attentive to diversity across the spectrum of differences; (2) seek to understand how their actions affect both local and global communities; and (3) address the world's most pressing and enduring issues collaboratively and equitably. Retrieved from the AAC&U website January 14, 2021.

development. These outcomes include learning another language or learning differences in business operations within a country's context. Clearly, these are useful educational gains, but students' learning could be expanded further and gain more when the experience is also grounded. This includes better understanding the country's history and culture, and most importantly, the underlying forces that highlight both differences and commonalities to the students' home countries. A depth of understanding of others who are different from oneself is foundational to realizing Inclusive Excellence as a lifelong goal of building cultural competence.

A parallel approach to educational effectiveness focuses on student engagement. Evidence of this type indicates that education abroad is a high-impact practice (HIP) that is effective in helping students achieve important learning outcomes. The ideas behind such HIPs have increasingly gained national attention since being introduced by Kuh (2008). AAC&U has also compiled a list of resources on education abroad specifically (Musil 2015), while other researchers and practitioners are recognized for leadership in researching the impact of all 11 HIPs (Kinzie et al., 2017). These resources will be of interest when developing the rationale for equitably expanding access to education abroad for historically underrepresented students.

As HIPs have been implemented more broadly and become the common shorthand for effective learning, it is important to understand what gives such practices their power. As Kuh (2008) describes them, HIPs:

- typically demand that students devote considerable time and effort to purposeful tasks.
- put students in circumstances that demand that they interact with faculty and peers about substantive matters.
- increase the likelihood that students will experience diversity through contact with people who are different than themselves.
- provide students . . . frequent feedback about their performance.
- help students . . . see how what they are learning works in different settings, on and off campus. (pp. 14–17)

Education abroad advocates and practitioners are passionate about their work because they believe that education abroad is a transformational learning experience. Kuh's work supports that intuitive conviction and illuminates some of the principles of good practice and design that make it so (Hovland, 2014). It is most important to note, however, that these practices have a high impact only when they are done well, as highlighted in the afterword (Clayton-Pedersen & Finley, 2010) of a study of 5 HIPs (Brownell

& Swaner, 2010). HIPs represent the best learning experiences that colleges and universities have to offer. Therefore, it is important that all students be encouraged and enabled to take advantage of them and that institutions identify and ensure equitable access to such experiences.

Sustained Institutional Change: The RIBS Model

Although much can be done on an individual level, we argue that a true shift toward inclusive practices in education abroad can only be achieved through sustained and successful institutional efforts. These efforts are the focus of the remainder of this chapter that is devoted to a detailed discussion of the RIBS model and its application. This model evolved from what was first conceptualized in Clayton-Pedersen's (1994) dissertation that focused on efforts to mobilize people who work on similar human development objectives. She observed that those institutions providing assistance to families in economic distress too often worked in parallel rather than in concert to move families to sufficiency. An earlier version of the RIBS framework was published in 2007 (Clayton-Pedersen & Dungy). Since then, the model has been refined through direct engagement with hundreds of campuses and nonprofit organizations.

The RIBS acronym stands for the following:

- ***R**aising awareness* among faculty, staff, and administrators of the institution's EDI challenges related to global learning and identify options to address them;
- ***I**ncreasing knowledge* about and understanding of these challenges to uncover its elements and the viable options required to address them effectively;
- ***B**uilding capacity* across the organization to identify and guide the essential tasks and professional development needed to achieve equitable outcomes using disaggregated data for assessment; and
- ***S**ustaining and evolving* successful efforts using relevant and effective assessment processes and tools, and using the narratives and data generated to reconfigure or eliminate elements that cannot demonstrate value in achieving their intended outcomes, while refining and expanding those that achieve their goals.

Each dimension of the RIBS model represents a scaffolding of institutional knowledge and action needed to accomplish various stated goals and to sustain the efforts successfully. RIBS enables stakeholders to develop shared understandings and common intellectual frameworks so they are in agreement regarding the elements necessary for success. The model encourages the kinds of robust collaborations necessary to engage the insights and practices of global learning and education abroad. It also offers a structure that generates insightful conversations about inclusion, diversity, equity, and excellence that informs the practices of global learning and education abroad.

The model also helps stakeholders recognize their overlapping and intersecting responsibilities for student success and positions students and their learning outcomes at the center of campus conversations. These then become important shared goals that are "owned" across traditional institutional divides between faculty, staff, administrators, managers, practitioners, and academic programs. Consequently, the RIBS model can be an efficient and effective means of acknowledging and addressing student learning, which takes place in the context of disciplines, departments, majors, and other less formal places and arrangements.

Applying the RIBS Model to Education Abroad

The RIBS action steps were initially conceived as a way for institutional leaders to identify, examine, and address the EDI challenges they faced. This model is equally well suited to offer education abroad stakeholders—including staff and faculty on campuses and working at education abroad provider organizations—a means to examine their programming critically. Its use can help stakeholders improve the design, practice, and assessment of education abroad in order to develop programs that lay a strong foundation for all students to make cultural competence a lifelong pursuit.

Although institutions vary in their structure and responsibilities, education abroad administrators may find themselves in a single-person office and have multiple personnel throughout a decentralized campus, one large staff that manages operations, or entities that function as a program provider partner for other institutions. Recognizing the vast difference in education abroad offices, this model is designed to assist readers in recognizing all stakeholders and consider who needs to be included in conversations. In addition, readers will find similarities between RIBS concepts and the recommendations found in The Forum's *Standards of Good Practice* (2020a); the RIBS model provides additional perspective on how the recommendations occur within institutional structures.

Raising Awareness: Education abroad professionals are most frequently tasked with raising awareness of education abroad and its value to a wide array of students. Those on the front lines, advisors in particular, are informed and well equipped to assist in identifying barriers and challenges in recruitment, application processes, and during the abroad experience. They can articulate students' rationale for participation as well as the challenges and benefits of their experiences—drawing on data, anecdotes, and other sources of information about their students. For these reasons, it has been argued that the education abroad field itself needs to become more diverse in order to best represent and advocate on behalf of a diverse student body (Charles & Wojenski, 2020).

At the same time, the full workload cannot rest on the shoulders of individual staff members, especially when it comes to transforming a whole system. It is just as important for leaders who oversee institutional improvement efforts to understand what needs to be done to achieve expected global learning outcomes among all students. In keeping with the values of Inclusive Excellence, there is general agreement that diverse communities of learners can increase learning for the entire community (Hurtado et al., 1999). Yet, diversity efforts have more often focused on compositional diversity, without concomitant attention to learning practices that promote educational equity and draw out the strengths of diverse learning environments.

To affect broader change, it is necessary to raise awareness across institutional structures, functions, and with intersecting groups. All leaders must understand the negative impact of inequitable educational opportunities when specific groups are underrepresented in HIPs like education abroad, as well as the value to campus and the institution's future of graduates who are globally and culturally competent. That awareness may focus on various facets of campus activity: developing overarching support structures and educational priorities advanced and supported by institutional leaders; evaluating whether existing abroad opportunities are accessed equitably and promote equitable learning outcomes abroad; and reviewing at the academic department level how education abroad, and other HIPs, are made explicit, relevant, and valuable to the student's degree, and available in all majors in their disciplines.

The support of institutional leaders at every level creates opportunities to advance campus-wide discussions on equity in education abroad, particularly now at junctures like the present, where EDI is top of mind on most campuses. When education abroad leaders can link this exploration to larger EDI conversations, it will position education abroad as a relevant illustration of how inequities occur and how they limit students' access to these educational outcomes. From the opening year convocations of college-level faculty, elevating education abroad participation as a facet of larger institutional priorities related to educational equity, quality, and access, positions it as a relevant opportunity within the scope of these campus discussions. This might involve having the President or Provost prioritize education abroad for the upcoming year (e.g., Western Kentucky University, 2013) or present awards to faculty or staff for work already done in this area (e.g., Grand Valley State University's "Internationalization Award," n.d.). Both of these examples can send a message for faculty and staff to shift their efforts and resources accordingly.

It is equally difficult to imagine that any efforts in student advocacy will be successful without involving faculty (who may also play a double role as staff). Faculty are instructors, advisors, and mentors, who know and understand students' lives. They are likewise integrally involved in curricular decision-making. Faculty senates and committees are ideal places to consider connections between students' experiences on campus and abroad, as well as strategies for increasing EDI in global programming. Some institutions like Western Michigan University (n.d.) have set up separate international education councils with an express charge of addressing diversity and inclusion. At the same time, faculty are themselves highly involved in implementing education abroad programs, as faculty leaders and instructors—a trend that has continued with the sharp increase in short-term and faculty-led programs (Institute of International Education, 2019). In this capacity, faculty are positioned to speak personally about the benefits that their students gain from overseas programming.

At the same time, institutions need to ensure that other key constituents are made aware of the importance of both education abroad and Inclusive Excellence, including parents, students, donors, and alumni. Each group requires a different communication strategy. It can be helpful, for example, to communicate core values to parents and prospective students during recruitment events and parent weekends. This might include presentations and marketing materials catered to various groups. Some institutions have translated this information into various languages (e.g., Spanish and Mandarin), to make the content more accessible. Similarly, presentations and discussions might take place during alumni gatherings and Trustees meetings. The more the stakeholder actors are involved, it is more likely that the narrative around education abroad will be shifted.

Increasing Knowledge: Once awareness has been raised, the next step is to gather more information and data. It is critical to understand students' needs and desires, existing individual and institutional barriers and challenges, and examples of where success has already been achieved. Otherwise, we may find that we are simply doing a lot of work without making any headway.

As with raising awareness, increasing knowledge must have a campus-wide reach to have the greatest impact. Here, it is helpful to start with diagnostic tools such as Sweeney's (2013) adaption of the AAC&U's Inclusive Excellence Scorecard (Williams et al., 2005), tailored to evaluate an institutions' progress toward equity and access in study abroad. Sweeney's scorecard includes four areas, each of which comes with a set of sample indicators: access and equity within study abroad, the campus climate, diversity within formal and informal curricula, and the learning and development of study abroad participants. This configuration supports the collection of data and information both at the campus level (e.g., race/ethnicity composition of faculty, staff, and students; concerns around discrimination and injustice on campus) and within education abroad units (e.g., diversity of students participating in education abroad; and resources and opportunities for reflection on race/ethnicity within predeparture/on-site/and reentry activities). Such analyses will demonstrate that all of these indicators are interconnected and part of a larger picture.

To answer the questions that Sweeney raises, leaders and staff need to know more about the students who are eligible to participate yet are missing from education abroad, as well as those who participate. Many of these data are already available, if not always mined sufficiently, through campus-wide information systems. These may include collecting information on self-reported race/ethnicity/gender; grades, majors/minors, graduation rates, and financial aid status; and education abroad databases including study destinations and initial interest versus actual participation. Data should be disaggregated by race, gender, and gender identity, as well as by ability status, disciplinary majors, and overall student demographics and economic status (i.e., recipients or nonrecipients of Pell government grants). It is also possible to obtain data from national and campus-wide surveys such as first-year, senior, NSSE, IPEDS, and program and course-level evaluations. Likewise, it is useful to conduct an analysis of messaging to current and prospective students through websites, marketing materials, and public announcements (Gozik, 2015).

At the same time, it is also crucial to hear directly from those students most affected. The majority of participants report positive education abroad experiences. However, through mechanisms such as interviews, focus groups, and surveys, it is important to identify and consult with students who do not provide positive feedback to discover what would have made their experiences more positive. Student returnees can help identify areas of support that would have made their experience more inclusive and equitable (Schulze, 2016). Findings can be disaggregated to determine if all students report similar experiences in academic, co-curricular programming, and housing (e.g., homestays, apartments with roommates from host countries, apartments with American roommates). Questions to consider include: In what areas do historically underserved and marginalized students report the need for assistance? Are resources readily available for these students when they arrive? What practices at home campuses and host institutions cause students to feel singled out and/or ostracized?

Just as importantly, it is essential to know more about students who chose *not* to go abroad. One might ask male students, for example, what hinders their plans to participate in education abroad, whether they value education abroad, and what would add value to education abroad for them (Lucas, 2018)? Similarly, are students of color, students from low-income families, and other underrepresented groups provided with opportunities that are most appealing or applicable to them?

Throughout this process, faculty and staff can be instrumental in digging deeper into students' experiences on individual programs. This can include tracking programs that have been more (or less) successful in recruiting and engaging a greater diversity of students. For example, the "Paris Noir" program at Boston College attracted a large number of students of color (Hackett, 2018), both from a number perspective and in determining where students feel most supported through curricular and co-curricular programming. The latter can be gleaned by talking to students during postreturn debriefing sessions and by analyzing their responses to postprogram evaluations. It is also essential to review outcomes assessment data to understand where students have met stated learning outcomes. Particularly important are outcomes data related to coping with ambiguity, relating to people who are different from oneself, and becoming more globally and/or interculturally competent. These can be measured by tools such as the Global Perspectives Inventory (GPI), the Intercultural Development Inventory (IDI), and the VALUE Rubrics.

Building Institutional Capacity: Once barriers to participation have been identified, key constituents need to work together to undertake the work of removing those barriers. This will entail exploring and enacting a variety of strategies that are necessary to make participation equitable for those who historically have been underserved. As outlined in Chapter 1 of this volume by Gozik and Barclay Hamir, building institutional capacity in this sense goes well beyond making a few superficial changes, and instead suggests broader, more holistic approaches that address structural changes.

Much of this work relies on establishing clear learning outcomes, as noted earlier, with particular attention to increasing awareness of diverse people and their perspectives and developing intercultural competence. If we do not know what students should learn and gain from programs, how can we confirm that programs and administrative structures that support them will be effective? A tremendous amount has already been written on learning outcomes assessment efforts in education abroad in (see Chapter 13 in this volume by Yngve and Brewer). This research repeatedly emphasizes the need to integrate learning outcomes into all stages of a student's education abroad process, including stating goals for students prior to departure (Bennett & Bennett, 2004). Once learning outcomes have been established, it becomes much easier to select other program components, such as courses, housing, and activities that align accordingly and add much more intentionality to programming (Gozik & Oguro, 2020).

Also important is making sure that there is sufficient funding to make student aid available, additional advising and support staff, and programs with broad appeal. In fact, the majority of institutions with high study abroad participation (i.e., 29%–100% of graduates studied abroad) were private (U.S. News & World Reports, 2020). This suggests that public institutions and those with smaller endowments and budgets may need to find creative fundraising strategies to make education abroad and study away offerings more inclusive. Obtaining sufficient funding involves enlisting the help of colleagues across the institution. For example, a perceptive chief financial officer (CFO) might suggest reallocating existing resources, or suggest a means of generating new resources, to support low-income students' abroad experiences. Other suggestions include the CFO offering enough seed money to build programs that show promise of eventually becoming self-sustaining. Development offices also can be strong partners in fundraising efforts, as can department chairs and office leaders who may have access to grants and scholarships. Financial aid officers can help the campus community understand financial aid rules and help students develop budgets. Advisors in education abroad offices can research, cull, and communicate funding opportunities including those offered through the U.S. Departments of State (e.g., Gilman, Boren, and Fulbright awards), the U.S. Department of Education, and through private organizations and donors.

In addition to finances, it is necessary to collaborate with colleagues to ensure that education abroad is effectively integrated into other academic and co-curricular programming on the home campus. Equity-minded and effectively developed cross-cultural engagement can sufficiently awaken learners' curiosity and desire to pursue developing their cultural competence as a lifelong endeavor. This would include courses that examine topics related to EDI and disciplines such as history, psychology, and sociology that examine the histories of different cultures and human behavior. Education abroad staff may have little control over the direction of curricula and other programming, yet they can collaborate with colleagues in departments to develop courses that complement education abroad experiences (e.g., pre-program courses on campus, senior seminars). The Duke Immerse program and Boston College's McGillycuddy-Logue Fellows program are examples of institutions that offer a sequence of abroad and on-campus activities that assist students in putting the pieces together.

Collaborations with other departments on campus can set clear road maps for students to incorporate education abroad activities into their majors/minors. This ensures that students can graduate on schedule while also gaining a global perspective. It is especially important for students in fields with little flexibility regarding sequencing coursework such as engineering, the health sciences, and education. Developing these strategies takes time, but they can achieve relatively quick outcomes in terms of participation rates, including for majors/minors that have historically been underrepresented in education abroad such as Boston University's engineering program (Pérez-Juez & Eisenberg, 2018).

To ensure that faculty and staff are prepared to support students and follow through on the aims outlined earlier, institutions need to offer sufficient professional development and resources. In the U.S., international education organizations like The Forum on Education Abroad, NAFSA, Diversity Abroad, and the Association of International Education Administrators (AIEA) offer such support. These offerings include conferences and workshops that can be tailored to institutional needs, opportunities to serve on committees that engage in discussions online and in person, and printed resources and workshops that can be tailored to institutional needs. Many also provide sharing opportunities within listservs, where institutional representatives can ask questions and gather information. Sister organizations have similarly been established in other regions (EAIE and APAIE) and countries (APUAF and APUNE). For more specific topics such as the development of intercultural competence, colleagues might consider attending Wake Forest University's annual WISE conference and the Institute for Cross-Cultural Teaching and Learning. It is also helpful to look beyond the international education community for events and professional development that can help inform the needs of specific groups of students.

At the same time, it is vital to recognize that building capacity means working with education abroad partners, including institutions, homestay families, and on-site staff that may be hired by a provider or the home campus. There are limitations regarding what can be done on the home campus, given that much of students' abroad experiences will take place overseas. There are also significant cultural differences that may affect the extent to which colleagues in other countries may understand and be able to respond to student needs. Similar to earlier, it is necessary to provide professional development and a space for cross-cultural dialogue (see the University of Minnesota example in Chapter 11 of this volume). Such preparations enable on-site staff to be better positioned to facilitate reflection opportunities that challenge students to examine their biases in host and home countries and identify similarities and differences in home and host communities that have been marginalized and underserved.

When assembled, each of the various components outlined lead to greater institutional capacity as well as to more holistic and systemic changes. Without clear learning outcomes, programmatic changes, broad campus support, and opportunities for professional development, it is unlikely that there be long-term, significant growth. At the same time, it is important to make sure that any modifications made are inclusive, equitable, and sustainable.

Sustaining Efforts: The fourth aspect of RIBS, sustaining the effort, is paramount. Sustaining and evolving inclusive and equitable education abroad practices begin in the first stage of the RIBS process by raising the community's awareness of the challenges and effects of exclusion and inequities in education abroad. Once the process of deep engagement by the campus community is established, institutional leaders and educators should consider the means by which the actions identified remain relevant and develop processes to address the diversity in the student populations who seek education abroad.

All stakeholders will need to collaborate to sustain efforts. Invite colleagues into the entirety of the education abroad process and find opportunities to collaborate throughout the entirety of students' experiences. It is important for historically marginalized and underserved students to have safe spaces where they can share their experiences and receive support. Historically marginalized and underserved students may not perceive personnel within education abroad offices as people to whom they can express their frustrations and challenges. Moreover, in general, students do not always see education abroad advisors as the most trusted sources of information (Stroud, 2015).

One challenge is staffing. We all know of that amazing colleague who begins a new program or initiative and then leaves, allowing the activity to disappear, falter, or fall into disarray. This is more likely to occur when strong efforts to collaborate across organizational lines are limited or nonexistent. The challenge of turnover makes it even more important for hiring officials to seek and hire candidates across the institution who demonstrate skills in collaboration and EDI, not just in one unit. Programming is also likely to continue when there is cross-unit professional development for staff, sufficient and long-term funding, and a full understanding across a unit/organization about the aims, policies, and practices of a given activity.

Equally important is a need to review programs and communication strategies on a regular and cyclical basis, thus closing the loop. It is all too easy to be caught up in the act of "doing," without taking time to ensure that one is still holding steady to previously established goals and evolving those that have ceased to serve their original purpose. Adding recurring check-in meetings and/or calendar reminders can serve as helpful reminders. With some auditing procedures, reviews may be built into existing processes. If not, a department or office may set up a timetable for more extensive evaluations, perhaps including colleagues from other areas of campus or other institutions. Any appraisal can and should include an analysis of students' experiences and attainment of learning outcomes and using the results to improve the programs.

Any program or initiative will need to adapt based on students' needs and/or institutional priorities. Yet, arbitrary means to increase the participation of those who historically have been marginalized will thwart efforts to make excellence inclusive in education abroad and undermine the very students this work seeks to engage. Instead, success requires that designers prioritize engaging members of these communities of students for their input regarding the barriers they face to participating in the programs. Better ensuring newcomers success requires being open to new ideas and practices that emerge from listening to the voices of a full range of diverse communities. This requires that we seek a better understanding of the needs and perspectives of all students, not just some students.

Likewise, it should be assumed that situations will arise that necessitate adjustments to the identified engagement strategies and activities. The recent pandemic is a perfect example of the need for educators to change course as needed. In all of these ways, sustainability may suggest that an activity needs to exist in perpetuity or remain unchanged. The programming itself is not the end goal. Instead, the goal is to serve as broad and diverse array of students while ensuring that all students have an opportunity to take full advantage of what the experience has to offer. Accordingly, sustainable practices must keep such long-end goals in mind.

Sustainability also requires creative approaches to reimagining the goals and methods that attract students to education abroad and appeals to students' interests and experiences so that they all can recognize its value to their personal, educational, civic, and professional futures. Consideration must likewise be given to devising means for campus community reflection on what makes existing models work, for whom they are working, and which processes require repair. Without such a soul-searching examination, we may miss the goal of broadening participation. That goal includes providing equitable and inclusive opportunities to those who previously have been overlooked.

Conclusion

This chapter does not present an Inclusive Excellence "2.0" per se, rather it returns us to the fundamentals of what was initially outlined by the AAC&U's Making Excellence Inclusive initiative in 2005. Taking education abroad as one slice of higher education, we have considered the extent to which making excellence inclusive has been realized while also developing a road map for expanding full participation, using the RIBS model developed by Clayton-Pedersen, one of the chief architects of the AAC&U's Inclusive Excellence initiative.

A primary reason that global learning is important for all students is that such experiences develop cultural competence. We must also be creative in reimagining the goals and methods of education abroad and study away so that all students can recognize its value to their educational and civic futures. Through well-designed experiences, students become more aware of their own cultural worldview, recognize their attitude toward cultural differences, understand different cultural practices and worldviews, and become more thoughtful in cross-cultural interaction. Another is that global learning experiences are among the well-researched, high-impact pedagogical practices. Yet, we must seek a better understanding of the needs and perspectives of all students to be able to extend the benefits of education abroad to those who do not have the resources to access these well-researched and powerful educational practices.

More must be done by program developers to ensure that all students recognize the dual advantages of education abroad and global learning outcomes by being realistic about how existing models work, and for whom. It is important, for example, for academic advisors to explain the value of education abroad to all students, not just those who request information. And to do so in ways that all students from underrepresented groups may gain an understanding of the long-term educational and career advantages from participation. We need to frame education abroad and study away within broader conversations about expanding notions of educational and institutional excellence that include effectively addressing the disparities that exist.

A higher education system that prioritizes the study of cultures, global challenges, and equity through education abroad and other global learning experiences can dramatically expand the number of U.S. citizens who develop a global worldview. This in turn can establish a national foundation for broader international and domestic cooperation, collaborative problem-solving, and mutual care and concern. Broadening global learning starts in the classroom, in the broadly diverse communities developed by indigenous people, slaves and their children, and immigrants to the U.S., and the capstone is an education abroad experience. This strategy could start small and grow based on research and assessments of the cost–benefit of improved global learning and improved collaboration across nations. The absence of a coordinated, global strategy to combat the 2020 COVID-19 pandemic is a timely example and opportunity to engage in a problem-based, global learning exercise. It offers a problem-based entry into the classroom to broaden participation in education abroad. This and similar strategies can move higher education closer to making excellence inclusive with respect to global learning and education abroad.

Education abroad and global learning, with their focus on cultural competence, are well aligned with the needs and expectations of an interconnected and interdependent world. They are also powerful models for the kinds of attitudes and aptitudes that are necessary for successful campus change efforts. Institutional team members need well-honed cultural competence in order to engage with multiple stakeholders and make excellence inclusive. Yet, access to such an experience requires that structures be in place to examine and mitigate the cost of this educational experience regularly to better ensure equitable participation. Also needed are means for institutions to address successfully reported negative experiences that are based on racial and ethnic identity and other dimensions of diversity across participant groups.

We hope that the practical suggestions mentioned earlier stimulate rich conversations. They can be summarized as variants on five basic questions that animate the work ahead.

1. Has my institution clearly articulated to students, faculty, and staff the outcomes and benefits of the global learning expected from its education abroad programming?
2. How are education abroad program objectives and global learning outcomes articulated and assessed?
3. How is information gained from the assessment process used to improve the programs?
4. How can these programs be designed and funded to offer equitable access to students who historically have been marginalized and underserved?
5. How might the content and practices of education abroad programs be redesigned to eliminate the inequities that historically marginalized students in the U.S. experience, ensuring they are not replicated or exacerbated in their abroad experiences?

A campus Inclusive Excellence framework should engage a great number of allies across the larger campus community in these questions as it moves explorations of EDI to the very core of definitions and metrics for institutional success. Professionals in the education abroad office should use the RIBS process to identify and align more fully their specific goals and objectives with the general priorities of an institution that is seeking to make excellence inclusive. Once these priorities are aligned, international educators are encouraged to seek help and borrow expertise from their campus allies. These allies include those who are engaged in institutional research, strategic planning, development, retention, academic affairs, financial aid, and student affairs areas focused on advocacy and social activism.

Such strategies can help education abroad professionals, faculty members, administrators, and students achieve the promises made in The Forum's recently released *Standards of Good Practice for Education Abroad* 6th edition, as well as in its newly revised *Code of Ethics:*

> We seek out opportunities to engage with diverse populations and perspectives, and do so with patience, understanding, humility, and respect, modelling the behavior we aim to cultivate in our learners. We endeavor to expand access to education abroad, and to create an environment of inclusivity that is open, respectful, and safe for all. We strive for equity in our treatment of all. We do not accept intolerance, and we work to eliminate inequities within our organizations and communities. Shared Values II C—Equity, Diversity and Inclusion. (The Forum, 2020, II, p. 3)

We do not assume that all those who manage the education abroad process and experiences have sufficient human resources to do *all* that is recommended in this chapter. This underscores the urgent need for collaboration across historical boundaries of offices, departments, and programs and institutions. The divisions within the U.S. should signal to the higher education community that we could use more cross-racial/ethnic and cross-cultural interaction within our country. Given that we are a nation made of indigenous people and people from all other nations, we should be able to develop and implement programs in which all students come to better understand the cultures of the world within our country.

References

Association of American Colleges and Universities. (2003). *Diversity digest.* https://www.colorado.edu/odece/sites/default/files/attached-files/rba08-14-11-2016-50802.pdf

Association of American Colleges and Universities. (n.d.). *Global learning VALUE rubric.* www.aacu.org/value/rubrics/global-learning

Bennett, J. M., & Bennett, M. J. (2004). *Developing intercultural sensitivity: An integrative approach to global and domestic diversity.* https://www.semanticscholar.org/paper/Developing-Intercultural-Sensitivity%3A-An-Approach-Bennett-Bennett/95bf57ec378d6f151cfab8799ce48b29a5de9c7b

Bennett, J. M. (2008). Transformative training: Designing programs for cultural learning. In M. Moodian. (Ed.), Contemporary leadership and intercultural competence: understanding and utilizing cultural diversity to build successful organizations. Sage Publishing. https://us.sagepub.com/en-us/nam/contemporary-leadership-and-intercultural-competence/book231703

Bensimon, E. M. (2004). The diversity scorecard: A learning approach to institutional change. *Change: The Magazine of Higher Learning, 36*(1), 44–52.

Bensimon, E. M., Dowd, A. C., & Witham, K. (2016, Winter). Five principles for enacting equity by design. *Diversity and Democracy, The Equity Imperative. 19*(1).

Boston College. (n.d.). McGillycuddy-Logue Fellows Program. Accessed at https://www.bc.edu/bc-web/offices/office-of-international-programs/mcgillycuddy-logue-center/fellows-program.html

Brownell, J., & Swaner, L (2010). Five high impact practices: Research on learning outcomes, completion, and quality. Association of American Colleges and Universities. https://www.aacu.org/publication/five-high-impact-practices-research-on-learning-outcomes-completion-and-quality

Charles, H., & Wojenski, C. (2020, September 9). To diversify education abroad participation, start with advisers. *International Educator.* Accessed at https://www.nafsa.org/ie-magazine/2020/9/9/diversify-education-abroad-participation-start-advisers

Clayton-Pedersen, A. (1992). *The elements of success: An implementation analysis of the Job Opportunities and Basic Skills (JOBS) Program in Tennessee.* [Doctoral dissertation, Vanderbilt University]. Vanderbilt Repository.

Clayton-Pedersen, A., Parker, S., & Smith Daryl. (2003). *The James Irvine Foundation's Campus Diversity Initiative. Diversity Digest, 7*(4).

Clayton-Pedersen, A., & Dungy, G. J. (2007). Developing effective collaboration. In J. Cook & C. Lewis (Eds.), *The divine comity.* National Association of Student Personnel Administrators (NASPA).

Clayton-Pedersen, A., Parker, S., Smith, D. G., Moreno, J. F., and Teraguchi, D. H. (2007). Appendix 2—Campus Diversity Initiative (CDI) Evaluation Project Institutionalization Rubric. Making a real difference with diversity: A guide to institutional change. Association of American Colleges and Universities. https://www.amazon.com/s?k=9780977921058&i=stripbooks&linkCode=qs

Clayton-Pedersen, A., & Musil, C. M. (updated 2017). *Making Excellence Inclusive: A framework for embedding diversity and inclusion into colleges and universities' academic excellence mission.* Association of American Colleges and Universities. https://www.bc.edu/content/dam/files/offices/diversity/2018keynoteresources/Making%20Excellence%20Inclusive%20(updated%202015).docx

Clayton-Pedersen, A., & Finley, A. (2010). Afterword: What's next? Identifying when high-impact practices are done well. In J. Brownell & L. Swaner (Eds.), Five high impact practices: Research on learning outcomes, completion, and quality. Association of American Colleges and Universities. https://www.google.com/books/edition/Five_High_impact_Practices/squRXwAACAAJ?hl=en

Duke University. (n.d.). *About Duke immerse.* Accessed at https://undergrad.duke.edu/programs/dukeimmerse

Goodwin, C. D., & Nacht, M. (2009). *Missing the boat: The failure to internationalize American higher education.* Cambridge University Press.

Gozik, N. (2015). Adapting the office mission and assessment practices to institutional needs. In Savicki, V. & E. Brewer (Eds.), *Assessing study abroad: Theories, tools, and practices* (pp. 162–179). Sterling, VA: Stylus.

Gozik, N., & Oguro, S. (2020). Beyond the gold standard: A review of program components in education abroad. In A. Ogden, B. Streitwieser, & C. van Mol (Eds.), *Education abroad: Bridging scholarship and practice* (pp. 59–72). Routledge.

Grand Valley State University. (n.d.). Faculty convocation. Accessed at https://www.gvsu.edu/provost/faculty-convocation-175.htm

Hackett, A. (2019, September). A different view of Paris 'Paris Noir' summer course gives students a chance to explore black history and identity in France. Accessed at https://www.bc.edu/bc-web/bcnews/nation-world-society/international/a-different-view-of-paris.html

Hoffa, W. (2007). *A history of U.S. study abroad: Beginnings to 1965.* The Forum on Education Abroad.

Hovland, K. (2014). *Global learning: Defining, designing, demonstrating.* Association of American Colleges and Universities.

Hurtado, S., Milem, J., Clayton-Pedersen, A., & Allen, W. (1999). *Enacting diverse learning environments: Improving the climate for racial/ethnic diversity in higher education. ASHE-ERIC Higher Education Report, Vol. 26, No. 8.* ERIC Clearinghouse on Higher Education.

Institute of International Education. (2019). *Open Doors report on international educational exchange.* Retrieved from https://opendoorsdata.org

Kinzie, J., Matross Helms, R., & Cole, J. (2017). A glimpse of global learning: Assessing student experiences and institutional commitments. *Liberal Education, 103*(2), n2.

Kuh, G., & Schneider, C. (2008). High-impact educational practices: What they are, who has access to them, and why they matter. Association of American Colleges and Universities. Item Detail – High-Impact Educational Practices (E-Title) (aacu.org)

Lucas, J. M. (2018). There and back again: A study abroad journey with men. In H. Barclay Hamir & N. Gozik (Eds.), *Promoting inclusion in education abroad: A handbook of research and practice* (pp. xxx). Stylus.

Milem, J. F., Chang, M. J., & Antonio, A. L. (2005). *Making diversity work on campus: A research-based perspective.* Association of American Colleges and Universities.

Musil, C. M. (2015). Service learning: Education's most powerful civic pedagogy. *The European Wergeland Center (EWC) Statement Series.* Retrieved from https://www.phbern.chsites/default/files/2019-10/EWC_Statement_Series_2015.pdf#page=7

Pérez-Juez, A., & Eisenberg, S. R. (2018). Engineers abroad: Opportunities for sophomores in international education. In H. Barclay Hamir & N. Gozik (Eds.), *Promoting inclusion in education abroad: A handbook of research and practice* (pp. xxx). Stylus.

Robinson-Armstrong, A., King, D., Killoran, D., & Fissinger, M. (2009). The equity scorecard: An effective tool for assessing diversity initiatives. *International Journal of Diversity in Organizations, Communities and Nations, 8*(6), 31–39.

Schulze, W. L. (2016). *Best practices for increasing diversity in study abroad: A manual for small private co-ed universities in the United States.* University of San Francisco Scholarship: A digital repository @ Gleeson Library https://repository.usfca.edu/capstone/347

Stroud, A. H. (2015). *Should I stay or should I go?: Factors impacting the decision to study abroad among students who have expressed intent.* University of Massachusetts-Amherst. https://scholarworks.umass.edu/dissertations_2

Sweeney, K. (2013). Inclusive excellence and underrepresentation of students of color in study abroad. *Frontiers: The Interdisciplinary Journal of Study Abroad, 23*(1), 1–21. https://doi.org/10.36366/frontiers.v23i1.326

The Forum on Education Abroad. (2020a). *Standards of Good Practice (6th Edition).* Retrieved from https://forumea.org/resources/standards-6th-edition

The Forum on Education Abroad (2020b). *Code of Ethics for education abroad.* Retrieved from https://forumea.org/resources/standards-6th-edition/code-of-ethics

U.S. News & World Reports. (2020, November 8). *Best colleges reviews: Study abroad.* https://www.usnews.com/best-colleges/rankings/study-abroad-programs

University of Southern California Center for Urban Education. (2020). *CUE racial equity tools.* Retrieved from https://cue.usc.edu

Western Kentucky University. (2013, August 23). https://www.wku.edu/presidentemeritus/convocation/2013.php

Western Michigan University. (n.d.). Faculty Senate/International Education Council. Accessed at https://wmich.edu/facultysenate/councils/international

Whitehead, D. (2017). Foreword in Nair, I. and Henning, M., *Models of global learning.* Association of American Colleges and Universities.

Witham, K., Malcom-Piqueux, L., Dowd, A., & Bensimon, E. M. (2015). *America's unmet promise: The imperative for equity in higher education.* Association of American Colleges and Universities.

Williams, D. A., Berger, J. B., & McClendon, S. A. (2005). *Toward a model of inclusive excellence and change in postsecondary institutions.* Association of American Colleges and Universities. https://operations.du.edu/file/9607

3

The Promise of Equity-Minded Practice: Lessons Learned from Higher Education for Education Abroad

Eduardo Contreras, Asabe Poloma and Ana M. Martínez Alemán

Introduction: Diversity, Equity, and Inclusion in Higher Education: Considerations for Education Abroad Today

At present, it is evermore imperative that college and university staff and faculty understand how higher education can respond to ongoing calls for racial, ethnic, and gender equity and how new challenges brought on by a global pandemic require new efforts to ensure educational equity and inclusion. In the United States, the tragic murders of Black Americans George Floyd, Ahmaud Arbery, and Breonna Taylor reminded us that the pernicious legacy of slavery and White supremacy continues to work against Black, indigenous, and people of color (BIPOC). The global COVID-19 pandemic presented institutions with innumerable fiscal, pedagogical, and technical challenges. In particular, the socioeconomic vulnerability of many BIPOC students has become conspicuous and will continue to demand urgent institutional attention and action in order to support access and student success. Although this vulnerability is not altogether new for BIPOC students, their postsecondary educational persistence will certainly be greatly impacted by their ability to access health care, housing, classroom resources, and technologies required for online courses.

Within this broader context of higher education, education abroad programs must also pivot and respond to calls for inclusive excellence and equitable access to global learning opportunities during these contemporary challenges. As colleges and universities reimagine overseas study for the postpandemic world, will the emerging and existing education abroad approaches and opportunities consider the needs of BIPOC students? How will college and university education abroad programs embrace frameworks for postsecondary equity, diversity, and inclusion (EDI) to achieve inclusive excellence that is beneficial to all students?

A centerpiece of global learning, inclusive excellence directs postsecondary institutions to commit to students' substantive engagement with difference (e.g., racial, cultural, and linguistic) in global learning (Doscher & Landorf, 2018). Increasing the number of BIPOC students in education abroad can certainly help institutions achieve inclusive excellence (Chang, 1999) but, as is the case in higher education generally, just improving compositional or structural diversity (i.e., increasing the raw number of BIPOC students) does not guarantee that the cross-race relationships necessary for substantive engagement will be formed (McPherson et al., 2001). However, research does indicate that structural diversity in higher education can lead to more close interracial relationships among students and that these relationships, "may notably shape post college behaviors, attitudes, and values" (Bowman, 2012, p. 134). It seems, then, that to achieve inclusive excellence in education abroad programs, colleges and universities must not only improve the participation rates of BIPOC students but also craft experiences that can motivate the development of interracial relationships and extend those experiences to relational engagement with cultural, racial, religious, and ethnic difference. To do so, education abroad practitioners should consider broader EDI frameworks in postsecondary education, as well as research-based evidence on BIPOC student experiences to guide the design of inclusive excellence in their programs that meet the unique needs of all students.

This chapter situates education abroad within EDI frameworks and research in order to understand best practices for inclusive excellence in higher education abroad. For the purposes of this chapter, we build on the work established in the opening chapter of *Promoting Inclusion in Education Abroad* (Hamir & Gozik, 2018) by utilizing the Inclusive Excellence framework outlined by the Association of American Colleges and Universities (AAC&U, n.d.). This framework calls on higher education to, "address diversity, inclusion, and equity as critical to the well-being of democratic culture" (AAC&U, 2013). Accordingly, this chapter opens with an overview of EDI frameworks in U.S. higher education and supporting empirical research. Research on equity and inclusion in education abroad programs is also discussed. Although these data and their implications are U.S. specific, the U.S. case may be informative to other national contexts. Borrowing from scholarship and success in other areas of higher education, the chapter concludes with four areas that can help advance inclusive excellence in education abroad.

Equity, Diversity, and Inclusion in U.S. Higher Education

Generally, EDI frameworks in U.S. higher education make distinctions between each of their grounding conceptual elements. Equity or equity-mindedness focuses on institutional policies and practices that have perpetuated gaps in BIPOC student achievement as a way of framing postsecondary change (Bensimon, 2007). Focusing responsibility for change on institutions rather than on assumed deficiencies in BIPOC students, equity-mindedness frames institutional diversity and inclusion as goals possible only through the transformation of organizational, cultural, pedagogical, and curricular norms and practices. By applying the principles of equity-mindedness and using tools that evaluate equitable practices, such as an equity scorecard (Bensimon, 2012; Bensimon et al., 2016), institutions can effectively move toward inclusive campus policies and practices. As a guide for institutional practices and policies, equity-mindedness propositions include (a) the development of a color-conscious (not color-blind) worldview; (b) awareness that normative discourses, practices, and policies are not neutral and likely have racially disparate effects; (c) willingness to accept responsibility for putting an end to racial and ethnic inequality on campus; and (d) an awareness that racism is both covert and overt, and that racialized patterns are embedded in institutional policies and practices (Bensimon et al., 2016). Consequently, institutional efforts to achieve inclusive excellence within the entire organization (e.g., structural, cultural, pedagogical, and/or curricular) require a form of assessment or accountability that moves beyond a compositional metric or race and ethnicity and toward a substantive discursive assessment of behaviors, strategies, administration, systems, and traditions.

Diversity is ordinarily understood to refer to structural diversity or the presence of racially and ethnically diverse groups on campus. As a goal for campuses to attain inclusive excellence, structural diversity is compositional and enumerative. The number of students, staff, and faculty from historically marginalized or minoritized racial and ethnic groups in higher education constitutes a measure of the extent to which a campus is diversified or multicultural. By virtue of some proportional representation, diverse campuses presume that racial and ethnic heterogeneity among students, staff, and faculty will set the course for attaining institutional inclusive excellence. Undoubtedly, racial and ethnic diversity among campus populations is not unrelated to achieving inclusive excellence, but an enumerative increase in "diverse" people does not guarantee the cultural changes necessary for institutions to be equitable and inclusive. Without organizational, cultural, pedagogical, and curricular change and accountability informed by equity principles (Dowd & Bensimon, 2015), compositional diversity will likely constitute assimilationist action that ostensibly accommodates minoritized identities to hegemonic norms (Martínez Alemán & Salkever, 2003).

In higher education worldwide, "inclusion" and "inclusive education" are most often associated with a call for paradigmatic change in primary and secondary education to include children with any form of disability but also as a framework to consider access and attainment for students "vulnerable to exclusion" (Messiou, 2017, p. 147). Immigrant, racial, ethnic, and indigenous groups, as well as students with behavioral or disciplinary issues, are among those likely to be excluded from full-access participation in education. However, as Messiou (2017) points out, educational inclusion is also framed by principles of "equity, participation, community and respect for diversity" (p. 147). Inclusive higher education worldwide now has broadened frameworks to include LGBQ, trans- and gender-diverse people (McKendry & Lawrence, 2020; Renn, 2017), and students with intellectual disabilities such as autism (Bethune-Dix et al., 2020), among the many historically marginalized groups discriminated against through inequitable practices and policies. In addition, the confluence of multiple identities that individuals in these many groups embody creates particular experiences that may challenge institutional inclusion efforts (Museus & Griffen, 2011). Conceptually, then, inclusive higher education is constituted by those principles in compositional or structural diversity and equity and equity-mindedness.

EDI in Higher Education Today

Racial and ethnic inequity and disproportional representation in U.S. higher education persists today. Despite this, there have been some improvements. Higher education has seen a significant increase in the number of students of color attending varied institutions over the past two decades. In addition, there has been slow but steady growth of ethnic and racial representation among the nation's faculty, as well as an uneven implementation of culturally inclusive and equity-minded pedagogy in postsecondary curricula.

Overall, U.S. colleges and universities have become increasingly populated by BIPOC students who now comprise roughly 45% of the domestic student population (Espinosa et al., 2019). Since 1995, Black, Asian, Latinx, and Native American undergraduate student enrollments have almost doubled in size with the most substantial growth occurring among Latinx populations. Colleges and universities continue to experience unprecedented rates of Latinx student enrollment, primarily at 2-year institutions, while Black undergraduate student enrollments have followed closely behind. Despite the increased representation of some Asian groups in undergraduate and graduate education, compared to Whites, large gaps in degree and type of degree attainment remain (Monarrez & Washington, 2020).

The increase in BIPOC student enrollment has not prompted a corresponding upsurge in their persistence to degree completion, raising concerns about institutional EDI efforts. Though the number of baccalaureate degrees and postsecondary certificates earned by Asian, Native American, Black, and Latinx students has increased (National Center for Education Statistics [NCES], 2019), graduation rates have not kept up with increases in enrollment. Just over half of the first-time, full-time undergraduate Latinx students who began their pursuit of a bachelor's degree graduate; completion rates among Black students (40%) and American Indian/Alaska Native students (39%) also fell short of their respective enrollment levels. Asian students, however, outpace all college completers (74%), including Whites (64%) (NCES, 2017). Together with the type of credential (e.g., bachelor's or associate's degree) and the field study (e.g., STEM vs. health care), the college completion gap between Whites and Black, Latinx, and Native American students correlates with social and economic mobility of these students. The long-term earnings potential of communities of color is negatively impacted by low college completion rates, exacerbating existing social and economic disparities between communities of color and Whites (Libassi, 2018). Consequently, though the compositional diversity of institutions has shown progress, the gaps in persistence and degree completion raise questions about the extent to which institutional structures (e.g., financial aid, pedagogy, curricular and co-curricular programs) are equitable by design and in practice.

To foster the success of BIPOC students, increasing the compositional diversity of faculty can be seen as an equity strategy primarily because engagement with faculty of color appears to have an impact on BIPOC student persistence. Doing so also serves a related inclusive function because BIPOC faculty serve as mentors and role models to BIPOC students, while also potentially broadening and making university curricula more inclusive to positively impact both the learning and development of BIPOC and White students (Banks & Dohy, 2019). However, the growth in faculty of color teaching, advising, and researching in U.S. colleges and universities has been slow. In 2016, approximately 21% of postsecondary faculty were faculty of color (Espinosa et al., 2019), an uptick of about 6% since 1998 (Schuster & Finkelstein, 2006). The slow increase in faculty compositional diversity relative to population demographics and BIPOC student enrollment undermines inclusive education's goal to realize the public purposes of higher education in a democracy (Martínez Alemán, 1999). The lack of adequate faculty compositional diversity limits students' experience with role models and mentors of color who often focus on racial and ethnic issues in their disciplinary studies, effectively frustrating and limiting opportunities to affect postsecondary institutional policies and practices (Antonio, 2002).

In the college and university classroom, faculty of color are often the agents of curricular and pedagogical change that enable intercultural competence (Madyun et al., 2013), a centerpiece of inclusion. Faculty of color often believe that the integration of topics and analyses of race in their courses is cognitively beneficial to students and thus imperative despite the negative consequences that this may have for their careers (Castillo-Montoya, 2020; Griffin et al., 2011). Nevertheless, scholars have also argued that an equity-minded, anti-racist, and inclusive pedagogy enacted by *all* faculty, not only positively affects students of color, yet also benefits *all* students (Dowd & Bensimon, 2015; Gannon, 2018). As Tuitt et al. (2016) point out, addressing racial inequities is possible when instructors evaluate disciplinary frames to determine norms of exclusion and inclusion while validating and attending to the varying social identities of their students. Also, U.S. inclusive, equity-minded, and anti-racist pedagogy is understood to positively influence postsecondary education comprehensively.

As emphasized elsewhere in this volume, inclusive pedagogy is an equity-minded and anti-racist pedagogy that requires faculty to engage in discerning and dismantling of their biases about knowledge claims and student engagement. To engage in equity-minded pedagogy, faculty should understand the difference between treating students equitably rather than equally. Because not all students have the same access to canonical knowledge and normative ways of disciplinary thinking, treating all students equally would mean that only those who do have access to scholarly and educational norms will achieve the course learning objectives. To engage in equitable instruction, however, students' varied funds of knowledge (academic and/or experiential) are valued as a means to learning (Kiyama & Rios-Aguilar, 2017).

To transform traditional pedagogy to equity-minded pedagogy and further inclusive goals, professional development for faculty that combines the scholarship of teaching with learning science and evidence-based teaching and curricular development has proven successful (Costino, 2018; Malcom-Piqueux & Bensimon, 2017).

Intersectionality: Moving toward a Holistic Framework of Education Abroad

Beyond the work that needs to be done with inclusive pedagogy, there is a need to focus on how student affairs can be attentive to and support the intersectional identities of students. Crenshaw (1989) notably theorized intersectionality as the mutually reinforcing influence of salient identities, namely, race and gender, in the marginality of Black women in policy making, and its racist and gendered enforcements. Yet, Crenshaw's (1989) emphasis on *experiences of policy impacts* on those at the margins she theorizes is often overlooked in discourses about intersectionality. By placing emphasis on how institutional policies and practices *contribute* to marginality and oppression, rather than merely understanding how minoritized students' identities are constitutively mutual (i.e., they effect each other interdependently), intersectionality presents an important analytical framework for student services practitioners and international educators that enables a path to inclusive excellence.

Frameworks of holistic, student-centered advising and support services emphasize the growing diversity and multiplicity of students' identities and experiences in U.S. higher education and require more collaboration and coordination between student affairs and academic affairs (Kuh, 1996; Martin & Murphy, 2000). Martin and Murphy (2000) highlight the ongoing need for bridging the gap between services focused on student learning (previously relegated to academic affairs) and student development (previously relegated to student affairs) across all university functions. Although student support services vary based on the type of institutions (e.g., 2- and 4-year institutions) and educational levels (e.g., undergraduate and graduate education), an overview of prevalent models among U.S. higher education institutions reveals some similarities. For example, student services and programs might include academic support services (e.g., academic advising, academic skills, learning services), peer advising and student leadership services, wellness and residential programs, career and preprofessional career advising, counseling services, accessibility services, and identity and affinity communities (e.g., for LGBTQ+ identifying folk, women, first-generation, low income, Black students, Chinese students), orientation programs, and campus involvement groups (e.g., student activities, clubs). These similarities notwithstanding, inclusive approaches, equity-minded frameworks, and anti-racist effectiveness of student support services also vary widely. The implications for equitable inclusion are timely and urgent, particularly as the fields comprising student support services consider the reformulations of student development in the era of remote and virtual education.

Along with other forms of global programming, education abroad benefits from drawing on intersectionality as an analytical frame to evaluate transborder learning opportunities and experiences for equity-mindedness. Does its norms, values, and practices restrict access to trans-cultural experiences? Do BIPOC students and other minoritized students have access to support networks while studying overseas? Do those support networks consider students' embodied positions, intersectional identities whose meaning can challenge situational norms? By going beyond representational or compositional diversity of BIPOC students engaged in education abroad, intersectional global education seeks to highlight, amplify, and integrate transnational perspectives on race, culture, and identity in advising, orientations, curricular developments, and global programming (e.g., international student programming, education abroad, language partnerships, mentor programs). In this context, intersectional global education is the intentional injection of culturally relevant frameworks that engage all students and foster a sense of belonging for BIPOC students studying abroad and serve as countertrends to an almost exclusive emphasis on Eurocentric models of education abroad. As has been demonstrated at Historically Black Colleges and Universities (HBCUs), when institutions acknowledge the intersectionality of race, gender, and other so-called marginalized identities, they demonstrate a sense of "communal responsibility" that aids in supporting BIPOC students along their nuanced identities and lived experiences (Suggs & Mitchell, 2011, p. 160). Within an education abroad context, intersectional frameworks have the potential to not only support the inclusion of participating BIPOC students but also could advance cross-cultural and transnational linkages between BIPOC communities around the world.

Equity, Diversity, and Inclusion in Global Programming

With an intersectionality framework in mind, EDI frameworks in higher education demand a more expansive and comprehensive understanding of the experiences of BIPOC students studying abroad, including international students who identify as BIPOC. The temporal, contextual, and situational identities of all students studying overseas must be taken into account when prevailing frameworks on student identity development place identity as central to students' process of self-authorship and development (Hemwall & Trachte, 1999), Yet, such frameworks are U.S. centric while simultaneously presuming that identity development experiences are globally relevant and culturally inclusive of BIPOC students' identity development processes. Furthermore, they overlook the process of identity reformulations that occur when students are overseas, including for BIPOC, LGBTQ+, and first-generation populations. Indeed, we know that for students studying overseas, whether inbound or outgoing, the transformational impact of their global education is situational, temporal, and contextual, informed by their curricular and co-curricular experiences as well as their social identities, positionalities, and locations.

Amidst the recent global COVID-19 pandemic and social movement against anti-Black racism, the U.S. government has deployed a coordinated set of policies (e.g., travel bans and restrictions, changes to visa policies for international students and scholars) that have had significant impact on internationalization and global programming (e.g., the elimination of Fulbright programs in Mainland China and Hong Kong). Drawing on the concept of global social justice, Tannock (2018) argues that legislative and institutional policies and geopolitics conditionally situate and differentiate "the global" from "the local" in ways that legitimize, rationalize, and normalize educational inequities. Such policies include differential tuition fees, a lack of access to financial aid and university scholarship opportunities, and social exclusion from community membership due to xenophobia and neo-racism (Lee, 2017; Tannock, 2018). In addition, Tannock (2018) argues that these disparities and inequities can have a disproportionate impact for low-income and international BIPOC students. Such policies imposed by the federal government on institutions of higher education may sabotage any efforts that education abroad offices (as well as others, including international student and scholar service units) put forth to provide equitable access and inclusive experiences for students studying abroad.

Existing scholarship and empirical evidence suggests that BIPOC students' education abroad experiences can often be upsetting and unnerving. Often, BIPOC students experience values and social and educational norms in the host country that challenge their identities, educational goals, and developmental expectations (Goldoni, 2017). For example, Goldoni references Tharps' (2008) account of her time spent in Spain where racism and sexism characterized her experiences. Though common in the U.S., the racist misogyny experienced by Tharps took on a different and particular character in Spain's sociohistorical context. Not surprisingly, Trans and gender expansive students studying abroad also find their identities challenged and unsupported (Michl et al., 2019). Though Sweeney's (2013) "inclusive excellence scorecard" does not fully encompass equity-minded principles, it does point to the need for more research on the experiences of BIPOC and other minoritized students studying abroad, and on the urgency to include equity practices in education abroad programs. For example, student services must prioritize new directions in inclusive support services that not only facilitate inclusive engagement and support for BIPOC students abroad but also center pedagogies for anti-racist self-development and learning through reflection and action. In addition, critical advising strategies that support students' sense of belonging, community building, and self-confidence, particularly as they learn to navigate and negotiate new learning environments and shifting institutional and geopolitical contexts, are essential (Puroway, 2016).

Advancing Equity and Inclusion in Education Abroad

The insights offered earlier from U.S. higher education can be informative for practitioners and researchers in education abroad who are seeking to advance inclusive excellence. In particular, the following four areas are important in helping the field advance inclusive excellence in education abroad: a focus on equity and equity-mindedness, a consideration of context and shifting demographics, an expansion of the basis for understanding student support services, and the incorporation of intersectionality into practice. Although the COVID-19 pandemic has forced colleges and universities to cancel the majority of education abroad programs, many institutions are using this crisis to find new ways to offer global educational experiences (Wood, 2020). Accordingly, as institutions are reimagining the future of education abroad, it would also be wise to consider the lessons learned from U.S. higher education to ensure that existing policies and practices are reformed to serve the widest array of students.

Focus on Equity and Equity-Mindedness

Scholars of higher education have similarly pointed out that the need to focus on equity and equity-mindedness is essential to advancing inclusive excellence in higher education. Treating all students equally is not the same as treating students equitably since not all students will have the same structures of support and access to the cultural capital associated with dominant groups. This does not mean, however, that traditionally marginalized students arrive on their campuses without cultural capital and funds of knowledge that can be leveraged for learning and engagement. As Malcom-Piquex and Bensimon (2017) have noted, there has long been an implicit and pernicious assumption in higher education that minoritized students, families, and communities are responsible for their knowledge deficits, rather than recognizing the social, educational, and economic inequalities imposed on generations of certain groups.

An equity-minded approach offers an alternative framework for addressing historical inequities and gaps in access to educational assets and opportunities for two primary reasons. First, it forces practitioners to consider past instances of oppression and systemic injustices in their institutions and in the work. An example of this can be acknowledging the elitist nature of education abroad. In the 1960s, education abroad practitioners in the U.S. increased the levels of scrutiny and control over who was accepted to study abroad in ways that made the practice of overseas study highly selective (Contreras, 2015). By knowing this history, contemporary practitioners can actively question long-standing practices that make the field less equitable. Second, an equity-minded approach may help professionals better acknowledge the rich strengths of BIPOC students. Although deficit narratives have prevailed in higher education and within the field of education abroad, BIPOC students bring with them a rich set of talents such as tenacity and resilience (Chambers & Chambers, 2011), as well as their own cultural capital. As Yosso (2005) notes, it is more productive and supportive to focus on the rich cultural, linguistic, navigational, social, and familial community cultural wealth that BIPOC students possess. In these two ways, an equity-minded approach rejects long-standing systemic inequities and embraces the strengths and assets of historically minoritized students.

Bensimon et al. (2020) describe a 2015 project by AAC&U called "Committing to Equity and Inclusive Excellence" that invited 13 U.S. colleges and universities together to establish practices that would use data to address inequities at their institutions. Several of the institutions involved in the project committed to holding a series of workshops that would invite faculty members to examine disaggregated student outcome data at an institutional and a course level. The course-specific data were relevant to the courses they were teaching so the faculty were able to see where the equity gaps existed within their own lessons. Through these structured opportunities, "[r]ather than being told by others where equity gaps exist and which student groups experience them, faculty were able to uncover gaps for themselves" (Bensimon et al., 2020, p. 78).

Borrowing from what has already been proven to be successful broadly in higher education, the type of equity-minded professional development described by Bensimon et al. can be applied to an education abroad context in similar ways. For example, faculty who lead programs abroad could be invited to analyze their syllabi and pedagogical practices with an eye toward addressing equity gaps. Similar workshops could take place at the staff level by inviting program coordinators and on-site administrators to make sense of program assessment data. (See also Chapters 9 and 14 of this volume, which consider ways in which an articulation of learning outcomes and analysis of outcomes assessment data can be employed from an inclusion standpoint.)

Even for those who are not so data minded, the work outlined here is a good reminder of the need for conversations and training that simply raise awareness. In addition, equity-minded study abroad practitioners should be encouraged to raise awareness of racial inequities in education abroad outcomes, acknowledge the community cultural wealth of BIPOC students, build understanding around these inequities and systemic inequalities, and seek evidence-based knowledge about what these inequities are on their own campuses (Center for Urban Education, USC., n.d).

Consider Context and Shifting Demographics

The data presented in this chapter on the broader U.S. context of higher education show that racial and ethnic student enrollment in postsecondary education has increased; however, the increase in faculty of color teaching, advising, and researching in U.S. colleges and universities has been slow. At many institutions throughout the U.S., higher education experts have shown that faculty are far less diverse than the students they teach. According to the Integrated Postsecondary Education Data System (IPEDS), faculty members who are Black or Latinx are underrepresented relative to the population of the U.S., and the percentage of these same groups in tenured categories is typically lower than in nontenured categories (Vasquez Heilig et al., 2019). It is also important to note that there is great diversity in the typology of colleges and universities that exist within the U.S. Indeed, there is a myriad of differences in demographics and missions between different types of institutions. By definition, a Minority Serving Institution (MSI) (e.g., HBCU, Asian American and Native American Pacific Islander Serving Institutions [AANAPISI], Tribal Colleges and Universities [TCU], or a Hispanic Serving

Institution [HSI]) will have different demographic representation in the student body than a Predominately White Institution (PWI).

Scholarship from other areas within higher education has demonstrated the need for institutions and practitioners alike to understand the history of race and ethnicity in the context of institutional mission. This approach enables education abroad faculty and administrators to be race-conscious (in an affirmative and anti-racist manner) and mindful of the present and historical context of exclusionary practices. In addition, an equity-minded framework can enable education abroad professionals to identify and understand the gaps in outcome measures along ethnoracial lines. In the context of education abroad, this is highly important since many studies have shown that students often have different motivational factors to study abroad based on their gender or racial/ethnic identity (Anderson, 2007; Brux & Fry, 2010; Bryant & Soria, 2015; Salisbury et al., 2011). For practitioners, this means attending to the distinct needs of their student body in ways that are mindful of structures, policies, and practices of education abroad that are exclusionary or perpetuate inequitable achievement rates or outcomes.

One way that education abroad practitioners can use data to understand their institutional context and needs of their students is by incorporating information from campus partners and university-wide data sets with an eye toward data that touch on EDI topics. Some of these data can be found in student surveys conducted by offices of institutional research, multicultural affairs, or student activities. Such data sets can be anything from the first-year student satisfaction surveys, to national data collection efforts such as the National Survey of Student Engagement (NSSE). In addition, campus climate surveys are instruments designed to capture how individuals perceive their treatment on campus, as well as the extent that certain groups experience harassment or discrimination (Hurtado et al., 2012). Campus climate surveys can also allow institutions to evaluate the degree to which given units or programs are succeeding in promoting equity. As Smith (2020) notes, assessing campus climate typically leads to policy recommendations and programmatic realignments in areas that are crucial to supporting inclusion and equity, particularly in the areas of ". . . hiring, teaching and curriculum, admissions, town-gown relationships, and community health" (p. 64). Practitioners would be wise to collaborate with offices that administer campus climate surveys to include education abroad in such assessments. In addition, they can utilize survey data to see which communities on campus, if any, are being either underserved or mistreated as well as to track the impact of education abroad participation on institutional equity goals and outcomes.

Whether it is tapping into campus climate survey data or other modes of assessment, a data-driven approach can help guide education abroad programs in directions that are mutually constitutive with institutional equity and inclusion priorities.

Expand the Basis for Understanding Student Support Services

A holistic, equity-oriented framework in student services is fundamental to fostering inclusive excellence in education abroad programs. Lessons learned from international students and scholars (ISS) support services are especially instructive here. At a minimum, it is essential for education abroad to consider student support in a nuanced manner to include both academic and student services. More specifically, academic support services should include academic advising, academic skills and learning services, extended service hours (in-person and/or virtual), and intervention plans for specific student population needs (e.g., first-generation, commuter), to name a few. Student support services should comprise wellness and residential programs, career and preprofessional career advising, mental health counseling services, accessibility services, financial advising, and identity and affinity programs. Of course, these services would be put in the context of education abroad, where students of all backgrounds have equitable access to the curricular and co-curricular aspects of their programs.

Rather than reinventing the wheel, education abroad offices benefit from further partnering with the array of campus services at their home institutions. An organizational commitment to coordinated and collaborative programming across education abroad programs and student services can provide the structural integrity to ensure equitable access. Designating clear and tangible collaborations between education abroad programs and other on-campus student services can broaden access and improve outcomes. For example, as colleges and universities seek ways to support students who are the first in their families to go to college, there is an opportunity for collaboration between units designated as "FGEN" centers and education abroad offices. The growing body of research focused on the first-generation students demonstrates that there are multiple avenues of partnership in this area (Gable, 2021; Gilman & Arch, 2020; Jack, 2019). Beyond collaboration with FGEN centers, education abroad can also partner with assessment efforts on campus. At the University of Portland, a Catholic liberal arts college in Oregon, the Office of International Education, Diversity, and Inclusion is partnering with the Office of Institutional Research to assess various high-impact practices including study abroad. Beyond looking at the data in the aggregate, this project will disaggregate data along various identity markers (e.g., race, ethnicity, gender, nationality, student-athlete and first-generation status) to determine the impact of high-impact practices and to understand whether there are equity gaps. The aim of this partnership will also be to assess empirically whether equitable access to services is provided and to see how, if at all, high-impact practices like education abroad are linked to student engagement and learning outcomes. The information from this assessment will be used to support regional assessment efforts and to improve practice in the service of all students. Data-driven assessments like this can provide education abroad offices with rationale for equitable decision-making.

It is especially beneficial for education abroad offices to team up with multicultural affairs/diversity offices to address the distinct needs of minoritized students (López-McGee & Contreras Jr., 2014). Research tells us that minoritized students' study abroad decision-making patterns vary significantly from those of White students. Among students of color, cultural capital, financial, and social concerns significantly affect student-choice parameters and their subsequent participation in education abroad (Murray Brux & Fry, 2010; Salisbury et al., 2011). An equity-minded, student-choice model for students of color can address these indicators. For example, an extended student services net can address the social, emotional, and economic factors that affect BIPOC students' decision to enroll in education abroad programs. Particularly, individual advising for minoritized students may undo the deficit perspective that can improve their participation in these programs (Harris & Harris, 2019; Perkins, 2020), in large part by drawing on their existing sources of cultural capital.

Equally critical in terms of nuanced student support is a more inclusive approach to providing frameworks for student identity development. Participation in education abroad programs has shown positive effects on students' identity and intellectual development (McKeown, 2009; Savicki, 2020). However, prevailing frameworks are most often U.S. centric and based on dominant, largely White, student identities (Contreras et al., 2020). Consequently, the field needs a more robust understanding of student identity development that considers distinct cultural and national contexts, and colonial and racist history. Although there has been some work in recent years to show what strengths BIPOC students bring to abroad programs (Hartman et al., 2020; Johnstone et al., 2020; Wick et al., 2019), more research is needed on how students develop within programs based on their distinct identities.

Incorporate Intersectionality into Practice

Finally, incorporating intersectionality into education abroad will support a wider array of students, researchers, and practitioners in the field and dismantle existing forms of oppression that are doubly damaging for individuals who are minoritized in more than one element of identity. As noted earlier, Crenshaw (1989) demonstrated that race and gender combined put Black women in a uniquely vulnerable space from a legal perspective. Moreover, she argued that it was necessary to understand the twofold impact of these two salient aspects of identity, in order to address the racist and gendered policies that worked against them. In the context of higher education, Gold (2011) offers examples of how intersectionality is addressed at a PWI using the lens of community cultural wealth (Yosso, 2005) by focusing on an academic support program that was created specifically for BIPOC students who identified as women. Among Gold's notable finding were that the students who participated in the program developed their communication skills by navigating different cultural settings under the guidance of an advisor who, as one student observed, "... sees what we don't have, and she pushes us into situations where we have to act and be a leader" (Gold, 2011, p. 67). The social and navigational capital that the students already possessed were amplified and enhanced by mentorship and guidance by the program advisors, which empowered the BIPOC women on their predominantly White campus.

The same principle of intersectionality holds true in education abroad, where students who embody more than one salient identity may be subject to discrimination in distinct, culturally specific ways. Accordingly, considering the intersection of identities of students will give practitioners a richer understanding of how to support inclusive excellence by valuing the community cultural wealth that students bring with them and valuing these talents on their own terms. Moreover, if programs are to enact inclusive education that is equity-minded, education abroad practitioners and researchers should acknowledge and understand their own levels of oppression and privilege. Understanding the internalized oppression that professional experiences based on their intersectional identities, as well as addressing unearned privileges, will be a means for practitioners and researchers to utilize their own positionality to advocate for others and dismantle existing systems of oppression (Contreras, 2020). Within the wider context of U.S. higher education, it is important for education abroad practitioners to also learn from peers in other fields and to understand the wide array of issues that BIPOC students face within colleges and universities.

Conclusion

We acknowledge that each of the four suggestions outlined earlier will come with its own set of challenges related to implementation, integration, and evaluation. Focusing on equity beyond equality and inclusive excellence beyond access calls on education abroad practitioners and the institutions they serve to break from deeply ingrained paradigms that focus on deficit thinking and normative compliance. Considering context, demographics and disaggregated data based on ethnicity, socioeconomic status, gender, gender identity, first-generation status, nationality, and disability will involve potentially painstaking and politically charged new norms of data collection. Expanding the basis of understanding for student support services to include academic support will require distinct academic units to move beyond silos and break traditional organizational schemes. Finally, incorporating intersectionality into practice will require individuals and institutions to reckon with decades, if not centuries, of institutional racism, sexism, and other forms of oppression. All of these suggestions will require tireless work by researchers and practitioners so that decisions can be informed by robust research.

Despite the challenges, this work is essential and necessary in providing a more equity-minded approach to education abroad that will serve all students. The difficulty of these efforts is magnified in the face of the current pandemic and financial crisis, yet so is the urgency. At present, there is an urgent need for the implementation of frameworks to advance inclusive excellence to serve those students on the margins, many of whom are now disproportionately impacted by COVID-19. The current global context also provides an opportunity. As novelist Roy (2020) has noted, this pandemic can be seen as a portal that offers us the chance to leave the old world for something new:

> We can choose to walk through it, dragging the carcasses of our prejudice and hatred, our avarice, our data banks and dead ideas, our dead rivers and smoky skies behind us. Or we can walk through lightly, with little luggage, ready to imagine another world. And ready to fight for it. (para. 48)

We offer the abovementioned suggestions as an invitation to imagine another world for inclusive excellence in education abroad—not just as part of the current pandemic, yet also beyond.

References

Association of American Colleges and Universities. (2013). *Making excellence inclusive.* https://www.aacu.org/making-excellence-inclusive

Anderson, B. D. (2007). *Students in a global village: The nexus of choice, expectation, and experience in study abroad.* [Doctoral dissertation, The University of Texas at Austin]. Retrieved from https://repositories.lib.utexas.edu/handle/2152/3176?show=full

Antonio, A. L. (2002). Faculty of color reconsidered: Reassessing contributions to scholarship. *The Journal of Higher Education, 73*(5), 582–602. DOI: 10.1080/00221546.2002.11777169

Banks, T., & Dohy, J. (2019). Mitigating barriers to persistence: A review of efforts to improve retention and graduation rates for students of color in higher education. *Higher Education Studies, 9*(1), 118–131.

Bensimon, E. M. (2007). The underestimated significance of practitioner knowledge in the scholarship of student success. *Review of Higher Education, 30*(4), 441–469.

Bensimon, E. M. (2012). The equity scorecard: Theory of change. In E. M. Bensimon & L. Malcolm (Eds.), *Confronting equity issues on campus: Implementing the equity scorecard in theory and practice* (pp. 17–44). Stylus.

Bensimon, E. M., Malcom-Piqueux, L., & McNair, T. B. (2020). In E. M. Bensimon & L. E. Malcom-Piqueux (Eds.), *From equity talk to equity walk: Expanding practitioner knowledge for racial justice in higher education.* John Wiley & Sons, Incorporated.

Bensimon, E. M., Dowd, A. C., & Witham, K. (2016). Five principles for enacting equity by design. *Diversity and Democracy, 19*(1), 1–8.

Bethune-Dix, L., Carter, E. W., Hall, C., McMillan, E., Cayton, J., Day, T., Vranicar, M., Bouchard, C., Krech, L., Gustafson, J., & Bauer, E. (2020). Inclusive higher education for college students with intellectual disability. In *Strategies for supporting inclusion and diversity in the academy* (pp. 309–328). Palgrave Macmillan, Cham.

Bowman, N. A. (2012). Structural diversity and close interracial relationships in college. *Educational Researcher, 41*(4), 133–135.

Bryant, K. M., & Soria, K. M. (2015). College students' sexual orientation, gender identity, and participation in study abroad. *Frontiers: The Interdisciplinary Journal of Study Abroad, 25*(1), 91–106. Retrieved from https://doi.org/10.36366/frontiers.v25i1.347

Castillo-Montoya, M. (2020). The challenges and tensions of equity-minded teaching. *Change: The Magazine of Higher Learning, 52*(2), 74–78.

Center for Urban Education, USC. (n.d.). *What is equity mindedness?* Retrieved from https://cue.usc.edu/about/equity/equity-mindedness/

Chang, M. J. (1999). Does racial diversity matter?: The educational impact of a racially diverse undergraduate population. *Journal of College Student Development, 40*(4), 377–395.

Chambers, C. R., & Chambers, C. R. (2011). *Support systems and services for diverse populations considering the intersection of race, gender, and the needs of black female undergraduates* (1st ed.). Emerald Group Pub. Ltd.

Contreras Jr., E. (2015). *Rhetoric and reality in study abroad: The aims of overseas study for U.S. higher education in the twentieth century.* [Doctoral dissertation, Harvard University]. ProQuest Dissertations Publishing.

Contreras Jr., E. (2020). View, voice, and visibility: A liberating framework for social justice in education abroad. In L. Berger (Ed.), *Social justice in international education* (pp. 137–154). NAFSA: The Association of International Educators.

Contreras Jr., E., & López-McGee, L. (2014). Diversity and internationalization in higher education: Finding common ground to increase access to and diversity in education abroad *IIE Networker, Fall,* 42–43. Retrieved from https://www.nxtbook.com/naylor/IIEB/IIEB0214/index.php#/p/42

Contreras, E., López-McGee, L., Wick, D., & Willis, T. Y. (2020). Introduction: Special issue on diversity, equity, and inclusion in education abroad. *Frontiers: The Interdisciplinary Journal of Study Abroad, 32*(1), 1–11. DOI: 10.36366/frontiers.v32i1.431

Costino, K. (2018). Equity-minded faculty development: An intersectional identity-conscious community of practice model for faculty learning. *Metropolitan Universities, 29*(1), 117–136.

Crenshaw, K. (1989). Demarginalizing the intersection of race and sex: A Black Feminist critique of antidiscrimination doctrine. *Feminist Theory and Antiracist Politics, University of Chicago Legal Forum, 1989*, Article 8.

Doscher, S., & Landorf, H. (2018). Universal global learning, inclusive excellence, and higher education's greater purposes. *Peer Review, 20*(1), 4–7.

Dowd, A. C., & Bensimon, E. M. (2015). *Engaging the "race question": Accountability and equity in US higher education.* Teachers College Press.

Espinosa, L. L., Turk, J. M., Taylor, M., & Chessman, H. M. (2019). Race and ethnicity in higher education: A status report. *American Council on Education.* https://www.acenet.edu/Research-Insights/Pages/Race-and-Ethnicity-in-Higher-Education.aspx

Gable, R. (2021). *The hidden curriculum: First generation students at legacy universities.* Princeton University Press.

Gannon, K. (2018, March). The case for inclusive teaching. *Chronicle of Higher Education.* https://www.chronicle.com/article/the-case-for-inclusive-teaching/

Garcia, S. E. (2020, June 17). Where did BIPOC come from? *The New York Times.* https://www.nytimes.com/article/what-is-bipoc.html

Gilman, I., & Arch, X. (2020). In I. Gilman (Ed.), *Academic library services for first-generation students.* Libraries Unlimited, an imprint of ABC-CLIO, LLC.

Goldoni, F. (2017). Race, ethnicity, class and identity: Implications for study abroad. *Journal of Language, Identity & Education, 16*(5), 328–341.

Griffin, K. A., Pifer, M. J., Humphrey, J. R., & Hazelwood, A. M. (2011). (Re)defining departure: Exploring Black professors' experiences with and responses to racism and racial climate. *American Journal of Education, 117*(4), 495–526.

Hamir, H. B., & Gozik, N. (Eds.). (2018). *Promoting inclusion in education abroad: A handbook of research and practice.* Stylus.

Harris, M. R., & Harris, J. W. (2019). Study abroad and college students of the African diaspora: Attitudes, access and barriers. *Eastern European Journal of Transnational Relations, 3*(2), 11–27.

Hartman, E., Nora, P. R., Ferrarini, C., Messmore, N., Evans, S., Bibi Al-Ebrahim, & John, M. B. (2020). Coloniality-decoloniality and critical global citizenship: Identity, belonging, and education abroad. *Frontiers: The Interdisciplinary Journal of Study Abroad, 32*(1) DOI: 10.36366/frontiers.v32i1.433

Hartwell, E. E., Cole, K., Donovan, S. K., Greene, R. L., Storms, S. L. B., & Williams, T. (2017). Breaking down silos: Teaching for equity, diversity, and inclusion across disciplines. *Humboldt Journal of Social Relations, 39*, 143–162. Retrieved from http://www.jstor.org.ezproxy-eres.up.edu/stable/90007877

Hemwall, M. K. & Trachte, K. C. (1999, March). Learning at the core: Toward a new understanding of academic advising. *NACADA Journal, 19*(1), 5–11.

Hurtado, S., Alvarez, C.L., Guillermo-Wann, C., Cuellar, M., & Arellano, L. (2012). A model for diverse learning environments: The scholarship on creating and assessing conditions for student success. In J. C. Smart & M. B. Paulsen (Eds.), *Higher education Handbook of theory and research* (Vol. 27, pp. 41–122). Springer Netherlands.

Jack, A. A. (2019). *The privileged poor: How elite colleges are failing disadvantaged students.* Harvard University Press.

Johnstone, C., Tiffany, L. S., & Malmgren, J. (2020). Academics as arbiters: Promoting equity and cultural responsibility in group-based study abroad. *Frontiers: The Interdisciplinary Journal of Study Abroad, 32*(2). DOI: 10.36366/frontiers.v32i2.470

Kiyama, J. M., & Rios-Aguilar, C. (Eds.). (2017). *Funds of knowledge in higher education: Honoring students' cultural experiences and resources as strengths.* Routledge.

Kuh, G. D. (1996). Guiding principles for creating seamless learning environments for undergraduates. *Journal of College Student Development, 37*(2), 135–148.

Lee, J. J. (2007). Neo-racism toward international students: A critical need for change. *About Campus, 11*(6), 28–30. https://doi.org/10.1002/abc.194

Libassi, C. J. (2018, May). *The neglected college race gap: Racial disparities among college completers.* Center for American Progress. https://www.americanprogress.org/issues/education-postsecondary/reports/2018/05/23/451186/neglected-college-race-gap-racial-disparities-among-college-completers/

Malcom-Piqueux, L., & Bensimon, E. M. (2017). Taking equity-minded action to close equity gaps. *Peer Review, 19*(2), 5.

Martin, J., & Murphy, S. (2000). *Building a better bridge: Creating effective partnerships between academic affairs and student affairs.* NASPA.

Martínez Aleman, A. M. (1999). Qué culpa tengo yo? Performing identity and college teaching. *Educational Theory, 49*(1), 37–51.

Martínez Alemán, A. M., & Salkever, K. (2003). Mission, multiculturalism, and the liberal arts college: A qualitative investigation. *The Journal of Higher Education, 74*(5), 563–596.

McKendry, S., & Lawrence, M. (2020). Trans inclusive higher education: Strategies to support trans, non-binary and gender diverse students and staff. In Gail Crimmins (Ed.), *Strategies for supporting inclusion and diversity in the academy* (pp. 201–221). Palgrave Macmillan.

McKeown, J. S. (2009). *The first time effect: The impact of study abroad on college student intellectual development.* SUNY Press.

McPherson, M., Smith-Lovin, L., & Cook, J. M. (2001). Birds of a feather: Homophily in social networks. *Annual Review of Sociology, 27,* 415–444.

Madyun, N. I., Williams, S. M., McGee, E. O., & Milner IV, H. R. (2013). On the importance of African-American faculty. *Higher Education: Implications and Recommendations. Educational Foundations, 27,* 65–84.

Messiou, K. (2017). Research in the field of inclusive education: Time for a rethink? *International Journal of Inclusive Education, 21*(2), 146–159.

Michl, T., Pegg, K., & Kracen, A. (2019). Gender x culture: A pilot project exploring the study abroad experiences of trans and gender expansive students. *Frontiers: The Interdisciplinary Journal of Study Abroad, 31*(2), 32–50.

Monarrez, T., & Washington, K. (June 18, 2020). *Racial and ethnic representation in postsecondary education.* The Urban Institute. Retrieved from https://www.urban.org/research/publication/racial-and-ethnic-representation-postsecondary-education

Murray Brux, J., & Fry, B. (2010). Multicultural students in study abroad: Their interests, their issues, and their constraints. *Journal of Studies in International Education, 14*(5), 508–527. doi: 10.1177/1028315309342486

Museus, S. D., & Griffin, K. A. (2011). Mapping the margins in higher education: On the promise of intersectionality frameworks in research and discourse. *New Directions for Institutional Research, 2011*(151), 5–13.

Payne Gold, S. (2011). Buried treasure: Community cultural wealth among Black American female students. In C. Renée Chambers (Ed.) *Support systems and services for diverse populations: Considering the intersection of race, gender, and the needs of Black female undergraduates* (*Diversity in Higher Education*, Vol. 8, pp. 59–72). Emerald Group Publishing Limited, Bingley.

Perkins, C. (2020). Rewriting the narrative: An anti-deficit perspective on study abroad participation among students of color. *Frontiers: The Interdisciplinary Journal of Study Abroad, 32*(1), 148–165.

Puroway, A. (2016). Critical advising: A Freirian-inspired approach. *NACADA Journal, 36*, 4–10.

Renn, K. (2017, April 10). LGBTQ students on campus: Issues and opportunities for higher education leaders. *Higher Education Today.* Retrieved at https://www.higheredtoday.org/2017/04/10/lgbtq-students-higher-education/

Roy, A. (2020, April 3). The pandemic is a portal. *The Financial Times.* Retrieved from https://www.ft.com/content/10d8f5e8-74eb-11ea-95fe-fcd274e920ca

Salisbury, M. H., Paulsen, M. B., & Pascarella, E. T. (2011). Why do all the study abroad students look alike? Applying an integrated student choice model to explore differences in the factors that influence white and minority students' intent to study abroad. *Research in Higher Education, 52*(2), 123–150. DOI: 10.1007/s11162-010-9191-2

Savicki, V. (Ed.). (2020). *Developing intercultural competence and transformation: Theory, research, and application in international education.* Stylus.

Schuster, J. H., Finkelstein, M. J., & Finkelstein, M. J. (2006). *The American faculty: The restructuring of academic work and careers.* Johns Hopkins University Press.

Smith, D. G. (2020). *Diversity's promise for higher education: Making it work* (3rd edition). Johns Hopkins University Press.

Suggs, V. L., & Mitchell, S. (2011). The emergence of women's centers at HBCUs: Centers of influence and the confluence of black feminist epistemology and liberal education. In C. Renée Chambers (Ed.), *Support systems and services for diverse populations: Considering the intersection of race, gender, and the needs of Black female undergraduates* (*Diversity in Higher Education*, Vol. 8, pp. 145–162). Emerald Group Publishing Limited, Bingley. https://doi.org/10.1108/S1479-3644(2011)0000008012

Sweeney, K. (2013). Inclusive excellence and underrepresentation of students of color in study abroad. *Frontiers: The Interdisciplinary Journal of Study Abroad, 23*(1), 1–21.

Tannock, S. (2018). *Educational equality and international students justice across borders.* Palgrave Macmillan.

Tharps, L. (2008). *Kinky gazpacho: Life, love & Spain.* Atria Books.

Tuitt, F., Haynes, C., & Stewart, S. (2016). *Race, equity, and the learning environment: The global relevance of critical and inclusive pedagogies in higher education.* Stylus.

Vasquez Heilig, J., Wong Flores, I., Barros Souza, A. E., Carlton Barry, J., & Barceló Monroy, S. (2019). Considering the ethnoracial and gender diversity of faculty in United States college and university intellectual communities. *South Texas College of Law Houston: Hispanic Journal of Law and Policy*, 1–31. Retrieved from http://www.stcl.edu/about-us/publications/hispanic-journal-2019/

Ward, H. (2017). *Internationalizing the co-curriculum: Internationalization and student affairs.* American Council on Education. DOI: 10.13140/RG.2.2.16876.46729.

Weick, K. E. (1976). Educational organizations as loosely coupled systems. *Administrative Science Quarterly, 21*(1), 1–19. DOI: 10.2307/2391875

Wick, D., Willis, T. Y., Rivera, J., Lueker, E., & Hernandez, M. (2019). Assets-based learning abroad: First-generation Latinx college students leveraging and increasing community cultural wealth in Costa Rica. *Frontiers: The Interdisciplinary Journal of Study Abroad, 31*(2). DOI: 10.36366/frontiers.v31i2.455

Wise, G., Dickinson, C., Katan, T., & Gallegos, M. C. (2020). Inclusive higher education governance: Managing stakeholders, strategy, structure and function. *Studies in Higher Education, 45*(2), 339–352.

Wood, S. (2020, June 26). Colleges cancel fall study abroad programs, look at new ways of global engagement. *Diverse Issues in Higher Education.* Retrieved from https://diverseeducation.com/article/180325/

Yosso, T. J. (2005). Whose culture has capital? A critical race theory discussion of community cultural wealth. *Race Ethnicity and Education, 8*(1), 69–91.

Lessons Learned

4

Inclusion Begins with Us: Developing Inclusive Organizational Cultures and Hiring Practices

Heather Barclay Hamir, Aileen Bumphus, Patricia Izek and Betty Jeanne Taylor

> *By the last week of the program I felt immense loneliness and sadness thinking, 'will there ever be a place where I feel like I belong?' In my solitude, I realized the importance of preparing students of color for the minority experience abroad as well as providing a space for them to unpack their experiences.... I longed to not only be heard but understood. (Burrow, 2019, p. 17)*

Efforts to advance equity, diversity, and inclusion (EDI) within education abroad often begin with approaches intended to recruit and enroll increasingly diverse student cohorts. Although that approach may yield a more diverse group of participants, it does not guarantee that they will have equivalent support or guidance, as the opening quote by Western Kentucky University student Ar'Meishia Burrow illustrates, leading to inequitable outcomes from the experience itself. To realize our ultimate goal that EDI informs all phases of the student experience, from recruitment to preparation to participation and reentry, we must focus on the common denominator across all those phases: ourselves. At every stage of the process, the expectations, beliefs, and biases of the individuals involved influence the student experience, as other chapters in this volume demonstrate. To truly advance EDI within education abroad requires active engagement of all staff to unpack and address implicit biases within the organizational cultures and hiring practices that shape our teams.

To embrace this work in earnest requires a collective acknowledgment of the beliefs that impede progress. Education abroad professionals are often passionate about the value of intercultural learning and embrace interactions with diverse cultures. These tendencies lend themselves to the adoption of EDI in principle as an extension of the core values already present within the profession yet, in practice, we continue to fall short of true adherence. An emphasis on EDI cannot be fully realized without unpacking the ways in which power, privilege, and oppression shape the current state of education abroad, with biases deeply entrenched in seemingly neutral facets of our work.

This chapter is predicated on the belief that all organizations—including those in education abroad—must do the hard work of internal reflection, unpacking implicit biases within our offices and selves to become inclusive organizations that successfully hire and retain a talented, diverse group of employees. As authors, we have experience with organizational change from multiple perspectives, both on a university campus and within a provider organization, and from the perspectives of education abroad, campus diversity and community engagement, and human resources. Collectively, we have significant firsthand experiences illustrating the incredible power of inclusivity within organizations and hiring practices, the challenges that can impede or prevent this work, and strategies described in this chapter to guide those committed to lasting, equitable, and inclusive change.

In the wake of George Floyd's murder, which sparked protests worldwide and the global expansion of the Black Lives Matter movement (Westerman et al., 2020), agreement with the principles of EDI without action to advance it is no longer sufficient. Employees, students, and members of the larger community expect action to materially improve how EDI manifests in the workplace and in their own experiences of belonging. When we are successful in bringing organizational culture and hiring into alignment with an emphasis on EDI, the corresponding change in assumptions, sensitivities, and understanding rapidly elevates work that supports the rich range of student identities across higher education.

The recent national dialogue in the U.S. on racism and anti-racist action has finally sparked real attention on the internal dynamics that must change in our offices and organizations (Charles & Wojenski, 2020; Contreras et al., 2021). This chapter intends to support these efforts through an overview of relevant literature on the value of diverse teams, concrete guidance on how to move toward an inclusive organizational culture, and strategies to address bias in the hiring process. While the guidance in this chapter relates to systemic issues that impact all historically marginalized groups, the authors reference Black, Indigenous, People of Color (BIPOC) throughout to elevate attention on groups with long histories of oppression and overt exclusion in U.S. society.

Importance of Diversity in the Workforce

The importance of diversity in the workplace is well documented when it comes to productivity and innovation, which translates into higher functioning organizations (Hunt et al., 2015a; Hunt et al., 2015b). McKinsey's groundbreaking analyses of the impact diversity has in the workplace found that:

> The companies in the top quartile of gender diversity were 15 percent more likely to have financial returns that were above their national industry median. Companies in the top quartile of racial/ethnic diversity were 35 percent more likely to have financial returns above their national industry median. (Hunt et al., 2015b, p. 7)

Studies have shown that inclusive teams make better business decisions and outperform nondiverse teams (Hunt et al., 2015a; Hunt et al., 2015b), while low gender and ethnic diversity correlate to a significant likelihood to be less profitable than more diverse companies (Dixon-Fyle et al., 2020). The same report concludes that, "...an emphasis on representation is not enough; employees need to feel and perceive equality and fairness of opportunity in their workplace. Companies that lead on diversity have taken bold steps to strengthen inclusion" (Dixon-Fyle et al., 2020, p. 2). While most education abroad entities are not profit driven like private corporations, they are generally invested in providing the best experience possible for their students. The significance of diversity within corporate teams provides compelling evidence of the richness a diverse education abroad team can provide students. One could also expect that a truly inclusive workplace will lead to an increase in retention. McKinsey also found that an emphasis on inclusion, "...improves employee satisfaction and also reduces conflict between groups, improving collaboration and loyalty" (Hunt et al., 2018, p. 26).

This significance is further reinforced by research on the benefits of treating customer diversity and inclusion as a strategic priority (Deloitte Australia & Australian Human Rights Commission, 2017, p. 12). While respect for customers seems obvious for any service sector, implicit biases and assumptions about individuals may result in students, faculty, or other constituents feeling unwelcome, as if they do not belong. Having a diverse group of employees can help ensure that customers' needs are being identified and met. At the same time, such research points to a conclusion that most companies have made by now: diverse teams, when that diversity is valued, are more productive and successful. Note that a diverse team is not necessarily one that is easier to manage. In fact, differences may create conflict since not all members will necessarily see eye to eye. Working through those differences of opinion allows space for the creativity that enriches our perspectives and improves our work.

Each year, the college-aged population becomes more diverse across multiple identity groups. In terms of race and ethnicity, the U.S. is projected to become a minority–majority nation within 25 years, with no single racial or ethnic group that represents more than 50% of the population (Frey, 2018). This transformation is driven by the significant increase in diversity within more recent generations (Cohn, 2016; Fry & Parker, 2018). The proportion of U.S. adults who identify as LBGTQ+ is also increasing steadily, rising from 3.5% in 2012 to 4.5% in 2018, due largely to self-reporting among millennials (Newport, 2018). Over the same period, the proportion of the U.S. population with a disability increased from 12.1% to 12.6%, including a significant increase among young adults aged 16 to 20 years (Erickson et al., 2020). Diversity is here, becoming more pronounced with each passing year. This is the context within which education abroad professionals work, and our ability to engage and value students for the strengths they embody will only be as strong as our own awareness, empathy, and experience allows. Looking inward is the first step in resetting our organizations and our professional field to meet the needs of the students we serve.

Laying the Groundwork: Developing an Inclusive Organizational Culture

Given the clear benefits of a diverse team, the trajectory of demographic change, and our field's intention to foster equity, it is imperative that we fully engage with and support diverse individuals for ethical and practical reasons. We know from data and anecdotal evidence that this is not often the case right now, as the quote from Ar'Meishia Burrow illustrates. So, where do we start? We argue that the first step, *before* focusing on diversity in hiring, is to begin by focusing on organizational culture, as articulated in Guiding Principle 4.4 (EDI) of The Forum on Education Abroad's *Standards of Good Practice for Education Abroad*, which states that, "Each organization should develop structures to examine, identify, and address systemic biases and deficiencies in its policies, practices, and programs" (2020, p. 25). Completing an internal evaluation to unpack implicit biases embedded within organizations and ourselves not only allows work groups to understand where they may have awareness gaps but also sets the stage for creating inclusive environments when hiring diverse, talented individuals. Several authors of this chapter are practitioners within the EDI change-agent space and, as a group, we recognize that this is hard work, and that change initiatives often fail because organizations are not nimble enough or are unwilling to unpack their own implicit biases as part of the process. If an internal evaluation is omitted or downplayed, any further actions are likely to be hobbled, if not derailed, by the underlying biases that shape beliefs, expectations, practices, policies, and systems.

There is no one right way to engage in this work. Campus climate assessments, where available, can serve as a useful framework; the less formal evaluations described later can provide similar insights. Campus climate in this context is defined as the current perceptions, attitudes, and expectations that describe the institution and its members (Peterson & Spencer, 1990) specifically as they relate to racial/ethnic diversity, which is composed of perceptions, behaviors, and expectations around issues of race, ethnicity, and diversity (Hurtado et al., 2008). Hurtado et al. (1998, 1999) offer a framework for understanding campus climate as a multidimensional construct influenced by the policies, practices, and behaviors of individuals within and beyond institutions. Several critical elements are particularly influential including the historical legacy of inclusion/exclusion, structural diversity, and the psychological and behavioral dimensions of climate (Hurtado et al., 1999). Although this framework is discussed most frequently in the context of race and ethnicity, the core concepts apply when considering how members of any marginalized group experiences their environment.

Historical Legacy of Inclusion/Exclusion

The historical legacy of inclusion/exclusion serves as the foundation of Hurtado et al.'s campus climate framework. BIPOC and other marginalized communities are often far more aware of an institution's historical legacy of inclusion and exclusion than their White counterparts. For much of higher education's history, "[c]ollege campuses across America were literally and figuratively shaped by the blueprints of racism ... helping to enshrine Jim Crow laws, segregation policies, and discriminatory practices through generations of American society" (McGuire, 2019, para. 3). This history impacts the extent to which members of a college community feel welcomed.

The following are sample questions to consider in unpacking the historical legacies that may influence an office, institution, or community:

- Who originally occupied the land where your institution/organization exists?

- Are there any ties to slavery and racial oppression evident at your institution historically, or enshrined through memorials (buildings, statues) or traditions, including campus anthems?
- How did your institution respond during emancipation, the implementation of Jim Crow laws and segregation, desegregation, the Civil Rights Movement, and the Black Lives Matter movement?

As BIPOC students, faculty, and staff confront systemic racism on campus, they also must engage in academic and social environments that perpetuate false stereotypes, exclusion, tokenizing, and bias incidents. Institutions may ignore that academic, social, and financial levels of support are affected by campus racial dynamics, yet this can negatively impact students' ties to the academic and social arenas of college (Saenz et al., 1999).

Structural Diversity

The next critical element, structural diversity, refers to the demographic makeup of the campus community relative to the larger population, including students, faculty, and staff at every level of the institution or organization, including leadership. When BIPOC do not see themselves reflected in the faculty and staff around them, they are less likely to feel that they belong, particularly if the institution has a history of racism. At the departmental or office level, the degree of structural diversity present among staff, including student workers, can reinforce or undermine a message of inclusion.

Working from this framework, departmental staff can deepen their awareness of the experiences of BIPOC and other marginalized communities by asking the following questions:

- Do your team members (including student employees), education abroad participants, and program materials reflect the campus population?
- For public or regional institutions, do your staff and students reflect the demographics of the region you serve?
- Are you trending toward an inclusive workforce throughout the levels of staff, management, and leadership?

Psychological and Behavioral Dimensions

The remaining two elements of campus climate as defined by Hurtado et al., the psychological and behavioral dimensions, form the fabric of day-to-day experiences on campus. Put simply, "[h]ow people are treated in institutional settings is the product of deeply rooted racialised (and gendered and classed) social practices that shape how they view themselves and the world around them and how they act in the world" (Powers, 2007, p. 155). Perceptions and interactions may adversely affect working and learning experiences and outcomes, including BIPOC students' feelings of alienation and lower institutional attachment (Cabrera & Nora, 1994; Hurtado et al., 1996). Those feelings will affect all interactions on campus, including how they perceive education abroad as an activity and as a department within the larger campus. Efforts to advance an EDI mission will be more effective when undertaken with full awareness of these dynamics.

To understand how an office or organization is perceived on these dimensions, consider the following:

- Survey stakeholders about their experience with your department/organization; do any experiences/perceptions run counter to a mission of EDI?
- When reviewing employment and student pipeline data, are specific groups more likely to be over- or under-represented?
- What strategies can you employ that promote the understanding of identity and the sense of belonging for underrepresented students?
- What inherent beliefs may be influencing policy and practice in ways that run counter to promoting EDI?

Common negative interpersonal interactions on college campuses have become known as microaggressions, first described by Pierce (1970) and widely discussed by Sue et al. (2007). The latter define microaggressions as "the everyday verbal, nonverbal, and environmental slights, snubs, or insults, whether intentional or unintentional, which communicate hostile, derogatory, or negative messages to target persons based solely upon their marginalized group membership" (Sue, 2010, p. 24). Individuals and work groups should consider how they perpetuate microaggressions, on departmental and individual levels, as part of their efforts to foster an inclusive organizational culture. Mechanisms for feedback should be provided to better understand how individuals are experiencing the department. Looking at the wider snapshot of university campus climate data, examples of problematic interactions could include stereotyping or tokenizing underrepresented staff and students, for example, through media and communications elements, service on committees, assumptions made about individuals' interests and experiences, and so on.

Creating an inclusive organizational culture depends on the willingness of the team to be vulnerable. Focusing on the external environment—the history of inclusion or exclusion, even the larger campus or community environment—is the easier area for exploration as it is external to our own deep-seated beliefs and biases. Internally, unpacking individual biases can be deeply uncomfortable work. However, every person has biases, and the courage to surface them is the only means to create a truly inclusive, equitable, and richly diverse community. Deliberate conversations about power, privilege, and oppression are necessary for understanding their implications and how they manifest within the department. Staff members who have engaged in critical self-reflection regarding their own identities and positionalities, and engaged with others via dialogue, are better prepared to interrogate how diversity is framed within the rhetoric of the department and institution.

The most crucial component of the abovementioned framework is what we do with the accrued knowledge it provides. "Faculty, staff and university administrators, in particular, have the obligation to reflect on their own perspectives and challenge themselves to become catalysts for change" (Taylor et al., 2014, p. 231). Particularly for individuals at predominantly White institutions (PWIs), in which Whites make up 50% or more of the student population, it is common that staff members may be unaware of the privilege their social identity holds, as well as the resulting bias that may be unintentionally informing their work. The campus climate framework creates new avenues to build that awareness and is most effective in tandem with deeper exploration of implicit bias and how it works. Implicit bias, also referred to as unconscious or unexamined bias, "... is the unconscious attitudes and stereotypes we hold about different groups of people that influence our actions" (Jackson, 2018, p. 2). Combatting implicit bias is especially important throughout the hiring process, where unexamined biases can disrupt an inclusive process at every stage, from the position description through to the final offer. A tremendous amount of work exists on implicit bias, including practical guides produced by the Kirwan Institute for the Study of Race and Ethnicity at The Ohio State University (2010), the University of Washington (2010), Harvard University (2011), and Stanford University (2019). As subsequent sections illustrate, efforts to hire and retain a more diverse team will fail without consistent attention on removing and mitigating the effects of implicit biases throughout the process.

Recruitment, Hiring, and Retention

As outlined in the previous section, the introspective work teams do to understand how power, privilege, and oppression influence education abroad lays the groundwork for addressing biases in the hiring process. Even searches that intend to prioritize the recruitment and hiring of diverse candidates, particularly BIPOC individuals, are challenged to eradicate biases that fundamentally shape the search from the first decisions about the position description. Take, for example, a search in which the hope is to hire a candidate from an historically marginalized community to join an education abroad team. A natural tendency is to list commonly required or preferred qualifications such as an advanced degree and experience studying abroad. Although seemingly innocuous, the impact of those two criteria alone substantially reduces the potential candidate pool. In 2017–2018, BIPOC individuals represented nearly 290,000 (35%) of master's degrees recipients (U.S. Department of Education & National Center for Education Statistics, 2019) and roughly 103,000 (30%) of study abroad participants (Institute of International Education, 2020). What is the likely percentage of individuals who are in both groups, especially considering that in each prior year these proportions were even lower? What percentages are interested in education abroad as a professional field? When we add in other desired qualifications, such as experience in an education abroad office or in higher education to reduce training needs, it is no wonder that searches often fail to identify a strong, diverse candidate pool. This convergence of factors seems to validate a common conclusion that the problem is with the larger candidate pool, instead of acknowledging that bias can impact every element of a search process.

The pernicious nature of implicit biases on hiring is clearly illustrated in a study of efforts to remove gender bias in orchestra hires (Goldin & Rouse, 2000). Orchestra leaders were successful only when they removed names from candidates' materials, set up screens to block evaluators' views of the musicians, and even eliminated the auditory cues made by candidate's footfalls, efforts we might consider extraordinary only because biases are so firmly entrenched in the hiring process. Despite attention on EDI in hiring, anti-Black and anti-Latinx racism in hiring remains largely unchanged over the past 30 years (Bertrand & Mullainathan, 2003; Quillian et al., 2017). Discrimination in hiring remains prevalent and requires agreement and cooperation among hiring managers and everyone involved in the search process to overcome.

Before discussing approaches to address bias throughout the hiring process, it is important to acknowledge that biases are and have shaped education abroad as a profession. The demographics of the profession suggest that affinity bias plays a strong role in hiring and retention. According to Davis (2020),

> Human beings—no matter their race, ethnicity, or religion—are united by a deep-seated desire to belong.... As such, we gravitate toward people like us—toward

> people who can empathize with our experiences and worldviews. This phenomenon is known as affinity bias. It is our tendency to connect with others who share similar backgrounds, beliefs, and interests. (para. 1)

Education abroad professionals are predominantly White and female (Gordon et al., 2019), serving a disproportionately White, female population of participants at a national level. That replication of identities suggests that there is work to be done both with student-facing *and* internal hiring/culture dynamics to break both cycles, as Charles and Wojenski (2020) suggest. The problem with diversity in hiring is not a lack of good applicants; it is how our own biases prevent us from sourcing and hiring good, diverse candidates. It is imperative that we recognize the bias inherent in our ideas of the "ideal candidate," which often translates into a candidate much like the persona of the field, for example, a White, female, liberal arts major. Very few hiring managers set out to fill roles with individuals who fit this profile, yet the norms of searches combined with the many subtle forms of bias that influence the process lend themselves to this outcome. Until we view the value add of diverse candidates as the "ideal" we seek, including different lived experiences, perspectives, ways of communicating, and strengths, we will continue to struggle and often fail in our hiring goals. The good news is that change is entirely within our reach through the organizational culture work described earlier, and purposeful attention to disrupting bias in each of the six stages of the hiring process described in subsequent sections: preparing, sourcing, screening, selecting, hiring, and onboarding.

Preparing

Preparing to recruit for a position entails securing approval for the job description and salary range. The job description itself creates opportunities to signal that EDI is embedded in a team's culture and values through direct messaging about the mission, if overtly referenced, and the priority the team places on engaging diverse constituents. Those elements can be integrated into position functions as well, through acknowledgment that part of the role is to engage with and support diverse groups. Beyond the descriptive, how one handles the remaining elements of the job description will convert words to actions, most directly through position qualifications, but also through salary data, and the inclusivity of language used throughout the job description.

As the earlier example illustrated, some of the most commonplace qualifications in education abroad can be problematic for offices that are serious about hiring a diverse team. In setting qualifications, required and preferred qualifications are often confused. Requirements should be *essential* to the position, meaning there is no capacity for training once hired; they represent skills or knowledge that a candidate will need on Day 1. In the prior example, study abroad experience is a required qualification to be considered for the position. To test if this is essential or preferred, committee members should ask themselves: What specific skill does study abroad experience bring that cannot be attained by other means? Increasingly, "studied, lived, or worked abroad" is used in searches to expand the potential candidate pool, yet the experiential emphasis still does not make clear what unique skills or competencies are derived by living outside the U.S. If this criterion represents intercultural competence, could that also be present in bi-cultural individuals living in the U.S.? We often establish qualifications that seem logical on the surface as a proxy for a suite of competencies or skills, yet the very experience is exclusionary, making the job qualifications exclusionary as well.

Common requirements that may hinder the goal of a broad and diverse applicant pool include degree requirements, especially advanced degrees, a required number of years of experience, and preferences for specific types of experience if that experience is not a prerequisite to be able to perform the intended work. It is helpful to review the position requirements one by one and ask the following: What skill does this requirement bring to the position? Can this skill be acquired in another way? Requirements should be as inclusive as possible to support the goal of attracting the most diverse applicant pool. Organizations such as NAFSA (2021) and Diversity Abroad (n.d.) provide resources to help identify key competencies versus experience that presumes competency development.

The inclusion or exclusion of salary also impacts who is likely to apply for a position. There is a tendency within education abroad to omit salary from postings, yet it is best practice to include at least a minimum starting salary. Jobseekers reviewing postings are most interested in salary and benefits (Glassdoor, 2018), and listing the salary range gives employers a competitive edge (Lewis, 2018). Failing to include some indication of compensation may hinder efforts to attract the candidates we seek at best and set candidates and searches up for failure at worst.

How position descriptions are worded and what is required to apply are further opportunities to appeal to a broader range of candidates. The phrasing of a position description can attract certain applicants while signaling to others that they do not belong (Born & Taris, 2010; Gaucher et al., 2011). Applications and augmented language services such as Datapeople (2021) and Textio (2021) can help assess preferences or biases that may be embedded in a job description. In addition, it can help to remember the following regarding language:

- Be intentional and inclusive, using "you," "we," and "us" and gender-neutral language
- Avoid idioms, jargon, and acronyms
- Avoid language requirements unless they are required to perform the position. Stating "proficiency in a foreign language" without specification may reinforce a sense of elitism. Alternatives could include "excellent communication skills" or "ability to speak, read, and write professional [specific language] where [specific language] relates to essential job duties."

When finalizing the position description, it is important to review the application requirements through the lens of inclusivity as a final check. Required application materials should reflect only what one needs to know or understand to screen a candidate. Recommendations or references are not necessary to screen candidates and may exclude individuals when taking into consideration who historically has access to mentors and colleagues who can provide a recommendation (see also Chapter 8 in this volume on applications). For this reason, some searches no longer request references at the time of application.

Sourcing

Hiring managers often feel a sense of urgency to fill a vacant position, yet the desire for speed may be contrary to inclusive hiring. Often, job descriptions are posted on the same job boards and through the same listservs and then search committees wonder why the pool is not more diverse. Although seemingly easier, this is how we replicate sameness in our candidate pools. Sourcing requires time, research, and relationship building. An inclusive hiring process can be slower and more focused on attention to detail to ensure the position is shared broadly, not simply to the usual places that have been used in the past. It is useful to begin by creating a realistic timeline, first figuring out when the new hire needs to start, and then moving backward from that date. If the timing is unrealistic, extend it.

Sourcing ideally starts well before a need to hire exists but, even without that groundwork, new avenues to reach more diverse candidates are available. Personal and professional networks, employee resource or affinity groups on campus, and community organizations can all be potential resources for recruitment. Relocation is expensive, and individuals already in the area may find a new opportunity attractive. In addition, one might consider reaching out to institutions known to graduate diverse students to share positions on their job board. Strategies to build those relationships could include visits, virtual or in-person, or internship placements with two or more students/candidates at a time to leverage the benefit of a cohort-style experience. Individuals with little or no representation want to make connections, and this will allow them to connect and potentially join the institution or organization in the future.

Within education abroad, Diversity Abroad's job board allows employers to reach a diverse audience interested in employment in the profession while the annual conference provides opportunities to connect with a broad range of talented and diverse people with a shared commitment to EDI. Sessions and interest groups related to EDI occur at several international education conferences, providing additional resources and colleagues with whom to network. Opportunities to welcome newcomers to the field present another space in which to be both a good ambassador for the profession and develop an expanded network. One never knows who will be searching for a position or have a colleague who is searching at some point down the road.

Screening

Screening can be a step that unintentionally eliminates the very candidates the committee seeks. From this point forward, the full search committee is typically engaged through the rest of the hiring stages, which requires a shared commitment to interrupting unconscious bias. To help bring awareness to bias and how it works, it is important to provide unconscious bias training to everyone involved in the process, ideally before discussing specifics about the search itself. In initial meetings, the search committee/team should discuss the goals for the search and the priority placed on bringing diverse perspectives to the team; establish a plan for dealing with or omitting social media, as it creates tremendous potential for biases to influence the committee; create a screening rubric aligned to the required qualifications listed for the position; and have screeners review the previously determined essential requirements, those necessary for Day 1 of work, to maintain focus on stated requirements when completing the rubric. At this and each subsequent stage in the process, the committee should be clear about what actions will be taken if the process does not yield a strong slate of diverse candidates.

Assuming the composition of the candidate pool meets the objectives for a richly diverse pool and screening can begin, screeners should attempt to screen for "inclusion" rather than "exclusion." The goal is not to narrow the applicant pool rapidly, rather it is to retain a broad, diverse candidate pool that meets the established requirements. There should be less elimination at this stage than may have occurred in previous searches. When possible, it is best to wait until all applications are in and the position is closed to begin screening in order to give all applicants the same unbiased opportunity.

The screening phase can be particularly challenging as the desire to secure a hire increases as the search moves forward. This sense of urgency can lend itself to a parallel assumption that, if the pool is not diverse, it is unlikely that a new search will yield better results because qualified diverse candidates are not available. It is necessary to address this assumption to disrupt the cycle of searches that end with hires that look remarkably similar to previous hires. In moving forward, the committee/team should keep in mind that implicit bias can be difficult to eradicate. To avoid this pitfall, one should ask, "This candidate was just screened out, did bias influence that decision?," and continue to monitor numbers and percentages of the pool's diversity to correct course throughout the process. This is not an easy process and is time-consuming. However, this work is crucial to move the best qualified candidates into the next stage of the process, the final selection.

Selection

With a healthy pool of applicants who meet the requirements, making them qualified candidates for the position, the final selection process is ready to begin. Options to refine the candidate pool to a reasonable number of finalists including phone, virtual, and in-person interviews. All three present their own risks with respect to potential bias. A phone interview would seem unbiased, yet a wide range of implicit biases manifest when we hear someone speak and instantaneous reactions can influence decisions (Anderson et al., 2014; Toy, 2019). The virtual video interview presents additional considerations, including who has access to a quiet, uninterrupted environment and the necessary broadband, not to mention the ease to present themselves naturally in the virtual world. Not all candidates may feel comfortable showing their surroundings. These factors speak to privilege.

In-person interviews also have opportunities for bias to encroach. Employers tend to evaluate how a candidate might assimilate into the culture, which reflects a preference for "cultural fit" versus "cultural add" in hiring (Rivera, 2012). Hiring for cultural fit is another manifestation of affinity bias. It is essential to consider instead which candidate is the best "cultural add," able to expand the team's perspectives to attract and serve an increasingly diverse population of college students. LinkedIn's (n.d.) checklist, "Interview questions to check for cultural add," suggests inviting candidates' reflections on their unique contributions to existing work groups, their observations of your office culture and values, and their thoughts on possible improvements.

Multiple studies show that a structured interview process using the same questions in the same order asked by the same interviewer(s) helps diminish bias (Brecher et al., 2006; Pogrebtsova et al., 2019). Consistency allows the committee to understand each candidate's strengths and potential gaps based on the same topics, instead of the idiosyncratic conversations that emerge in unstructured interviews. Scheduling time to debrief as a group immediately after the interview call allows the committee to compare notes while the interview is fresh, including asking clarifying questions to evaluate whether bias played a role in assessing the candidate's responses. Norming discussions about the influence of biases in the search before and during the hiring process can help remove the stigma of its presence while strengthening the process and its outcomes.

Interviews present an opportunity to explore the candidate's understanding and commitment to EDI while also demonstrating the hiring manager's and team's own commitment. It is important to have at least a question or two around these vital topics. How candidates answer can reveal whether they understand the role EDI plays in the profession and whether they are ready to be allies and advocates in this arena. Portland State University's (n.d.) "Interview Questions Regarding Diversity" guide offers helpful sample questions. At the same time, BIPOC candidates and others passionate about EDI are eager to see how the organization/hiring team values diversity. Valuing diversity is more than what is conveyed verbally and in writing; candidates will also assess whether they see others with whom they can identify, both in the organization and nearby, and whether diverse identities are represented among leaders as well as staff. As McKay and Avery (2006) note,

> [I]t may be reassuring for minority job seekers to encounter other in-group members. A minority presence within the organization may signal that the organization values diversity and does not discriminate. Likewise, a minority presence in the surrounding community may signal that the community values diversity. (p. 402)

Both parties are interviewing each other, yet candidates considering relocation are also evaluating how comfortable they will feel in the new environment. This might include accounting for factors such as access to relevant goods and services. Being open and prepared to offer resources for smoothing the transition is an important step in welcoming diverse hires to the community. The lessons of the pandemic and an extended period of working remotely also point to opportunities for candidates to ease their way into a new community through virtual transition activities.

One final aspect to consider: Often, search teams work hard to ensure that there is a diverse candidate at the final stage of the process to consider for hire. Everyone will usually feel accomplished in bringing a missing voice forward for consideration. However, research on gender bias in hiring shows that, if only one diverse (i.e., female) candidate is in a final pool of four, the diverse candidate effectively has a zero chance of hire (Johnson et al., 2016). It is best to have more than one diverse candidate at the selection stage of the process to offer an opportunity for hire and counteract difficult-to-detect biases influencing the process.

Hiring

Once the search is complete, bias has been mitigated to the greatest extent possible, and an offer is ready to be made, it is time to think about "retention." The way that the offer is presented and communicated will influence the candidate's perception of how they are valued. For the most positive candidate experience, it is important to:

- Emphasize the benefits, especially those most important to the candidate. Mention the use of holidays, especially if flexible, and share the less visible benefits of employment in the department and institution or organization.
- Make explicit connections that signal the candidate will feel supported as an employee. Provide a list of campus organizations, affinity groups, or community groups to all candidates and offer to make connections. Ask if they are interested in a mentor and provide one if they are.
- Learn about their interests and demonstrate interest in their professional development.
- Anticipate a counteroffer and see it as a positive move from the candidate.
- Be transparent about the probation period and assessment. This demonstrates that one sees the candidate succeeding and as part of the team.

An inclusive work environment is one where an employee feels seen for who they are, heard by others, and truly valued. There is no better place to confirm the inclusive workplace than at the offer stage and in the next stage, onboarding.

Onboarding

Onboarding may seem like an unusual place to think about turnover, yet it is the foundation upon which employees build investment in their work and team. When hires result in turnover, it costs about one-third of the position's salary through lost productivity, knowledge loss, and search-related expenses (Agovino, 2019). Year after year, research also shows that over three quarters of those losses are preventable (Mahan et al., 2020). Onboarding is an opportunity to reinforce that a new employee made the right choice in accepting the offer. This involves engaging key stakeholders in the process, as well as having existing staff take the lead in reaching out to the new employee and getting to know them.

It is also important to reinforce inclusivity within organizational culture by "managing perceptions about fair treatment and access, facilitating assimilation through mentorship and affinity groups, and training and holding managers accountable for creating inclusive cultures" (Grillo & Kim, 2015, p. 4). Onboarding should include clear information on how the organization reinforces an inclusive organizational culture. If an onboarding module or framework does not exist, it can be helpful to develop one session for all employees so that the entire team has shared expectations of community behavior.

For those engaged in remote work, onboarding is especially essential in retaining a new hire (Mauer, 2020), beginning with the technology necessary for success in the position, training modules, and structured opportunities for members of the team to connect with the new hire. Offering mentorship and connections to affinity groups, if available, can be valuable, including professional associations that may be applicable as well as the potential for attending conferences in the future. A manager can share how assignments are given and the opportunity for career development. Holding managers accountable for creating inclusive cultures may prove to be more of a challenge, and they may need help. An internal group dedicated to EDI can serve as a resource, potentially offering an opportunity for learning and growth around these topics for the entire team to reinforce and expand the shared journey toward being an inclusive, equitable organization.

Conclusion

While this chapter focuses on offering tangible steps that individuals and teams can pursue to build an inclusive organizational culture and hiring strategy, it rests on the assumption that collectively we will do the work to unpack and disrupt our own biases. The implications of this work are profound for the profession: Imagine how even our application process for education abroad might change if we used the strategies described here. What will the profile of our employees be like if we can eradicate bias in hiring? How will our conscious and subconscious "ideal candidate" shift, and what would happen if every hire was a cultural add hire?

The answer will vary for each institution, yet the likely commonality is change toward more inclusive organizations that better align with the needs and interests of our increasingly diverse younger generations. The process of self-examination, both personal and organizational, requires a level of introspection that may at times seem difficult, though it is already a growth process with which we are very familiar. Year after year, this introspection is exactly what we ask of our students to help them set aside their cultural assumptions, check their instinct to evaluate local cultures based on their inherent cultural preferences, and reflect on what they are experiencing in order to grow and adapt. This is a deeply personal and sometimes painful process that can feel threatening to the student's worldview, and it is fundamentally the same process that we, as educators, must also pursue to unpack the biases and structures that impede the realization of truly inclusive organizations and hiring practices.

The tangible outcome of this process allows for a more innovative education abroad team that benefits from its collective staff diversity. Longstanding programs are refreshed while new and future programs are positioned to attract more students from a more representative range of backgrounds and cultures. The rich diversity of these cohorts in turn deepens the learning for all as they form richly diverse communities who learn from and with each other in the new cultural context of their program. It is a journey to reach that end goal yet, as Ar'Meisha Burrow reminds us, even when we fall short, that only means we must work harder, for the sake of the students we strive to serve, the colleagues within our organizations, and the larger society to which we all belong.

References

Agovino, T., (2019). To Have and to Hold. *HR Today: The Society for Human Resource Management.* Retrieved from https://www.shrm.org/hr-today/news/all-things-work/pages/to-have-and-to-hold.aspx

Anderson, R. C., Klofstad, C. A., Mayew, W. J., & Venkatachalam, M. (2014). Vocal fry may undermine the success of young women in the labor market. *PLoS ONE, 9*(5), e97506. https://doi.org/10.1371/journal.pone.0097506

Bertrand, M., & Mullainathan, S. (2003, July 28). *Are Emily and Greg more employable than Lakisha and JAMAL? A field experiment on labor market discrimination.* http://www.nber.org/papers/w9873.

Born, M. P., & Taris, T. W. (2010). The impact of the wording of employment advertisements on students' inclination to apply for a job. *The Journal of Social Psychology, 150*(5), 485–502. https://doi/abs/10.1080/00224540903365422.

Bragger, J. D., Kutcher, E., Morgan, J., & Firth, P. (2002). The effects of the structured interview on reducing biases against pregnant job applicants. *Sex Roles, 46*, 215–226. https://doi.org/10.1023/A:1019967231059

Brecher, E., Bragger, J., & Kutcher, E. (2006). The structured interview: Reducing biases toward job applicants with physical disabilities. *Employee Responsibilities and Rights Journal, 18*(3), 155–170. https://doi.org/10.1007/s10672-006-9014-y

Burrow, A. M. (2019). *From the hill to the world: Increasing diversity abroad through intentional outreach.* Western Kentucky University. https://digitalcommons.wku.edu/cgi/viewcontent.cgi?article=1841&context=stu_hon_theses

Cabrera, A. F., & Nora, A. (1994, January). College students' perceptions of prejudice and discrimination and their feelings of alienation: A construct validation approach 1. *Review of Education Pedagogy and Cultural Studies, 16*(3–4), 387–409. https://doi.org/10.1080/1071441940160310

Charles, H., & Wojenski, C. P. (2020, September 9). To diversify education abroad participation, start with advisors. *International Educator.* https://www.nafsa.org/ie-magazine/2020/9/9/diversify-education-abroad-participation-start-advisers

Cohn, D. (2016). *It's official: Minority babies are the majority among the nation's infants, but only just fact tanks news in the numbers.* Pew Research Center. https://www.pewresearch.org/fact-tank/2016/06/23/its-official-minority-babies-are-the-majority-among-the-nations-infants-but-only-just/

Contreras, E., Montgomery, M., & Sevilla-Garcia, H. (2021, January 5). *An antiracist framework for education abroad.* NAFSA. https://www.nafsa.org/ie-magazine/2021/1/5/antiracist-framework-education-abroad

Datapeople. (2021). *Language analytics for job descriptions: Treat candidates like they're people.* https://datapeople.io/language-analytics-for-job-posts/

Davis, J. (2020). The bias against difference. *Psychology Today.* https://www.psychologytoday.com/us/blog/tracking-wonder/202006/the-bias-against-difference

Deloitte Australia & Australian Human Rights Commission. (2017). *Missing out: The business case for customer diversity.* Deloitte. https://www2.deloitte.com/content/dam/Deloitte/au/Documents/human-capital/deloitte-au-hc-business-case-diversity-27Feb2017.pdf

Diversity Abroad. (n.d.). https://www.diversitynetwork.org

Dixon-Fyle, S., Dolan, K., Hunt, V., & Prince, S. C. (2020, May). *Diversity wins: How inclusion matters.* McKinsey & Company. https://www.mckinsey.com/featured-insights/diversity-and-inclusion/diversity-wins-how-inclusion-matters

Erickson, W., Lee, C., & von Schrader, S. (2020). *Disability Statistics from the 2018 American Community Survey (ACS).* Cornell University Yang-Tan Institute. https://www.disabilitystatistics.org

Frey, W. H. (2018, March 14). *The US will become 'minority white' in 2045, census projects.* Brookings Institute. https://www.brookings.edu/blog/the-avenue/2018/03/14/the-us-will-become-minority-white-in-2045-census-projects/

Fry, R., & Parker, K. (2018, November). *Early benchmarks show 'Post-Millennials' on track to be most diverse, best-educated generation yet.* Pew Research Center. https://www.pewsocialtrends.org/2018/11/15/early-benchmarks-show-post-millennials-on-track-to-be-most-diverse-best-educated-generation-yet/

Gaucher, D., Friesen, J., & Kay, A. (2011). Evidence that gendered wording in job advertisements exists and sustains gender inequality. *Journal of Personality and Social Psychology, 101*(1), 109–128. http://gender-decoder.katmatfield.com/static/documents/Gaucher-Friesen-Kay-JPSP-Gendered-Wording-in-Job-ads.pdf

Glassdoor. (2018, July 25). *Salary and benefits are most important for U.S. workers and job seekers looking at job ads, according to Glassdoor survey.* https://www.glassdoor.com/

about-us/salary-and-benefits-are-most-important-for-u-s-workers-and-job-seekers-looking-at-job-ads-according-to-glassdoor-survey/

Goldin, C., & Rouse, C. (2000, September). Orchestrating impartiality: The impact of "blind" auditions on female musicians. *American Economic Review, 90*(4), 715–741. https://doi.org/10.1257/aer.90.4.715

Gordon, A., Johannes, W., and Ledesma, E. (2019). *2019 survey of diversity & inclusion among international educators.* https://www.diversitynetwork.org/page/Research_Reports

Grillo, M., & Kim, H. K. (2015). *A strategic approach to onboarding design: Surveys, materials, & diverse hires.* Cornell University. https://hdl.handle.net/1813/74358

Harvard University. (2011). *The Implicit Bias Association Test (IAT).* https://implicit.harvard.edu/implicit/education.html

Hunt, V., Layton, D., & Prince, S. (2015a, January). *Why diversity matters.* McKinsey & Company. https://www.mckinsey.com/~/media/McKinsey/Business%20Functions/Organization/Our%20Insights/Why%20diversity%20matters/Why%20diversity%20matters.pdf

Hunt, V., Layton, D., & Prince, S. (2015b, February). *Diversity matters.* McKinsey & Company. https://static1.squarespace.com/static/5b3b875dcef372fc7822d05f/t/5b4ae84d70a6ad5e777005ba/1531635794833/McKinsey+Diversity_Matters_Full_Report.pdf

Hunt, V., Yee, L., Prince, S., & Dixon-Fyle, S. (2018). *Delivering through diversity.* McKinsey & Company. Retrieved from https://www.mckinsey.com/business-functions/organization/our-insights/delivering-through-diversity?cid=other-eml-nsl-mip-mck-oth-1802

Hurtado, S., Carter, D. F., & Spuler, A. (1996). Latino student transition to college: Assessing difficulties and factors in successful college adjustment. *Research in Higher Education, 37*(1), 135–157.

Hurtado, S., Clayton-Pedersen, A. R., Allen, W. R., & Milem, J. F. (1998). Enhancing campus climates for racial/ethnic diversity: Educational policy and practice. *The Review of Higher Education, 21*(3), 279–302. DOI: 10.1353/RHE.1998.0003

Hurtado, S., Griffin, K. A., Arellano, L., & Cuellar, M. (2008). Assessing the value of climate assessments: Progress and future directions. *Journal of Diversity in Higher Education, 1,* 204–221.

Hurtado, S., Milem, J., Clayton-Pedersen, A., & Allen, W. (1999). *Enacting diverse learning environments: Improving the climate for racial/ethnic diversity in higher education* (ASHE-ERIC Higher Education Report, Vol. 26, No. 8). The George Washington University, Graduate School of Education and Human Development.

Institute of International Education. (2020). Profile of U.S. study abroad students, 2000/01-2018/19. *Open Doors Report on International Educational Exchange.* https://opendoorsdata.org/data/us-study-abroad/student-profile/

Jackson, V. W. (2018). *Institutional interventions to prevent implicit bias from undermining organizational diversity.* Kirwan Institute for the Study of Race and Ethnicity. http://kirwaninstitute.osu.edu/wp-content/uploads/2018/04/Combating-Implicit-Bias-in-the-workplace.pdf

Johnson, S. K., Hekman, D. R., & Chan, E. T. (2016, April 26). If there's only one woman in your candidate pool, there's statistically no chance she'll be hired. *Harvard Business Review.* https://hbr.org/2016/04/if-theres-only-one-woman-in-your-candidate-pool-theres-statistically-no-chance-shell-behired

Kirwan Institute for the Study of Race and Ethnicity. (2015). *Understanding implicit bias.* The Ohio State University College of Social Work. http://kirwaninstitute.osu.edu/research/understanding-implicit-bias/

Lewis, G. (2018, June 19). This job description heatmap shows you what candidates really care about (and what they ignore). *LinkedIn Talent Blog.* https://business.linkedin.com/talent-solutions/blog/job-descriptions/2018/job-description-heatmap

LinkedIn. (n.d.). *Checklist: Interview questions to assess for culture add.* https://business.linkedin.com/content/dam/me/business/en-us/talent-solutions-lodestone/body/pdf/checklist-3-culture-add_new.pdf

Mahan, T. F., Nelms, D. A., Jeeun, Y., Jackson, A., Hein, M., & Moffett, R. (2020). 2020 retention report: Trends, reasons & wake up call. *The Workforce Institute.* https://workinstitute.com/retention-report/

Mauer, R. (2020, April). Virtual onboarding of remote workers more important than ever. *HR Magazine Society for Human Resources Management.* https://www.shrm.org/ResourcesAndTools/hr-topics/talent-acquisition/Pages/Virtual-Onboarding-Remote-Workers.aspx

McGuire, P. (2019). How higher education can atone for its long history of racism. *The Chronicle of Higher Education, 65*(38), A40.

McKay, P., & Avery, D. (2006). What has race got to do with it? Unraveling the role of racial ethnicity in job seekers' reactions to site visits. *Personnel Psychology, 59*(2), 395–429.

NAFSA. (2021). https://www.nafsa.org

Newport, F. (2018, May 22). In U.S., estimate of LGBT population rises to 4.5%. *Gallup.* https://news.gallup.com/poll/234863/estimate-lgbt-population-rises.aspx?g_source=link_NEWSV9&g_medium=TOPIC&g_campaign=item_&g_content=In%2520U.S.%2c%2520Estimate%2520of%2520LGBT%2520Population%2520Rises%2520to%25204.5%2525

Peterson, M. W., & Spencer, M. G. (1996, Winter). Understanding academic culture and climate. *New Directions for Institutional Research, 1990,* 3–18. https://doi.org/10.1002/ir.37019906803

Pierce, C. (1970). Offensive mechanisms. In F. B. Barbour (Ed.), *The Black seventies* (pp. 265–282). Porter Sargent.

Pogrebtsova, E., Luta, D., & Hausdorf, P. A. (2019). Selection of gender-incongruent applicants: No gender bias with structured interviews. *International Journal of Selection and Assessment.* https://onlinelibrary.wiley.com/doi/abs/10.1111/ijsa.12270

Portland State University, (n.d.). *Interview questions regarding diversity.* https://www.pdx.edu/hr/sites/www.pdx.edu.hr/files/Interview%20Questions%20Regarding%20Diversity.pdf

Powers, J. M. (2007). The relevance of Critical Race Theory to educational theory and practice. *Journal of the Philosophy of Education, 41*(1), 151–166.

Quillian, L., Pager, D., Hexel, O., & Midtbøen, A. H. (2017). Meta-analysis of field experiments shows no change in racial discrimination in hiring over time. *Proceedings of the National Academy of Sciences, 114.* https://doi.org/10.1073/pnas.1706255114

Rivera, L. (2012). Hiring as cultural matching: The case of elite professional service firms. *American Sociological Association, 77*(6), 999–1022. https://doi.org/10.1177/0003122412463213

Saenz, T, Marcoulides, G. A., Junn, E., & Young, R. (1999). The relationship between college experience and academic performance among minority students. *International Journal of Education Management, 13*(4–5), 199–207.

Stanford University. (2019). *Stanford encyclopedia of philosophy.* Center for the Study of Language and Information. https://plato.stanford.edu/entries/implicit-bias/

Sue, D. W. (2010). *Microaggressions in everyday life: Race, gender, and sexual orientation.* Wiley.

Sue, D. W., Capodilupo, C. M., Torino, G. C., Bucceri, J. M., Holder, A. M. B, Nadal, K. L., & Esquilin, M. (2017, May–June). Racial microaggressions in everyday life: Implications for clinical practice. *American Psychologist, 62*(4), 271–286. https://doi.org/10.1037/0003-066X.62.4.271

Taylor, B. J., Miller, R. A., & García-Louis, C. (2014). Utilizing intersectionality to engage dialogue in higher education. In D. Mitchell, Jr., C. Simmons, & L. Greyerbiehl (Eds.), *Intersectionality & higher education: Theory, research, and praxis.* Peter Lang.

Textio. (2021). *Augmented writing.* https://textio.com/

The Forum on Education Abroad. (2020). *Standards of good practice for education abroad, sixth edition.* https://forumea.org/resources/standards-6th-edition/

The Work Institute. (2020). *2020 retention report: Insights on 2019 turnover trends, reasons, costs & recommendations.* http://info.workinstitute.com/en/retention-report-2020

U.S. Department of Education & National Center for Education Statistics. (2019). *Table 323.20 Master's degrees conferred by postsecondary institutions, by race/ethnicity and sex of student: Selected years, 1976–77 through 2017–18.* https://nces.ed.gov/programs/digest/d19/tables/dt19_323.20.asp

University of Washington. (2010). *ADVANCE Center for Institutional Change.* https://www.engr.washington.edu/lead/biasfilm/materials/key-concepts.html#:~:text=Unexamined%20Bias%3A%20A%20form%20of,on%20bias%2C%20holding%20them%20accountable

Westerman, A., Benk, R., & Greene, D. (2020, December 30). *In 2020, protests spread across the globe with a similar message: Black lives matter.* NPR. https://www.npr.org/2020/12/30/950053607/in-2020-protests-spread-across-the-globe-with-a-similar-message-black-lives-matt

Zivkovic, M. (2020, July 20). 6 Types of unconscious bias in hiring and how to combat them. *togglhire.* https://toggl.com/blog/unconscious-bias

5

Equity-Minded Program Design for Inclusive Excellence

Malaika Serrano, David Wick and Devin Walker

In the context of the COVID-19 pandemic and racial, environmental, and economic justice crises, a growing number of educators have sought to acknowledge and address the biases and systemic injustices within our communities and in our work. This is no different for those who work in education abroad, helping students to study, work, volunteer, and conduct research abroad. At the same time, the field remains entrenched in approaches and practices that were not designed to foster equity and justice or to advance inclusive excellence. Although new topics, locations, and scholarships with the goal of expanding access have been added to program offerings, the underlying structures of individual programs reflect models that are not optimized to serve historically minoritized students or to confront systemic inequities in home or host communities.

How do we reimagine education abroad program design for the 21st century and center equity, diversity, and inclusion (EDI)? We believe that it is vital to look outside the field of education abroad toward other fields that position equity and justice as core values and competencies. Disciplines including education, sociology, psychology, and social work provide guidance on design for inclusion, belonging, quality, and equity (Abe, 2020; Bensimon et al., 2016; Chavez et al., 2003; Tervalon & Murray-Garcia, 1998; Williams et al., 2005). We leverage these multidisciplinary perspectives throughout this chapter because they powerfully inform design for EDI and because they are rarely cited by education abroad practitioners and scholars, including those who have been engaging in EDI work for decades.

To apply insights from the interdisciplinary fields mentioned previously, we propose a three-step process for (re)designing education abroad programs that are equity-minded and based on inclusive excellence tenets:

(1) Shift our mindset toward equity and inclusive excellence
(2) Articulate equitable and inclusive program learning goals
(3) Align program components to goals

Such an approach aligns well with The Forum on Education Abroad's *Standards of Good Practice* (2020b). As a membership association that has been recognized by the U.S. Department of Justice and the Federal Trade Commission as the U.S. standards development organization (SDO), The Forum establishes practice standards for the field of education abroad. The sixth edition of the *Standards* for the first time emphasizes EDI as a guiding principle and EDI concepts are woven throughout subsequent clauses and subclauses. Given this significant and recent change to the field's *Standards*, and the current justice-related crises, this chapter demonstrating how equity-mindedness and inclusive excellence can guide program design is both timely and essential for education abroad professionals.

We have organized this chapter into three main sections based on the stages of program design. First, we present frameworks for shifting our mindset toward cultural humility, equity, and inclusive excellence. We then discuss approaches to articulating developmental program learning objectives. In the final section, we examine examples of practice for aligning education abroad program components to equity-minded and inclusively excellent learning goals. Our introductions and positionality serve as context for the subsequent discussion of this three-step program design process.

Author Positionality

A commitment to equity and inclusion requires us to acknowledge our identities, backgrounds, and experiences and their impact on our work. This is a critical step that influences our ability to design for equity and inclusive excellence. We present our profiles to help readers understand our perspectives and biases.

Malaika Marable Serrano comes to this work from the perspective of an African American, (currently) able-bodied, heterosexual, cisgender woman, with Southeastern U.S. roots and strong ties to Latin America. Since studying abroad in Australia and teaching English in Venezuela, she has worked in a number of administration and teaching roles, including leading a service-learning program to the Dominican Republic, where students explored and critically reflected on how identities inform our approaches to addressing social inequalities.

Devin Walker comes to this work as a Black, able-bodied, heterosexual, cisgender man who grew up with a White mother and Black father in Los Angeles, California. Going to the University of Wisconsin–Madison for college taught him how to be comfortable with discomfort and how to navigate racially homogeneous spaces. He studied abroad three times as an undergraduate and taught English in Korea for 2 years prior to attending graduate school at The University of Texas at Austin. Over the past 8 years, he has helped the Division of Diversity and Community Engagement at UT-Austin take over 400 students to South Africa and China, 80% of whom self-identify as Black or Latin(x), and 45% who identify as first-generation students.

David Wick comes to this work as a White, heterosexual, cisgender male with a chronic physical disability. His parents were teachers who taught him to see education as a human right and a force for social justice. He has worked with youth exchange and in varied higher education organizations and institutions. Each of these contexts provided insights into the differences between his lived experience and that of his students. He has studied the ways that international education systematically excludes and underserves marginalized and minoritized students. His recognition of these systemic educational failings has guided his teaching, research, practice, and thinking about equity-minded education abroad program design.

Step 1: Shifting our Mindset as Program Designers

How do we shift our mindset from familiar, current, or traditional approaches to equity-minded program design and implementation?

As a first step in designing programs for inclusive excellence, we ask readers to pause, reflect, and reconsider what we have always believed to be true for education abroad programs. As international educators, we often pride ourselves on being intercultural and/or having achieved intercultural competency, that is, the ability to relate and communicate effectively with individuals who do not share the same culture, ethnicity, language, or other common experiences as our own (The Forum on Education Abroad, 2020b). This position is problematic in that it supports a myth that cultures are monoliths (Doerr et al., 2021; see also Chapter 10 of this volume) and implies that we are already able to design for perspectives, experiences, and needs that differ from our own. To disrupt our thinking about education abroad program design, we must begin with self-work, which we break down here into three areas: reorienting ourselves with cultural humility, changing our systems, and recognizing inclusion as essential for educational excellence.

Reorienting Ourselves With Cultural Humility: Cultural humility helps us shift our mindset away from the status quo and invites us to "maintain an interpersonal stance that is other-oriented (or open to the other) in relation to aspects of cultural identity that are most important to the [other person]" (Hook et al., 2013, p. 2). Further, with cultural humility we recognize the ways we may have benefited from (un)earned privilege and/or unconsciously supported ideas and systems that predominantly reward White, middle/upper-middle class, legacy college students and penalize students from marginalized and minoritized communities. Developing cultural humility, the perpetual and self-critical awareness of our identities (Hook et al., 2013; Tervalon & Murray-Garcia, 1998), helps us to challenge and change our perspective. This combined with the other two tenets of cultural humility—(a) recognition and challenging of power imbalances and (b) partnering to advocate and advance institutional accountability (Abe, 2020; Tervalon & Murray-Garcia, 1998)—reorients our thinking about program design.

Awareness of our implicit biases and how they impact the entire program lifecycle (i.e., design, recruitment, selection, preparation, on-site, postprogram engagement, assessment, and refinement) moves us toward equity-minded design. In recognizing the powerful impacts of implicit biases, we may be able to confront them to design and facilitate programs that are more equitable and just.

Changing Our Systems With Equity-Mindedness: In addition to cultural humility, the concept of equity-mindedness presents a powerful framework for confronting systemic inequities in education (Bensimon et al., 2016). This framework can be used in many ways, including faculty development (Costino, 2018), program design (Bensimon et al., 2016), and assessment and evaluation (Harris III & Bensimon, 2007). Equity-mindedness intersects with inclusive excellence (American Association of Colleges and Universities [AAC&U], n.d.), the central idea of this volume, and can be articulated as following:

> The perspective or mode of thinking exhibited by practitioners who call attention to patterns of inequity in student outcomes. These practitioners are willing to take personal and institutional responsibility for the success of their students, and critically reassess their own practices. It also requires that practitioners are race-conscious and aware of the social and historical context of exclusionary practices in American Higher Education. (The Center for Urban Education, n.d.-b, para. 1)

Equity-mindedness provides an interdisciplinary approach to reimagining education abroad program design and assessment, one that begins with an acknowledgment that the current system has not been designed with marginalized and minoritized students at the center (see also Chapter 1 in this volume). According to The Center for Urban Education, "educational reform must acknowledge and foreground the policies and practices contributing to disparities in educational achievement and abstain from blaming students for those accumulated disparities" (n.d.-a, para. 1). Deficit mindsets place blame on historically minoritized communities. The latter has been evident in education, relative to students' demographic representation (Bensimon et al., 2016; Clayton-Pedersen & Musil, 2009; Costino, 2018; Whitehead, 2015). Equity-mindedness reminds us that underrepresentation is not an outreach or access problem, but instead a systemic design problem.

Each of the five following principles for enacting equity by design applies directly to education abroad program design and thus guides us to question and change systems and structures (Bensimon et al., 2016):

- Principle 1: Clarity in language, goals, and measures is vital to effective, equitable practices.
- Principle 2: "Equity-mindedness" should be the guiding paradigm for language and action.
- Principle 3: Equitable practice and policies are designed to accommodate differences in the contexts of students' learning—not to treat all students the same.
- Principle 4: Enacting equity requires a continual process of learning, disaggregating data, and questioning assumptions about relevance and effectiveness.
- Principle 5: Equity must be enacted as a pervasive institution- and system-wide principle.

In line with these principles, we must first describe and define what we mean with our language and what we seek to achieve in education abroad programs. The terms and definitions section of The Forum's *Standards* (2020b, pp. 10–21) includes definitions for terms such as equity, diversity, and inclusion (EDI), each of which is central to this approach to program design. Institutions and organizations can use these definitions as starting points for establishing their definitions to provide the clarity in language, goals, and measures that grounds equity-minded work.

The second and third principles compel us to center our efforts on the pursuit of equity rather than equality. In doing so, we acknowledge the history of inequity, racism, and exclusionary practices. We further recognize how privilege and oppression disproportionately harm minoritized students including Black, Indigenous, and People of color (BIPOC). Once we acknowledge the context and reality of systemic inequity, it becomes clear that we must accommodate student differences in all aspects of design to achieve equality in outcomes for students, partners, and hosts. These principles also place the responsibility of disrupting systems of inequity on institutions, organizations, offices, and individuals rather than on the minoritized students and their communities.

Taken together, Principles 4 and 5 underscore the importance of seeing equity-mindedness as an ongoing process that requires us to adapt all systems including design and assessment. When we question our assumptions about what we do, how we do it, and how well it works, we begin to see the impacts of inequity. This approach to assessment and evaluation, combined with a disaggregation of data, requires us to constantly call all aspects of our work into question.

These five equity-minded principles present a shift in education abroad narratives and conventional wisdom around access, participation, and achievement gaps between White and BIPOC students. Previously, institutions and organizations were excused from acknowledging systemic inequality in program design, recruitment, and implementation (Lopez & Louis, 2009; Wick et al., 2019; Yosso, 2005). In an international education context, these narratives centered deficits and blamed students for not considering education abroad or for not being successful applicants. With such principles in mind, we note, for example, that rigid deadlines and timelines, particularly for applications (see Chapter 8 of this volume) and funding, often require access to capital, long before a student's financial aid arrives. In addition to the considerations for program design in this chapter, an equity-minded approach requires questioning fee structures, payment schedules, housing options, host countries, program leaders, training, outreach efforts, student support, parent engagement, applications, selection processes, host community engagement, assessment, and evaluation.

Recognizing Inclusion as Essential for Excellence: Building on cultural humility and equity-minded perspectives, education abroad program design for equity and inclusion must also respond to concerns about quality and depth of learning. With the goal of promoting "access, student success, and high-quality learning" (AAC&U, n.d., para. 1; see also Chapter 2 of this volume), the concept of inclusive excellence addresses these concerns directly.

First coined by the AAC&U, inclusive excellence is characterized by the following:

(1) A focus on student intellectual and social development. Academically, it means offering the best possible course of study for the context in which the education is offered.
(2) A purposeful development and utilization of organizational resources to enhance student learning. Organizationally, it means establishing an environment that challenges each student to achieve academically at high levels and each member of the campus to contribute to learning and knowledge development.
(3) Attention to the cultural differences learners brings to the educational experience and that enhance the enterprise.
(4) A welcoming community that engages all of its diversity in the service of student and organizational learning. (Williams et al., 2005, p. vi)

Within this definition, there is a natural connection between inclusive excellence and education abroad. Whitehead (2015) explains that global learning "prepares students to critically analyze and engage with complex global systems, their implications for the lives of individuals, and the sustainability of the earth" (para. 2). Inclusive excellence requires that institutions and organizations systematically integrate EDI, an approach that is crucial to disrupting systemic inequity and guiding the development of inclusive programming, as we continue in Step 2.

Step 2: Program Learning Goals

What strengths, goals, and needs do students possess, and how will we leverage these through equity-minded program learning objectives?

Once we have interrogated our biases, perspectives, and beliefs, we are ready to continue with the program design cycle by articulating equity-minded inclusively excellent goals and associated developmental learning objectives. This approach prepares us to construct program learning goals that are aligned with The Forum's *Standards* clauses on EDI (2020b, p. 25). Although each program should have learning outcomes tailored to its learners, institutions, subject matter, and context, to design for EDI, we must define developmental, equity-minded learning outcomes that advance inclusive excellence across all programs in a given office or organization. Learning outcomes designed for EDI are a necessary first step toward equity-minded assessment (Harris III & Bensimon, 2007; see also Chapter 14 of this volume, focusing on assessment and the construct of belongingness). These equity-minded assessments must also measure the impacts on the host communities (Hartman & Chaire, 2014; Lough & Toms, 2018).

To achieve inclusive excellence and equitable learning outcomes, it is necessary to design learning experiences that address the strengths and needs of each student. This requires an understanding of who they are (Bensimon et al., 2016), the strengths they bring (Glass & Holton, 2021; Yosso, 2005), and their developmental needs (Williams et al., 2005). Drawing on psychological and educational development theory, developmental needs can be categorized into three domains—social identities, cognitive, and psychosocial (Wick & Trujillo, 2018)—which we explore here.

Social Identities and Development: To illustrate the first of the three domains, social identities, let us begin with the following example. Students sit around a table working quietly. They are asked to create a social identity wheel (Social Identity Wheel, n.d.) and to respond to a series of reflective questions. Using the wheel, they are asked to describe their gender, sexuality, ability, race, ethnicity, nationality, first language, and other identities. Reflection prompts include: Which of these identities are you most aware of in this room? Which of these identities has the greatest impact on your learning at your home institution? How might you experience these identities differently while studying abroad?

The abovementioned setting may not immediately seem like the start of a predeparture session for an education abroad program, but it can be. Such an examination of social identities is vital because all our identities are tied to historical, political, economic, and cultural realities and inform our relationships to all educational experiences. When we are in a new group, such as a study abroad cohort or a host family, different aspects of our identities become more or less significant to our experience (Abes et al., 2007). In this context, our sense of self and understanding of our identities may come under stress (Butler, 2019). At the same time, shifts in identity can also create powerful opportunities for growth and learning (Doerr et al., 2021; Wick et al., 2019; Willis, 2015). To balance the potential stress associated with navigating a new environment as international educators, it is necessary to integrate identity-based critical self-reflection into learning and provide students with tools for navigating their identities in new contexts. Models for social identities (Abes et al., 2007) illustrate how the salience of each of our identities shifts based on external factors. Circling back to informing learning outcomes,

> Faculty program leaders and in-country staff who support education abroad programs should engage in self-reflective work alongside the students. This recognition will create a feeling of openness, trust, and support for students, as well as foster an experience that is learner centered. (Serrano, 2020, p. 161).

Cognitive Development: To achieve inclusive excellence and equity-minded education abroad program learning goals, we must consider the cognitive capacity of the learners to engage with the program context and content. Cognitive capacity relates to our ability to think, solve problems, and understand the world around us. We must also consider the perspectives and experiences that students, especially marginalized and minoritized students, bring to the learning experience (Doerr, 2018; Wick et al., 2019; Yosso, 2005). As required by *Standards* subclause 6.2.3, "supporting student understanding of the social, historical, political, economic, linguistic, cultural, and environmental contexts"' includes a broad range of topics that we must approach developmentally to ensure that every student can learn.

Supporting student learning after the time abroad is also encouraged in *Standards* subclauses 6.3.3 and 6.3.6 that recommend "continuing local and global engagement in culturally-relevant, ethical and reciprocally-beneficial activities." Taken together, these elements suggest that, to advance inclusive excellence, we must design increasingly complex culturally relevant equity-minded learning experiences before, during, and after the time abroad that are beneficial to both students and host communities (Lough & Toms, 2018). For example, before a program begins, we can guide students to describe and define their social identities, while abroad we can support participants as they analyze and critique social identity construction and performance in the host country, and after the program we can work with returnees to reframe and debate identity-based policies and cultural practices.

Psychosocial and Intercultural Development: Frameworks for learning about diversity and difference (Chavez et al., 2003) and intercultural learning and development remind us to assess knowledge and skill related to human difference before we guide students to further development. Here too we must be careful to consider the psychosocial skills that marginalized and minoritized students bring to education abroad (Doerr 2018; Wick et al., 2019; Yosso, 2005). By connecting social identity development and recognition of structural inequity to psychosocial development, we embody the principles of equity-mindedness and critically examine how these power imbalances impact our interpersonal and intercultural relationships. Most importantly, an equity-minded and inclusively excellent developmental approach to psychosocial and intercultural development requires us to recognize the knowledge and skills in these domains that immigrants and other marginalized and minoritized students possess.

The *Standards* imply a developmental progression for psychosocial development and intercultural learning. Subclause 6.1.9 requires that we "prepare participants to navigate the cultural transition and to engage in culturally-relevant, ethical, and reciprocally-beneficial activities in relation to the local community" (The Forum on Education Abroad, 2020b, p. 32). Furthermore, 6.1.9.2 indicates that we are expected to communicate "the significance of identities ... in relation to the program context" (The Forum on Education Abroad, 2020b, p. 32). Similar requirements are included in *Standards* clauses 6.2.5 and 6.2.6 related to intercultural interactions and identity negotiation abroad. Finally, the *Standards* recommend postprogram creation of learning opportunities and continuing global and local engagement. Together these elements connect psychosocial and intercultural development and require that we provide structured support for student learning and host community reciprocity (Lough & Toms, 2018) in these areas before, during, and after international experiences.

Model Learning Objectives: Writing learning objectives that can apply across all education abroad activities presents challenges. Each program design team must write and refine learning objectives that reflect the goals, strengths, and needs of their students, partners, and host communities. As noted earlier, international educators must also articulate developmental learning objectives before, during, and after the time abroad. A few examples that may be of use as a starting point include the following:

- Students will model critical self-reflection to deepen and expand their understanding of themselves in the world.
- Students will practice working collectively and interculturally to identify and confront equity and justice concerns in their communities and around the world.
- Program participants will demonstrate empathy, humility, and authentic caring in their relationships with their fellow students and with those they interact with on-site.
- Students will collaboratively design solutions to equity and justice issues that apply varied perspectives and sources of knowledge.

These sample objectives show how student learning must begin with critical self-examination, similar to our discussion of developing critical consciousness as part of cultural humility (Abe, 2020). They also center equity and inequity (Bensimon et al., 2016), recognize the cultural differences learners bring, and respond to the ways those differences shape their interpretations of their actions and impacts (Williams et al., 2005). These samples provide a grounding for our exploration of program components. To advance equity and inclusive excellence, an equity-minded assessment plan that examines student learning, home, and host community impacts is essential (Harris III & Bensimon, 2007; Hartman & Chaire, 2014; Lough & Toms, 2018).

Step 3: Program Component Alignment

How do all activities and structures of your program reflect equity-mindedness and advance inclusive excellence?

Education abroad programs consist of many interrelated components, all of which must be designed intentionally to contribute to equity-minded learning goals. These program components include a range of formal and informal structures. Helpfully, Gozik and Oguro (2021) differentiate between five major education abroad program components: (a) modes of instruction, (b) housing, (c) extra- and co-curricular activities, (d) experiential learning, and (e) student support services. Here, we use these program components as a starting point, though change the categories and add additional layers, to emphasize EDI and belonging for equity and inclusive excellence.

Building programs for inclusive excellence, and ones that model the *Standards*, requires an integration of student agency in learning objectives. Moreover, the ideas behind inclusive excellence and student development theory emphasize the need for students to be seen as active participants in their own learning (Magolda, 2008; Mezirow, 1997; Williams et al., 2005). Guiding students to design their own learning goals as part of the application process helps faculty and program coordinators align student interests and needs with the program components like assignments, site visits, guest speakers, and so on. Similar approaches to empowering student agency include the establishment of community pacts or group norms, prior to departure or soon after arriving in-country. For virtual programs, dedicating time during the first-class meeting to having these conversations demonstrates prioritization of students' developmental and belonging needs. Creating these opportunities for students to shape program learning goals and program design contributes to development of culturally responsive (Ladson-Billings, 1995) learning environments.

Curricular Offerings: The Forum's *Standards* ask us to consider the following: "How do the curricular and co-curricular programming, including assigned readings, excursions, and guest speakers include diverse perspectives and practice inclusive pedagogy?" (4.4.k). This question ties into the work of inclusive pedagogy and curricular design, which is a student-centered approach to creating and fostering equitable learning environments (Florian,

2015). This framework drives the prioritization of EDI in instructional spaces. Both the teacher and the student have a shared responsibility in the learning process; self-awareness and reflection are critical to fostering inclusive programs (Florian, 2015).

To help illustrate an inclusive design, let us imagine the following case study, which we build upon throughout this section:

> *'Urban Economic Development' in Cape Town, South Africa* is a 4-week faculty-led Maymester program, hosted by a diversity division within a large public institution in the South. The program was conceptualized when the international office approached the diversity division to collaborate on a program which would attract students who are traditionally underrepresented within study abroad. This program has run five times between 2014-2019 taking on average 56 students a year, over 80% of whom identified as Black or Latinx. Students stayed together in a hostel or hotel, students engaged in community-based global service-learning two days a week and took classes three days a week at the University of Cape Town. Students also participated in varied co-curricular activities in and around Cape Town exploring how communities negatively impacted by apartheid contribute to economic development. Both faculty leaders are Black men, a point that has been raised with the in-country program provider, with a request for more female guest speakers, to even out the perspectives.

This example illustrates the importance of diversifying the curriculum. By recognizing the gendered and cultural perspectives of program leaders, it becomes clear that other voices are needed. Moreover, it is important to include additional perspectives in ways that demonstrate they have similar weight and value to the voices of those who are already working in the program. In addition to bringing voices into the conversation, we must also guide students to recognize the biases in how they listen, in the sources they seek, and in the perspectives that they have. Each of these skills is connected to the learning objectives outlined earlier related to intrapersonal, interpersonal, and intercultural growth. In this chapter, we emphasize design elements related to equity and inclusive excellence. For curricular examples of subject area content and coursework, we refer readers to other chapters in this book.

Accommodations as an Inclusive Learning Space: Students often spend more time at their places of residence, which can include homestays, residence halls, hotels, hostels, campsites, and so on, than anywhere else while abroad. Dynamics of gender, race, sexuality, and other social markers must all be thoroughly engaged when considering the various housing choices. As we consider housing through an equity-minded lens, we must also realize that safety is not a neutral term and means something very different for people depending on the body they occupy (Crenshaw, 1989; Willis, 2015).

In addition, each housing choice has a different impact on student learning outcomes and on support structures and needs.

To provide one illustration of inclusive excellence in housing, let us consider homestays. The homestay experience, it is argued, is an essential and "classic example of the immersion model" (Berg et al., 2012, p. 44). However, these goals are not always actualized. Without proper training, preparation, and expectation setting for students, host families, and homestay organizations, homestays can have particularly negative effects on everyone involved (Schmidt-Rinehart & Knight, 2004). For the South Africa program, homestays were briefly considered but ultimately decided against, due to the large number of students, the daily travel considerations, and the high level of petty crime within Cape Town.

It is critical that the recruitment and selection process of host families is conducted with an inclusive excellence lens and organizational values around EDI and belonging are communicated early and often. To support Fair Trade learning and ethical engagement, reciprocity is central to the relationship for all stakeholders (Hartman & Chaire, 2014; Lough & Toms, 2018) and must be continuously assessed. Host families and community members should be consulted and equitably compensated for their time and expertise.

In addition to vetting host families for safety and security, program developers must also facilitate mutually beneficial opportunities for intercultural communication and learning between students and hosts prior to arrival. For example, institutions and education abroad organizations can integrate the social identity exercise mentioned earlier in the chapter, as a training tool for host families and on-site staff. Such exercises allow all parties to develop vocabulary and greater awareness of dimensions of diversity that are salient to the U.S. students they are receiving in their homes and at their institutions. Providing opportunities for host families and on-site staff to engage in critical self-reflective work, as well as examine how EDI presents in their contexts, will better equip them to receive and support an increasingly diverse U.S. student body and will extend the opportunity for intrapersonal and intercultural learning to the host community.

Extra- and Co-Curricular Activities: Activities such as visits to museums, historical and cultural sites, day tours, hikes/walks, cultural events and performances, and sporting events are ideally meant to enhance student learning. When planning such activities in the host country, equity, social justice, and inclusion should be at the heart of all decisions (Bensimon et al., 2016; Clayton-Pedersen, 2019; Clayton-Pedersen & Musil, 2009; Hartman et al., 2018; Lough & Toms, 2018; The Forum on Education Abroad, 2020b); this aligns with the Forum *Standards* and Fair Trade Learning (Hartman & Chaire, 2014).

Physical activity

Equity-minded design principles remind us that equitable practice and policies are designed to accommodate differences in the contexts of students' learning—not to treat all students the same (Forum, 4.4 b). Co-curricular activities like nature walks, hikes, and other physical activities create an opportunity for informal engagement among students, team building, and self-efficacy (Simpson & Grimes, 2020). However, physical activities also create opportunities for some students to feel marginalized, isolated, and hyper-aware of their physical limitations. Program coordinators, faculty members, and staff should create alternative options for students who may find the entire physical activity daunting but still want to participate and achieve similar learning outcomes.

Coming back to the Cape Town example, let us imagine that there are multiple hikes and/or long walks when visiting historical and cultural sites. To ensure that all students feel safe, supported, and included whatever their physical characteristics, hidden disabilities, or physical limitations, we might incorporate the following guidelines:

- Every hike or walk has multiple destinations. For example, students can climb to the top of the mountain if they so choose, but we also identify a midway point that is scenic for students who do not choose to continue on. At least one staff member per hike stops at the midway point, and one continues to the higher point.
- One staff member is always in the back with the last student. Therefore, when a student gets exhausted or falls behind, they are not alone. This also serves as a safety measure.
- Staff members rotate the role they play on hikes. If a staff member is in the back on one hike, they will have the option to hike as far as they want on the next hike. This ensures that the work is equitably distributed among staff and does not fall on those who are traditionally looked at as caregivers.

With different program learning outcomes, we may also take other approaches to adapting student engagement. For example, let us imagine a program that requires students to move from meeting to meeting each day requires navigation of multiple transportation systems and walking. The travel time provides essential opportunities for students and faculty to connect, as we noted related to hikes. The physical demands also present different challenges for each student. As with our approach to hikes, instead of simply encouraging students to opt out, it is possible to design other ways for students to participate and achieve the learning objectives. We can design programs so that students participate in a percentage of meetings or activities and are expected to skip some to work on reflection and projects. In addition, to bring all voices to meetings, groups can prepare collaboratively and have one or two students who serve as facilitators and others who are note-takers. In these ways, all student voices shape the conversations with partners and all students have access to the insights, whether or not they attend. These approaches not only increase accessibility but also create a more collaborative and egalitarian learning experience, one that reflects the intrapersonal, intergroup, and intercultural learning objectives of the program.

In addition, an equity-minded approach helps us to adapt existing program decision-making based on incidents that arise. Prior to departure, for example, it might be that we have a student on the Cape Town program who has broken her ankle and is physically limited, often wearing a boot. Collectively, the staff as well as the student can plan for each excursion and what support will look like. The student may at first consider not participating at all. To accommodate the student, it could be that the location of the hike is changed or that discretionary funds are used to purchase tickets for her to take the gondola lift up the mountain with a staff member. Operating out of an equity-based framework requires that we do not treat all students the same (Bensimon et al., 2016) and instead leads us to adjust the procedures and resources to meet individual student needs.

Cultural and historical site visits

The second principle of Bensimon et al.'s equity-minded model invites us to reconsider the "sociohistorical context of exclusionary practices and racism in higher education and the impact of power asymmetries on opportunities and outcomes, particularly for African Americans and Latinas/os" (2016, para. 12). Cultural and historical site visits, for instance, can be places where violence has taken place against particular races, cultures, and communities. This suggests a diverse group of students will experience the site in very different ways. It is essential to create spaces for dialogue where students can critically interrogate relations of power, identity, and history prior to visiting the site. It is equally important to create opportunities for dialogue and reflection after visiting such sites so that students have the opportunity to learn from one another and the various ways in which they may have experienced a site.

Back to our case, prior to visiting the District Six museum in Cape Town, a memorial to the forced movement of 60,000 inhabitants of various races to District Six during Apartheid in South Africa in the 1970s, a group might discuss the relationship between Apartheid and histories of forced relocation and Jim Crow Laws in the U.S., as well as current patterns of gentrification. Creating space for this discussion prior to the site visit allows for students to share some of their own families' experiences, setting a tone of active engagement prior to entering the museum. Through dialogue, both before and after the site visit, students are better able to understand how exclusionary practices based on White supremacy operate on a global level. They make connections between what was happening in Cape Town and how that mirrored histories and current realities of certain groups within the U.S. All students are challenged to reflect on their identities in relation to power, privilege, and oppression, which ultimately opens the door for powerful dialogues and intercultural communication.

This form of inclusive pedagogy focuses on student voices and experiences creating an environment that promotes social justice where all students feel valued. Cape Town offers unique opportunities to discuss race, power, inequity, and oppression, given the severity of Apartheid, yet similar themes can be explored in all parts of the world. While South Africa may seem like a natural place to explore these issues, other locations can similarly offer a starting point for such discussions.

Experiential Learning: Ethical Engagement With Community, Work, and Research: The program component of experiential learning includes community-based global learning, internships, and research (Gozik & Oguro, 2021). Central to program design is beginning partnerships by learning about the partner's goals, strengths, and needs. Recent publications including the latest edition the *Standards* by The Forum, *Social Justice and International Education* (NAFSA, 2020), and a special issue of *Frontiers: The Interdisciplinary Journal of Study Abroad* (Contreras et al., 2020) all emphasize the need to design for equity in impacts on all participants in education abroad experiences. The National Association of Colleges and Employers (NACE) has also incorporated Principles for Creating Equity by Design and inclusive excellence as core tenants to their approach in developing equity-minded practitioners (Clayton-Pedersen, 2019). This aligns with the *Standards* related to collaboration and transparency (clauses 4.2.1–4.2.4) and with the *Standards* related to ethics (clauses 4.3.1–4.3.7). By designing our experiential components for mutual respect and mutual benefit, we can advance equity-minded and inclusively excellent education abroad programs.

We are using the term *community-based global learning* for our discussion of what is sometimes called service learning to reframe this as an equity-minded practice. Framing these activities in this way places an emphasis on mutual benefit, support for students and communities pre- and post-engagement, and long-term sustainable relationships that can contribute to Fair Trade Learning (Hartman & Chaire, 2014; Hartman et al., 2018; Lough & Toms, 2018). Such approaches emphasize equity and ethics as the starting point for relationships and insist on emphasizing justice in our approaches. By beginning with these considerations, rather than student learning goals, we develop partnerships that may lead to standards-aligned learning opportunities. These concepts are integrated into many of the prompts for self-assessment (The Forum on Education Abroad, 2020a) including: "What steps do you have in place to respect and promote each partner's values?" (4.2.b), "How does each partner benefit from the partnership?" (4.2.c), "Who determines the benefits to each partner?" (4.2.d), and "How do responsible parties follow ethical practices in teaching, work, service/volunteering, and research?" (4.3.d).

Returning to the example of South Africa, it might be that each student participates in a community-based global learning experience with a local business or organization to support their efforts twice a week. Prior to arriving in the host country, students could be paired with partners based on the desired skill sets of the partners and student learning needs and competencies. In addition to fulfilling partner needs, students could be required to interview stakeholders within the organization and the surrounding community. This would help them learn about organizational strengths and opportunities for improvement. They might equally be asked to complete a related final project, with examples ranging from a social media campaign to a community cleanup, architectural rendering, academic curriculum, leadership training, and so on, depending on the student's skill level. After the program ends, group leaders would follow up with partners to ensure their goals were met through the partnership and to integrate their feedback into future planning. In this way, the program would be designed to respond to community partner and student strengths, goals, and needs.

Holistic Student Support through Identity and Career-Oriented Workshops

The *Standards* ask us to consider: "How do advising materials and resources intentionally address the needs and concerns related to the identities of historically underrepresented and historically underserved students?" (4.4.h). Holistic support starts at the program ideation stage and extends far beyond the completion of the program. What holistic support looks like will likely vary across programs, from advising materials, to mental health services, to financial support, to staff support, to identity-based workshops, to career workshops, and so on, because each group will need something different. However, all students should feel like their identities and career goals are being supported during and after the program.

To successfully support students while abroad, it is essential to develop open lines of communication through team-building exercises and critical conversations around identity, privilege, and power prior to departure. As noted earlier, team-building and identity-based workshops provide necessary opportunities for students to open up with one another, become more aware of their biases, challenge each other, support one another, and build their intercultural communication skills prior to being in another country (Vavrus & Pekol, 2015). Another important factor of holistically supporting students is a diverse staff presence. If fiscally possible, a strong staff presence helps ensure that all students have someone they feel connected to both abroad and on the home campus. Student identities are more malleable while abroad, something that presents transformational learning and mentoring opportunities. Such support can happen through individual meetings, workshops, and informal gatherings.

Returning once again to South Africa, toward the latter end of the program, we might facilitate workshops that help students connect their experiences to tangible skills they have developed. A month after the faculty-led program, we could have an informal gathering at the professor's house to help students reflect on their experiences, identify transferable skills, and describe the support relationships developed. These gatherings would affirm to the students that we care about their holistic development as people and encourage them to attend additional postprogram personal and professional competency workshops so that they can make the most out of their experiences abroad.

Closing Thoughts

We began this chapter on education abroad program design for equity and inclusion with the assertion that the first step toward equity-mindedness and inclusive excellence is self-work. To transform education abroad, we must acknowledge that the field of education abroad was created and centered around White, Eurocentric norms and not designed for the strengths, needs, and goals of marginalized and minoritized students (see also Chapter 1 in this volume). To ensure that education abroad serves *all* students, we must begin from a place of cultural humility, while keeping in mind injustice and inequity in the systems and contexts where we work. Accordingly, in this chapter, we have presented a model for centering equity as the starting point for program design. This model draws from the principles of inclusive excellence, as developed by the AAC&U and subsequently integrated within The Forum's *Standards*.

We see program design as a cycle that continues with equity-minded outcomes assessment with approaches such as the Equity Scorecard (Harris III & Bensimon, 2007). Likewise, the *Standards* guide us in "assess[ing] student learning related to portfolio and program learning goals and disaggregate data by student demographics such as gender, socioeconomic status, race, and ethnicity to check for equitable outcomes for all students" (The Forum on Education Abroad, 2020). Assessment for inclusive excellence, with a focus on belongingness, is described in greater detail in Chapter 14 of this volume.

Drawing from the examples mentioned previously, as well as best practices in the field, we end with a few questions that can be useful in approaching program design from an equity-minded standpoint:

- As professionals, how can we model authenticity and vulnerability?
- How will we intentionally create ethical, respectful, and mutually beneficial communities within student cohorts and with home and host communities?
- In what ways can we integrate safe spaces for inclusion and belonging and brave spaces for dialogue, perspective-taking, and growth?
- How have we leveraged reflective practices before, during, and after the time abroad to foster intrapersonal, interpersonal, and intercultural growth?
- How can we ensure that host communities, including local establishments and people, are reaping sustainable economic, environmental, social, and educational benefits from our programs?

Writing this chapter has reaffirmed our belief in the potential of education abroad to increase equity, model inclusive excellence, and positively impact home and host communities. We are convinced that our field can advance EDI by shifting our mindset, articulating equity-minded and inclusively excellent learning objectives, and aligning all program components to these goals.

References

Abe, J. (2020). Beyond cultural competence, toward social transformation: Liberation psychologies and the practice of cultural humility. *Journal of Social Work Education, 56*(4), 696–707. https://doi.org/10.1080/10437797.2019.1661911

Abes, E. S., Jones, S. R., & McEwen, M. K. (2007). Reconceptualizing the model of multiple dimensions of identity: The role of meaning-making capacity in the construction of multiple identities. *Journal of College Student Development, 48*(1), 1–22. https://doi.org/10.1353/csd.2007.0000

American Association of Colleges and Universities. (n.d.). *Making Excellence Inclusive.* American Association of Colleges and Universities. https://www.aacu.org/making-excellence-inclusive

Association of American Colleges and Universities. (2009). *Global knowledge VALUE rubric.* Association of American Colleges and Universities. https://www.aacu.org/value/rubrics/global-learning

Bensimon, E. M., Dowd, A. C., & Witham, K. (2016). Five principles for enacting equity by design. *Diversity and Democracy, 19*(1). https://www.aacu.org/diversitydemocracy/2016/winter/bensimon

Berg, M. V., Paige, R. M., & Lou, K. H. (2012). *Student learning abroad: What our students are learning, what they? Re not, and what we can do about it.* Stylus Publishing, LLC.

Berger, L. (Ed.). (2020). *Social justice and international education: Research, practice, and perspectives.* NAFSA: Association of International Educators.

Chavez, A. F., Guido-DiBrito, F., & Mallory, S. L. (2003). Learning to value the "other": A framework of individual diversity development. *Journal of College Student Development, 44*(4), 453–469.

Clayton-Pedersen, A. R. (2019). *Inclusive excellence: challenges & solutions for higher education & employers.* 2019 NACE Conference and Expo, Walt Disney World Swan and Dolphin Resort. https://www.naceweb.org/uploadedfiles/files/2019/conference/inclusive-excellence-materials-from-the-nace19-session-presentation.pdf

Clayton-Pedersen, A., & Musil, C. M. (updated 2017). *Making Excellence Inclusive: A framework for embedding diversity and inclusion into colleges and universities' academic excellence mission.* Association of American Colleges and Universities. https://www.bc.edu/content/dam/files/offices/diversity/2018keynoteresources/Making%20Excellence%20Inclusive%20(updated%202015).docx

Contreras, E., López-McGee, L., Wick, D., & Willis, T. Y. (2020). Introduction: Special issue on diversity, equity, and inclusion in education abroad. *Frontiers: The Interdisciplinary Journal of Study Abroad, 32*(1), 1–11.

Costino, K. (2018). Equity-minded faculty development: An intersectional identity-conscious community of practice model for faculty learning. *Metropolitan Universities, 29*(1), 117–136.

Crenshaw, K. (1989). Demarginalizing the intersection of race and sex: A black feminist critique of antidiscrimination doctrine, feminist theory and antiracist politics. *The University of Chicago Legal Forum,* 139.

Doerr, N. M. (2018). 'Global competence' of minority immigrant students: Hierarchy of experience and ideology of global competence in study abroad. *Discourse: Studies in the Cultural Politics of Education, 0*(0), 1–15. https://doi.org/10.1080/01596306.2018.1462147

Doerr, N. M., Puente, D., & Kamiyoshi, U. (2021). Global citizenship, identity and intercultural competence. In A. C. Ogden, B. Streitwieser, & C. Van Mol (Eds.), *Education abroad: Bridging scholarship and practice* (pp. 119–134). Routledge.

Florian, L. (2015). Conceptualising inclusive pedagogy: The inclusive pedagogical approach in action. In *Inclusive pedagogy across the curriculum*. Emerald Group Publishing Limited.

Glass, C., & Holton, M. (2021). Chapter 7: Student development—Reflecting on sense of place and multi-locality in education abroad programmes. In A. C. Ogden, B. Streitwieser, & C. Van Mol (Eds.), *Education abroad: Bridging scholarship and practice*. Routledge.

Gozik, N., & Oguro, S. (2021). Program components:(Re) considering the role of individual areas of programming in education abroad. In A. C. Ogden, B. Streitwieser, & C. Van Mol (Eds.), *Education abroad: Bridging scholarship and practice*. Routledge.

Harris III, F., & Bensimon, E. M. (2007). The equity scorecard: A collaborative approach to assess and respond to racial/ethnic disparities in student outcomes. *New Directions for Student Services, 2007*(120), 77–84.

Hartman, E., Kiely, R. C., Friedrichs, J., & Boettcher, C. (2018). *Community-based global learning: The theory and practice of ethical engagement at home and abroad*. Stylus Publishing, LLC.

Hartman, E., & Chaire, C. (2014). Market incentives and international volunteers: The development and evaluation of fair trade learning. *Journal of Public Scholarship in Higher Education*, 4, 31–68.

Hook, J. N., Davis, D. E., Owen, J., Worthington Jr, E. L., & Utsey, S. O. (2013). Cultural humility: Measuring openness to culturally diverse clients. *Journal of Counseling Psychology, 60*(3), 353.

Ladson-Billings, G. (1995). But That's just good teaching! The case for culturally relevant pedagogy. *Theory Into Practice, 34*(3), 159–165. JSTOR.

Lopez, S. J., & Louis, M. C. (2009). The principles of strengths-based education. *Journal of College and Character, 10*(4).

Lough, B. J., & Toms, C. (2018). Global service-learning in institutions of higher education: Concerns from a community of practice. *Globalisation, Societies and Education*, 16(1), 66–77. https://doi.org/10.1080/14767724.2017.1356705

Magolda, M. B. B. (2008). Three elements of self-authorship. *Journal of College Student Development, 49*(4), 269–284.

Mezirow, J. (1997). Transformative learning: Theory to practice. *New Directions for Adult and Continuing Education, 1997*(74), 5–12.

Schmidt-Rinehart, B. C., & Knight, S. M. (2004). The homestay component of study abroad: Three perspectives. *Foreign Language Annals, 37*(2), 254–262.

Serrano, M. (2020). Social justice-centered education abroad programming: Navigating social identities and fostering conversations. In L. M. Berger (Ed.), *Social justice and international education* (pp. 155–172). NAFSA: Association of International Educators.

Social Identity Wheel. (n.d.). University of Michigan. https://sites.lsa.umich.edu/inclusive-teaching/sample-activities/social-identity-wheel/

Tervalon, M., & Murray-Garcia, J. (1998). Cultural humility versus cultural competence: A critical distinction in defining physician training outcomes in multicultural education. *Journal of Health Care for the Poor and Underserved, 9*(2), 117–125.

The Center for Urban Education. (n.d.-a). *Equity by design: five principles*. University of Southern California. https://cue.usc.edu/equity-by-design-five-principles/

The Center for Urban Education. (n.d.-b). *What is equity-mindedness*? University of Southern California. https://cue.usc.edu/about/equity/equity-mindedness/

The Forum on Education Abroad. (2020a). *Meeting the Standards of Good Practice for Education Abroad: Prompts for Self-Assessment*. The Forum on Education Abroad.

The Forum on Education Abroad. (2020b). *Standards of Good Practice for Education Abroad*. The Forum on Education Abroad.

Vavrus, K., & Pekol, A. (2015). Critical internationalization: Moving from theory to practice. *FIRE: Forum for International Research in Education, 2*(2), 5–21.

Whitehead, D. M. (2015). Global learning: Key to making excellence inclusive. *Liberal Education, 101*(3). https://www.aacu.org/liberaleducation/2015/summer/whitehead

Wick, D., & Trujillo, S. (2018). *Refining practice: Using student development theory for inclusion and success in education abroad.* CEA.

Wick, D., Willis, T. Y., Rivera, J., Lueker, E., & Hernandez, M. (2019). Assets-based learning abroad: First-generation Latinx college students leveraging and increasing community cultural wealth in Costa Rica. *Frontiers: The Interdisciplinary Journal of Study Abroad, 2.*

Williams, D. A., Berger, J. B., & McClendon, S. A. (2005). *Toward a model of inclusive excellence and change in postsecondary institutions.* Citeseer.

Willis, T. Y. (2015). "And Still We Rise…": Microaggressions and intersectionality in the study abroad experiences of Black women. *Frontiers: The Interdisciplinary Journal of Study Abroad, 26,* 209–230. eric.

Yosso, T. J. (2005). Whose culture has capital? A critical race theory discussion of community cultural wealth. *Race Ethnicity and Education, 8*(1), 69–91. https://doi.org/10.1080/1361332052000341006

6

Passing the Mic: The Role of Outreach, Messaging, and Marketing in Building Inclusive Excellence in Education Abroad

Brett Berquist, Jennifer Calvert Hall, Shelley Jessee and Michelle Foley

Much has been written on the importance of promoting equity, diversity, and inclusion (EDI) in education abroad (EA). From the first overseas programming to focus specifically on recruiting students of color in 1979, UCEAP and Michigan State (López-McGee et al., 2018), our field's commitment to diversity has grown to include a wide range of individual and group differences. This work has been furthered in the development of field-wide *Standards of Good Practice* (The Forum on Education Abroad, 2020) and numerous guides and other resources (e.g., Association of American Colleges and Universities [AAC&U], 2020; Coleman et al., 2020; Diversity Abroad, 2020).

At the same time, the literature is short of concrete examples of how to adapt existing approaches to include a more diverse student population, and particularly in ways that challenge the status quo. In this chapter, we look specifically at one set of practices within the EA process—outreach, messaging, and marketing—with a goal of promoting inclusive excellence. As originally articulated by the AAC&U, inclusive excellence goes beyond the explicit marketing to encompass the "informal curriculum" and the overall campus climate to support diverse students and their learning (Milem et al., 2005). A corresponding inclusive excellence scorecard (Williams et al., 2005) links EDI to student development. When adapted to EA, such a tool can include racial, ethnic, and national identities (Sweeney, 2013), operating under the premise that efforts to increase access to and participation in EA require a comprehensive and holistic approach to be effective.

To illustrate these points, we provide case studies of how three organizations have developed inclusive excellence in outreach, messaging, and marketing for EA within their individual contexts: the University of Auckland (UoA) in New Zealand; The Fund for Education Abroad (FEA), a U.S.-based nonprofit EA scholarship provider; and CET Academic Programs (CET), a U.S.-based program provider organization. Throughout these cases, we highlight the need to amplify student voices—not to simply have students parrot what we want them to say, yet rather to communicate in authentic ways that show the good and bad and ultimately allow for dialogue within and between diverse groups of students. "Passing the microphone (mic)" to students may seem unsettling at first, yet until we allow students to speak honestly with other students, as educators, we ourselves will not learn how to build inclusive programming, and fellow students will not benefit from opportunities to reflect honestly about their overseas experiences.

Although each institution and organization is different, it is hoped that examples offered here are helpful for practitioners and scholars alike in rethinking their approach to outreach, messaging, and marketing in EA.

Challenging Dominant Narratives: Reframing the Benefits of Education Abroad

Since the University of Delaware's first study abroad program, taking U.S. students to France in 1923, EA has been perceived as aligned with the Grand Tour of Europe and its elitist approach of discovering other cultures to learn about oneself. This is seen as the ultimate extension of liberal arts in higher education as a rite of passage, and historically one reserved primarily for White, female students in the humanities. The core message or value proposition reinforces this positioning of EA as a reflection of or a means to achieve social status, often billed with the goal of becoming "global citizens" (Gore, 2005).

The concept of global citizenship is a contested discourse that is increasingly flowing into national strategies (Brigham, 2011; Education New Zealand, n.d.). It can be useful in advancing our understanding of international learning beyond foreign language and culture to encompass broader visions of globalization and internationalization (Lewin, 2009). This federating power, however, also can minimize our attention to the range of motivations and outcomes that different groups of students may seek from an EA experience. EDI marketing seeks to identify and validate the range of student motivations by developing multiple value propositions and ensuring these are represented in messaging and marketing. At the same time, authors like Zemach-Bersin have taken the field to task for the commercialization of the experience, where EA is positioned as a commodity, an entitlement, and a nonacademic adventure, which is reinforced through the field's practice of employing marketing and imagery akin to the travel industry (2009). While Zemach-Bersin's comments are centered on the U.S. experience abroad, pointing out parallels to American exceptionalism and neocolonial theory (Ogden, 2008), such messaging can be found in other countries where institutions seek to promote the benefits of EA.

Recently, we have seen a proliferation of studies that seek to reframe the narrative on EA, with a recognition that mainstream messages around EA may not appeal to students who have been underrepresented historically (Twombly et al., 2012). For example, scholars have observed that graduate students have different goals and motivations compared to their undergraduate counterparts, with a greater focus on research and professional development (Dirkx et al., 2014). Similarly, there is evidence that males, on the whole, are motivated more by career benefits and less by marketing that positions EA as fun and seemingly frivolous, with images of students jumping in the air in front of landmarks (Lucas, 2009). Students of color may be less convinced of the need to participate in programs that broadcast intercultural learning, given that many are already used to code switching on a daily basis as they navigate multiple cultures (Boulden, 2019; Perkins, 2017). They may also be concerned about racism and how they would fit in culturally overseas (Perkins, 2017). Part-time students, mature students, and first-generation students too may be looking for more concrete benefits, while also taking into consideration family obligations, for example, the importance of *whānau* (family) in the EA decision process for Māori and Pacific students (Faure-Kilgannon et al., 2019).

While many of the extant case studies come from the U.S. context, similar concerns have appeared elsewhere. Over the past several decades, there have been greater successes in other countries that can serve as models for reframing EA. Many of these examples involve career-readiness strategies, with concrete, practical ways that students can grow by studying, interning, and/or conducting research abroad. For example, Australian universities have been engaged in EA in earnest for approximately 15 years and surpassed U.S. participation rates in 2016 (Potts & Anderson, 2018). Initial expressions of the Australian agenda echoed U.S. rhetoric positioning EA as "a key part of preparing graduates for professional life in a global society of the twenty-first century" (Adams et al., 2011). Importantly, they also emphasized "professional" growth, with a focus on skills development. Subsequent Australian-led research on EA has focused on employability outcomes for participants and advanced our understanding of benefits as well as priorities in this context (Potts, 2015). Similar priorities appear to be a key driver for New Zealand EA participation (Faure-Kilgannon et al., 2019; Wunderman, 2017).

Even with the successes that have been achieved, more can and needs to be done to shift the narrative. EA is broadly recognized in the literature as a high-impact practice, which has the ability to prepare students for life and careers postgraduation, by offering the opportunity to develop adaptability, independence, global mindedness, language proficiency, and intercultural awareness (Barclay Hamir & Gozik, 2018, p. 7). However, the focus on broad and often seemingly abstract learning outcomes alone can impede our attention on identifying what motivates different groups of students. Without understanding these nuances, we cannot be effective in our efforts to reach them and to encourage them to pursue these opportunities. To achieve EDI in EA, we need to reconsider existing outreach, messaging, and marketing strategies to ensure that they align with what students want and need to gain from learning in another cultural context.

Outreach, Messaging, and Marketing: An Integrated Approach

Outreach, messaging, and marketing are common terms in our modern vernacular. For the purposes of this chapter, we define *outreach* as the process of engaging with students and communities in a spirit of partnership to explore shared needs and potential outcomes. *Messaging* is the core content that posits a value proposition for the services/experiences proposed. Much of the literature has focused on the need to segment the traditional EA message to recognize and validate different needs and motivations resulting from different backgrounds, levels of cultural capital (Bourdieu, 1997), socioeconomic status, and identity. Lastly, *marketing* is the process of reaching prospective students and the structured manifestation of key messages through advertising and other channels. In everyday use, it is common for these terms to be interchangeable, but in fact each means something different, and those nuances are important in developing a holistic approach. EDI strategies can be more effective if viewed with attention to the interconnection and how each piece influences the other.

As we look at the overall institutional climate of support and the role the "informal curriculum" plays in supporting EDI (Milem et al., 2005), a comprehensive analysis of EA outreach, messaging, and marketing is a natural component. From the research literature on marketing, the concept of Integrated Marketing Communication (IMC), which attempts to look at the positioning of an organization through "every means of communication, and the coherent use of multiple channels" (Gordon-Isasi et al., 2020), can provide a useful lens. This approach is typically affiliated with goals to increase revenue and as such may seem at odds with the personal development goals that are core to EA. Nevertheless, we see value in the way that IMC encourages us to examine multiple components, such as consistency and synergy of communication planning, intraorganization integration, message consistency, continuous planning and monitoring, stakeholder-centered strategic focus, and organizational alignment (Gordon-Isasi et al., 2020, p. 61).

Case Studies

In the next section, short case studies illustrate how three different EA organizations changed aspects of their outreach, messaging, and marketing for more holistic alignment toward the EDI goals they set. The cases are from a nonprofit scholarship provider, a for-profit EA program provider, and a comprehensive university located outside the U.S. They are intended to offer the reader a range of examples for potential application to their organizational context.

Case #1: Messaging for Inclusive Excellence: The Fund for Education Abroad

Based in Washington, DC, FEA is the only independent study abroad scholarship provider in the U.S. dedicated solely to increasing access and diversity in EA. FEA accepts applications from U.S. undergraduates from all 50 states, the District of Columbia, and Puerto Rico, who are attending all types of institutions, including public, private, and 4-year and 2-year colleges and universities. The existence of FEA is a testament to the financial barriers EA has traditionally posed for low-income students of color and first-generation college students. Given that financial barriers are among the most often cited concerns for underrepresented students considering EA, messaging to assuage these concerns is a topic FEA has actively engaged in since its inception in 2010.

While an EDI mission has always been central to the organization, over time staff have developed a messaging strategy that speaks honestly and directly to students, both to encourage EA participants to apply for funding, yet more broadly to help both applicants and recipients of funding understand the value of overseas study experiences. Not surprisingly, they have discovered that using students' own voices in this work has been most effective in the recruitment of underrepresented students. The use of blogs, video (vlog) and written, has been central to this work.

Over 5,000 students who visit the FEA website each application cycle have open access to a repository of FEA Scholar experiences via the Scholar Blog, which is prominently featured on the landing page. Each scholarship recipient is expected to produce blog entries, which are shared online with students, donors, and institutional contacts. The blogs document scholars' experiences before, during, and after their time abroad, allowing applicants to see themselves having similar experiences and facing the challenges, triumphs, and growth FEA scholars articulate. FEA was intentional in the design of its blogging curriculum and requires that scholars agree to abide by the stated guidelines prior to receiving funding.

While students may share an array of experiences, staff have found it useful to provide guiding questions, allowing for blog entries to be more structured and purposeful. This has been especially important in allowing students to connect what they are learning abroad with future careers, thus reinforcing the skills that students build during their time abroad. Conceptualized as part of a curriculum, the questions focus on eight characteristics, which are drawn from a survey published by the National Association of Colleges and Employers (NACE) related to the competencies that employers seek from college graduates. These traits include "critical thinking/problem solving; oral/written communications; teamwork/collaboration; digital technology; leadership; professionalism/work ethic; career management; and global/intercultural fluency" (NACE, 2019).

Among the many examples of student responses to the prompts, Chelsea De Mesa, an FEA scholar from the California State University, East Bay who studied abroad in South Korea, stated in her poststudy abroad vlog:

> I feel that I've become more independent...and improved my problem-solving capabilities. In general, I feel more capable as a person. I think any employer would like a worker who is proactive and self-disciplined, and is able to connect with people

> from different cultures ... especially since in the United States, we value diversity. (De Mesa, 2019)

Similarly, FEA scholar Kevin Sanchez completed his study abroad during COVID-19 with a virtual internship in France. Preparing for its end, he highlighted the development of his communication skills in the following post:

> As a Gilman and FEA scholar, my experiences and lessons are being shared with students who may study abroad or, like me, participate in a virtual opportunity. Therefore, they can draw on these weekly blog posts to relate to and understand that the challenges and successes of virtual programs are more common than they realize. I do hope future scholars take away from these posts that virtual experiences are not a perfect substitute for being physically abroad, but can offer very valuable lessons and be worthwhile for professional development. (Sanchez, 2021)

FEA scholars are invited to continue their relationships with FEA as alumni and encouraged to engage as volunteer ambassadors on their campus or as members of an Alumni Council leadership body, which itself serves as a pipeline to the FEA Board of Trustees. At any given time, two board seats are filled by alumni serving 2-year limited terms as trustees. In these volunteer leadership roles, at all levels of the organization, student and alumni voices are featured on the FEA website, communicating to incoming cohorts and applicants the difference the FEA scholarship and study abroad experience made in their lives. By amplifying the voices, experiences, and lessons learned from alumni, FEA underscores its commitment to inclusion at all levels of the organization and keeps students' voices at the center of its work.

Case Study #2: Marketing for Inclusive Excellence: CET Academic Programs

CET Academic Programs is a study abroad organization that has been developing and delivering innovative educational programs abroad since 1982. Today, CET offers a varied portfolio of semester, summer, and short-term customized programs around the world for college, high school, precollege, and gap-year students. Like FEA, CET develops student-generated content to amplify diverse voices in EA, thus allowing students from underrepresented communities to see themselves in the study abroad experience. A first step in this effort is making sure the photos and images in CET materials feature diversity. The next is to think creatively about how one might encourage and actively seek out student-generated content from underrepresented populations. Then, once one has the content, how is it used in program messaging and marketing to help students from heretofore underrepresented or underserved identity groups see that study abroad is possible for and relevant to them?

CET conducts an annual audit of its web pages and brochures for visibly diverse identities in their photo representation. The marketing team keeps a record of each page/printed piece and tallies the photos per page that feature various visible identities. Quantifying the visual representation of identity helps them see in clear detail where they are succeeding and where they are falling short in accurate program representation. For example, implementing an audit showed that some pages did not feature any photos of Black students. If a Black student only visited that page on the website, how would they see themselves in the EA experience? This system helps keep all parties accountable and takes a critical eye toward materials.

When CET reviews the audit and makes changes to materials based on the results, they are careful not to over-represent the visible diversity of any particular program. For example, if the enrollment data show that a program's typical racial background is 75% White, 15% Black, 5% Asian, and 5% Other racial identities, the marketing team avoids overly featuring photos of students of color. If a piece over-represents diversity on a program, it can create dissonance for participants when they arrive on-site and meet the rest of their cohort. CET strives to accurately reflect the reality of its programs while always pushing to promote EDI and increase participation among underrepresented student groups.

CET's Student Correspondent program serves to highlight the student experience, while also supporting students to see themselves as ambassadors for EA. Each CET program has one blogger and one photographer per term, each of whom document their experience on the program, in their host city, and with their cohort. Care is taken to ensure that cohorts represent a variety of identities and are not only telling the stories of the majority. Correspondent entries are not only shared with the family, friends, and community of the authors, but with future students considering studying abroad with CET. The photos are used in CET's marketing materials and shared with institutional partners and at study abroad fairs. The correspondent program is designed intentionally to offer a leadership and skill-building opportunity to students so that CET actively engages and supports the labor and knowledge creation of the students in the program. Often, student correspondents list their participation in the program on the resumes, shining a light on their reflection and work completed as part of the program. All CET students are invited to apply to the correspondent program each term and are not paid.

Student correspondents are free to write and document any part of their experience they wish, but they are also provided with suggested reflection questions each month from CET. These questions help students reflect beyond the day to day of their experience and synthesize the skills and personal growth they are building while abroad. Sample topics include first impressions (e.g., "Whether it is about your classes, the city, assignments, roommates, etc., tell us anything you had tell a friend back home. Have any of your identities impacted how you are perceived in your host country?"), academics (e.g., "How is class or even college life in general different compared to your U.S. campus?"), housing (e.g., "Introduce us to your local roommate. What are the rewards and challenges of living with someone from the host culture?"), and a day in the life of the student (e.g., "Tell us about your daily routine. Tell us about each of your classes, your favorite spots to eat lunch, how long you spend studying, and what you do at home with your roommates."). The submissions from student correspondents are posted on the CET website, but they are also used in a number of other ways. Quotes are used in program catalogs, entries are featured on CET social media, and study abroad advisors receive regular updates of blogs from their students. This ensures the content reaches a wide audience and lives on beyond the static blog entry.

CET also offers all alumni the opportunity to share a Perspective Piece, a personal essay that touches upon experiences a student has had as a minority group member abroad. These essays provide support and one-of-a-kind insight from students (CET, 2019). Perspective Pieces are raw, unfiltered, and honest. The experiences portrayed in these essays are not always positive, but they can serve to provide feedback to CET on what they can do better to support students on their programs, offer an outlet for reflection and conversation for the author, and serve as an invaluable resource for future students who hold similar identities.

To facilitate peer-to-peer mentorship, CET maintains an Identity Abroad Support Network (CET Academic Programs, September 2019). Sustained by their alumni, CET connects incoming students with alumni of programs who have identities that informed and shaped their experiences abroad. The relatively low commitment (in terms of time spent) makes this an easy way for students to stay engaged with the CET community, as well as share their experience with students who could benefit from the examples provided by program alumni. All CET applicants have access to the Identity Abroad Support Network in their application portal, and CET advisors often connect applicants to program alumni in the network during advising sessions.

Blogs about student identity, Perspective Pieces, and Identity Abroad Support Network information are shared publicly on program-specific diversity and inclusion web pages on CET's website. These pages seek to be a hub of information that shares details on the local climate on issues from gender, race, sexuality, and ability as well as a central place to find identity-related student-generated content. Collecting student-generated content helps CET avoid tokenization in its marketing materials. The student correspondents who blog and take photos for CET know that their photos will be used in marketing materials in the future and sign off on this when they are accepted into the program. The students choose what to submit to CET, giving them active control over the images that may be used for marketing in the future. CET's goal is to achieve inclusive excellence by inviting and listening to the voices of students and to follow their lead on the topics, experiences, and motivations for EA most pertinent to their respective student journeys.

Case #3: Outreach Partnerships Driving Inclusive Excellence: The University of Auckland

In the third case, the UoA is New Zealand's largest university with approximately 44,000 students, 20% of whom are international. Auckland, the country's largest city, is also one of the most multicultural in the world with 41.6% of Aucklanders born in another country (Statistics New Zealand, n.d.). Diversity participation targets focus especially on Māori and Pacific Islander students, which represent approximately 14% of the student body. Bridging and preparation programs aim to increase access, retention, and completion rates for this demographic. The importance of Māori and Pacific cultures is inherent in the University's strategic documents and communications and is embodied by appointed senior leaders, including the Pro Vice-Chancellor Māori and Pro Vice-Chancellor Pacific. In 2021, moreover, the university moved toward the implementation of navigation labels in *te reo* Māori across its website, along with a new dual name (Māori and English) for the university gifted by Ngāti Whātua Orākei, the local *iwi* (tribe).

New Zealand graduates are among the most mobile in the world (Berquist & Moore, 2019), but this has traditionally occurred after graduation. To provide more opportunities for current students, UoA was the first university in New Zealand to set a participation target for learning abroad in its strategic plan for 2020 (UoA, n.d.). When a new director joined the University after leading EA at Michigan State University, he saw an opportunity to define clear goals and to establish outreach efforts in alignment with the strategic direction of the institution. The International Office joined The Forum on Education Abroad and undertook training on the *Standards of Good Practice*, signed on to the Institute for International Education (IIE)'s Generation

Study Abroad movement, joined FEA's Access Advisory Board, and joined and trained with Diversity Abroad.

Recognizing that they did not have the necessary resources in-house, the International Office engaged a marketing agency to develop a clear brand brief that focused on key value statements, leading to the rebranding of the EA program as "360 International." The office understood the need to ensure that all students, including those who were historically underrepresented, were able to go abroad. In addition to market research to understand Māori student motivations and drivers, staff consulted with students, their families, Māori and Pacific community leaders, and conducted a review of policies and funding support. Through this holistic process, they learned that certain myths, for example, that EA will delay graduation, has little career benefit, and is focused primarily on language acquisition and the adventure of travel, were particularly prevalent among this population. For Māori and Pacific community members, it also became clear that any change would need to involve the *whānau* (family), reversing the institution's previous outreach and marketing efforts for EA which targeted only the student, not their larger community.

The 360 International team built strong links with the Māori community and developed dedicated messaging to enable aspiring participants to articulate the benefits and convince their *whānau* of the value. Most importantly, they hired a new adviser from the Pacific community who understood the challenges and motivations of this population, was well connected to useful campus and community networks, and who could personally speak to the experience the team sought to encourage Māori students to consider. A Māori student peer adviser joined the team at the same time.

In addition to changes to ensure this student segment could identify with student and staff advisors, concurrently, marketing materials were developed that feature student and staff individual profile images that include their *iwi* affiliation. A full wall poster of the director of Māori Studies featured prominently at the entrance to the student help center for several weeks and a 10-m-long billboard on a high-traffic street in the heart of campus featured a Māori EA scholarship recipient during a strategic point in the semester. This helped make students aware of the possibilities to participate and scholarship funding, while also allowing them to imagine themselves as future participants.

Extensive collaboration across the institution, from the Equity Office to the Tuākana network (a dedicated peer mentorship network for Pacific and Māori students), student associations and groups, the Planning Office, Academic Services, eight academic faculties, to senior university leadership, resulted in a carefully considered strategy. The lengthy consultation process established shared goals and understanding from community leaders, crucial to the project's success. The goal of the Māori learning abroad participation and inclusion strategy is embodied in the Māori proverb *Ko te pae tata, whakamaua, kia tînā, Ko te pae tawhiti, whaia, kia tata,* translated as "Secure the horizons that are close to hand and pursue the more distant horizons so that they may become close" (Faure-Kilgannon et al., 2019).

Given the prevalence of the postgraduation overseas experience in New Zealand (Berquist & Moore, 2019), university staff were initially skeptical that students desired to learn abroad during their studies. Students, however, reported high interest but a dearth of infrastructure and information beyond semester exchange opportunities (see Raby, 2006, for similar results among U.S. community college students). In promoting this agenda across campus, the 360 International team increased outreach through key community networks, revised policy to simplify the process, increased funding, and clarified messaging that spoke to student motivations that were identified through the formal marketing research process. The "brand bowtie" developed with an external marketing agency sets out differentiators, values, a customer value proposition, and a positioning statement (see Figure 6.1) informed through market research and consultation. This has empowered consistent messaging across the different marketing manifestations of the brand, be it through advertisements, flyers, social media posts, and presentations. The brand is now firmly established throughout the UoA ecosystem.

The team's learning was multiplied when they hosted Diversity Abroad's Global Institute for Inclusive Leadership and then a group of First Nations students working with Māori students in partnership with the University of Victoria. The work has contributed to the EA strategy being developed by the New Zealand Ministry of Education Te Tāhuhu o Te Mātauranga and the indigenous learning abroad strategy in development by Te Puni Kokiri Ministry of Māori Development and Te Kāhui Amokura, a committee of Universities New Zealand Te Pôkai Tara that focuses on improving outcomes for Māori students.

This case shows how deep collaboration with Māori students and community leaders, formal market research and brand development, and a holistic analysis of the ecosystem allowed the international office to develop a pathway toward EDI in their specific context. This work has been recognized by the EA field through the Diversity Abroad 2019 Diversity and Inclusion award for outreach marketing and recruitment, the 2020 Universitas21 award, and was shortlisted for the 2021 PIEoneer award for championing diversity.

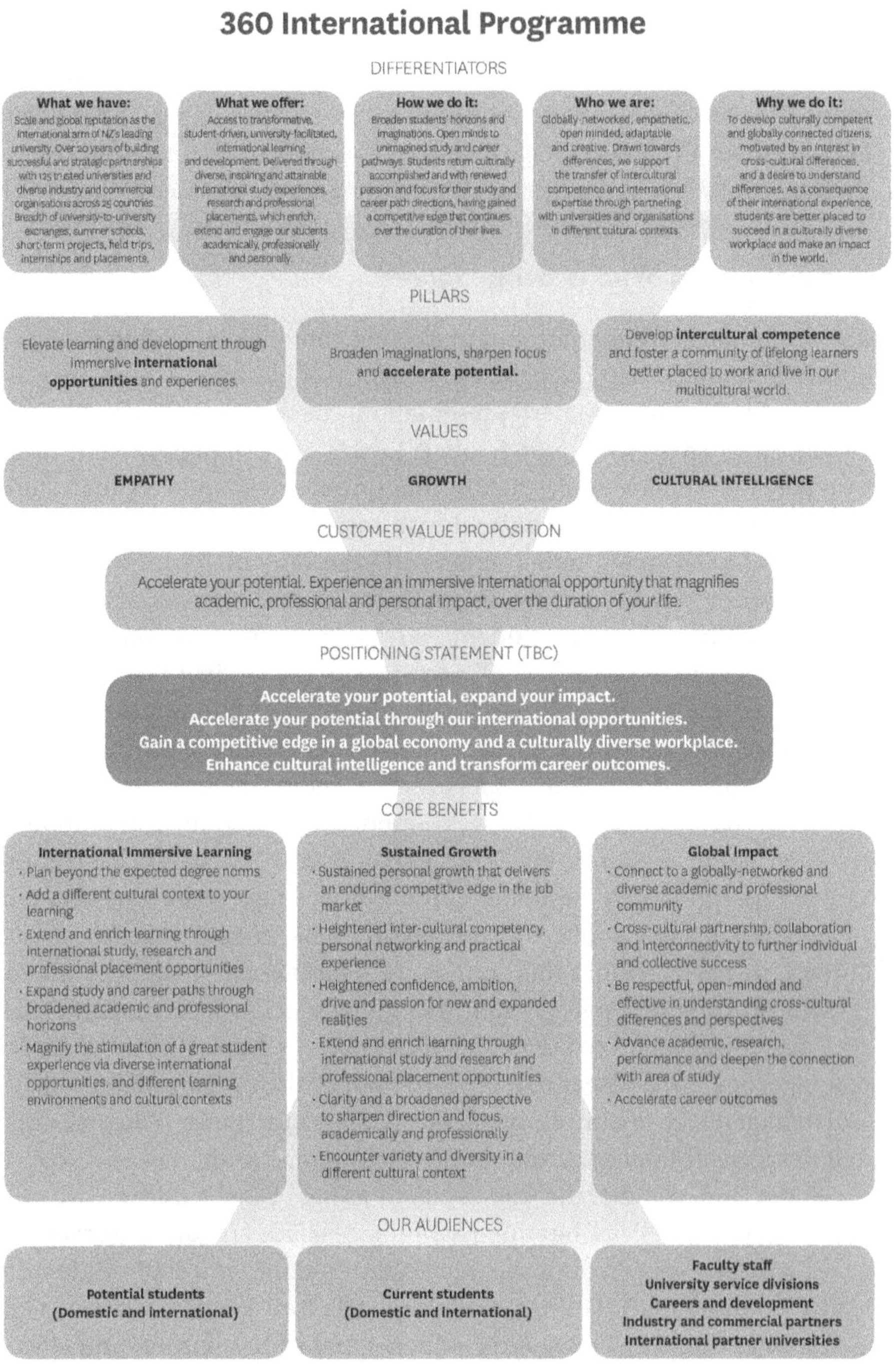

360 International Programme

DIFFERENTIATORS

What we have:
Scale and global reputation as the international arm of NZ's leading university. Over 20 years of building successful and strategic partnerships with 125 trusted universities and diverse industry and commercial organisations across 25 countries. Breadth of university-to-university exchanges, summer schools, short-term projects, field trips, internships and placements.

What we offer:
Access to transformative, student-driven, university-facilitated, international learning and development. Delivered through diverse, inspiring and attainable international study experiences, research and professional placements, which enrich, extend and engage our students academically, professionally and personally.

How we do it:
Broaden students' horizons and imaginations. Open minds to unimagined study and career pathways. Students return culturally accomplished and with renewed passion and focus for their study and career path directions, having gained a competitive edge that continues over the duration of their lives.

Who we are:
Globally-networked, empathetic, open minded, adaptable and creative. Drawn towards differences, we support the transfer of intercultural competence and international expertise through partnering with universities and organisations in different cultural contexts.

Why we do it:
To develop culturally competent and globally connected citizens, motivated by an interest in cross-cultural differences, and a desire to understand differences. As a consequence of their international experience, students are better placed to succeed in a culturally diverse workplace and make an impact in the world.

PILLARS

Elevate learning and development through immersive **international opportunities** and experiences.

Broaden imaginations, sharpen focus and **accelerate potential.**

Develop **intercultural competence** and foster a community of lifelong learners better placed to work and live in our multicultural world.

VALUES

EMPATHY | **GROWTH** | **CULTURAL INTELLIGENCE**

CUSTOMER VALUE PROPOSITION

Accelerate your potential. Experience an immersive international opportunity that magnifies academic, professional and personal impact, over the duration of your life.

POSITIONING STATEMENT (TBC)

Accelerate your potential, expand your impact.
Accelerate your potential through our international opportunities.
Gain a competitive edge in a global economy and a culturally diverse workplace.
Enhance cultural intelligence and transform career outcomes.

CORE BENEFITS

International Immersive Learning
- Plan beyond the expected degree norms
- Add a different cultural context to your learning
- Extend and enrich learning through international study, research and professional placement opportunities
- Expand study and career paths through broadened academic and professional horizons
- Magnify the stimulation of a great student experience via diverse international opportunities, and different learning environments and cultural contexts

Sustained Growth
- Sustained personal growth that delivers an enduring competitive edge in the job market
- Heightened inter-cultural competency, personal networking and practical experience
- Heightened confidence, ambition, drive and passion for new and expanded realities
- Extend and enrich learning through international study and research and professional placement opportunities
- Clarity and a broadened perspective to sharpen direction and focus, academically and professionally
- Encounter variety and diversity in a different cultural context

Global Impact
- Connect to a globally-networked and diverse academic and professional community
- Cross-cultural partnership, collaboration and interconnectivity to further individual and collective success
- Be respectful, open-minded and effective in understanding cross-cultural differences and perspectives
- Advance academic, research, performance and deepen the connection with area of study
- Accelerate career outcomes

OUR AUDIENCES

Potential students
(Domestic and international)

Current students
(Domestic and international)

Faculty staff
University service divisions
Careers and development
Industry and commercial partners
International partner universities

Fig. 6.1

Discussion and Lessons Learned

The cases presented here are unique to their context, yet they also provide models for how others might approach outreach, messaging, and marketing in EA through an inclusive lens. In this final section, we outline a few common themes from the case studies for EA practitioners to consider in their work.

Understanding Who Is Being Served

Before outreach, messaging, and marketing could begin, staff in each of the abovementioned cases recognized a need to determine whom they were serving. In discussing underrepresentation, the American Council on Education (ACE) advises HE professionals to ask "underrepresented in relation to what?" (Coleman et al., 2020). This question reminds us that student demographics should be managed with regard to student experiences and educational outcomes rather than with the aim of mirroring particular national or local demographic distribution. For EA professionals, we are not engaged in diversifying the student body per se; rather, our aim is to ensure access to EA opportunities for all segments of the student body with which we are working. The question also highlights the fact that what is considered "underrepresented" varies significantly from one setting to another, based on an array of historical, political, social, and economic factors.

As we have seen, the FEA was founded expressly to serve underrepresented students within the U.S., and thus EDI has been baked into its mission and practices. Awardees come from a range of institutional types, ranging from large public universities to small private colleges, to study abroad providers. Within this context, FEA has aimed to support "students of color, community college, and first-generation college students" (n.d.). As a for-profit EA provider, CET similarly serves a wide array of students coming from U.S. colleges and universities. For their part, staff have defined EDI to include "academically qualified students of all races, religions, origins, abilities, gender identities, and sexual orientations" (n.d.).

At the UoA, some of the same student groups listed earlier are identified as part of EDI practices, but there are nuances based on differing realities in New Zealand. Equity groups include Pacific students and staff; students and staff with disabilities; Lesbian, Gay, Bisexual, Transgender, Intersex, Queer, *Takatapui*+ (LGBTIQ *Takatapui*+) students and staff; refugees; and students from low socioeconomic backgrounds. *Takatapui* is an example of how language and culture need to be taken into consideration. Roughly translated as having an "intimate companion of the same sex," the concept might be boiled down to "lesbian" or "gay" in the U.S.; however, it refers to someone who is both Māori and a member of the LGBT+ community, thus combining culture and gender in ways that are in fact difficult to fully translate, yet which matter considerably to those who identify as such. Just as importantly, the UoA acknowledges the distinct status of Māori as *tangata whenua* and is committed to partnerships that acknowledge the principles of Te Tiriti o Waitangi (University of Auckland Equity Office, n.d.), the 1840 treaty that established relations between Māori and the Crown and that underpins government and education priorities as reflected in the Education and Training Act of 2020 (Ministry of Education Te Tāhuhu o te Mātauranga, 2021).

Understanding who needs to be served is not just about looking up statistics. In each of the cases, staff partnered with others to gauge their constituencies and determine need. In establishing EDI goals, it is thus essential for EA professionals to consult widely to understand the students they serve and what matters most to key constituents, including organizational leaders and other community members.

Tailored Messaging

Having defined priority targets, the challenge is then to reach each population with a differentiated message that is appropriate to students' motivations and needs. Previous studies have shown that U.S. minority students have similar levels of interest in EA but significantly lower actual participation rates (Cole, 1991; Kasravi, 2018; Perkins, 2017; Simon & Ainsworth, 2012). Although financial barriers are a common factor, a more complex analysis of Bourdieu's concept of habitus and cultural capital allows for the identification of challenges that minority students face in navigating the "micro-political processes" necessary to take up an EA experience (Simon & Ainsworth, 2012).

For institutions with long-established EA programming, recalibrating the message to reflect different student priorities and accepting that the established set of core value statements in our field may not be the primary interest of under-engaged student segments can be difficult but nonetheless necessary to achieve EDI goals. Previous studies have demonstrated that the core message of EA as a fun, transformative, experience of personal development and transformation will not speak as strongly to students with motivations and concerns distinct from the EA mainstream (Dirkx et al., 2014; Lucas, 2009; Miller-Idriss et al., 2019; Perkins, 2017; Twombly et al., 2012). It is necessary to ensure that our outreach, messaging, and marketing is connecting with the students we seek to serve, not only heard by those already predisposed to study abroad.

In the case of FEA, for example, staff recognized a need to help students translate their overseas experiences into skills that are marketable to future employers and graduate schools. Doing so is important for students (and their families) who might not initially see the value of EA; demonstrating its benefits as a high-impact practice that can prepare students for a complex and globally connected world is one way FEA seeks to support the populations it serves. Likewise, the CET correspondents program provides students with prompts that address some of the fears that underrepresented students might have regarding EA. At the same time, the organization adapts its programming to the needs of individual identity groups, acknowledging that the same messaging will not resonate with all students.

Giving Students an (Authentic) Voice

Lastly, these cases remind us of a simple truth: Students want to hear from students. Today's students understandably distrust messaging that feels inauthentic. Moreover, they learn about programs and services through social media and prefer to see content generated by students (The Access Platform, 2019). As we have seen, two of the abovementioned case study organizations have established peer advisors to fill this need and all three have developed online blogging for current EA students and alumni to share their experiences directly through their own voices.

Many institutions have increased their outreach with limited resources through developing a peer advisor program. At the UoA, a key turning point occurred when a Māori student peer advisor joined the team, along with a Pacific Island advisor. CET also has used a network of peer advisors as well as program alumni to support participants during and after their program, and FEA has established a meaningful scholar blog program asking the scholars to respond to guided questions to generate meaningful content aimed to encourage prospective students to identify with the scholars' experiences.

Peer-to-peer strategies can be most effective when historically underrepresented or underserved students see others they can identify with through balanced representation in marketing collateral, peer advisors, and staff. The ability to identify with someone from a similar background, culture, or demographic is frequently reported as a key influencing factor in the higher education decision process (Hakkola, 2015; Lucas, 2009; Miller-Idriss et al., 2019; Perkins, 2017; Sweeney, 2013). It is not uncommon to hear some students share their dismissal of EA as "not for people like me." Seeing another student or staff they perceive to be like them is often a first step in supporting determined students to start their journey. The case studies in this chapter share concrete steps taken to ensure representation of more students in marketing collateral while taking care against over-representation or tokenization.

Just as importantly, staff in each of the cases have learned that the messaging needs to ring true. A canned marketing ploy will only go so far if it does not resonate with its targeted audience. CET's Perspective Series is a good example of how students' unfiltered stories can be raw at times, not always in line with exactly how an advisor might want to portray a potential overseas experience. However, other students typically appreciate the honesty and will have greater confidence in what they are reading. Likewise, in the peer-to-peer activities mentioned earlier, it is necessary to coach volunteers/workers so that they understand the goals of outreach, marketing, and messaging, yet not so much that their own opinions and voices are stifled.

Conclusion and Next Steps

In the pursuit of inclusive excellence, we believe that it is essential that communications strategies and initiatives are designed to be both sustainable and accountable in partnership with the communities EA serves and engages. Given that institutional and organizational practices are an essential part of student success, teams must be strategic and self-reflective in how they are serving diverse student groups. As Fisher et al. (2019) note, "Inclusive education is essentially about intentional pedagogy and systemic practice meant to eliminate barriers that prevent individuals or groups from participating in a learning community" (p. 69). What is more, "radical inclusion" insists that education "can only realize [its] transformative potential if we make [it] for everyone" (p. 83). As such, there is a clear call to action for EA professionals to take on the charge of inclusive excellence through outreach, messaging, and marketing efforts that meet students where they are.

To deliver the support that students historically underrepresented in EA need to enroll and succeed in programming abroad, institutions and providers need "to critically examine and reimagine their entire institutional response to and conceptualization of who these students are," and, accordingly, recalibrate their communications and the very nature of their relationships with these students, parents, and communities (Ward et al., 2014, p. 563). In the pursuit of inclusive excellence, EA professionals "must be partners of the students in their relations with them" (Freire, 1970).

There is a continued need for the international education community to look holistically at real and perceived barriers to participation in EA for underrepresented students, to understand different motivations for different segments, and to develop differentiated or tailored messaging. The traditional value proposition for mainstream EA may not be of interest to underrepresented students. Undertaking market research with target student groups is essential to understand their motivations and perceived barriers. This can inform the development of appropriately differentiated messaging. The approach to outreach should also be adapted to work in partnership through existing networks and associations. The importance of community and family should be considered in the design of an outreach effort. Where possible, undertaking outreach with staff and students with whom the underrepresented student can identify should be prioritized. Outreach is most effective when undertaken in partnership.

Balanced representation is important for effective recruitment. Marketing materials should also be differentiated to reflect the messaging developed with target segments. Care should be taken to avoid over-representation or tokenization of underrepresented students in imagery used. Student voices are valued sources of information to reach prospective students. Student speakers and writers can be invited to address themes defined as important to the outreach goals through structured framework or guidance when inviting them to speak, blog, or post social media content through channels coordinated by the EA team.

In this chapter, we advocate that marketing adjustments should be part of a holistic approach to address system barriers within the campus culture. This makes it challenging to isolate variables and to establish a direct cause and effect of changes to outreach, messaging, and marketing. Success is most often defined as a quantified decrease in the participation gap in EA by underrepresented segments of the student body previously defined as priority segments. Future research that collaborates with marketing and market research disciplines would be beneficial to further our understanding of these factors. Lastly, we leave practitioners with a series of questions that they might ask themselves in developing an outreach, messaging, and marketing plan for EA. Seemingly straightforward, these questions are fundamental for making sure that we develop comprehensive strategies that are tailored to the needs of our students.

Guiding Questions

Questions to ask in designing outreach initiatives:

- Given your unique context, how are you thinking about "diversity"? Which intersections and identities are included? Which are not included, and why?

- Whom are you trying to reach?
- Where do they go for information?
- What do they want to know?
- What are the assumptions about EA among community members?

Guiding questions for outreach partnering:

- Who is your target audience?
- What resonates with them? Where do they get information about study abroad?
- Where do you get your information about the concerns students face? About their expectations for EA?
- Which channels do you use to recruit students? Who speaks for the organization/program?
- Who's experience abroad is represented in presentations and marketing collateral? How are destinations depicted? Which perspectives are left out?
- How do you receive feedback on your messaging, marketing, and outreach efforts? How often? What processes are in place to make changes?

Guiding questions to integrate student voices in EA messaging:

- How do you determine the value propositions used to promote EA with a specific audience? Through which channels do you ascertain student interests and priorities related to EA?
- Have you identified differentiated talking points that are aligned to these priorities? Where do these show up?
- What language do you use to set student expectations, address student/family concerns, and discuss the value of EA opportunities?
- Whose voices amplify these messages? Which channels do you use to communicate these messages? Can you include student perspectives during presentations?
- At information sessions, do you gather information from students about their career interests? Do you share stories of alumni who have entered different fields, and how their experience abroad shaped their career trajectory?
- Do you engage students from communities you hope to reach in leadership roles? Do you empower their voice to speak for your programs?

References

Adams, T., Banks, M., & Olsen, A. (2011). International education in Australia: From aid to trade to internationalization. In R. Bhandari & P. Blumenthal (Eds.), *International students and global mobility in higher education: National trends and new directions.* Palgrave Macmillan.

Association of American Colleges and Universities. (2019). *Making excellence inclusive.* Retrieved from https://www.aacu.org/making-excellence-inclusive

Barclay Hamir, H., & Gozik, N. (2018). Making the case for inclusion in education abroad. In H. Barclay Hamir & N. Gozik (Eds.), *Promoting inclusion in education abroad. A handbook of research and practice.* Stylus.

Berquist, B., & Moore, A. (2019). Internationalization and employability – The case of the kiwi overseas experience (OE). In R. Coelen & C. Gribble (Eds.), *Internationalisation and employability in higher education.* Routledge.

Boulden, K. (2019). *Inclusivity in higher education: Black student experiences with study abroad marketing.* (Accession no. 22618128) [Doctoral dissertation, Capella University]. ProQuest Dissertations Publishing.

Bourdieu, P. (1997). The forms of capital. In A. H. Halsey (Ed.), *Education: Culture, economy and society* (pp. 241–258). Oxford University Press.

Brigham, M. (2011). Creating a global citizen and assessing outcomes. *Journal of Global Citizenship & Equity Education, 1*(1), 15–43.

CET. (n.d.). *Our approach to diversity, equity, & inclusion.* Retrieved from https://cetacademicprograms.com/about/diversity-inclusion/

CET Academic Programs. (2019, September 17). *Support a diverse community abroad.* Retrieved from https://cetacademicprograms.com/alumni/identity-abroad-support-network/

CET Academic Programs. (2019, October 30). *Submit a perspective piece.* Retrieved from https://cetacademicprograms.com/alumni/perspective-pieces/

Cole, J. (1991). Opening address of the 43rd international conference on educational exchange. In *Black students and overseas programs: Broadening the base of participation.* Council on International Educational Exchange. Retrieved from https://files.eric.ed.gov/fulltext/ED340323.pdf

Coleman, A., Lewis Keith, J., & Webb, E. (2020). *Engaging campus stakeholders on enrollment issues associated with student diversity: A communications primer.* College Board, Education Counsel, American Council on Education. Retrieved from https://www.acenet.edu/Documents/Student-Diversity-Communications-Primer.pdf

De Mesa, C. (2019). After a whole year in Korea! (Return video). Retrieved from https://fundforeducationabroad.org/journals/whole-year-korea-return-video/

Dirkx, J., Janka Millar, K., Berquist, B., & Vizvary, G. (2014). Graduate student learning abroad: Emerging trend? *International Higher Education, Fall*(77).

Diversity Abroad. (2020). *Global equity & inclusion guidelines for education abroad* (2nd edn). Retrieved from https://www.diversitynetwork.org/DIVaPublic/01-Resources-Services-Pages/03_Global-Equity-Inclusion-Guidelines.aspx

Education New Zealand. (n.d.). *International education strategy. He Rautaki Mātauranga a ao 2018–2030.* Retrieved from https://enz.govt.nz/assets/Uploads/International-Education-Strategy-2018-2030.pdf

Faure-Kilgannon, L., Moore, A., & Berquist, B. (2019). *Increasing Māori participation in learning abroad.* University of Auckland. Retrieved from https:auckland.ac.nz

Fisher, L., McFarland, M., Smith Arthur, D., Estevez, M., & Kimberling, M. (2019). Radical inclusion: Broadening university communities. *The Journal of General Education, 67*(1–2), 68–85.

Freire, P. (1970). *Pedagogy of the oppressed* (30th Anniversary ed.). The Seabury Press.

Gordon-Isasi, J., Narvaiza, L., & Gibaja, J. (2021). Revisiting integrated marketing communication (IMC): A scale to assess IMC in higher education (HE), *Journal of Marketing for Higher Education, 31*(1), 58–90.

Gore, J. E. (2005). *Dominant beliefs and alternative voices: Discourses, belief, and gender in American Study Abroad.* Routledge.

Hakkola, L. (2015). *Shifting the lens: A critical examination of diversity discourses in college recruiting.* (Accession no. 3728157) [Doctoral dissertation, University of Minnesota]. ProQuest Dissertations Publishing.

Kasravi, J. (2018). Students of color and study abroad: From barriers to results. In H. Barclay Hamir & N. Gozik (Eds.), *Promoting inclusion in education abroad. A handbook of research and practice.* Stylus.

Lewin, R. (Ed.). (2009). *The handbook of practice and research in study abroad: Higher education and the quest for global citizenship.* Routledge.

Lopez-McGee, L., Comp, D., & Contreras, E. (2018). Underrepresentation in education abroad: A review of contemporary research and future opportunities. In H. Barclay Hamir & N. Gozik (Eds.), *Promoting inclusion in education abroad. A handbook of research and practice.* Stylus.

Lucas, J. (2009). *Where are all the males? A mixed methods inquiry into male study abroad participation.* (Accession no. 3381358) [Doctoral dissertation, Michigan State University].

Milem, J., Chang, M., & Antonio, A. (2005). *Making diversity work on campus: A research-based perspective.* Association of American Colleges and Universities.

Miller-Idriss, C., Friedman, J., & Auerbach, J. (2019). *Jumping, horizon gazing, and arms wide: Marketing imagery and the meaning of study abroad in the USA. Higher education* (Vol. 78:6). Springer.

Ministry of Education Te Tāhuhu o te Mātauranga. (2021). *The Education and Training Act 2020: Te Tiriti o Waitangi.* Retrieved from https://www.education.govt.nz/our-work/legislation/education-and-training-act-2020/the-education-and-training-act-te-tiriti-o-waitangi/

National Association of Colleges and Employers. (2019). *Career readiness for the new college graduate.* Retrieved from www.naceweb.org/uploadedfiles/pages/knowledge/articles/career-readiness-fact-sheet-jan-2019.pdf

Ogden, A. (2008). The view from the Veranda: Understanding today's colonial student. *Frontiers: The Interdisciplinary Journal of Study Abroad, 15,* 35–55.

Perkins, C. (2017). *Students of color studying abroad: A qualitative description of the factors that influence participation and the perceived impact of participation.* (Accession no. 10276848) [Doctoral dissertation, Widener University]. ProQuest Dissertations Publishing.

Potts, D. (2015). Understanding the early career benefits of learning abroad programs. *Journal of Studies in International Education, 19*(5), 441–459.

Potts, D., & Anderson, K. (2018, October 16). *Fake news and study abroad: don't believe everything you read.* Retrieved from https://www.ieaa.org.au/blog/fake-news-and-study-abroad

Raby, R. (2006, Fall). Community college study abroad: Making study abroad accessible to all students. *IIE Networker,* 39–40.

Salisbury, M. (2012). We're muddying the message on study abroad. *Chronicle of Higher Education, 58*(42), A23. Retrieved from http://chronicle.com/article/Were-MuddyingtheMessage-on/133211/

Sanchez, K. (2021). *Sustainable thinking (blog).* Retrieved from https://fundforeducationabroad.org/journals/week-5-sustainable-thinking/

Simon, J., & Ainsworth, J. W. (2012). Race and socioeconomic status differences in study abroad participation: The role of habitus, social networks, and cultural capital. *ISRN Education,* 21. Article ID 413896. DOI: 10.5402/2012/413896

Statistics New Zealand. (n.d.). *Census quick stats about a place: Auckland region.* Retrieved from https://www.stats.govt.nz/tools/2018-census-place-summaries/auckland-region#birthplace

Sweeney, K. (2013). Inclusive excellence and underrepresentation of students of color in study abroad. *Frontiers: The Interdisciplinary Journal of Study Abroad, 23,* 1–21.

The Access Platform. (2019). Collaborate: Using students as content creators. ThinkTAP Research paper #2. Retrieved from https://www.theambassadorplatform.com/white-papers

The Forum on Education Abroad. (2020). *Standards of Good Practice for Education Abroad, Sixth Edition.* The Forum on Education Abroad.

Twombly, S., Salisbury, M., Tumanut, S., & Klute, P. (2012). Study abroad in a new global century: Renewing the promise, refining the purpose. *ASHE Higher Education Report, 38*(4).

University of Auckland. (n.d.). *Strategic Plan 2013–2020.* Retrieved from https://cdn.auckland.ac.nz/assets/central/about/the-university/how-the-university-works/policy-and-administration/strategic-plan-2013-2020.pdf

University of Auckland Equity Office. (n.d.). *About equity.* Retrieved from https://www.auckland.ac.nz/en/about-us/about-the-university/equity-at-the-university/about-equity/what-is-equity.html

Ward, E. G., Thomas, E. E., & Disch, W. B. (2014). Mentor service themes emergent in a holistic, undergraduate peer-mentoring experience. *Journal of College Student Development, 55*(6), 563–579.

Williams, D., Berger, J., & McClendon, S. (2005). *Toward a model of inclusive excellence and change in postsecondary institutions.* Association of American Colleges and Universities.

Wunderman, T. (2017). Brand Bowtie for University of Auckland rebrand of education abroad.

Zemach-Bersin, T. (2009). Selling the world. Study abroad marketing and the privatization of global citizenship. In R. Lewin (Ed.), *The handbook of practice and research in study abroad.* Routledge.

7

Reimagining Inclusive Practices through Appreciative Advising in Education Abroad

Nikki Bruckmann, Opal Leeman Bartzis and Chris Van Velzer

Consider the scenario of two consecutive appointments for an education abroad advisor. The first student advisee, Marcus, made an appointment at the insistence of his faculty advisor to explore education abroad options that would allow him to complete an internship related to his business administration major. As a first-generation college student, he knew options for a semester abroad existed, but the destinations his peers casually referenced (e.g., Australia, Costa Rica, China, and Chile) seemed distant both geographically and logistically. He has no passport, has never travelled far from his home state prior to university, and has flown on a plane only once. College is already a new world to him, so why would he cross oceans to thrust himself into another potentially daunting set of unknown realities? How would he pay for it? Would his financial aid transfer, and would studying abroad delay his graduation?

Marcus is followed by Shelly, female, environmental science major who has dreamt of studying in Florence since she was young based on her mother's college experience abroad. Shelly comes to the advising session with a clear idea of the program she has selected, how she can graduate on time by fulfilling general education electives, and a list of questions about application materials and visa requirements. She has also prepared a basic budget outlining projected personal and travel expenses after taking into account program fees.

What constitutes effective education abroad advising for these two students considering their individualized needs and the different stages of hesitation and determination each brings to their advising session? In the balance between application materials, deadlines, credit transfer, and financial aid policies, among others, is there time and priority to engage diverse student identities holistically and help them explore how their broader educational, personal, and career goals might inform not only where they might study abroad but also what experiences they will actively seek out when there? Education abroad advising does not simply end once students depart but continues postprogram as they unpack their experiences. What additional support will they each need for continued learning and reflection? Pertinent to the topic of this volume, how might an inclusive approach to advising inform these interactions?

Advising for education abroad typically exists within broader academic advising structures that span the entire postsecondary education of a student, and some basic background of advising approaches are helpful to note here. For example, borrowing from traditional academic advising frameworks, Marcus and Shelly have unique needs and opportunities based on their backgrounds that could benefit from both *prescriptive* and *developmental* advising strategies (Barbuto et al., 2011; King, 2005; Grites, 2013). Prescriptive strategies, named for their directive nature, might include advising that dictates the paperwork, administrative, or logistical responsibilities a student needs to complete for course registration and credit transfer (Crookston, 2009). At the same time, both students can and should be engaged through *developmental* advising strategies (Crookston, 2009; O'Banion, 2009). Originally proposed as the contrast to prescriptive advising strategies, developmental advising places the advisor as a student-centered teacher or mentor, focused on the development of the whole student, including academic, personal, and professional goals (Crookston, 1972).

Broadly speaking, developmental advising is not a theory or singular model, but rather a set of practices or strategies in advising. These practices are primarily defined by a shared relationship between advisors and advisees that is focused on holistic (i.e., educational, personal, professional) student success (Grites, 2013). Although developmental advising is widely endorsed, it is potentially difficult to implement into a single, coherent, integrated system (Gordon, 2019). Furthermore, although developmental approaches were initially proposed as a remedy to the shortcomings of prescriptive advising, research has shown that many underrepresented student populations are more satisfied with prescriptive approaches where expert information and guidance is proffered (Anderson et al., 2014). The need for practical advice and direction often first draws students to an advising session (Jordan et al., 2013) and may be what students want and expect. But if students are only advised on application requirements, visa procedures, and credit transfer processes, when do crucial conversations begin about the broader purpose of their sojourn: cross-cultural engagement in host communities, expanding global perspectives, and potentially being exposed to new ideas and opportunities that will radically shape their future academic, personal, and professional plans?

Balancing such prescriptive and developmental advising needs is a fundamental challenge. Education abroad advisors may be inclined (like their advisees) to beg the question, "but what should I actually do?" as they prepare to meet with a student. Options abound through the application of documented advising approaches such as motivational-interviewing approach (Hughey & Pettay, 2013), emphases on self-authorship (Schulenberg, 2013), and models focused on strengths-based (Schreiner, 2013), proactive (Varney, 2013), and praxis (Hemwall & Trachte, 2009) advising. Are all of these developmental strategies equal in their potential to encourage and serve diverse student populations in education abroad?

This chapter looks at how two institutions, Michigan State University (MSU) and the Institute for Study Abroad (IFSA), have implemented various advising techniques to promote inclusivity. All fall under the umbrella of what has been termed *appreciative advising*, an advising model that implicitly supports inclusion by guiding students through stages that allow them to reflect on their unique strengths and assets, and design actionable plans that can be achieved. Examples from the two cases explored here—one a large, state university located in East Lansing, Michigan, and the other a program provider based in Indianapolis, Indiana, and serving institutions across the United States—demonstrate the wide applicability and flexibility of appreciative advising for education abroad.

An Inclusive Approach to Advising

If a new advising term could be suggested by this chapter, it would be "inclusive advising." However, this approach does not invoke an entirely new or distinct advising model; rather, it underscores the importance (and possibilities) of infusing inclusive practices throughout any advising strategy. An inclusive approach overtly emphasizes practices that affirm students' identities as assets in the advising process. Drawing on resource pedagogies, this fundamentally enlists an advisor to help identify the skills and knowledge embedded in a student's cultural identity—what Moll and Gonzalez (1994) termed *funds of knowledge*—and empower students to employ them toward a successful study abroad sojourn, or to redesign advising structures to utilize these strengths. In one sense, any developmental model of student advising that claims to develop students holistically would be impossible without taking into consideration students' unique identities. Nevertheless, an inclusive approach makes this effort explicit and, in doing so, fosters self-understanding of identity and the collective strength embedded within the diverse identities of others—that is, the hallmark of making excellence inclusive as developed by the Association of American Colleges and Universities (AAC&U, n.d.).

Although Marcus and Shelly do not represent all students who enter the doors of an advisor's office, their situation, needs, and opportunities represent the intersection of several possibilities for reimagining inclusive practice in education abroad advising. Inclusive advising must be oriented to diverse student identities, and it should reorient institutional structures where they still (though not always) cater to questions and needs of historical majorities in education abroad: White, affluent, cis, female participants. It is paramount to acknowledge that inclusive advising aims to do more than increase participation from students like Marcus, whose background includes several underrepresented populations in education abroad (e.g., male, first generation). The goal is to support students of all backgrounds in co-creating a plan that will leverage the opportunities and strengths present in their own identities with intentionality among their peers and host community abroad. To this point, Shelly can still benefit from exploring how her own identity will inform her education abroad experience.

It follows that in the context of advising for education abroad, explicitly focusing on inclusive advising approaches is a natural extension of equity-minded values that the AAC&U articulates. Inclusion plays a vital role in not only honoring and inviting shared strengths inherent in diversity but also actively sustaining and fostering those strengths in line with broader inclusive pedagogy—what Paris (2012) termed *culturally sustaining pedagogy*. Beyond elevating diverse strengths, inclusive advising also exposes barriers to access and retention by recognizing diverse student needs. The advising scenarios of Marcus and Shelly above demonstrate the importance of effective and flexible support for diverse student populations. Marcus is at risk of forgoing study abroad altogether because he doubts it is feasible for him and has little external support to encourage considering education abroad. In contrast, Shelly has support and is logistically prepared, but will benefit from critically reflecting on how her personal, academic, and professional goals are aligned with her current plans.

Emphasizing inclusion—"the active, intentional, and ongoing engagement with diversity ... in ways that increase awareness, content knowledge, cognitive sophistication, and empathic understanding of the complex ways individuals interact within systems and institutions" (AAC&U, n.d.)—also broadly prepares and supports learning outcomes surrounding intercultural competency. Self-awareness of one's own cultural identity, which influences and is in turn influenced by many intersections of identity, is foundational to intercultural competency and appreciation of cultural values in others (Deardorff, 2016). Inclusive advising fosters this by helping students discern the unique ways their own identity shapes opportunities and possibilities for their own sojourns, and how their identity might reshape ways they will interact with (and live among) diverse peers and host communities abroad.

Next, we turn to the application of inclusive advising practices within an established model of advising that is both relevant and practical in education abroad: *appreciative advising*. Although appreciative advising does not overtly focus on inclusion, it is a pragmatic and effective example of how inclusive practices can be applied and integrated into advising.

Appreciative Advising

Appreciative advising is a form of academic advising based on positive psychology, positive counseling, and appreciative inquiry as a research form (Bloom & Martin, 2002; Cooperrider, 1998; Howell, 2010). It aims to authentically cultivate advisor-student rapport through a relationship-building approach that places students at ease and provides them with individualized guidance. This strategy enables consideration of students' personal goals, visualization of their preferred outcomes, and ultimately self-authorship of their futures (Van Velzer & McCullers, 2020).

Appreciative advising traditionally employs six stages that each begin with the letter "D": Disarm, Discover, Dream, Design, Deliver, and Don't Settle (Bloom & Martin, 2002). These stages are an expansion of the 4D model of appreciative inquiry from organizational development theory (which used discover, dream, design, and deliver), to which Bloom et al. (2008) added the first and last phases (Disarm and Don't Settle). In the Disarm stage, advisors seek to place students at ease. In the Discover stage, students become aware of new possibilities. The Dream stage prompts students to envision themselves taking part in identified activities. Students and advisors jointly map out a plan for reaching goals in the Design stage, and the Deliver stage describes student progress toward them. Finally, Don't Settle is a reminder to keep working toward a realization of dreams.

Some students come to the advising experience with a developed understanding of their options and concrete ideas about next steps; such students may enter the continuum around the Design phase. Others are unaware of opportunities and benefit most from exploratory conversations and exposure to new ideas, thus entering the continuum earlier, at the Discover and Dream phases. Some have developed plans, but conversations with an appreciative advisor will cause the student to realize these plans are based on the expectations of others. They may need to revisit the early phases of Discover or Dream to reconsider their own personal hopes and priorities. This is to say that advisees may not need to go through all phases, and phases do not always have to be followed sequentially (Bloom et al., 2013). The appreciative advisor meets students where they are in their decision-making processes to establish a starting point, helps them visualize the journey from the outset, and encourages further progression with intentionality.

Ideally, the appreciative advisor cocreates a learning plan with students that includes personal, academic, and professional goals and actively supports them on their ensuing journeys. This begins with helping students strip away the expectations that may have been placed on them externally and which may have seeped into their psyches unchecked (Braunstein, 2009). Sample questions include: "What kind of career would feel the most meaningful to you, and why?"; "Describe situations that make you feel successful," or "What is a personal goal that you may not have verbalized to anyone before?"; and "How would it make you feel to realize that personal goal?" In response, students are given the opportunity to pause and reflect, and the potential value in stepping back for a moment cannot be overestimated.

Appreciative advising is effective not only in interactions that focus on structured outcomes such as the development of a learning plan but also in unexpected situations wherein the advisor functions as a mentor for life challenges. Rather than approaching perceived obstacles within a problem-solving framework, appreciative advising strategies instead focus on embracing possibilities (Habley & Bloom, 2007). Strengths are built upon, rather than weaknesses mitigated. Ultimately, students learn how to recognize and then harness their own skills, perspectives, and dispositions to turn challenges into opportunities. Through such awareness, they come to understand that they possess the tools and resources to constructively deal with obstacles that will inevitably come their way.

These basic principles and practices complement several intended outcomes of education abroad such as the development of personal agency and responsibility. However, appreciative advising can also build inclusive approaches within an education abroad office or organization by reconceptualizing the student experience and redesigning the ways in which all aspects of student services are delivered. A review of current processes and procedures may reveal areas that have unintentionally created access issues for education abroad applicants. It is imperative, therefore, to concentrate on the goal of the experience first, that is, the holistic thriving of all student learning, and then identify the necessary steps to help all students reach that goal, considering what is needed along the way to assist the student. Akin to backward curriculum design (Wiggins & McTighe, 1998), this outcomes-focused approach includes intentionality in the provision of content and concepts throughout the student's interactions with the education abroad office.

Appreciative Advising in Education Abroad

By its very nature, the education abroad application process tends to be transactional. There are typically many forms, compulsory signatures, transcripts, procedural tasks, visa applications, travel plans, and other steps to complete. The experience of applying can be driven almost exclusively by such administrative obligations; in other words, most students have a list of prescriptive advising needs to navigate while applying to, and preparing for, an education abroad experience. In fact, the excitement of preparing to enter an unfamiliar culture and new educational system can be overshadowed by bureaucracy and requirements when students are not accompanied by an advisor who is co-creating their education abroad experience.

Although there are myriad developmental strategies that might be employed, appreciative advising, when applied with inclusive practice, is uniquely poised to facilitate holistic thriving in all students while simultaneously priming diverse identities to be supported in a strength-based approach to the education abroad sojourn itself—supporting deeper development of intercultural skills, personal growth, and academic learning.

For inclusive practice, the completion of appreciative advising stages is less important than the consistent development and application of an appreciative mindset. Consider the vast and varied potential for inclusive excellence when an appreciative approach is applied to evaluating all components of education abroad operations. For example, application prompts such as "describe your previous international travel" may serve as a deterrent by implying that only students with significant travel experience are qualified for education abroad. An appreciative approach might instead ask students to describe how they see themselves in an education abroad setting or to explain how they believe education abroad will enhance their college degree.

Taken a step further, how often are students explicitly invited to reflect on how aspects of their identities might inform their choice of program location (e.g., based on ethnic heritage) or ways that could be particularly rewarding for them to engage with local host communities (e.g., involvement in a shared or new religious community, or in community-based organizations and academic communities around social issues that are important to them)? Subtle suggestions can have a profound impact on possibilities students might consider for their sojourn but can just as easily be overlooked in narratives of exotic locations, personal travel, and the rush to prepare the logistics of getting to their site.

Another example of applying an inclusive and appreciative mindset involves revising protocols for responding to situations in which students find themselves struggling personally or academically. Students can be asked to reflect on and articulate the specific personal skills that have helped them succeed in the past and to think about how they might apply those skills to resolve their current situation. In such an approach, students can build on personal strengths and recognize their power to affect the outcome of the challenge at hand. Similarly, students who traditionally would be denied admission to a program because they do not quite meet the minimum requirements of an education abroad program due to extenuating circumstances may instead be permitted to participate with the addition of an ongoing support plan. Their education abroad program may include periodic check-ins with on-site staff or virtual check-ins with their home institution's education abroad office; these meetings may be structured in such a way that the student recognizes the accompaniment on their education abroad journey of caring individuals who are not anticipating their failure but rooting for their success. The field of education abroad and appreciative advising share the aims of accessibility and inclusion. Equity, diversity, and inclusion (EDI) underpin appreciative advising insofar as the characteristics that may be indicated by student identities are recognized as genuine assets, as opposed to deficits that require mitigation. First-generation college students, for example, often display resilience and grit; underrepresented and minoritized students often possess determination and tenacity; and students with financial challenges are typically resourceful and demonstrate resolve. Although some populations of students may feel that they are unprepared, appreciative advising strategies disrupt that line of thinking and encourage students to understand that embedded in their identities are unique life experiences (and subsequently developed skills) that position them for success.

Centrality of Identity

Identity is central to the content and praxis of inclusive excellence and is aptly the primary focus of an appreciative mindset. Inclusive excellence encompasses practices that intentionally draw out and benefit from the strengths and perspectives of diverse identities as they interact with social, cultural, geographical, and intellectual communities (Clayton-Pedersen et al., 2010). The more a person reflectively understands the unique value that comes through the complexity and intersections of their own identity, the more apt they are to recognize, value, and collaboratively draw on the strengths that are represented in the unique identities of others.

Skillful deployment of appreciative advising techniques can encourage students not only to consider how their identities are constructed but also open new possibilities for students to imagine how various aspects of their own identities and those of the diverse host communities (and peers abroad) will interact. For example, the question "How might your identity shape a new, unique understanding of your local host community?" opens possibilities for thinking strategically about how some aspects of identity may be particularly salient abroad. Other questions may guide students to consider how identity can, and should, inform how they prioritize their learning goals, whether academic, personal, or professional. These learning goals may appropriately be very different for a first-generation student, a Black woman, an Asian heritage student, a White male, or a student with a disability.

Accordingly, at MSU, education abroad program coordinators and the office of international health and safety recently collaborated on the creation of "Identity and Cultural Awareness," an online educational module encompassing predeparture orientation and reentry resources. The module introduces topics like social identity, intersectionality, and bias, while the student engages in critical reflection surrounding their own identities and assumptions. Further, the module encourages peer-to-peer support and is accompanied by thoughtfully compiled resources for students of various identities. The goal of this module and the entire predeparture and reentry series is to prepare students to engage in global perspective taking, which is paramount to MSU's institutional mission of cultivating globally engaged citizen leaders ready to change the world (MSU, 2020).

Different Starting Points of Identity Reflection

Although an appreciative advising model can foster inclusive practices at the advising stage, a central challenge is the reality that all students will begin at varying stages of understanding their own identities. These different starting points are often reflections of the identities themselves. Students whose primary identities encompass majority groups (e.g., White, cis-gendered, high socioeconomic status, not living with a disclosed disability) already dominate education abroad participation in a U.S. context (Institute of International Education, 2019) and may have less prior reflection on their identities precisely because they occupy majority experiences. Asking a first-generation, Latino/a, queer student to consider how their identity may shape their experiences in Europe will likely be very different than the initial response of a straight, White, wealthy, female student. In contrast to majority students, non-majority students may have deep awareness of aspects of their identities, which may already be shaping anxieties and opportunities in their decision to participate in education abroad or their selection of an education abroad site (Brux & Fry, 2010). On the other hand, the student among a majority group may not be as aware of their unique identities and can similarly benefit from the same advising techniques. Rather than focusing on a deficit-based model of advising, appreciative advising can help students recognize the unique strengths and capacities they have for learning abroad as they engage with diverse communities (Van Velzer & McCullers, 2020).

Even asking questions around how identity might influence an experience abroad can be an impetus for students to begin considering important questions around power and privilege. For majority and non-majority students alike, education abroad is an opportunity packaged in privilege and social capital. Host communities can easily become exotified or commodified, serving as little more than "community props" in the backdrop of a student experience, rather than rich human sources of diversity that are to be engaged with (Van Velzer, 2017). Appreciative advising can shape even the most crucial reflections such as these to consider how each individual's sources of relative privilege exist as opportunities to exercise solidarity, embodying "power with" and "power on behalf of"—rather than "power over"—marginalized global communities (Slimbach, 2018). Within an intentionally inclusive framework, appreciative advising can and will invite students to consider all aspects of their identity; how that identity is positioned within a cross-cultural context is crucial to understand if inclusion is genuinely to produce excellence.

Implementing Appreciative Advising: Structural and Institutional Factors

Applying an appreciative mindset to inclusive advising practices is not merely an effort of individual advisors; similarly, although an education abroad office may serve as the primary driver of practice, cross-departmental and institution-wide collaboration is a crucial mechanism for sustaining inclusive practice. The range of institutional structures, sizes, and programs themselves create fundamental challenges that resist a single model of implementation. Thus, the decision to adopt appreciative advising as a framework for education abroad services cannot rest with a single individual or unit but must be an underlying concept that permeates from a committed core to other parts of the institution. Ideally, implementation of the strategy is a collective effort with institution-wide support.

Implementing inclusive advising does not have to mean an immediate overhaul or cultural shift; significant progress can be made with a few small steps. The following sections represent actionable areas of focus that are practical examples of how a proactive application of inclusive and appreciative advising strategies may be implemented.

Changes in mission and mindset. A shift toward inclusive advising is prefaced by two foundational practices in order to ensure the success of sustained efforts. Articulating a commitment that captures the localized needs for inclusive practice to ensure that sustained efforts to change are successful (The Forum on Education Abroad, 2020) and recognition that a commitment to inclusion likely requires the thoughtful revision of prior advising scripts to reflect a more inclusive, appreciative mindset.

Understanding these needs, MSU's Office for Education Abroad (OEA), for example, began a realignment of operations with a clearer mission on what they hoped to achieve. Staff engaged in a 6-month process, which was distilled into the following six values: put students first; think innovatively; promote diversity, equity, and inclusion; maintain an educator mindset; hold one another accountable; and work with integrity and professionalism. Embodying a strength-based approach to their work, these values have since served as the foundation for a revised vision of providing "high-quality learning abroad programs and excellent services to cultivate globally-engaged citizen leaders who are ready to change the world," as well as a new mission statement, declaring that "our global educator mindset combines with campus and international partnerships to position learning abroad as a high impact practice that fosters student success" (Michigan State University Office for Education Abroad, 2020).

Articulate a commitment to appreciative advising. Advisors can begin with a collective agreement, working together with leadership and team members on impactful advising, outlining a key statement and guiding principles across all student experiences. For example, at IFSA, the following statement is made public on the website:

> We consider where your students are coming from, not just where they are going. In fact, we believe that true global learning requires us to engage the whole student, celebrating the diverse identities and abilities they bring to their learning communities. From creative funding to individualized support, our approach expands access and helps students consider the intricacies of personal identity with their destination in mind. Welcoming people of all communities, identities, and abilities enriches the discussions we have together, enhancing the education abroad experience for everyone. (IFSA, 2021)

A collective agreement is a needed fulcrum to direct the effort of inclusive practice and is paramount to sustaining and assessing such an effort (The Forum on Education Abroad, 2020).

Rewrite the advising script. Beginning with an appreciative advising model, it is important for the advising team to revise their advising sessions to include more open-ended, positive questions. By doing so, they can evaluate current interactions with students to ensure they have the opportunity to drive the conversation. By interrogating traditional advising approaches that might focus on where students wish to go, and the materials and tasks needed to get there, invite students to explore who they already are, who they hope to become, and where they might best leverage their unique strengths and experiences.

Such an approach was taken by IFSA in 2016 based on the recognition that previous advising conversations had largely been transactional in nature and mostly predetermined by personal biases or previous experiences advising on topics or locations. Through trainings by appreciative advising experts and practice sessions with one other, the team adapted a new philosophy to advising. Advisors sought to accomplish an appreciative advising call with each of their students. With a list of open-ended questions to focus the conversation, the goal of each call was to assure the advisor engaged the student and allowed them to drive the conversation for a meaningful and personal exchange. Changing conversations with students to open-ended questions grounded in appreciative advising impacted every aspect of student interaction.

This approach redirected conversations to what was most salient for the student, centering around their goals, outcomes, and concerns for their experience abroad, while inviting their experiences, backgrounds, and identities to shape their planning and goals. This new approach to advising deepened the program advisors' relationships with their students, going beyond transactional interactions, allowing the advisor and student to personally connect. In turn, individually focused conversations created space for students to surface concerns and questions more organically and allowed advisors to understand misconceptions early in the process, up to and include students who had selected programs that were not, in fact, a good fit for them.

Similarly, MSU education abroad staff became acquainted with the tenets of appreciative advising and noted the obvious connections between its underlying principles and the aims of education abroad at the university. Through a series of prompts, MSU advisors inserted personal messaging from their first point of interaction with students and participated in the creation of video clips, welcoming students to the education abroad journey. Staff in the education abroad business office revised their preset student communications, removing, as an example, deficit-based language that could be perceived as impersonal pursuit of unpaid accounts in favor of a supportive tone and offering thoughtful ideas for resolution. Throughout the initial semester of professional development and implementation, the program development team read articles each month that focused on the use of appreciative advising to support various populations of students and discussed methods of application to the MSU advising model.

Reimagining operational structures and policies. Integration of an inclusive and appreciative advising mindset quickly points to many areas of practice beyond student that would benefit from this approach. For example, at MSU, this underpinning philosophy significantly changed the way in which the education abroad office conceived its outreach activities, placing greater emphasis on events and advising in the campus locations students most often occupy. There are many implications of inclusive approaches to all phases of the education abroad experience, which are discussed elsewhere in this volume. There are several facets of the experience that noticeably benefit from an appreciative advising approach, which we discuss in greater depth here.

Reconceptualizing phases of the journey. At MSU, the OEA website serves as the hub for program and services information, as well as a promotional tool; thus, the decision to embrace appreciative advising as a philosophy meant a redesign of the website through an appreciative advising framework was imperative. Navigational headers for the revised website were adapted to reflect the key stages of appreciative advising that complemented the basic stages of the education abroad process. The Discover, Dream, and Design phases were represented in a localized interpretation as Explore, Plan, and Apply. The Deliver phase was retooled as a set of on-site support mechanisms that included linked learning modules and a separate database for student travelers. Thus, the presentation of services was reorganized.

Revising application materials. Education abroad as a field has historically catered to majority White, female, affluent, traditional students (Bhandari & Chow, 2009; Simon & Ainsworth, 2012), and a closer examination of long-standing application materials and processes often carries an inherent bias toward these students. Infusing a strength-based appreciative advising mindset simultaneously means revisiting eligibility criteria to ensure alignment, including fundamental criteria such as GPA, faculty recommendations, the necessity of requiring official transcripts (and costs to the students of acquiring them), to name a few. When appreciative advising informs essay requirements, they are transformed from mechanisms to exclude students into a means for students to indicate interests and reflect on their goals for the experience. Inviting students, faculty, and staff to review proposed application materials is a valuable means to interrogate how language and application processes may unintentionally exclude or present barriers to diverse applicants. It becomes necessary to root out language that assumes knowledge or experience and to focus on prompts that are framed as opportunities to elaborate on lived experiences, skills, and talents.

Prearrival preparation. Inclusive advising resources that are available to students at all stages of the education abroad process (i.e., program exploration, applying to programs, preparing to go abroad, on-site experiences, and return) serve several important functions. First, for institutions and offices that do not have the capacity to require or offer individual in-person advising sessions for all students, resources may represent a primary source of delivery for advising itself. In addition, for all offices, advising resources can function to affirm, encourage, and celebrate diverse constructions of identity, or provide narratives of underrepresented student participation in programs. Even for majority students, such resources may help broaden their own awareness of how diverse identities will experience education abroad differently.

For example, students embody many identities and lived experiences that shape their goals and trajectories abroad. By presenting students with an inclusive advising worksheet before or during an advising appointment, students can self-select from a wide range of identity topics that are important to them. Are they interested in learning about LGBTQ+ resources or faith communities in their host country? This approach invites a relevant and personalized conversation driven by the student, but even considering the diversity of identity topics that may not be prescient to them, all students can be invited to consider how these topics will intersect with their experience abroad.

Prearrival materials can and should explicitly address privilege and power dynamics in the host country and any site-specific contexts that can help prepare students for their time abroad (e.g., local race relations, LGBTQ+ safety, cultural points of knowledge pertaining to non-White, heterosexual, or cis-gender students). Identity-related activities can help students consider their upcoming experience more deeply, such as the classic identity wheel activity (Social Identity Wheel, 2020) to encourage students to critically reflect on their identities and how they might navigate them abroad. Diversity Abroad offers multiple resources to students and advisors. For example, their Abroad360 is a comprehensive resource that includes micro-learning and advising modules, online workshops, and country-specific Diversity and Inclusion Guides (Diversity Abroad, 2021). These can be provided as optional resources or woven into the application and acceptance process itself.

It is helpful to create or collaborate with partners to develop inclusive resource guides. For example, IFSA's student engagement team created a resource bank of identity-related frequently asked questions based on topics students raised during the application. Complemented by student stories and quotes, the team partnered with resident staff experts to develop guides for programs around the world that address a wide range of topics such as athletics, disabilities, faith communities, family considerations, finances and scholarships, first-generation college students, gender, Greek life, LGBTQ+, STEM, race and ethnicity, veteran status, and work-study abroad. At the beginning of the application process, students have the option of self-selecting any of these advising topics as areas of interest, which can then be integrated into advising appointments with the guides providing a concise list of resources for students to explore and educate themselves on each topic.

While abroad. In addition to preparing students for their time abroad, appreciative advising also enhances the on-site experience. For example, at IFSA, the learning plans and notes from the students appreciative advising call provide insights to on-site staff on each student's individual goals. The individual learning plans help on-site staff better prepare for incoming students and how to best support them for their time abroad. As part of student engagement while abroad, resident staff hold at least three check-in meetings at the beginning, middle, and end of the program, utilizing an appreciative advising approach to help students reflect on their stated goals, consider whether they remained accurate and/or achievable, map out a plan to pursue said goals, and draw on staff networks and knowledge to help students get started. Meetings toward the end of the program support students in transitioning their goals back to the home campus by focusing on next steps to continue learning and development. The implementation of these meetings has strengthened student relationships with on-site staff, assisted students in reflecting on their experiences abroad, and helped students make purposeful choices about how to invest their effort abroad with the support and guidance of on-site staff.

Reentry. Departure from the international study site does not signal the end of the education experience, but more accurately indicates the beginning of a process of cognitive unpacking that is integral to student learning (Rowan-Kenyon & Niehaus, 2011; Walters et al., 2017). This recognition prompted increased focus on the postprogram aspects of education abroad. MSU created online educational modules delivered through the university learning management system that explicitly prompt students to reflect on knowledge gained and skills developed and to articulate ways to apply these to the remainder of their college careers and beyond (Larkin, 2008). There was an inherent acknowledgment that the student's learning plan did not conclude with the program end date; instead, the careful thought that went into the development of this evolving document would accompany the student through their return home and be applied to continued personal, academic, and professional learning. In these ways, the new website reflected and continues to support inclusive practices and an appreciative advising approach.

Inclusive collaboration. Advising relies on the premise that students will seek guidance when exploring or planning education abroad opportunities. As such, modeling an inclusive approach requires campus partnerships across institutional units, actively understanding the relative commitments of inclusive practice in partners and foreign host institutions, and leveraging the stories and experiences of diverse alumni.

Leveraging campus partnerships. Whether or not inclusive excellence is widely embraced or implemented throughout an institution, campus-based education abroad administrators and offices may find success in linking appreciative advising strategies to specific campus partnerships. Obvious connections exist between professional goal setting and career services offices, for example. Learning plan entries that indicate activities such as volunteering and service learning may resonate with offices of community-engaged learning, and units focused on supporting particular types of students will recognize the value of appreciative advising for its focus on building skills and abilities rather than alleviating perceived disadvantages. The principles of appreciative advising resonate with a variety of stakeholders. Varied units may find that appreciative advising complements their goals and visions. Collaborating with a wide range of offices such as financial aid, diversity and inclusion, community engagement, student success, and multicultural and disability service offices can result in new, mutually beneficial approaches (see Chapter 5 on Messaging, Outreach, and Marketing).

Leveraging alumni. Perhaps the most powerful resource in the appreciative advising toolbox is program alumni. Listening to and learning about the challenges and successes from students themselves also enables advisors to continue to evolve practices and resources. Education abroad alumni also assist in the advising process by storytelling and making their experience relatable to others. Creating a peer-to-peer advising program can normalize and elevate student voices and experiences with myriad identities. Peer-to-peer advising across interest topics, when also framed in an appreciative advising model, can be particularly powerful ways for students to learn from one another; applicants hear from past participants directly, but past participants also have the opportunity to continue reflective learning from their own experience. During advising appointments, in digital resources and at education abroad events, diverse peer advisors highlighting their own unique experiences abroad can inspire prospective participants.

This modeling can occur in the form of blog posts, videos, social media posts, or student-led webinars. *UNPACKED: A study abroad guide for students like me* (Student Stories – IFSA, n.d.) models inclusive student storytelling as a lens through which students are empowered to lead discussions and pull otherwise marginalized narratives to the center stage. Stories go beyond the typical transformational narrative and speak to the complicated responsibilities, hesitations, and goals of those less represented in education abroad programs around the world. Similarly, the Illinois Abroad Ambassadors site of the University of Illinois at Urbana–Champaign (University of Illinois, 2020) provides personal accounts of education abroad alumni that are grouped, with permission, according to identity areas such as first-generation college student, student of color, student athlete, high financial need, transfer student, LGBTQIA+, and accessibility. Prospective education abroad applicants are invited to contact the alumni with whom they identify for a direct conversation. Students, often unmoved by traditional marketing, can begin to see themselves and their own responsibilities, hesitations, and goals within the context of education abroad through the experiences of their peers. Alumni perspectives, in their many forms, can help education abroad feel less daunting for all students considering an opportunity abroad.

Conclusion

Education abroad offices play a critical role in determining the quality of programs and experiences available to their students. While taking an institutional inventory of education abroad program offerings, are strength-based developmental programs and inclusive excellence established parts of evaluating approved programs? This creates a strategic opportunity to align commitments and goals related to inclusive excellence with institutions and providers that share this alignment and actively foster inclusive practices on-site. For example, beyond advisors who are engaging in an appreciative advising model, how are faculty abroad and across campus trained on how to navigate the identity needs of U.S. students? Are they prepared to respond effectively to potential conflict or concerns around group dynamics? Returning to the narratives that opened this chapter, when Marcus and Shelly arrive at their respective sites, how will their unique strengths and identities not only be honored, but actively engaged and encouraged by staff and faculty on-site? Will they be engaged and encouraged as they navigate their new worlds and experiences?

If inclusive practices are to be successful in dismantling historical patterns of majority student participation in education abroad, much of the work must begin by embedding inclusive practices within the advising process itself. This chapter has underscored the particular alignment of appreciative advising and inclusive excellence and ways that an appreciative mindset not only serves to support greater compositional participation but also fosters the excellence that comes from drawing on the strengths of diverse identities and experiences.

In the spirit of that rich diversity, what matters most is a personal commitment as advisors and educators to do the self-work required by their own identities and lived experiences in confronting dynamics of power, privilege, their own histories, and the histories of study abroad. As our own perceptions of intersecting identities and the global societal implications of race, class, gender, sexuality, religion, abilities, age, and many other factors become more nuanced, so too it expands our repertoire for understanding and inviting the identities and perspectives of students into experience abroad.

References

Association of American Colleges and Universities. (n.d.). *Making excellence inclusive.* Retrieved from https://www.aacu.org/making-excellence-inclusive

Anderson, W., Motto, J. S., and Bordeaux, R. (2014). Getting what they want: Aligning student expectations with perceived advisor behaviors. *Mid-Western Educational Researcher, 26*(1), 27–51.

Barbuto, J. E., Story, J. S., Frits, S. M., & Schinstock, J. L. (2011). Full range advising: Transforming the advisor-advisee experience. *Journal of College Student Development, 52,* 656–670.

Bhandari, R., & Chow, P. (2009). *Open doors 2009: Report on international educational exchange.* Institute of International Education.

Bloom, J., & Martin, N. A. (2002). Incorporating appreciative inquiry into academic advising. *The Mentor: An Academic Journal, 4*(3). Retrieved from https://journals.psu.edu/mentor/article/view/61701/61346

Bloom, J. K., Hutson, B. L., & He, Y. (2013). Appreciative advising. In P. Jordan, M. A. Miller, & J. K. Drake (Eds.), *Academic advising approaches: Strategies that teach students to make the most of college* (pp. 83–99). Jossey-Bass.

Bloom, J. K., Hutson, B. L., & He, Y. (2008). *The appreciative advising revolution.* Stipes.

Braunstein, M. (2009, March 4). Advising honors students within the appreciative advising framework. *The Mentor: An Academic Advising Journal.* Retrieved from http://dus.psu.edu/mentor/old/articles/090304mb.htm

Brux, J. M., & Fry, B. (2010). Multicultural students in study abroad: Their interests, their issues, and their constraints. *Journal of Studies in International Education, 14*(5), 508–527.

Clayton-Pederson, A., O'Neill, N, & McTighe Musil, C. (2010). Making excellence inclusive: A framework for embedding diversity and inclusion into colleges and universities' academic excellence mission. AAC&U. Crookston, B. B. (2009). A developmental view of academic advising as teaching. *NACADA Journal, 29*(1), 78–82. (Reprinted from *Journal of College Student Personnel, 13,* 1972, pp. 12-17; *NACADA Journal, 14*(2), 1994, pp. 5–9).

Cooperrider, D. L. (1990). Positive image, positive action: The affirmative basis of organizing. In S. Srivasta & D. L. Cooperrider (Eds.), *Appreciative management and leadership: The power of positive thought and action in organizations* (pp. 91–125). Jossey-Bass.

Deardorff, D. K. (2016). Identification and assessment of intercultural competence as a student outcome of internationalization. *Journal of Studies in International Education, 10*(3), 241–266. http://doi.org/10.1177/1028315306287002

Diversity Abroad. (2021 February 15). *Abroad360 international education virtual advising.* https://www.diversitynetwork.org/page/abroad360

Grites, T. (2013). Developmental academic advising. In P. Jordan, M. A. Miller, & J. K. Drake (Eds.), *Academic advising approaches: Strategies that teach students to make the most of college.* Jossey-Bass.

Gordon, V. N. (2019). Developmental advising: The elusive ideal. *NACADA Journal, 39*(2), 72–76.

Habley, W. R., & Bloom, J. L. (2007). Giving advice that makes a difference. In G. L. Kramer (Ed.), *Fostering student success in the campus community* (pp. 171–192). Jossey-Bass.

Hamir, H. B., & Gozik, N. (Eds.). (2018). *Promoting inclusion in education abroad: A handbook of research and practice.* Stylus.

Hemwall, M. K., & Trachte, K. C. (1999). Learning at the core: Toward a new understanding of academic advising. *NACADA Journal, 19*(1), 5–11.

Howell, N.G. (2010). *Appreciative advising from the academic advisor's viewpoint: A qualitative study.* (Doctoral dissertation). Available from Educational Administration: Theses, Dissertations, and Student Research. 21. https://digitalcommons.unl.edu/cehsedaddiss/21

Hughey, J., & Pettay, R. (2013). Motivational interviewing: Helping advisors initiate change in student behaviors. In P. Jordan, M. A. Miller, & J. K. Drake (Eds.), *Academic advising approaches: Strategies that teach students to make the most of college.* Jossey-Bass.

Institute for Study Abroad. (2020, August 23). *Inclusive excellence expanding opportunity.* Retrieved from https://www.ifsa-butler.org/inclusive-excellence/#sct-7

IFSA CHART. (2020, August 23). *CHART curriculum hub: An academic resource tool.* https://portal.ifsa-butler.org/chart/CH_Login?projectId=null

Institute of International Education. (2019). *Open doors 2019: Report on international educational exchange.* Retrieved from https://www.iie.org/opendoors

Jordan, P., Miller, M. A., & Drake, J. K. (Eds.), (2013). *Academic advising approaches: Strategies that teach students to make the most of college.* Jossey-Bass.

King, M. C. (2005). *Developmental academic advising.* Retrieved from http://www.nacada.ksu.edu/Resources/Clearinghouse/View-Articles/Developmental-Academic-Advising.aspx

Kuh, G. (2008). *High impact educational practices: What they are, who has access to them, and why they matter.* American Association of Colleges and Universities.

Michigan State University Office for Education Abroad. (2020, August 10). *Education abroad overview.* Retrieved from https://educationabroad.isp.msu.edu/about/overview/

Moll, L., & Gonzalez, N. (1994). Lessons from research with language minority children. *Journal of Reading Behavior, 26*(4), 23–41.

Larkin, M. (2008, February 6). Creating reflection on international experiences through appreciative advising. *The Mentor: An Academic Advising Journal.* Retrieved from https://journals.psu.edu/mentor/article/view/61547/61199

O'Banion, T. (2009). An academic advising model. *NACADA Journal, 29*(1), 83–89. (Reprinted from *Junior College Journal, 42,* 1972, *62, 63, 66–69; NACADA Journal,* 1994, *14*(2), 10–16).

Paris, D. (2012). Culturally sustaining pedagogy: A needed change in stance, terminology, and practice. *Educational Researcher, 41*(3), 93–97.

Schreiner, L. (2013). Strengths-based advising. In P. Jordan, M. A. Miller, & J. K. Drake (Eds.), *Academic advising approaches: Strategies that teach students to make the most of college.* Jossey-Bass.

Schulenberg, J. K. (2013). Academic advising informed by self-authorship theory. In P. Jordan, M. A. Miller, & J. K. Drake (Eds.), *Academic advising approaches: Strategies that teach students to make the most of college.* Jossey-Bass.

Simon, J., & Ainsworth, J. W. (2012) Race and socioeconomic status differences in study abroad participation: The role of habitus, social networks, and cultural capital. *International Scholarly Research Notices.* Retrieved from https://www.hindawi.com/journals/isrn/2012/413896/

Slimbach, R. (2018). *Using power well.* Unpublished manuscript. Azusa Pacific University.

Student Stories – IFSA. (2020, August 23). *UNPACKED: A study abroad guide for students like me.* Retrieved from https://www.ifsa-butler.org/unpacked/

Social Identity Wheel. (2020). *Program on intergroup relations and the spectrum center.* University of Michigan. Retrieved from http://sites.lsa.umich.edu/inclusive-teaching

The Forum on Education Abroad. (2020). *Standards of good practice in education abroad* (6th edn). The Forum on Education Abroad.

University of Illinois. (2020). *Illinois abroad & global exchange: Illinois Abroad Ambassadors.* Retrieved from https://studyabroad.illinois.edu/ambassadors.html#

Van Velzer, C. M. (2017, July). Inclusive excellence: Learning from and listening to our local host communities. Institute for Study Abroad Annual Conference, Indianapolis, IN. USA. Retrieved from https://www.youtube.com/watch?v=0-lTFeY6UgY&feature=youtu.be

Van Velzer, C. M., & McCullers, M. S. (2020). Speaking for themselves: Student self-authorship in education abroad. *Diversity Abroad: The Global Impact Exchange*. Retrieved from https://www.diversitynetwork.org/resource/resmgr/documents/summer_2020_gie.pdf

Varney, J. (2013). Proactive advising. In P. Jordan, M. A. Miller, & J. K. Drake (Eds.), *Academic advising approaches: Strategies that teach students to make the most of college*. Jossey-Bass.

Wiggins, G., & McTighe, J. (1998). What is backward design? In *Understanding by design* (1st edn, pp. 7–19). Merrill Prentice Hall. Retrieved from https://web.archive.org/web/20160721163755/http://www.fitnyc.edu/files/pdfsBackward_design.pdf

8

Dismantling Exclusive Practices: Education Abroad Applications as a Tool for Inclusion

Taylor Woodman, Jeremy Gombin-Sperling and Qimmah Najeeullah

Although research has noted the importance of thoughtful application processes to enhance access and inclusion in education abroad (EA; Butler et al., 2018; Whatley & Raby, 2020), the process itself, including relevant requirements and procedures, is an under-researched and under-reviewed area within the field that deserves attention. Applications are a critical factor that determines who does or does not participate in EA programming. However, process updates are often updated only for efficiency but not for equity. Many organizations and universities operate from an understanding that the application process is innately neutral, often implementing inherited and nonempirically informed methods (Liu, 2011). In failing to critically reflect on how normative requirements and protocols can reproduce and further an elite and noninclusive narrative of EA, we, as professionals, advocates, and scholars ultimately may inadvertently be exacerbating the exclusion of students who are both marginalized and underrepresented in EA, despite the best of intentions.

In this chapter, we take a critical look at the application process to reframe the EA application from a tool for exclusion to a tool for inclusion that can leverage the strengths of students, in order to cultivate an inclusive and formative educational experience. In referencing students who are underrepresented and marginalized in study abroad, we refer primarily to students of color, LGBTQ+ students, first-generation students, low-income students, students with disabilities, and students who sit at multiple intersections of these identities. Other groups such as men, and more specifically White men, are not part of this definition; while underrepresented in study abroad, their social position prevents them from encountering systemic barriers or marginalization that hinders their participation (Simpson & Bailey, 2020).

Our analysis is the only known work solely dedicated to EA applications, which led us to review both practitioner-based resources and scholarly articles to provide an overview of the current context and framing of EA application processes. Within this review, we examine standard application components (i.e., eligibility standards and selection procedures) and related processes and structures (e.g., advising, financial aid) that can impact applicants' abilities to complete an application, let alone ponder the possibility of beginning one. We interrogate our field's hidden curriculum and the subsequent assumptions and biases that manifest within application practices, to bring about awareness that can inform a set of new standards. Lastly, we offer recommendations to reframe the application process from an equity-minded perspective. We generally are referring to examples from the United States, which is a unique context; however, the recommendations provided here can be applied to other cultural contexts.

Global Rationale for Equity, Diversity, and Inclusion

The structural barriers that are prevalent throughout the application process and policies in the culture of EA administration are indicative of those faced by marginalized groups more generally in the United States. Although there has been a significant diversification of students participating in EA and those in EA staff positions, the field as a whole remains predominantly White and often middle class to upper class (Cohen, 2001; Diversity Abroad, 2019). This lack of diversity is especially striking in a field that promotes itself on the benefits of cross-cultural and intercultural exchange. As with the EA program application process, access to the decision-making table is often steeped in established metrics that speak more to a person's level of similitude to the current dominant culture than one's potential to navigate and foment substantial connections with communities abroad.

Objectives around EA have increasingly aligned with broader neo-liberal reforms within universities that focus on the student as a global consumer (Bolen, 2001)—a stance that contrasts with growing global youth-led movements. These movements articulate an inevitable transformation of U.S. values that prioritize environmental consciousness, anti-materialism and anti-consumerism, and gender and racial equity and justice. Such a divergence is indicative of disconnects between the historical structures of U.S. international education, the resistance of many leaders in international education toward systemic reconfigurations that would reshape the field, and the emerging awareness and needs of the core stakeholders—the students themselves. Until we recognize the unequal access to resources and opportunities baked into our educational system, let alone social and political systems, inclusion in international education will remain ever distant. Likewise, we must also shift our lens to recognize how EA remains primarily, though not entirely, steeped in a geopolitical modality that often reproduces a harmful narrative that positions predominantly White and Western modes of education and administration as superior to all other forms of knowledge production and practice (Hartman et al., 2020).

Therefore, we see it as a moral obligation to leave no piece of the EA puzzle unexamined. Any component of a system is a product and indicative of the histories and social dynamics, which brought it into being. As we intend to reveal through a critical analysis of EA application processes and components, we must unlearn and unravel the inequities embedded in what have become normative.

Unpacking the Hidden Curriculum

To reimagine a more inclusive and formative EA application process, we incorporate the concept of the hidden curriculum as a primary analytical frame for this chapter. The hidden curriculum refers to the messages and norms that educational practices and processes implicitly reproduce and instill in students (Margolis, 2001). Through a critical lens, the hidden curriculum plays an insidious and unrecognized role in the maintenance of power within institutions, reifying the ability and entitlement of those with the most privilege—predominantly White students, staff, and faculty—to maintain unequal access to the majority of resources and opportunities offered by colleges and universities (Jay, 2010; Patton, 2016). Even those who feel they are doing the "right" thing, and who want to be allies to marginalized students, may inadvertently be promoting inequality and enabling harm by not considering and correcting for the historic inequities built into EA.

When we apply the hidden curriculum to EA applications, we are looking at application components not as neutral criteria, but rather as subjects that carry their own political histories within the growth and expansion of the EA field (Giroux, 1983, Zemach-Bersin, 2007).

While few studies have analyzed EA's hidden curriculum, the critical work that has been produced demonstrates the necessity of expanding this research to the application aspect of EA. Most notably, Ficarra (2017) has applied the framework of a hidden curriculum to investigate institutionalized study abroad portfolios (ISAPs), defined as "the compilation of study abroad programs that a university promotes to its students that take place in particular locations focusing on specific academic disciplines" (p. 2). Ficarra's analysis of ISAPs relates to application processes in that both reflect experiences that take place *before* a study abroad program begins. Her analysis reveals that factors such as program availability/location, corresponding disciplines, promotion materials, and internationalization missions play a role in "situating [students] in a way that is either transformative or serves to reify privileged neo-imperial positions" (p. 2).

Within the three institutions she studied, Ficarra found that 63% of the programs offered within ISAPs were based in Western Europe, where programs in sub-Saharan Africa constituted only 4%. Moreover, programs in sub-Saharan Africa centered almost entirely on service learning and development compared with Western Europe where nearly every discipline was available to students with the noted absence of service learning. International experiences operate in ways that reinforce global dispositions, attitudes, and actions previously formed in students (Larsen, 2014). Given the institutionalized relationships between non-Western communities and colonial powers are still dynamic and under-acknowledged, such international experiences often have conceited, savior-based motivations for engaging in service abroad programs. The potential of these practices to perpetuate the dichotomies of developed/underdeveloped and rich/poor and reproduce neo-colonial power relations under the disguise of helping and cross-cultural learning is dangerously high and has been thoroughly documented (Heron, 2007; Tiessen, 2008; Zemach-Bersin, 2007).

The goals of Ficarra's project and similar initiatives are not solely about critique; her deep engagement with ISAPs and ours with applications are calls to EA offices to critically reflect and consider the potential harm that our institutionalized discourses and practices may have on students. This includes students with identities from marginalized communities, and in parallel, the collective harm caused by the unconsciousness and resistance of majority-minded/White students.

Application Components as Structural Barriers

Dissecting how the seemingly normal and benign components of EA applications contribute to the maintenance of social stratification helps us realize the extent to which oppressive mechanisms are baked into our institutions (Gramsci et al., 1992; Hall et al., 1983) and are often replicated and unintentionally promoted throughout internal systems, and by well-intentioned practitioners. Relevant to our analysis, we recognize how dominant application processes can present multiple levels of struggle that result in students from marginalized social positions either not submitting an application or even beginning one. When we refer to the application process, we are looking at the actors, resources, and materials with which a student must interact in order to apply for a program. We also focus on how these elements themselves interact with one another in shaping the experience a student has throughout the process. To illustrate these points, we focus our discussion on EA application process and materials, the role of the EA advisor, eligibility requirements, financial considerations, and selection procedures.

Education Abroad Application Process and Materials

The application initiates the student's decision to participate in an EA experience. Despite the importance of this stage in the overall EA application process, scholarly and practitioner-based resources rarely treat applications critically. In many ways, the application is simply taken for granted as a neutral mechanism or needed step to gain basic information about a student (Welton et al., 2018). The dedication of most scholarship and practice is given to the partnership, orientation, and programming that occur in pursuit of the program. This is not to say that applications have not evolved over time. EA application procedures have shifted alongside general higher education trends, including reducing student application burdens through the use of the Common Application by U.S. colleges and universities, reducing or eliminating nonessential criteria such as letters of recommendation, lowering application fees, and developing holistic review procedures for applications (Bastedo et al., 2018). Recent developments, like the section on equity, diversity, and inclusion, in The Forum on Education Abroad's revised *Standards of Good Practice* (2020) ("The Forum's Standards"), have opened critical space to reimagine application procedures.

Despite these advances, issues persist around the various administrative procedures and the purpose of the application itself. Extending Ficarra's work beyond the portfolio of program offerings, the operationalization of the hidden curriculum intersects with a set of cumbersome, bureaucratic processes and acknowledges recent developments in the field. Oftentimes, a student enters a process that includes multiple actors leading to a series of steps and procedures across organizations with various biases and competing priorities. Integration and collaboration across organizations can be quite minimal, leading to duplication, confusion, and fatigue. It is also common for students to complete multiple applications, one for the home school and another for a provider or host institution, thus adding to the amount of paperwork required. Administrative burdens can lead to student attrition during the application phase, and especially for student communities that have traditionally been underserved or underrepresented. Many of these students are on campuses with low-resourced EA offices and collectively lack the institutional support and/or attention needed to navigate unclear terrains that are often assumed by many administrators to be straightforward and easily understood.

As with other elements of EA, institutional stakeholders typically do not make efforts to establish consensus on the purpose of the application (Dodds, 2008). For instance, advisors and program administrators may see the application as a mechanism to support enrollment capacity requirements, thereby using the process to remove students from the applicant pool. In contrast, international partners may seek information on academic level and cultural understanding to determine best curricular placement. Further complicating these partnerships is the rise of third-party providers that add an additional administrative layer and opportunity for misalignment.

Throughout this investigation, a closer examination of the underlying assumptions within the application procedures and an intentional revision of the application with international partners is needed (Willems et al., 2019).

Role of the Advisor

The EA advisor can serve as both a gatekeeper and a motivator for application instruction and content. For many students, other than applying for college or a job, the EA application may be one of the only processes that necessitates strict adherence for successful qualification, while also requiring a contemplative look at their lives and skills, alongside an assessment of their potential. As such, it is essential that advisors refrain from seeing themselves as a "gatekeeper" when deciding whom, and to what degree, to support an interested student. Part of this involves being careful about automatically judging whether a student might be "prepared" or "mature" enough for a given experience. This concept of maturity is often classed, racialized, and gendered, in which administrators holding more privileged social positions may apply unequal and burdensome expectations on students holding marginalized identities (Smith et al., 2008).

Within their own critical reflections, EA advisors need to address the structural factors that have limited access to global education for underserved and underrepresented students. While an advisor's bias may be unintentional, it can result in treating the presence of Black and brown professionals as exceptions rather than as required and celebrated members of the field. Yet more importantly, it robs the world of talents and perspectives that will ensure more substantive connections, collective visioning, holistic solution building, and thoughtful education programming.

Offices should also provide relevant training to advising staff. The expectation by the EA community has been for advisors to independently adapt to this trend without the insight and training to create informed and welcoming environments needed to do so (Lentz, 2018). Students from marginalized communities are often in the position of being their own advocates and may be hesitant to rely on their preexisting support networks, especially if those networks are already struggling for resources (Griffin Bassas, 2015). With this in mind, it is important for advisors to be considerate of the work, family, and program realities of a diverse audience. Furthermore, this type of critical reflection can be cultivated through training and honest dialogue, not only with advising staff but also with faculty members and peer mentors involved in the EA application cycle. These other parties, like EA advisors, can play a pivotal role in a students' entryway into EA, and their adherence to a critically reflective advising approach ensures a more holistic experience of inclusion for students—especially those that are most marginalized.

Eligibility Criteria

EA, like most academic programs, employs an admission-based system to determine participation, utilizing the concept of eligibility in order to establish a neutral and "equal" playing field in the application process. Despite assumptions of fairness, eligibility criteria come with their own set of inherent inequities, which enable greater access and a wider availability of programs to students privileged by dominant policies in U.S. higher education.

Grade Point Average

Nearly every EA program employs grade point average (GPA) as a key criterion in student selection. The weight of the GPA in determining application decisions can vary, where some institutions may automatically exclude applicants if they lack a listed GPA or weigh decisions more highly in favor of those who meet or exceed it. There is a significant difference between a minimum GPA requirement—one that establishes a baseline of academic commitment and responsibility—and a competitive minimum requirement that discourages an "average" student from considering applying, which may involve ranking candidates without taking other factors into consideration. Some institutions have intentionally lowered their overall GPA minimum requirement to increase access, in some cases down to a 2.0 within a 4.0 scale, the minimum level required for a student to remain in good academic standing, allowing them access to financial aid (Campbell et al., 2015).

EA professionals have long drawn much of their guidance from higher education admissions, a field that uses GPAs as a primary criterion in their decision-making processes around accepting, waitlisting, or rejecting students (Leonard & Jiang, 1999). There is an assumption that GPAs serve an indicator of a student's academic ability and, therefore, a predictor as to how well a student may or may not perform (Noble & Sawyer, 2004). Essentially, it is the assumption that students with higher GPAs are stronger academically and better prepared and thus deserve greater access to opportunities. Despite research showing the false nature of this claim (Dyer & Breja, 1999; Van Overschelde & López, 2019), many programs still commit to this narrative.

What is perhaps more damaging about this rhetoric is how it ignores systemic inequities that impact student academic performance disproportionately. The GPA narrative reifies the meritocracy myth in higher education—the idea that one's success in educational settings is solely determined by the individual effort a student makes, rather than the complex interaction of systems, biases, and cultural factors that impact the barriers students of varying identities across race, gender, class, sexuality, ability, and other identities may encounter throughout the entirety of their educational experience (McNamee & Miller, 2014).

Rather than relying solely on GPA, advisors can also encourage the expansion of self-selection application components that allow students to share their stories. This would further demonstrate the preparedness and understanding they already possess for participation in EA experiences—ultimately applying an asset-based approach (Yosso, 2005), which can help acknowledges the various forms of capital that minoritized students bring to an abroad experience. In addition, it is helpful to have alternative review processes of applications that include different perspectives, such as having alumni reviewers. Research points to how the inclusion of students in review protocols typically reserved only for staff and/or faculty can create more collaborative environments and highlight perspectives too often excluded from processes in higher education (Tran, 2018). Once a student completes a program, they know exactly what qualifications are required to manage the dynamics present in that particular host community/institution and/or program structure. Feedback from alumni would offer EA advisors a unique insight into a new applicant and would account for the varying factors of life and value students navigate as they invest in going abroad.

Application Essays

Often, applications for competitive EA programs include multiple essays and/or short answer questions requesting a student to share relevant personal history, accomplishments, or a statement of purpose. Some units collect these writing assignments without actually reading them or only using them in cases where two applicants are very close in other factors like GPA. The idea is that an extra hurdle ensures that students are indeed serious about a given program, yet the additional step may be serving unintentionally as a barrier for participation and not just for those who lack "seriousness."

When writing assignments are taken into consideration, they are generally scrutinized for grammar, writing style, and structure rather than the story trying to be told. This implicit bias creates an added barrier that most often affect speakers of English as a second language (Kanno & Varghese, 2010) or those who speak variants and dialects of English that U.S. higher education institutions tend to delegitimize (Morrison & Bryan, 2014). For international students, scholars such as Seelen (2002) have shown that earlier performance in school-level English is not strongly correlated with academic performance within the U.S. higher education system. Rather, Seleen finds that the effectiveness and support of teachers across subjects in college are the most crucial correlating factors for the success of English learners.

Further, students from under-resourced school systems and communities are often first-generation students who require more remedial support in some areas and are conditioned to be less confident in their academic abilities (Stebleton & Soria, 2012). Lacking a parent or mentor to proofread an application and offer strategic recommendations can determine the fate of an otherwise qualified student. Therefore, like the GPA, focusing on characteristics of an application that highlights the quality of previous education or access to education raises questions of equity when college itself often is designed to help bridge such academic gaps.

EA professionals might consider other mechanisms to gather student motivations and potential for an EA experience, such as short videos, audio recordings, and virtual interviews. Moving beyond written personal and project statements can also address the different cognitive and learning styles that impact student understanding and mediate access to information so students can choose the most appropriate strategies (Evans et al., 2010) for their learning and the expression of their ideas.

It may similarly be possible to permit students to submit materials in a language other than English. Expanding the language options widens the pool for who is a part of the selection process and offers a solution to language inequity and English "quality." This will naturally insist that advisors reach out to EA community members with relevant language skills and diverse perspectives. The expanded view of the applicants will also require more nuanced essay questions and prompts that will ensure a more vibrant image of a student's qualifications—again taking an asset-based approach rather than focusing on deficiencies.

Financial Considerations

Financial considerations impact all aspects of the EA process and the application phase is no different (Doyle et al., 2010). Before a student starts the application, social and economic messages of EA as an elite activity can already deter lower income and working-class students from applying. One of the first factors that applicants encounter is application fees and deposits, which are administered to ensure again that students are committed to going abroad. The application fee may vary widely, from a few dollars to a hefty amount, and is due upon submission of the application. Such fees may be used to generate revenue, with the goal of covering administrative costs and/or funding other initiatives, including scholarships for students with financial need (Whalen, 2008). They may also be used to deter students from submitting multiple applications, thus overwhelming the system. Deposits are usually due after a student has been admitted, to secure a student's spot on a program. Some deposits are collected up front in the form of a check, credit card payment, or charge to the student's account, while others are only charged if the student withdraws, serving more as a penalty rather than an actual deposit.

Despite the perceived benefits of both, fees and deposits can place an undue burden on students. High-need students may not have the available funds needed, requiring that they either forego EA entirely or seek funding from family or through a financial aid office, all requiring additional work and causing potential anxiety or embarrassment. In addition, the amounts due early in the process further the narrative of EA as an elite activity requiring wealth to participate (Simon & Ainsworth, 2012).

In addition to the costs associated with applications, students will have questions about how to finance their EA experience. While many federal financial aid packages transfer, institutional and state aid has a number of caveats based on program affiliation. For instance, a school may have a home-school tuition model that supplies different information than a program cost sheet or an international institution's tuition and fees information. In addition, certain types of financial aid transfer, while others do not. For example, the veteran's educational assistance program, Yellow Ribbon, requires numerous documents and approvals and can be denied by new federal interpretations of existing policy (NAFSA, 2020). Students unable to acquire sufficient funding through personal means and institutional resources often seek out external scholarships. This additional labor adds competing deadlines that operate outside normal university timelines to a student's workload. Many competitive national scholarship applications are also due months in advance, which requires a student to carefully plan for their EA experience before the application even opens. Although these financial considerations are not specific to applications, they are part of a larger context that provides a bearing on whether or not students apply for programs, and it is critical that stakeholders understand this context.

Passport Access

As an extension of the financial barriers noted, one of the most common requirements is the possession of a passport, often assumed to be a U.S. passport. While students do not need to have a passport to apply to programs nor is it a requirement for admission, it is a requirement upon acceptance and thus can be viewed as part of the application and onboarding process.

Beyond EA, passports are a reflection of the global system of surveillance, border control, and regulations that police the entry and exit of bodies across nation-states (Salter, 2006). The geopolitical power that predominantly White Western countries like the United States maintain and impose on a global stage ensures that the possession of a U.S. passport guarantees facilitated access to the majority of nations worldwide (Neumayer, 2006). At the same time, passports signal higher socioeconomic class, education level, and mobility. The assumption of U.S. passport possession ultimately disadvantages a wide variety of student access to EA. Students of lower socioeconomic status who may struggle to afford the fees associated with a passport, or whose families have an underlying discomfort with the screening process required to acquire one, are prevalent in minority serving institutions and community colleges all over the United States where just 3.4% of students study abroad during their undergraduate careers, compared to a 10.4% participation rate for students across all institutions nationally (Redden, 2018).

International students and legal permanent residents in the United States may experience barriers or barred entry from certain EA sites due to the country of origin of their passport—let alone the challenges of visa reentry policies to the United States (Twombly et al., 2012). In addition, undocumented students without possession of Advanced Parole and Deferred Action for Childhood for Arrivals (DACA) status cannot go abroad or return to the United States (Albrecht et al., 2018; Butler et al., 2018); and even those who do have this status may be concerned that regulations will change while they are abroad, preventing them from returning to the United States. While EA itself cannot alter some of these unequal realities, it is important to be aware of their consequences and prepared to assist students in supplying accurate information and resources. This can involve helping to cover the costs of passports for those with U.S. citizenship, a measure that has proven effective in advancing the participation of many underrepresented student communities in study abroad (Engel, 2017). An advisor can also provide assistance in locating resources for those with DACA or international statuses, such as affordable and easily accessible legal counsel with expertise in these areas.

Letters of Recommendation

As with essays, letters of recommendation are often a questionable requirement in applications. These letters may tell reviewers little about the student, as recommenders typically do not provide negative evaluations. Just as importantly, recommendations can be a means of inequity because many students from minority/under-resourced communities struggle to build relationships with faculty and supervisors due to class, cultural, gender, or generational differences. All of this is within the backdrop of historic racism and discrimination prevalent in college advising and working environments. For these reasons and others, many have argued for the removal of letters of recommendation altogether from admission processes (Iwen, 2019).

If an organization decides to maintain this practice, it is important for family and friends to be able to weigh in; the application process should allow for anecdotal stories and personal windows into potential applicants to be shared by those who know the applicant best. The idea that only those who see the academic or professional side of an applicant are valuable undermines the fact that the growth and challenges of an EA experience is in the day-to-day relationships with host community members, which go well beyond students' professional and academic skills and experiences. It can also be helpful to give more guidance to reviewers through forms and rubrics, which allow for nuance and prompt recommenders to highlight strengths of applicants that are not always captured by more traditional application procedures and questions.

Selection

Selection is the final step and barrier in a student's application process for an EA program. The diversity or lack thereof within a pool of applicants is often a reflection of the confluence of how engaged an institution has been in creating equitable EA policies and practices to support student participation (Perdue, 2018; Salisbury et al., 2011). Even in a situation where strong representation exists among students who are underrepresented or underserved in EA, biases among those making application decisions can present additional challenges.

Who is involved and how decisions are made vary considerably. For programs with sufficient capacity, including those that are at risk of not running without enough students, it may be that any student who meets the minimum qualifications is automatically admitted. Other programs are more competitive, with limited space. Those admitting students can range from a lone EA advisor or faculty member to a committee, though the latter is more unusual unless funding is attached. In addition, overseas partner institutions or third-party providers may be involved, unless the program is run entirely by the home institution.

Regardless of the type of program, it is important for anyone helping to select students to be fully aware of their own biases and assumptions. It is also necessary to diversify the groups who are ultimately making admissions decisions (Sensoy & DiAngelo, 2017). Engaging with the selection phase with a lens that recognizes the interplay of power and bias helps us see how much there is in fact to untangle when it comes to shifting dominant application processes in EA toward one of equity and inclusion (see Chapter 4 on hiring and organizational culture within this volume and The Forum's *Standards* 4.47).

Toward a New Application

The application process is ripe with opportunities for our work to create new entry points for future students. We recommend two important first steps forward in advancing inclusive excellence within EA applications: alignment and the development of a critical mindset.

The Importance of Alignment

One of our primary recommendations by which institutions can shift their application processes is by reflecting on how well their current policies and practices align with any public commitment to inclusive excellence ideals (see The Forum's *Standards* 4.14 & 4.43). Many, if not all, institutions of higher education in the United States espouse some discourse in which they assert their ongoing dedication to diversity such as through strategic plans, mission statements, and/or other documents (Patel, 2015). Although these statements remain important, it is often the case that institutions do not implement actions, policies, and accountability measures that would give such words meaning and substance (Ahmed, 2006). Our call for alignment is, therefore, a call for institutions to reflect critically on whether or not they are doing justice not only to their mission for diversity, but more importantly justice for the students these statements aim to support and recognize. As an institution begins this analysis, it is important to keep in mind that the mission-inclusive praxis relationship is dialogical, not linear. As offices and institutions engage in alignment work, reviewing effective policies and practices in application systems could lead to changes in a mission statement, and the goals of a mission statement may impact how new elements of the application process form, or how old ones are reborn.

What is critical in this alignment process is that there is representation from the communities that our inclusive work is trying to reach. Often, the individuals designing statements, policies, and practices represent the most privileged in an institution (Iverson, 2007). EA offices must work diligently to include the expertise of students, staff, and/or faculty from marginalized communities in their planning (see The Forum's *Standards* 4.45), being cognizant of not placing these same groups in a tokenized and overburdened position, but rather one where power is shared across the different social positions of individuals on such a committee (Faulkner et al., 2021). Collectively, these recommendations around alignment can move application system redesign toward the equity of inclusive practices.

Alignment in Practice

Whether one is a university EA advisor or a third-party administrator, what is produced reflects the belief system that guides one's EA program. To operationalize alignment within application procedures, one must establish a baseline of qualities and outcomes. During the first stage of the process, consensus building and norming priorities within the collective body of actors within the application process to both build and evaluate applications. Below are a set of questions to aid in conceptulizing a new way forward in application development that demands that both international educators critically reflect on their biases while providing guidance on a new set of evaluative procedures.

Questions to Build Applications
What can I ask students to disrupt my assumptions about them or expose my implicit bias about them and their communities and/or identities?
What do we want the students to be able to do as a result of this learning experience?
How can I collect insight into a student if they struggle with writing and/or expressing themselves? If they struggle with expression in English?
How can I assess a student's self-awareness of who they are and their impact in the world?
What are all of the qualities a student needs to be successful in this program? What does successful completion of this program look like?

Questions to Evaluate Applications
Does this applicant show awareness of, or the capacity to, responsibly address critical issues that are at the forefront of our society with a host country national?
Has this applicant considered/demonstrated responsibility for their own learning or leadership in teaching others?
Will the host community expand in their understanding of the United States by interacting with this student? What are additional ways to gather or showcase this information?
Will this experience assist this student in achieving the goals they have articulated for themselves?
Does this student show the capacity to handle the stress (emotional & environmental), rigor (academic/linguistic), social and analytical demands, and critical engagement requirements of this EA experience?

As these questions are asked and answered, educators should be allowed to follow the direction of the conversation and ensure others share varying points of view. As a result, more questions may arise and more time may be needed to sift through the information you may gather about yourself and the perspectives, fears, and commitments of your colleagues. At its core, inclusion is a contemplative exercise and needs to be a conscious investment in the quality and sustainable impact of your EA programming. The outcomes/findings of this exercise should be recorded and revisited as the next phase of application structuring and content building is reached.

In addition to considering the macro purposes of the application itself, applications can be scrutinized for efficiency and quality of instruction, order of components, and the word choice or phrasing of essay/statement questions. These details establish a hierarchy of information: what the applicant needs to value about themselves and what an evaluator believes is important about people. For example, if we always put demographic information first (i.e., zip code, race, gender, major, etc.), the "box" is being built around demographic information before an individual is able to express their authentic identity. Instead, one might begin with an essay or statement to allow an applicant to share who they are. Moreover, it is possible for a student to create their own submission, with more flexible prompts. Providing exploratory space fuels creativity instills a sense of trust in their readiness and ensures accountability for their submission.

Additional forms of alignment can occur through attention to the student experience. This can include everything from providing starter language to assist students in initiating tricky discussions to exercises and questions to inspire applicants to uncover and share uncomfortable and new information about their life experiences. The latter can help challenge or expand the existing narrative of their identity group(s) and highlight the importance of their presence as a contribution to their EA cohort, host community, and community(ies) in the United States. Engaging students within an application redesign is a crucial step to better understand the shifting student demographics and needs of your university population.

Developing a Critical Mindset

Recommendations toward building inclusive and equitable applications and application processes in EA start with the acknowledgment that the dominant systems in which EA operates, as well as the dominant practices in which most EA administrators and scholars engage, are built on inequitable foundations and histories. EA and international higher education are not separate from, but rather a critical component of the colonial and imperial projects of predominantly White Western nations like the United States in establishing a global hegemony that attempts to situate the rest of the world in a subordinate geopolitical position, while also benefiting and securing the place of elites along lines of race, gender, class, ethnicity, nationality, sexuality, ability, religious affiliation, and other systems of difference (Zemach-Bersin, 2007). These systems manifest in the construction of the hidden curriculum that perpetuate inequity within EA. As *critical educators,*we are responsible for identifying, acknowledging, and rectifying inequities and their impact on the institutions and global communities we serve. Our commitment is to *inclusive excellence,* which dictates that we operate from an understanding that the creation of a more supportive environment addresses endemic issues of power and privilege and enhances the learning experience for all students through the process of learning with and from each other (AAC&U, 2019). We must also remember that the work of critical educators is not solely about critique; critical work can and should be healing work, a series of exercises to support institutions in recognizing how systemic inequity has harmed and at times robbed the humanity and dignity of minoritized communities, thus illuminating our obligation to dismantle and unlearn such models so that being able to show up in one's fullness is no longer a privilege, but rather part of a normalized liberatory praxis (McGee & Stovall, 2015).

Concluding Thoughts

This chapter focused the efforts of a critical mindset on the application process and encouraged us to apply a similar lens to all structural aspects of their work and involvement in EA. We all come to this work from various vantage points, based on our own level and type of privilege (Wijeyesinghe & Kendall, 2017). Inclusion is an ongoing contemplative process that requires many of us to simultaneously learn to advocate for and support structurally disadvantaged communities underrepresented in EA with whom we do not share affinity or experience and to advocate for those with whom we do. While it may be daunting for some to consider and wrestle with the histories of inequity on which the field of EA was built, utilizing our agency to tackle the elements under our purview such as the application process is one crucial step in the direction of inclusive excellence, and our ability to harness that momentum within our organizations and across our field could support us collectively and holistically in institutionalizing a culture of inclusion across EA. EA creates power. However, to do so as an act of inclusion, means we have to critique what has been/we have created, adjust our lenses, and maintain a commitment to ongoing reflection and adaptation of our practices. While we know that this work will not be a panacea for all issues of inequality within EA, we must find our starting points, with the application process as one example analyzed in this chapter. Our collective work around inclusive practice matters, and when we realize the potential we have to effect change, a world where equity is the organizing principle becomes all that more possible.

References

Ahmed, S. (2006). Doing diversity work in higher education in Australia. *Educational Philosophy and Theory, 38*(6), 745–768.

Albrecht, T., Palacios, A., & Siefken, D. (2018). Undocumented students and access to education abroad. In H. Barclay Hamir & N. Gozik (Eds.), *Promoting inclusion in education abroad: A handbook of research and practice* (pp. 164–184). Stylus & NAFSA.

Association of American Colleges & Universities. (2019). *Making excellence inclusive.* Retrieved August 1, 2020, from https://www.aacu.org/making-excellence-Inclusive

Bastedo, M. N., Bowman, N. A., Glasener, K. M., & Kelly, J. L. (2018). What are we talking about when we talk about holistic review? Selective college admissions and its effects on low-SES students. *The Journal of Higher Education, 89*(5), 782–805. https://doi.org/10.1080/00221546.2018.1442633

Bolen, M. (2001). Consumerism and U.S. study abroad. *Journal of Studies in International Education, 5,* 182–200.

Butler, P. E., Madden, M., & Smith, N. (2018). Undocumented student participation in education abroad: An institutional analysis. *Frontiers: The Interdisciplinary Journal of Study Abroad, 30*(2), 1–31. https://doi.org/10.36366/frontiers.v30i2.409

Campbell, C. A., Deil-Amen, R., & Rios-Aguilar, C. (2015). Do financial aid policies unintentionally punish the poor, and what can we do about I? *New Directions for Community Colleges, 2015*(172), 67–76. https://doi.org/10.1002/cc.20164

Cohen, M. (2001). The Grand Tour. Language, national identity and masculinity. *Changing English, 8(*2), 129–141. https://doi.org/10.1080/13586840120085685

Diversity Abroad. (2019). *Survey of diversity & inclusion among international educators.* https://www.diversitynetwork.org/page/Diversity_Inclusion_InternationalEducators_Survey2019

Dodds, A. (2008). How does globalisation interact with higher education? The continuing lack of consensus. *Comparative Education, 44*(4), 505–551.

Doyle, S., Gendall, P., Meyer, L. H., Hoek, J., Tait, C., McKenzie, L., & Loorparg, A. (2010). An investigation of factors associated with student participation in study abroad. *Journal of Studies in International Education, 14,* 471–490.

Dyer, J., & Breja, L. (2003). Problems in recruiting students into agricultural education programs: A Delphi study of agriculture teacher perceptions. *Journal of Agricultural Education, 44.* DOI: 10.5032/jae.2003.02075

Engel, L. (2017). Underrepresented students in US study abroad: Investigating impacts. *IIE Mobility Research and Impact.* https://www.iie.org/Research-and%20Insights/Publications/Underrepresented-Students-and-Study-Abroad

Evans, C., Cools, E., & Charlesworth, Z. (2010). Learning in higher education – How cognitive and learning styles matter. *Teaching in Higher Education, 15*(4), 467–478.

Faulkner, S. L., Watson, W. K., Pollino, M. A., & Shetterly, J. R. (2021). "Treat me like a person, rather than another number": University student perceptions of inclusive classroom practices. *Communication Education, 70*(1), 92–111. https://doi.org/10.1080/03634523.2020.1812680

Ficarra, J. M. (2017). Curating cartographies of knowledge: Reading institutional study abroad portfolio as text. *Frontiers: The Interdisciplinary Journal of Study Abroad, 29*(1), 1–14.

Giroux, H. A. (1983). *Theory and resistance in education: A pedagogy for the opposition.* Bergin & Garvey.

Gramsci, A., Buttigieg, J. A., & Callari, A. (1992). *Prison notebooks.* Columbia University Press.

Griffin Bassas, C. (2015). Advocacy fatigue: Self-care, protest, and educational equity. *Windsor Yearbook of Access to Justice, 32*(2), 37–64.

Hall, S., Slack, J. D., & Grossberg, L. (2016). *Cultural studies 1983: A theoretical history.* Duke University Press.

Hartman, E., Reynolds, N. P., Ferrarini, C., Messmore, N., Evans, S., Al-Ebahim, B., & Brown, J. M. (2020). Coloniality-decoloniality and critical global citizenship: Identity, belonging, and education abroad. *Frontiers: The Interdisciplinary Journal of Study Abroad, 32*(1), 33–59.

Heron, B. (2007). *Desire for development: Whiteness, gender and the helping imperative.* Wilfrid Laurier University Press.

Horsthemke, K. (2008). Scientific knowledge and higher education in the 21st century: The case against 'indigenous science'. *South African Journal of Higher Education, 22*(2), 333–347.

Iverson, S. V. (2007). Camouflaging power and privilege: A critical race analysis of university diversity policies. *Educational Administration Quarterly, 43*(5), 586–611.

Iwen, M. (2019, April 10). Letters of recommendation: Just say no. *Inside Higher Ed.* https://www.insidehighered.com/advice/2019/04/10/letters-recommendation-reaffirm-entrenched-systems-bias-and-exclusion-opinion

Jay, M. (2003). Critical race theory, multicultural education, and the hidden curriculum of hegemony. *Multicultural Perspectives, 5*(4), 3–9.

Kanno, Y., & Varghese, M. M. (2010). Immigrant and refugee ESL students' challenges to accessing four-year college education: From language policy to educational policy. *Journal of Language, Identity & Education, 9*(5), 310–328. https://doi.org/10.1080/15348458.2010.517693

Kendall, F. E., & Wijeyesinghe, C. L. (2017). Advancing social justice work at the intersections of multiple privileged identities. *Student Services, 2017*, 91–100. https://doi.org/10.1002/ss.20212

Larsen, M. (2014). Critical global citizenship and international service learning. *Journal of Global Citizenship & Equity Education, 4*(1).

Lentz, A. (2018). Integrating student development theory into education abroad advising. *Capstone Collection.* Retrieved from https://digitalcollections.sit.edu/capstones/3120

Leonard, D. K., & Jiang, J. (1999) Gender bias and the college predictors of the SATs: A cry of despair. *Research in Higher Education, 40*, 375–407.

Liu, A. (2011). Unraveling the myth of meritocracy within the context of us higher education. *Higher Education, 62*(4), 383–397.

Margolis, E. (2001). *The hidden curriculum in higher education.* Routledge. http://link.library.utoronto.ca/eir/EIRdetail.cfm?Resources__ID=1052727&T=F

McGee, E. O., & Stovall, D. (2015). Reimagining critical race theory in education: Mental health, healing, and the pathway to liberatory praxis. *Educational Theory, 65*, 491–511. https://doi.org/10.1111/edth.12129

McNamee, S. J., & Miller, R. K. (2004). *The Meritocracy Myth.* Rowman & Littlefield.

Morrison, S., & Bryan, J. (2014). Addressing the challenges and needs of English-speaking Caribbean immigrant students: Guidelines for school counselors. *International Journal for the Advancement of Counselling, 36*(4), 440–449. https://doi.org/10.1007/s10447-014-9218-z

NAFSA: Association of International Educators. (2020, January 30). *Collegial conversation: Changes to benefits for education abroad.* https://www.nafsa.org/professional-resources/browse-by-interest/changes-veterans-benefits-education-abroad

Neumayer, E. (2006). Unequal access to foreign spaces: How states use visa restrictions to regulate mobility in a globalized world. *Transactions of the Institute of British Geographers, 31*(1), 72–84.

Noble, J. P., & Sawyer, R. L. (2004). Is high school GPA better than admission test scores for predicting academic success in college? *College and University, 79*(4), 17–22.

Patel, L. (2015). Desiring diversity and backlash: White property rights in higher education. *The Urban Review: Issues and Ideas in Public Education, 47*(4), 657–675.

Patton, L. D. (2016). Disrupting postsecondary prose: Toward a critical race theory of higher education. *Urban Education, 51*(3), 315–342.

Perdue, J. (2018). Black students, passports, and global citizenship: Developing research-based strategies to increase black student interest and participation in global learning on university campuses. *College Student Affairs Journal, 36*(1), 80–93.

Redden, E. (2018, September 11). *HBCU students abroad. Inside higher education.* https://www.insidehighered.com/news/2018/09/11/hbcus-seek-grow-study-abroad-participation

Salisbury, M. H., Paulsen, M. B., & Pascarella, E. T. (2011). Why do all the study abroad students look alike? Applying an integrated student choice model to explore differences in the factors that influence white and minority students' intent to study abroad. *Research in Higher Education, 52*(2), 123–150.

Salter, M. B. (2006). The global visa regime and the political technologies of the international self: Borders, bodies, biopolitics. *Alternatives – Amsterdam then New York Then Guildford then Boulder, 31*(2), 167–190.

Seelen, L. P. (2002). Is performance in English as a second language a relevant criterion for admission to an English medium university? *Higher Education, 44*(2), 213–232.

Sensoy, O., & DiAngelo, R. (2017). "We are all for diversity, but. . .": How faculty hiring committees reproduce whiteness and practical suggestions for how they can change. *Harvard Educational Review, 87*(4), 557–580.

Simon, J., & Ainsworth, J. W. (2012). Race and socioeconomic status differences in study abroad participation: The role of habitus, social networks, and cultural capital. *ISRN Education, 2012,* 1–21. WorldCat.org. https://doi.org/10.5402/2012/413896

Simpson, J. J., & Bailey, L. E. (2020). Men's experiences in short-term study abroad: Masculinity, temporality, and vulnerability. *Gender and Education,* 1–17. https://doi.org/10.1080/09540253.2020.1735312

Smith, L., Foley, P. F., & Chaney, M. P. (2008). Addressing classism, ableism, and heterosexism in counselor education. *Journal of Counseling & Development, 86*(3), 303–309.

Stebleton, M. J., & Soria, K. M. (2012). Breaking down barriers: academic obstacles of first-generation students at research universities. *Learning Assistance Review, 17*(2), 7–20.

The Forum on Education Abroad. (2020). *The standards of good practice for education abroad* (6th ed.). Dickinson College. Retrieved from https://forumea.org/resources/standards-6th-edition

Tiessen, R. (2008). Small victories but slow progress. *International Feminist Journal of Politics, 10*(2), 198–215. DOI: 10.1080/14616740801957547

Tran, D. (2018). *Recruiting, training, and co-creation with PGR student reviewers on an academic journal.* University of Greenwich. http://gala.gre.ac.uk/id/eprint/19791/1/18940%20TRAN_Recruiting_Training_and_Working_with_PGR_Student_Reviewers_2018.pdf

Twombly, S., Salisbury, M., Tumanut, S., & Klute, P. (2012). Study abroad in a new global century: Renewing the promise, refining the purpose. *ASHE Higher Education Report, 38*(4), 1–168.

Van Overschelde, J. P., & López, M. M. (2018). Raising the bar or locking the door? The effects of increasing GPA admission requirements on teacher preparation. *Equity & Excellence in Education, 51*(3–4), 223–241.

Welton, A. D., Owens, D. R., & Zamani-Gallaher, E.M. (2018). Anti-racist change: A conceptual framework for educational institutions to take systemic action. *Teachers College Record, 120*(14), 1–24.

Whalen, B. (2008). The management and funding of U.S. study abroad. *International Higher Education, 50.* https://doi.org/10.6017/ihe.2008.50.8005

Whatley, M., & Raby, R. L. (2020). Understanding inclusion and equity in community college education abroad. *Frontiers: The Interdisciplinary Journal of Study Abroad, 32*(1), 80–103. https://doi.org/10.36366/frontiers.v32i1.435

Willems, J., Coertjens, L., Tambuyzer, B., & Donche, V. (2019). Identifying science students at risk in the first year of higher education: The incremental value of non-cognitive variables in predicting early academic achievement. *European Journal of Psychology of Education: A Journal of Education and Development, 34*(4), 847–872. https://doi.org/10.1007/s10212-018-0399-4

Yosso, T. J. (2005). Whose culture has capital? A critical race theory discussion of community cultural wealth. *Race Ethnicity and Education, 8*(1), 69–91.

Zemach-Bersin, T. (2007). Global citizenship and study abroad: It's all about US. *Critical Literacy: Theories and Practices, 1*(2), 16–28.

9

Decolonizing Education Abroad: Grounding Theory in Practice

Santiago Castiello-Gutiérrez and Nick J. Gozik

Introduction

Research and practice have demonstrated that education abroad (EA) programs can have long-lasting and profound meaning for students within higher education. Researchers have traced the potential for such programming to increase students' academic development (McKeown et al., 2021), proficiency in other world languages (Jackson et al., 2021), intercultural awareness (Deardorff & Arasaratnam-Smith, 2017; Doerr et al., 2021), and future employability (Wiers-Jenssen et al., 2021). Despite these positive outcomes, internationalization activities, and specifically EA, have not been equal for all actors involved. Historically, EA in the United States began and continues to be perceived by many as an elitist activity reserved primarily for White (Institute of International Education [IIE], 2020b; Sweeney, 2013), affluent students (IIE, 2020b; Lörz et al., 2016; Whatley, 2017). While much has changed over the past several decades, due to both demographic shifts within higher education and efforts by those in the field of EA, inequities persist (Netz et al., 2020).

Increasing attention has been devoted to inequities, both for the students involved (e.g., through the work of inclusive excellence, as explored in other chapters in this volume) and the local communities and organizations that are impacted by EA (e.g., Ficarra, 2019, 2021). Through the lens of decolonization, scholars have acknowledged the role of EA in exacerbating and widening power disparities, including those that exist between the Global

North and Global South (e.g., Adkins & Messerly, 2019; Brewer & Ogden, 2019; Tiessen et al., 2018; Woolf, 2007; Zemach-Bersin, 2010). Such an approach helps us to understand how EA fits within a broader historical context. As a result of centuries of oppression and power disparities, scholars point out that every form of international engagement—including cooperation in higher education—can be considered as a non-neutral endeavor (Leal et al., 2020; Lee, 2021) and that EA is no exception. From this perspective, higher education in the United States in general, and internationalization in particular, has and continues to be a colonizing endeavor (Lee, 2021; Stein, 2018). Who participates in EA programs and how participants perceive and interact with their host culture can reinforce neo-colonial practices (Ogden, 2008; Woolf, 2007).

In this chapter, we begin by exploring the origins and meaning of decolonizing EA and its connection to equity-driven work within global programming. Next, we focus on concrete and practical strategies for how a decolonization lens can be applied at various stages of the EA process. Although there has been some initial scholarship on the decolonization of EA, extant publications have rarely drilled down to the level of how this framework can be applied on a daily basis and, most importantly, how it can be threaded holistically and intentionally at each step of a student's journey from initial advising, to going abroad, and in returning from overseas. Accordingly, we believe that this chapter serves as a useful guide for scholars and practitioners alike seeking to move the field of EA beyond the status quo, for the benefit of all actors involved.

Decolonizing Education Abroad

So, what exactly is a decolonization approach, and what does that look like in EA? At its core, decolonial education looks to analyze the ongoing violence of colonization that has created current global inequities and an attempt to work against it through education (Smith, 2013). Decolonization, as an epistemology and framework, has its origins in the Latin American movement of the late 1990s against the hegemonic discourse and practices that framed modernity as a universal, inherently benevolent, and ahistorical concept (Leal & Moraes, 2018). It also stems from postcolonial thinking in Asia and Africa that exposed and denounced Eurocentrism (Gandhi, 2019). Scholars use this framework to (1) highlight and denounce the underlying causes for the power disparities between different regions/actors, and (2) flip deficit perspectives that place the formerly colonized as inferior, as in need, and as lacking.

The internationalization of higher education is often seen as a neutral endeavor where partners (in this case, higher education institutions) interact as equals in an ahistorical and apolitical vacuum. But decolonial and post-colonial scholars have amply documented that this is not the case; history and current politics have an important effect in making internationalization a primer tool for soft power, and an inherently power disbalanced activity (Thondhlana et al., 2021; Trilokekar, 2021). Therefore, in relation to EA, and in an attempt to decolonize it, we first need to acknowledge EA's past and current role in (neo)colonialism.

Analyzing the historical patterns of who participates in EA programs from the United States, in what kind of programs, for how long, and the most common destinations, shows how there is much risk in EA serving as perpetuator of colonial and neo-colonial legacies. For example, over half of U.S. students who participate in EA programs do so in a European country, with 80% of them in one of six countries: the United Kingdom, Italy, Spain, France, Germany, and Ireland. If also including Canada, Australia, and New Zealand, 6 out of 10 U.S. students choose to study abroad in a Western, developed country (IIE, 2020a). While these countries are certainly multicultural and diverse representations of the world, the imbalance in destinations replicates the center-periphery patterns of the colonial era.

What students do while in country also makes a difference. Unless intentional programming has been put in place, students have had less of a propensity to move outside touristic patterns, often with minimized levels of cultural or linguistic immersion. It can be quite easy to stay within one's comfort zone, without frequenting, for example, neighborhoods where immigrants/migrants might inhabit or where locals do not speak English as readily, thus missing out on meaningful learning opportunities (Holm & Zilliacus, 2009). An EA experience in a multicultural setting can still be monocultural in its curriculum and design, which also poses the risk to exacerbate perceptions of EA as academic tourism (Breen, 2012; Michelson & Álvarez Valencia, 2016).

Adding to these challenges, the length of programming has shortened over time. In the past 10 years, the percentage of U.S. students abroad for an academic year has decreased by half, while enrollments have doubled for programs of less than 2 weeks (IIE, 2020b). This results in over half of the participating students having an EA experience of fewer than 8 weeks. And while a shorter experience can potentially be more inclusive of students with limited resources, it also means that programs need to be planned carefully to ensure that students do in fact have an intercultural experience. Most of these programs are faculty led and/or cohort oriented, making students more prone to stay inside their "bubble."

EA programs need to evolve if they are to fulfill their promise of developing students into what is often referred to as "global citizens." But how can EA be transformed? From the perspective of local communities, EA can have a positive impact, such as with the exchanges that take place between host family members and international students. There are certainly instances where community-based learning strategies and/or collaborative research projects, when done well, can be fruitful for all involved. At the same time, there is great risk in local communities missing out on these benefits, and particularly when the transactions are one sided, within a customer-service model.

Within this context, how can EA be transformed? Adkins and Messerly's (2019) definition of decolonization of EA serves as an excellent starting point by identifying the main issues with current colonial frameworks in EA and suggesting some characteristics that a decolonial lens should have:

> To decolonize education abroad programming, then, is to eliminate approaches that are one-sided, ethnocentric, touristic, uncritical, oversimplifying of cultural complexity, and operating within the "savior complex" (particularly in community-based learning programs). Instead, approaches are respectful, reciprocal, critically self-reflexive, involve building long-term relationships, and seek to understand and interact holistically with local institutions and cultures and individual hosts–in all their profound complexities. (p. 75)

This approach ideally should be part of a larger strategy aimed at making sure that colleges and universities in the United States establish comprehensive and, most importantly, equity-driven internationalization strategies (George Mwangi & Yao, 2021).

Throughout this chapter, we explore how decolonial approaches can further complement the work of inclusive excellence within EA, as explored elsewhere in this volume. In doing so, we suggest how to apply Adkins and Messerly's (2019) definition of decolonization of EA throughout the different stages of the EA process, from the vantage point of students. We first identify some of the most common stages and then provide guidance on how to start using a decolonial lens as well as an inclusive excellence one at each stage. The complexity of applying decolonizing practices is such that it would be highly naive and egocentric to think that there is a single route to follow (Woolf, 2021). There is no single recipe for decolonize the entire EA process, for as Stein and da Silva (2020) note:

> To seek within decolonial critiques a prescriptive (re)solution would route them back into the same set of colonial entitlements that they seek to challenge. In other words, this would result in the mobilization of decolonial critiques toward creating more of the same (while believing that we are doing something different). (p. 562)

So, while we acknowledge the risks and limitations of suggesting some actions, we believe that, to start moving forward in at least "gesturing toward decolonial futures" in EA (Stein et al., 2020), it is imperative to reflect and theorize about the many ways in which EA is perpetuating local and global inequities and start implementing alternative practices that attempt to make right some of EA's systemic and systematic wrongs.

An Equity-Driven Approach to Education Abroad

As conceptualized here, the EA process begins with the design of an overseas program and ends with reentry activities and outcomes assessment. In this section, we present examples and suggestions for five stages of this process: developing a program mission & goals, curricula, marketing & recruitment, predeparture, on-site programming & activities, and outcomes assessment (see Figure 9.1). The goal is not to cover all stages or activities within each, and instead to provide illustrations of what might be reexamined, as part of an overall EA trajectory. Programs will look different, including everything from faculty-led programs abroad designed by the home institution to programs created by a host institution and curated to attract international students to the direct enrollment of visiting students in host institutions. Rather than prescribing one set of solutions, it is hoped that the logic introduced here can then be applied to other points along the continuum and for a myriad of program types.

Developing a Mission & Goals

With a goal of providing as many students as possible with an international experience—on its own a worthy cause—higher education institutions nonetheless often lose sight of the *why* and focus mostly on the *how* (Deardorff, 2014). In line with The Forum on Education Abroad's *Standards of Good Practice* (2020), it is important to begin the development of any

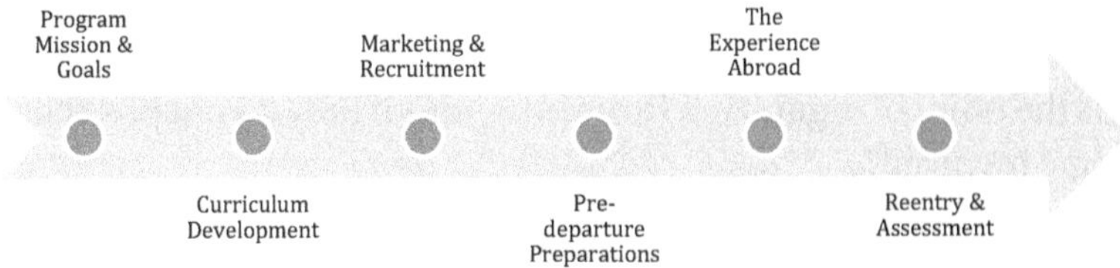

Fig. 9.1 Education abroad process.
Note: Not all stages are included; the diagram reflects the stages as outlined in the text of this chapter.
Source: Authors.

new program by establishing a clear mission and student learning outcomes (Gozik, 2015, see also Chapters 5 and 14 in this volume). Doing so ensures that all program components (Gozik & Oguro, 2021) align around well-defined purpose, ensuring that we maximize student learning and use resources effectively.

From a decolonization perspective, a more focused vision can assist institutions in seeing the longer term impact of programming. When key performance indicators revolve singularly around the number of students participating in EA, it is only natural to expect that institutions will turn to market-like practices to provide their students, oftentimes seen more as consumers and less as learners, with the best possible experience. Within this scenario, it can be tempting to only select options, such as locations, activities, schedules, that are most attractive from a consumer standpoint (Miller-Idriss et al., 2019; O'Toole, 2018). The continued growth of short-term programs is one example of how market forces have shifted many campuses' offerings. While such programming can be greatly beneficial, as noted earlier, a shorter time on the ground typically makes immersion and the ability to engage with locals more challenging, preventing either students and/or the host community from truly benefitting. There is a risk of reinforcing colonial ideals of entering a new place for one's advantage, to take from it any and all kinds of resources for an individual benefit, often at the expense of others.

In developing a program mission and learning outcomes, then, it is important to apply a decolonization strategy from the outset. The language of decolonization can be explicitly referenced or at least implied. It is also highly useful to collaborate with local partners to gain new perspectives and adjust models in ways that better serve students and the host community. The fact that the home institution needs to serve internally as the organizer and manage certain aspects of the program does not imply that it cannot include other partners. For example, courses can be co-designed and co-taught by local and visiting faculty and the program can be open to students from other partner institutions (also locally, from the home country, or a third location). These steps certainly imply a significant time investment, but then again, what is the point of organizing these programs if they do not positively impact everyone involved?

GUIDING QUESTIONS:

- Who needs to be at the table during the design process? Will members of the host community be included?

- Why is this specific EA program relevant and important?
- Why was this specific location selected as a destination? Were the rationales mostly about potential to recruit students appealing to their tastes? Based on the program's topic?
- What opportunities will participants have to experience and reflect on the local culture beyond a touristic gaze?
- What opportunities will participants have to interact, share, and learn with local actors?
- Who is the home institution partnering with locally to provide services? Could these relationships balance or further exacerbate inequities in the local community?

The Curriculum

Considerable attention has gone into exploring ways of decolonizing curricula in higher education, the bulk of which can be easily applied to EA. Much of this work, as Charles (2019) notes, began in the 1990s with a focus on an "inclusive curriculum" and continued with the notion of "decolonizing the university," stemming from a 2011 conference on this theme in Malaysia. More recently, the idea of "decolonization of the curriculum" has come about from advocacy in South Africa, where students at the University of Cape Town in 2015 called for the removal of a statue of Cecil Rhodes (Chaudhuri, 2016), coupled with other demands to recenter education, to make it more inclusive and centered in African culture, history, and thought. If "decolonization of the curriculum" started in a specific cultural and historical context, scholars and practitioners have found the primary tenets to be applicable in a variety of settings, including in the United States.

Bryn Mawr professor Chanelle Wilson (2021) explains that a decolonizing framework begins by acknowledging:

> that knowledge is not owned by anyone ... [it] is collectively produced and human beings of all races, ethnicities, classes, genders, sexual orientations, and disabilities have as much right as elite white men to understand what our roles and contributions have been in shaping intellectual achievements and shifting culture and progress. (para. 6)

Such an approach requires us both to validate the voices of "Others" and to deconstruct places/cultures in their multiple layers (Woolf, 2021), and in doing so to recognize other knowledges and ways of knowing as valuable. The latter requires stepping away from stereotypes and mainstream representations or simplified understandings of a culture or nation, as well as analyzing their history from multiple perspectives. In both cases, the EA experience will ideally encourage students to understand and appreciate multiple perspectives. This can be accomplished by ensuring, for example, that reading lists include marginalized and/or non-Western thinkers, something that can be gauged by an audit of syllabi and classroom materials.

From a pedagogical perspective, Wilson additionally observes that "decolonising requires sustained collaboration, discussion and experimentation among groups of teachers and students, who themselves have power to make things happen on the ground and think about what might be done differently" (n.d.). While faculty normally are viewed as constructors and conveyors of intellectual content, this approach turns the tables, recognizing that all actors have knowledge and experience that can benefit others in learning. Among these actors, we need to involve both students and the local community/experts. Regarding the former, students can contribute to discussions on curricular changes and the development of new classes. In the classroom, common practices include having students work in small groups, present readings, and offer arguments through opinion pieces and debates. Another strategy includes asking students to post questions/areas of interest before classes and then constructing lesson plans around those questions, allowing students to drive the content delivery. Likewise, one of the benefits of teaching in another country is to include local experts and students, who can provide other perspectives, including those that may challenge how the same content might normally be taught on the home campus.

Whatever the application, the goal is to continually mix up how we teach, driven by both students' needs and interests. Shifting practices will feel risky at first, and there will be some lessons/disciplines where less flexibility is possible. However, decolonization requires experimentation and confidence to rethink and revise what we teach—something that fits well with the experiential nature of EA.

GUIDING QUESTIONS:

- In what ways does the curriculum include the perspective from local voices/epistemologies?
  - Whose voices and perspectives are centered?
  - Are these voices from the inside or interpreted from outside?
- How is the program balancing different versions of the history surrounding the destination site, its culture, and its people?

Marketing & Recruitment

The way EA programs are marketed has been amply criticized for its consumeristic and touristic approach (Bolen, 2001; Ficarra, 2017; Zemach-Bersin, 2010; see also Chapter 6 in this volume). These portrayals of going abroad as an adventurous and exotic endeavor (Ogden, 2008) can affect the ways in which students view their own participation. In community-based learning programs, for example, without careful program design and descriptions, students who are being recruited might get a sense of participating in such program out of a self-need to "help" (Nordmeyer et al., 2016; Onyenekwu et al., 2017), often within what is referred to as a "White savior complex." Especially when students are in a location that is a current or former colony of the home institution's country, the program's materials (descriptions, images, etc.) need to be mindful of the history between the "home" and "host" cultures.

Meaningful changes to marketing practices can happen by selecting different perspectives in photo materials. For example, one might use an image taken when a local student or teacher is talking while a study abroad participant is listening, as opposed to one when the latter is centered and seems to be "instructing" a local group. These types of representations, especially when there is a history of colonization between some of the actors' identities (e.g., local or visiting students' nationality, race, and language) or other forms of power disparities (e.g., gender), are deeply important in challenging often unspoken and unquestioned notions of superiority.

In addition, we might consider how students will be affected by marketing practices. The literature around students of color has already shown differences in their experiences abroad (Engel, 2017; Lee & Green, 2016; Murray Brux & Fry, 2010; Wick et al., 2019); therefore, institutions need to be mindful of what the EA program might trigger for different students. For example, overemphasizing a specific EA program as a "heritage" experience might reinforce assumptions about the students' relation to a certain region. Posters with pictures of African American students studying abroad in Africa, or Latin*[1] students in Central or South America might imply that only/mostly students from these backgrounds will benefit from this particular program, that they will "fit right in." These assumptions do little to complicate historical, racial, and ethnical complexities associated with

[1] Latin* is used here to capture a wide array of Latin identities, similar to the use of "LatinX," while also acknowledging some of the concerns that the "x" presents in the latter (Salinas, 2020).

mobility and migration, while also compartmentalizing students based on their racial/ethnic identities.

GUIDING QUESTIONS:

- How is the EA program being depicted through marketing materials?
  - What is the intention of the marketing materials? Is the language being used inclusive? Market/adventure oriented?
  - Who is being targeted as a potential participant? Why?
- How are the host country/region, and its culture and values being depicted?
  - What are our sources for such information?
- Who/what is visible in photos, videos, and other media? Who/what is missing?

Predeparture Preparation

A careful EA program design needs to include a space where the home institution facilitates opportunities for students to start learning more about the destination country. Deconstructing the complexities of the place and its people, culture, and history is key to a successful and more meaningful intercultural experience. Most importantly, at this stage, students should start receiving information from different (and oftentimes conflicting) sources so they can gain a broader perspective.

Through a decolonization lens, some of the main issues that impede students from immersing more fully into a country and its culture stem from having a unilateral perspective about its complex past and present. In a faculty-led program going to Vietnam, for example, it will be necessary to recognize that the perspective that U.S. students will have about the war and postwar period in Vietnam will vary from that of students in Vietnam. Current Vietnamese students' understandings of the United States will also differ from that of students in neighboring Cambodia in light of differing views on the region's and the United States relationship with China (Vance, 2021). Such views should be considered and addressed before, during, and even after the EA program so that students can form a more balanced understanding of complex issues of interconnected global history(ies) and geopolitics.

One of the challenges to predeparture is that orientation sessions are often short and heavy with logistical content, such as packing instructions and health and safety information, making it difficult to get to the weightier conversations needed for a decolonization approach to be successful. Some institutions have addressed this problem by extending orientations to include lectures and presentations by experts, including faculty and staff from the host country (either those already on campus or who are available to present from overseas via online technology), as well as changing orientation so that logistical pieces are assigned to students to do on their own, thus freeing up space for dialogue and content in in-person meetings. In addition, some campuses have required predeparture courses such as for short-term, faculty-led programs, to extend the academic content that takes place on the ground, and/or created opportunities for students to further reflect through reentry coursework and seminars. Whichever strategies are employed, it is necessary that the faculty and staff involved are themselves aware of and prepared to implement a decolonization approach—something that likely will require additional training sessions (Absolon, 2019; Layne et al., 2020). It is crucial, then, to provide training and spaces for instructors to "examine their attitudes toward other cultures, including appreciating other cultural viewpoints as well as understanding their motivation to teach in a foreign context" (Gopal, 2011).

Finally, as EA program cohorts continue to become more diverse, it is fundamental that institutions integrate their students' prior experiences into the preparation for the EA experience. Predeparture orientations should not be unidirectional, as participants bring with them a myriad of "funds of knowledge" (Moll et al., 1992) based on their identities and lived experiences. As expressed by Manning et al. (2020, p. 45): "As educators, how do we decide what to include in these trainings [predeparture orientations] if we do not know what our students are bringing to the table?"

GUIDING QUESTIONS:

- What preconceived ideas and biases might students have about the host destination?
  - How are participating students being familiarized to the history, traditions, and social context of their host destination?
  - Are students being provided with a contextualization of the host country's history? From whose perspective?
- How are students being encouraged to investigate on their own the host destination, particularly in relationship to their specific interests as well as the goals of the EA program? How are students' prior

experiences and knowledge being valued as part of the global learning experience?
- What are the preconceived ideas and biases that might push the institution to recruit certain students more strongly based on their demographics?

The Experience Abroad

As noted earlier, students from the United States and other developed countries who participate in EA programs in the developing world have been documented to feel the need to "help," thus perpetuating a White savior complex. More common—and perhaps more harmful—is an implicit assumption that host society members should adapt local systems and services to program leaders and students' stated needs (Barros, 2016; Moreno, 2021; Olcon, 2020). Among many examples, this can include requiring that courses be taught in English, that certain services be offered, and that academic calendars be shifted to align with the home school's dates. The temptation to ask for these accommodations is understandable; it is much easier to offer program features that are attractive to students and courses that align easily with those on the home campus. At the same time, the negotiations that take place are typically asymmetrical, with little thought to those in the host country; they also tend to be apolitical and ahistorical, without consideration for power disparities and geopolitical tensions. By shifting the perspective, a decolonial approach can "find inspiration for de-centering the privileged traveler and rethinking the composition of the learning communities in education abroad contexts" (Adkins & Messerly, 2019, p. 75).

Working collaboratively with partners on the ground, one might consider adding curricular and co-curricular components that help students understand their host communities in new ways. In Florence, for instance, it is natural to include visits to the Uffizi and the Duomo, two important cultural and historical sites. Excursions might also be added to Prato, 20 minutes away and home to Italy's second largest Chinese community, or to a local migrant/immigration center serving immigrants from Sub-Saharan Africa. Doing so complicates students' understanding of the place, while also deconstructing notions of what represents "culture" in Italy. Even with more traditional activities, there is space to help students think critically about what they are consuming, down to the food itself. A pasta dinner in Italy easily elicits a conversation about where the ingredients stem from, with influences from the Middle East/North Africa (diffusion of pasta throughout Italy) and the Americas (origin of tomatoes). Likewise, one can discuss the ways Italian cuisine has been adapted in places like Eritrea, Ethiopia, and Somalia through Italian colonization, yielding dishes such as noodles that are served with *suugo suqaar*, an often meat-enriched, *xawaash*-spiced tomato sauce (Gebreyesus, 2020).

Despite the best intentions of being inclusive in terms of access to EA program while also taking a decolonizing approach in interactions with local actors and hosts, tensions will arise. Sometimes, institutions themselves might unintentionally come to be viewed as neo-colonizers. For example, housing may be provided by local providers who may or may not rely on binary rooming assignments. In such situations, asking a local partner to adopt the home institution's norms around gender identity and inclusion might be a way of imposing cultural norms in a setting in which they might conflict sharply with local norms. That said, although it is a complicated collection of issues, it is possible to discuss the needs of our students with local partners in a way that is respectful of local norms and approached as a problem to solve in a mutual manner. Nevertheless, there are cultural settings in which binary gender is still unquestionable and raising such a concern may do more harm than good—even potentially putting students' safety in jeopardy.

The on-the-ground experience involves many components, and so these examples provide a glimpse into the overall set of considerations that need to be considered. Importantly, they demonstrate a need to both help students reflect critically, using a decolonizing lens, while also finding ways to work with and respect local community members—something that allows program designers to model what they expect of their students.

GUIDING QUESTIONS:

- How is the program promoting participants' meaningful intercultural experiences?
- How are participating students being familiarized to the history, traditions, and social context of their host destination regarding issues of EDI?
- Are there any spaces for students to individually or collectively reflect/decompress?

Outcomes Assessment

Much good work has been done on outcomes assessment in EA, with the goal of not simply relying on anecdotal data to determine the success of programs and students in achieving stated outcomes. At the same time, this area of work remains largely an inward-looking endeavor, and one that seldom considers the impact (positive and negative) that EA might have on the host institution/community. Therefore, a program should also be evaluated to determine the extent to which faculty, staff, and students are integrated into and able to connect with a local community.

Assessment tools likewise present opportunities for reflection, thus continuing the work that takes place in predeparture and while on-site (see also Chapter 14 in this volume). Adding a related, open-ended question to a post-program evaluation can give students a chance to consider how their understanding of their host country evolved over the course of their program, thus both allowing for the student to be assessed, while also giving them a chance to reflect (and learn) even more (Ash & Clayton, 2009; Savicki & Price, 2015). Similarly, students might be prompted to contemplate their experiences through blogs, journals, and final projects, all of which can provide data for assessment (Savicki & Price, 2017).

At the same time, we may think more about the learning outcomes' key indicators that have come to be widely accepted in EA, such as around the goal of developing intercultural awareness and global citizenship. While scholarship and practices on ways to measure intercultural competencies are abundant, there is a general lack of focus on critiquing this outcome's definition. As Glass (2021) notes,

> It is not that debate about the normative ideals of globally competent graduates are unimportant. It is that such intense—and often exclusive—focus on normative aspects of global competence tend to obscure critical assumptions about whether changing individuals' beliefs and values through educational processes actually produces the world envisioned–or, more concerning, might even reproduce the geopolitical realities that education for global competence aims to address...we ignore our responsibilities if we challenge the content but not the 'hidden' structural frame shaping the discourse on global competence. (p. 170)

So, institutions need to go beyond simply stating that EA will increase a set of preconceived opinions of what constitutes the desired profile of an "interculturally competent" individual.

Global citizenship is equally elusive (Koyama, 2015) and, just as importantly, can pose a large risk of perpetuating colonial disparities by erasing history and placing the student (the "global citizen") above any local or national border—able to navigate and exercise their agency at a global scale. But as stated by Blanco (2021, p. 1): "Neither the global nor citizenship are neutral concepts, and both come with long histories of violence, oppression and exclusion." Therefore, EA programs should think carefully about the terminology they use. One possibility is to educate students as "global selves" (Killick, 2015), who are aware of their role, privilege, and position in the local landscape and also aware of the "global stratifications and inequities that prevent the idealized global citizenship of being viable in practice" (Koyama, 2015, p. 4).

Lastly, we might consider *who* is doing the assessment. Typically, assessments are conducted by faculty or staff, often on the home campus. Opportunities can exist for local community members to be involved in both the development of learning outcomes, as part of program design, and the actual assessment of students. Host families, internship or research supervisors, local students, and host country faculty, for example, might complete surveys or provide other types of input that can offer a 360 view on a student's progress. Who else would be more fitting to help to determine the extent to which a participant has learned to become adaptable, respectful of local norms and values, linguistically proficient, and, just as importantly, mindful of historical/political (post)colonial realities that shape the local landscape?

Assessment is often viewed in neutral terms, as a "scientific" and "objective" mechanism of evaluation. But, of course, no system is perfect, and the tools and terminology we use can be more harmful than good, particularly from a decolonization approach. Keeping this lens in mind is a good first step in drafting and revising assessment plans and in ultimately selecting tools for evaluation.

GUIDING QUESTIONS:

- What are the key indicators against which we assess a program's success? What are they measuring?
- How do we reconsider outcomes assessment, not just from the perspective of the home campus/students, yet also from the local community? Who is involved in both the establishment and the scope of program/learning outcomes?
- How is the partner institution/community included in the assessment process? Are they given the opportunity to provide feedback?

Conclusion

Throughout this chapter, and as a complement to other chapters in this volume that focus on inclusive excellence, we have highlighted the importance of establishing a decolonial approach to EA. This has included dissecting a sample of points along the EA process where faculty and staff can work to ensure that overseas programming is rooted in the self-awareness of the past and ongoing inequities and power imbalances. By sharing reflection questions, we hope this chapter assists scholars and practitioners in their individual and collective journey gesturing toward a decolonial future, toward an alternative path to engage globally "beyond the modern/colonial political, economic, social, intellectual, ecological and relational systems" (Stein & da Silva, 2020, p. 562).

In conclusion, we want to stress how decoloniality is a journey (Stein et al., 2021), not a destination. Decoloniality should not become just another fad in the evolution of theories and practices around international education. Following the important critique marshaled by Tuck and Yang (2012), it is imperative that we avoid trafficking in "decolonization" as simply a metaphor to describe a narrow set of pedagogical practices or curricular changes, as important as these issues may be. Indeed, within the United States alone, any claim to be "decolonizing" our educational practice will remain merely aspirational until traditional territories, government, and self-determination of native peoples are honored and restored through the recognition of treaties and in accordance with the 2007 United Nations Declaration on the Rights of Indigenous Peoples. To commit to decolonization as a normative ethic and imperative, therefore, requires that we be responsive to this agenda, both in relation to our program sites abroad, and to our host or sponsoring institutions—particularly when these are located in settler-colonial countries from the Anglo-American World.

This implies that our responsibility to and for oppressive power relations must extend beyond our students and immediate classroom dynamics to encapsulate a broader set of constituents to whom we are connected. It includes breaking from a more extractive model of teaching and knowledge production—a model that is common to the academy at large, and that is reproduced when students run the risk of appropriating local knowledge as part of a curated educational experience without meaningful consent, collaboration, or effort toward the articulation of mutual long-term benefit. Instead, we can proceed by allying ourselves with grassroots actors and communities, and by grounding our teaching, learning, and operational practices in the needs and priorities they identify. Doing so can allow us to leverage our educational programs and institutions to make modest contributions toward the broader transformation of our relationships to space, to place, and to one another—a project that includes our students and that, in its realization, holds transformative possibilities for the nature of education itself.

Acknowledgments

The authors would like to thank Roger Adkins, Clau Castaneda, and Geoffrey Boyce for their valuable insight in structuring the outline for this chapter. Their previous scholarly and experiential work in decolonization of EA also served as a basis for this text.

References

Absolon, K. (2019). Decolonizing education and educators' decolonizing. *Intersectionalities: A Global Journal of Social Work Analysis, Research, Polity, and Practice, 7*(1), 9–28.

Adkins, R., & Messerly, B. (2019). Toward decolonizing education abroad: Moving beyond the self/other dichotomy. In E. Brewer & A. C. Ogden (Eds.), *Education abroad and the undergraduate experience: Critical perspectives and approaches to integration with student learning and development* (pp. 73–94). Stylus Publishing, LLC.

Ash, S. L., & Clayton, P. H. (2009). Generating, deepening, and documenting learning: The power of critical reflection in applied learning. *Journal of Applied Learning in Higher Education, Fall,* 25–48.

Barros, S. R. (2016). Power, privilege, and study abroad as "spectacle." *Internationalizing Teaching and Teacher Education for Equity: Engaging Alternative Knowledges Across Ideological Borders, 57.*

Blanco, G. L. (2021). Global citizenship education as a pedagogy of dwelling: Re-tracing (mis)steps in practice during challenging times. *Globalisation, Societies and Education,* 1–11. https://doi.org/10.1080/14767724.2021.1899800

Bolen, M. (2001). Consumerism and US study abroad. *Journal of Studies in International Education, 5*(3), 182–200.

Breen, M. (2012). Privileged migration: American undergraduates, study abroad, academic tourism. *Critical Arts, 26*(1), 82–102.

Brewer, E., & Ogden, A. C. (Eds.). (2019). *Education abroad and the undergraduate experience: Critical perspectives and approaches to integration with student learning and development.* Stylus Publishing, LLC.

Charles, E. (2019). Decolonizing the curriculum. *Insights, 32,* 1–7. https://doi.org/10.1007/978-3-030-14284-1_5

Chaudhuri, A. (2016, March). The real meaning of Rhodes Must Fall. *The Guardian.*

Deardorff, D. K. (2014). Why engage in mobility? Key issues within global mobility: The big picture. In B. Streitwieser (Ed.), *Internationalisation of higher education and global mobility* (pp. 35–42). Symposium Books.

Deardorff, D. K., & Arasaratnam-Smith, L. A. (2017). *Intercultural competence in higher education: International approaches, assessment and application.* Routledge. https://doi.org/10.4324/9781315529257

Doerr, N. M., Puente, D., & Kamiyoshi, U. (2021). Global citizenship, identity and intercultural competence: Student identities in education abroad. In A. C. Ogden, B. Streitwieser, & C. Van Mol (Eds.), *Education abroad: Bridging scholarship and practice* (pp. 119–134). Routledge, Taylor & Francis Group.

Engel, L. C. (2017). *Underepresented students in US study abroad: Investigating impacts.* Institute of International Education.

Ficarra, J. M. (2017). Curating cartographies of knowledge: Reading institutional study abroad portfolio as text. *Frontiers: The Interdisciplinary Journal of Study Abroad, 29*(1), 1–14.

Ficarra, J. M. (2019). *Producing the global classroom: Exploring the impact of US study abroad on host communities in San Jose, Costa Rica and Florence, Italy*. Syracuse University.

Ficarra, J. M. (2021). Move over Medici!: Exploring the impact of US student power in Florence through host perspectives. In G. Malfatti (Ed.), *People-centered approaches toward the internationalization of higher education* (pp. 75–90). IGI Global.

Gandhi, L. (2019). *Postcolonial theory: A critical introduction*. Columbia University Press.

Gebreyesus, R. (2020, October). How colonialism brought a new evolution of pasta to East Africa. *KQED*.

George Mwangi, C. A., & Yao, C. W. (2021). US higher education internationalization through an equity-driven lens: An analysis of concepts, history, and research. *Higher Education: Handbook of Theory and Research, 36*, 549–609.

Glass, C. R. (2021). The hidden frame: National security, economic competitiveness, and the worldwide race for global competence. In J. J. Lee (Ed.), *U.S. power in international higher education* (pp. 170–186). Rutgers University Press.

Gopal, A. (2011). Internationalization of higher education: Preparing faculty to teach cross-culturally. *International Journal of Teaching and Learning in Higher Education, 23*(3), 373–381.

Gozik, N. J. (2015). Assessing study abroad: Closing the loop. In V. Savicki & E. Brewer (Eds.), *Assessing study abroad: Theories, tools, and practices* (pp. 57–82). Stylus.

Gozik, N. J., & Oguro, S. (2021). Program components: (Re)considering the role of individual areas of programming in education abroad. In A. C. Ogden, B. Streitwieser, & C. Van Mol (Eds.), *Education abroad: Bridging scholarship and practice* (pp. 59–72). Routledge, Taylor & Francis Group.

Institute of International Education (2020a). *OpenDoors 2020 fast facts*. https://opendoorsdata.org/fast_facts/fast-facts-2020/

Institute of International Education. (2020b). *Detailed duration of U.S. Study abroad 2005/06-2018/19*. Open Doors Report on International Educational Exchange. http://www.iie.org/opendoors

Jackson, J., Howard, M., & Schwieter, J. W. (2021). Language proficiency: Developmental perspectives and linguistic outcomes of education abroad. In A. C. Ogden, B. Streitwieser, & C. Van Mol (Eds.), *Education abroad: Bridging scholarship and practice* (pp. 92–105). Routledge, Taylor & Francis Group.

Killick, D. (2015). *Developing the global student: Higher education in an era of globalization*. Routledge, Taylor & Francis Group.

Koyama, J. P. (2015). The elusive and exclusive global citizen. In *UENSCO MGIEP* (Issue December). https:/www.researchgate.net/publication/293815119

Layne, P., Glasco, S., Gillespie, J., Gross, D., & Jasinski, L. (2020). #FacultyMatter: Faculty support and interventions integrated into global learning. In N. Namaste & A. Sturgill (Eds.), *Mind the gap: Global learning at home and abroad* (pp. 135–147). Stylus.

Leal, F. G., & Moraes, M. C. B. (2018). Decoloniality as epistemology for the theoretical field of the internationalization of higher education. *Education Policy Analysis Archives, 26*, 87.

Lee, J. A., & Green, Q. (2016). Unique opportunities: Influence of study abroad on Black students. *Frontiers: The Interdisciplinary Journal of Study Abroad, 28*(1), 61–77. https://doi.org/10.36366/frontiers.v28i1.380

Lee, J. J. (2021). *U.S. power in international higher education*. Rutgers University Press. https://doi.org/9781978820784

Lörz, M., Netz, N., & Quast, H. (2016). Why do students from underprivileged families less often intend to study abroad? *Higher Education, 72*(2), 153–174. https://doi.org/10.1007/s10734-015-9943-1

Manning, S., Frieders, Z., & Bikos, L. (2020). When does global learning begin? Recognizing the value of student experiences prior to study away. In N. Namaste & A. Sturgill (Eds.), *Mind the gap: Global learning at home and abroad* (pp. 43–54). Stylus.

McKeown, J. S., Celaya, M. L., & Ward, H. H. (2021). Academic developing: The impact of education abroad on students as learners. In A. C. Ogden, B. Streitwieser, & C. Van Mol (Eds.), *Education abroad: Bridging scholarship and practice* (pp. 77–91). Routledge, Taylor & Francis Group.

Michelson, K., & Álvarez Valencia, J. A. (2016). Study abroad: Tourism or education? A multimodal social semiotic analysis of institutional discourses of a promotional website. *Discourse & Communication, 10*(3), 235–256.

Miller-Idriss, C., Friedman, J. Z., & Auerbach, J. (2019). Jumping, horizon gazing, and arms wide: Marketing imagery and the meaning of study abroad in the USA. *Higher Education, 78*(6), 1091–1107.

Moll, L. C., Amanti, C., Neff, D., & Gonzalez, N. (1992). Funds of knowledge for teaching: Using a qualitative approach to connect homes and classrooms. *Theory into Practice, 31*(2), 132–141.

Moreno, R. (2021). Disrupting Neoliberal and neocolonial ideologies in US study abroad: From discourse to intervention. *Frontiers: The Interdisciplinary Journal of Study Abroad, 33*(2), 93–109.

Murray Brux, J., & Fry, B. (2010). Multicultural students in study abroad: Their interests, their issues, and their constraints. *Journal of Studies in International Education, 14*(5), 508–527.

Netz, N., Klasik, D., Entrich, S. R., & Barker, M. (2020). Socio-demographics: A global overview of inequalities in education abroad participation. In A. C. Ogden, B. Streitwieser, & C. Van Mol (Eds.), *Education abroad: Bridging scholarship and practice* (pp. 28–42). Routledge, Taylor & Francis Group.

Nordmeyer, K., Bedera, N., & Teig, T. (2016). Ending white saviorism in study abroad. *Contexts, 15*(4), 78–79.

O'Toole, L. (2018). *The political cultures of american study abroad initiatives in Latin America and Spain* [Doctoral dissertation]. The University of Arizona.

Ogden, A. C. (2008). The view from the veranda: Understanding today's colonial students. *Frontiers: The Interdisciplinary Journal of Study Abroad, 15*, 35–55.

Olcon, K. (2020). Confronting whiteness: White US social work students' experiences studying abroad in West Africa. *Journal of Teaching in Social Work, 40*(4), 318–335.

Onyenekwu, I., Angeli, J. M., Pinto, R., & Douglas, T.-R. (2017). (Mis) Representation among US study abroad programs traveling to the African continent: A critical content analysis of a teach abroad program. *Frontiers: The Interdisciplinary Journal of Study Abroad, 29*(1), 68–84.

Salinas, C. (2020). The Complexity of the "x" in Latinx: How Latinx/a/o students relate to, identify with, and understand the term Latinx. *Journal of Hispanic Higher Education, 19*(2), 149–168. https://doi.org/10.1177/1538192719900382

Savicki, V., & Price, M. V. (2015). Student reflective writing: Cognition and affect before, during, and after study abroad. *Journal of College Student Development, 56*(6), 587–601.

Savicki, V., & Price, M. V. (2017). Components of reflection: A longitudinal analysis of study abroad student blog posts. *Frontiers: The Interdisciplinary Journal of Study Abroad, 29*(2), 51–62.

Smith, L. T. (2013). *Decolonizing methodologies: Research and indigenous peoples*. Zed Books Ltd.

Stein, S. (2018). Confronting the racial-colonial foundations of US higher education. *Journal for the Study of Postsecondary and Tertiary Education, 3*, 77–96.

Stein, S., Ahenakew, C., Jimmy, E., Andreotti, V., Valley, W., Amsler, S., Calhoun, B., & The Gesturing Towards Decolonial Futures Collective. (2021). *Developing stamina for decolonizing higher education: A workbook for non-indigenous people.* https://higheredotherwise.net/resources/

Stein, S., Andreotti, V. D. O., SuŽa, R., Amsler, S., Hunt, D., Ahenakew, C., Jimmy, E., Cajkova, T., Valley, W., Cardoso, C., Siwek, D., Pitaguary, B., D'Emilia, D., Pataxó, U., Calhoun, B., & Okano, H. (2020). Gesturing towards decolonial futures. *Nordic Journal of Comparative and International Education (NJCIE), 4*(1), 43–65. https://doi.org/10.7577/njcie.3518

Stein, S., & da Silva, J. E. (2020). Challenges and complexities of decolonizing internationalization in a time of global crises. *ETD-Educação Temática Digital, 22*(3), 546–566.

Sweeney, K. (2013). Inclusive excellence and underrepresentation of students of color in study abroad. *Frontiers: The Interdisciplinary Journal of Study Abroad, 23*(1), 1–21.

The Forum on Education Abroad. (2015). *Standards of good practice for education abroad.* The Forum on Education Abroad. https://forumea.org/wp-content/uploads/2014/08/Standards-2015.pdf

Thondhlana, J., Abdulrahman, H., Chiyevo Garwe, E., & McGrath, S. (2021). Exploring the internationalization of Zimbabwe's higher education institutions through a decolonial lens: Postcolonial continuities and disruptions. *Journal of Studies in International Education, 25*(3), 228–246. https://doi.org/10.1177/1028315320932319

Tiessen, R., Roy, P., Karim-Haji, F., & Gough, R. (2018). Expanding our understanding of ethical considerations in north-south student mobility programs: Insights for improved institutional practice. *Journal of Global Citizenship & Equity Education, 6*(1), 1–21.

Trilokekar, R. D. (2021). International education as soft power: A history of changing governments, shifting rationales, and lessons learned. In J. J. Lee (Ed.), *U.S. power in international higher education* (pp. 23–41). Rutgers University Press. https://doi.org/10.36019/9781978820814-002

Tuck, E., & Yang, K. W. (2012). Decolonization is not a metaphor. *Decolonization: Indigeneity, Education & Society, 1*(1), 1–40.

Whatley, M. (2017). Financing study abroad: An exploration of the influence of financial factors on student study abroad patterns. *Journal of Studies in International Education, 21*(5), 431–449. https://doi.org/10.1177/1028315317697798

Wick, D., Willis, T. Y., Rivera, J., Lueker, E., & Hernandez, M. (2019). Assets-based learning abroad: First-generation Latinx college students leveraging and increasing community cultural wealth in Costa Rica. *Frontiers: The Interdisciplinary Journal of Study Abroad, 31*(2 SE-Research Articles). https://doi.org/10.36366/frontiers.v31i2.455

Wiers-Jenssen, J., Tillman, M., & Matherly, C. (2021). Employability: How education abroad impacts the transition to graduate employment. In A. C. Ogden, B. Streitwieser, & C. Van Mol (Eds.), *Education abroad: Bridging scholarship and practice* (pp. 135–150). Routledge, Taylor & Francis Group.

Wilson, C. (2021). *Revolutionizing my syllabus: The process.* https://www.brynmawr.edu/inside/academic-information/research/centers-institutes/teaching-learning-institute/creating-rethinking-syllabi-open-learning/revolutionizing-my-syllabus-process

Woolf, M. (2007). Impossible things before breakfast: Myths in education abroad. *Journal of Studies in International Education, 11*(3–4), 496–509.

Woolf, M. (2021). Coda. In J. Christian, M. Woolf, C. Colon, A. Gristwood, & S. Parker (Eds.), *Empires of the mind? (Post)Colonialism and decolonizing education abroad. CAPA Occasional Publication Series, Paper No. 9* (pp. 190–197). CAPA: The Global Education Network.

Zemach-Bersin, T. (2010). Selling the world: Study abroad marketing and the privatization of global citizenship. In *The handbook of practice and research in study abroad* (pp. 325–342). Routledge.

10

Flickers of Difference: Living and Learning with Others through Inclusive Classroom Projects

Neriko Musha Doerr and Yuri Kumagai

Introduction

How could we make global education more meaningfully inclusive? This chapter tackles the question by moving away from conventional categories such as race, gender, or class that treat these categories in rigid and often binary ways. Instead, we suggest a new approach to difference and inclusiveness that incorporates fluidity, layeredness, and even contradictions. We suggest a new concept, "flickers of difference"—a notion that understands difference as situated, relative, and layered that emerges in a specific moment in combination with and at the intersections of various axes of commonality and difference (e.g., difference of the first born and the baby that becomes significant only in relation to each other and only when it is discussed in that manner, whereas the same two people can be seen as "same" in terms of race or class in other situations) building on the framework of multiscalar networks that sees an individual to be connected to diverse networks of people and viewpoints, some of them may contradict with each other (Çağlar & Glick

Schiller, 2017). We call for encouraging students to investigate what has shaped a specific and contextual difference within a flexible framework of inclusivity that can be applied in a wide array of global learning contexts, including education abroad.

We illustrate such practices by drawing on two classroom projects: one engaging in dialogue with someone holding an opposite point of view on a topic, which may even be considered offensive or hateful, and the other discussing diverse readings of signs from another country, including interpretations that are incorrect in light of the intended message. By examining these projects, we demonstrate the benefits of inclusive classroom practices for the students as well as teachers. While both of these cases are based in U.S. classrooms, they offer much that can be applied to the context of education abroad, helping to expand and reconsider existing practices.

This chapter suggests ways to move away from a conventional binary view of difference in education abroad represented in the notion of "immersion," which conceptually separates students' home and host societies, in favor of more flexible notions of relationality and multiscalar networks (Çağlar & Glick Schiller, 2017). We suggest that education abroad instead use notions that are more conducive to student learning, in any moment of experiencing and engaging with difference, to identify commonality in other aspects, understand what has shaped our interlocutors' viewpoints through dialogue, examine one's own assumptions, and learn to relate to diverse individuals. Through the process, students learn about the complexity of individuals and the connections they forge with others. In short, we suggest a framework of inclusive practice rooted in living with and learning from difference.

Exploring Inclusive Classrooms in Global Education

Diverse understandings of global education exist, from learning to take responsibility for sustainability in environmental, social, and ethical terms on a global scale (Haigh, 2008), to elites learning to become cosmopolitans working for a collective good (Torres, 2015). Shared is the understanding that education abroad occupies the central place in global education, as a "living laboratory" that pushes students to get involved in the holistic learning process via border-crossing on "every level – intellectual, psychological, and emotional" (Laubscher, 1994, p. xiv).

Nonetheless, Doerr (2017) has argued elsewhere the importance of broadening our definition of "global education." Drawing on the notion of "regimes of mobility" (Glick Schiller & Salazar, 2013), which points out the double standard in the depiction of global mobility—whereas those in privileged positions (e.g., often White, middle or upper class professionals or education abroad students) are celebrated as "global citizens," while others (e.g., non-White, lower class immigrants or refugees) are often viewed with suspicion as "illegal"—Doerr (2012, 2017, 2020) has suggested the need to consider and value all cross-border learning. While Doerr has previously focused specifically on shedding light on the skills and competence of students with minority and immigrant backgrounds, this chapter expands the scope of difference to that of political viewpoints (first project) and the reading of signs in a linguistic landscape (second project).

Strategies for providing global perspectives to the classroom are not new. It is now nearly 20 years since "Internationalization at Home" as a concept first emerged in Europe, focusing on the integration of international/cultural dimensions into formal and informal curricula for domestic learning environments (Beelen & Jones, 2015). This chapter adds deeper theoretical footing to the rationale for inclusive practices at home: In addition to recognizing other kinds of differences, we also argue for the need to see these differences as fluid and layered, that is, what we refer to as "flickers of difference." Moving away from a model whereby teachers decide what constitutes productive and useful diversity (Fender, 1997), the class projects described in this chapter encourage students to engage even with what are often dismissed as "uncritical" or "incorrect" viewpoints so they can understand and work together to improve society.

In the United States, where education abroad continues to prevail in global education (Beelen & Jones, 2015), this chapter offers an alternative kind of program that can be introduced before, during, and after education abroad, or serve as an alternative for students not going overseas. Considering diverse cross-border learning, such as through classroom projects that focus on negotiating difference in political opinion (first project) and on analyzing linguistic landscapes of another language (second project), the projects described here encourage students to engage in dialogue with diverse viewpoints and negotiate with them, aiming at fostering inclusive practices anywhere.

In short, this chapter offers inclusivity to global education in terms of the kind of difference (i.e., beyond national, cultural, race, etc.), the degree of difference (i.e., even "uncritical" and "incorrect" ones) as well as the understanding of difference (i.e., fluid and layered) through our notion of "flickers of difference." This notion also adds to the discussion of education in general as well (see later in this chapter).

Inclusive Classrooms

Inclusiveness in education abroad fits into a much broader literature on strategies for promoting greater access to education. This topic has been investigated in at least two ways. On the one hand, those who view schooling as an equalizer, which provides knowledge needed to succeed in the society, seek to widen access to "success" in education. The Head Start program in the United States, for example, was designed to provide children from low socioeconomic backgrounds with the skills needed to succeed in school, with an understanding that these are not always provided at home. Although well meaning, this position assumes that the "knowledge needed" is something neutral, rendering those who lack it as deficient; in short, it fails to acknowledge the knowledge that these students do already have (Doerr, 2020). Similarly in education abroad, seeking to increase minority group participation risks suggesting they are deficient in skills such as "intercultural competence," a learning outcome commonly stated for education abroad, if their intercultural competence gained through other means, such as immigration to the United States or living in a bilingual household, is ignored (Doerr, 2020). On the other hand, those who view schooling as reproducing inequality seek inclusiveness in what is considered "legitimate" knowledge, arguing that such constructions are based on what the dominant group members in the society already have and view as important, giving advantage to the dominant group members and reproducing a structure of dominance (Bourdieu & Passeron, 1977).

There are several ways this way of thinking has been challenged, with the ultimate goal of making schooling inclusive to all students, not only in participation but also in success. Multicultural education has sought to expand what is considered legitimate knowledge in schools, as well as how students should learn (D'Amato, 1993). Although there are various practices (Kincheloe & Steinberg, 1997), multicultural education in general "recodes practices represented as "deficiencies" as "distinctive learning styles" and as "strengths upon which to build." It validates students' experiences and "cultural referents" as worthy of classroom study and activity (Olneck, 2000, p. 324). Nonetheless, the school's power over deciding what constitutes legitimate knowledge and learning practices remains the same (Olneck, 2000).

Whiteness studies advocate investigating the cultural invisibility of what is considered legitimate knowledge, revealing that it is based on the dominant group's worldviews, not "neutral" or "universal" knowledge (Baldwin, 1984; Frankenberg, 1997; Hooks, 1992; Roediger, 1991). Though this work has come later than multicultural education (McIntyre, 1997), it has provided a strong rationale for the further development of the latter.

Regarding education abroad, these first two approaches mean questioning cultural bias in the "desired" outcome for overseas study, that is, who decides what (e.g., "global competence") and how (e.g., through immersion) to gain it. This chapter suggests subverting such biases by exploring other possibilities through engaging in dialogue with those with different political viewpoints (first project) or with different interpretations of linguistic signs (second project).

While the first two approaches render schools as places of knowledge to be imparted to students thus reproducing status quo, Freire (1970) argues that education should ultimately be about transforming society, offering what he calls "problem-posing" education. Freire, and the advocates of the Critical Pedagogy inspired by him, value knowledge held by both teachers and students and urge all participants to share their knowledge in working together to transform the society for the better (Giroux, 2007). This approach values all types of knowledge and not just that represented in curricula, multicultural, or otherwise.

Building on these approaches, if also critiquing them at times, this chapter offers a new way to frame experience of "difference" in general, which can be also applied to the education abroad context. The following sections introduce several theoretical frameworks toward that end.

Multiscalar Networks

The approaches surveyed previously assume the supremacy of the categories they use—such as race or class or their specific combinations—treating them as the defining life experience of the individual. The notion of multiscalar networks (Çağlar & Glick Schiller, 2017) challenges this monolithic, somewhat coherent model of individuals. Çağlar and Glick Schiller (2017) argue that individuals develop diverse networks of people, and with it, knowledge and viewpoints, based on their various subject positions, which can be traced along multiple scales, such as ethnic, business, political, religious, and neighborhood, hence the term "multiscalar." Importantly, any of these networks may overlap or contradict each other. At the same time, this model does not rest with individuals alone—the intersectionality of their subject positions—and focuses on connections, or networks, forged through each subject position (Çağlar & Glick Schiller, 2017). Through these networks, individuals' lives are crisscrossed with diverse convictions and social interactions.

In the context of education abroad, the notion of multiscalar networks allows us to move away from a binary view of culture that portrays students' experience as jumping into the life of "cultural Other" through immersion. Instead, we can investigate diverse ways students connect with people through their similarities and differences at several levels. For example, Doerr (2020) has documented elsewhere how a group of students who studied abroad in Sierra Leone related to the people there by drawing on various networks/subject positions—Muslims, non-White, and from developing countries—permitting students to seek commonalities with those in their host country, while also moving past more simplistic notions of what constitutes Sierra Leonean culture. Unlike cultural binary models, this approach conceptualizes encounters in education abroad as individuals with diverse subject positions relating to others through networks these subject positions afford.

Noticing (Cultural) Difference

Not all networks get noticed and highlighted. For example, McDermott and Varenne (1995) argue that, in the society where everyone uses sign language, being unable to hear is not considered a disability or even difference because nobody would notice who can or cannot hear. It is not the physical makeup of the ear but the sociocultural environment in which verbal communication prevails that "disables" deaf people, rendering them "different." What we consider "difference"—race, class, and so on—are then merely some of many differences (e.g., blood type, the shape of a toe) that have come to be highlighted in our current sociocultural environment. This perspective pushes us to investigate the wider sociocultural contexts that make us notice a particular difference—in education abroad, "cultural difference."

What difference is considered "cultural" is also arbitrary though can have a significant impact. Doerr (2013) shows that in a study abroad program, when keeping pornographic magazines or not saying "please" were seen as not cultural but mere youthful bad behavior, they were punished; whereas when putting wet laundry in their room to dry or refusing to eat nonspicy food were considered as cultural differences, they were welcomed more positively as "cultural learning" moments and accommodated by host families. This is despite that appropriateness of keeping pornography may differ culturally, for example, seen as a male biological need in Japan (Luschmann, 2019), or how some languages do not have a separate word like "please" to show politeness (Doerr, 2013).

We thus need to question taken-for-granted "cultural difference" in education abroad and instead investigate what made us notice the difference and see it as (not) "cultural" by shifting our attention to wider discourses and structural setups.

Flickers of Difference

Although the notion of multiscalar networks allows us to see complexity of the individual and the analysis of sociocultural conditions that diversely push us to notice certain differences allows us to relativize differences, the category in question can still be perceived rigidly, for example, a network of "Koreans" based on a nation-state ideology that highlights national difference. To move away from this rigid conceptualization, this chapter draws on the work of Volosinov (1973), who argues that the meaning of individual words cannot be grasped in a stable form, such as a fixed term that appears in a dictionary, because the meaning emerges only when a conversation occurs. Rather, it is more like we only see light (i.e., meaning of the word) when the light switch is turned on (i.e., during a conversation), although the meaning of the word draws on a legacy of earlier utterances. Similarly, in talking about differences, we suggest moving away from static categories and instead view the notion of difference as something that emerges and gets noticed in specific contexts (see Doerr, 2018), which are nonetheless built on wider structural arrangements, historically and in the present. We call this new way of seeing difference as "flickers of difference."

In the context of education abroad, we urge students to focus on the specific flicker of difference and analyze on what axis of difference in the multiscalar networks it is located (e.g., "woman" connection is situated in the axis of gender differences), what sociocultural and structural arrangement pushed them to notice that axis of difference, and what specific context allowed that flicker of difference to emerge. Moving away from a home-host society binary with their associated "cultures" assumed in the notion of "immersion," students can instead investigate the flickers of difference they see in their encounters with others. Students then can think about education abroad experiences as constituted through multiscalar networks that stretch across the globe and sociocultural environments that make them matter.

Inclusivity Beyond Judgment

One remaining issue in this approach is the treatment of difference that is rendered problematic. The third educational approach discussed earlier, Freirean Critical Pedagogy, often rejects "uncritical" knowledge in classrooms, Anderson (2000) critiques. We suggest applying the notion of cultural relativism to such differences seen as "uncritical" or "incorrect" in the spirit of inclusive practices. Cultural relativism suggests that the observer tries to understand others' practice in its original context rather than applying our own cultural standard to judge it, based on the understanding that our ways are not better than others, though there are some issues as discussed (Abu-Loghod, 2002). The two projects introduced below are applications of this approach in classrooms.

Project 1: Living with Difference

The first project was aimed at nurturing student skills to live with difference and carried out by Doerr in an *Introduction to Anthropology* class in fall 2018 and spring 2019 at a public, liberal arts college of approximately 6,000 students in the Northeastern United States. This project could be translated to an education abroad program, before, during, or upon students' return.

Doerr introduced the project in order to show students theories such as cultural relativism are not only reserved for classroom learning but should be applied to daily life, in all of its complexity; that "difference" exists in a myriad of forms even though race, gender, and class were often the primary focus of the discussions; and that one does not have to study abroad to learn to live with difference. It is important to have opportunities for students to acknowledge this latter point in a college where education abroad is promoted yet not everyone can participate. Moreover, learning to reach out to those with different viewpoints can be fruitful where such conversations either often become too emotional or are avoided altogether.

For the project, students were tasked with identifying one person they knew (e.g., a relative, neighbor) with opposite views from them on a particular topic (e.g., immigration, Black Lives Matter, abortion) and to interview them about their views and how their background may have helped to shape their perspectives. Students asked themselves the same questions, exploring what shaped their own views. They also had to connect their discussion to one class reading to deepen their analysis, as well as suggest one workshop that could encourage conversations between those with different viewpoints, in order to apply their class learning to the "real world" (for details, see Doerr, 2022).

Before starting the project, the class discussed the complexity of cultural relativism, that is, what we consider "cultural" is arbitrary and the act of labeling something cultural itself has loaded effects as mentioned. Calling political standpoints "cultural" is a conscious act of being inclusive about what can be "culturally relativist" (Doerr, 2013). Students investigated how their interviewee's as well as their own subject positions influenced their views, as encouraged in the aforementioned Critical Pedagogy (Giroux, 2007), and questioned what is "normal" to them, as advocated by Whiteness studies (Baldwin, 1984; Frankenberg, 1997; Hooks, 1992; Roediger, 1991).

The class also discussed the fact that it may not be possible to be fully culturally relativistic, as it is necessary to take a stand against some practices such as genocide. How to do so was the issue. The class watched a documentary, *Accidental Courtesy* (Ornstein & Ornstein, 2016), in which an African American musician and activist, Daryl Davis, talks with the leaders of White supremacist groups. Through dialogue that humanizes his interlocutors (rather than shunning them as "ignorant" or "stupid"), Davis challenges White supremacist ideology and practices, which causes his interlocutors to leave their organizations. This was the goal of the project—to engage in conversation with the different view, even problematic ones, to collaboratively transform society for the better.

Each student presented their work in class and the entire class discussed the topic. At times, conversations became heated, triggered by a student's presentation. The exchange of ideas allowed for a good illustration of how to promote inclusive practices in the classroom—inclusive of kinds of "differences," diverse viewpoints even "uncritical" ones, and the venue in which we are expected to encounter "differences" (i.e., beyond the education abroad context).

The following are two cases chosen because of their contrasting conditions. Data are drawn from students' final papers. (Pseudonyms are used to retain students' anonymity.)

John: Connecting Despite Opposition

In the first case, John interviewed his father with whom he had been estranged after revealing that he is gay. For this assignment, John met with his father twice to discuss the issues of gun control and the Black Lives Matter movement. He carefully chose public venues for the sake of his "safety in case [his father's] anger became uncontrollable." This concern over safety shows how some political issues are so divisive that even talking about them can cause emotional outbursts. At the same time, his case also shows how such division can nonetheless be managed, hence the importance of conversation and inclusive practices. All students were told not to risk their personal safety for the sake of completing the project; if they felt unsafe, they were instructed to end the interview right away and that they would not be penalized for doing so.

In his first meeting, focused on gun control, John was "taken aback" when his father said that school shootings are the State's fault and not due to loose gun control laws. John tried not to show his anger and ended the interview. To make sense of the first conversation, John drew on a class reading on social constructions of masculinity (Pascoe, 2009) and analyzed how his father's upbringing affected his views:

> My father grew up in the time when boys played with toys guns and dirt and girls helped out with motherly things and had dolls. This is why I believe that my father believes in so much in being entitled to the 2nd amendments rights to bear arms even though, he himself doesn't even own one... I thought somewhere in his 61 years he would have begun to see the change and how society is moving forward, but he just wants to stay in the past.

Although John understood that his father is largely shaped by earlier social norms, he also recognized that his father has chosen not to adapt to societal changes.

A month later, John met with his father again and raised the issue of the Black Lives Matter movement (Coates, 2020). Holding back his tears because he "cared so much about [the cause]," John challenged his father who asserted that police brutality is "fake news" and "a hoax." This caused his father to shut down and become very upset, "believ[ing] that he [had] raised me wrong." John's father appeared to feel that he could have better shaped his son's opinions, leading to a sense of failed parenting and betrayal, John analyzed.

John reported that the project had some positive effects:

> This project although upsetting my father, did bring us back together and reconnect for the first time since my mother passed away. It was difficult for me to talk to him-but I felt that during this project we somehow grew closer since I was starting to learn about his views ... this was a great start.

Based on his experience, though not directly, John suggested a workshop in which participants would begin by reaching consensus on some topic, for example, on a favorite sports team, to help foster "a more open mindset" on both sides. This suggests, first, that being open to different perspectives depends on one's relationship to another person, not on the viewpoint itself. Accordingly, an inclusive environment needs to start with the fostering of good relationships. Second, it also implies that one may disagree with someone about one topic yet may agree on others. It can thus help to start by looking for commonalities, that is, points of connection, rather than immediately jumping to demonize the "other." This is exactly what Davis did with White supremacist leaders in his documentary.

Inclusive classrooms based on acceptance of diverse viewpoints start with seeing each other as complex individuals with multiple subject positions and perspectives, some of which may be shared—an aspect discussed with the notion of multiscalar networks—which may manifest itself as connections as well as difference in a specific moment, as we have described as "flickers of difference." Focusing on shared connections can help avoid binary "us versus them" confrontations and instead encourage meaningful dialogue.

Rose: Learning from Oppositions

Rose had a positive relationship with her father whom she interviewed about gun control. Her father wants less gun control for the following reasons: the existence of the Second Amendment to the U.S. Constitution, which protects the individual right to keep and bear arms; a belief that gun violence is caused because of a person, not the gun; and a conviction that gun control legislation is ineffective as criminals can procure weapons illegally. His views were shaped by having grown up hunting and later serving in the U.S. Marine Corps and working as a police officer and a firearms instructor at the police academy.

Rose grew up around guns but never liked hunting due to a love of animals, which led her to become vegetarian. Learning about gun violence and growing up with social media shaped her views on gun control legislation: Only law enforcement and the military should have access to assault rifles and there should be pre-purchase training on gun use and mental health checks.

Neither side changed their views through this project, but Rose commented repeatedly that she learned much from the interview because her father is knowledgeable about the topic. This suggests one's respect for the interviewee's expertise is important in making the dialogue productive. Drawing on class readings (Appadurai, 1990; Lassiter, 2014), Rose felt that their shared family connection allowed her and her father to have "common ground to speak on," while exposure to different aspects of the same cultural environment created difference: experience versus social media.

Inclusive Practices in Education Abroad: From Living with Difference Project

Both cases suggested that, when people with different viewpoints engage in dialogue, it is important that they can relate with each other at some level. In education abroad, we can apply this framework and urge students to focus on commonality beyond "cultural difference." Questioning not only the "cultural" explanations but also the assumption of its monopoly over difference and its static aspect, we urge education abroad students to use aforementioned frameworks of multiscalar networks and "flickers of difference" to focus on specific layered difference emerged contextually.

This is not to ignore differences but contextualize them and understand how these differences emerge and be recognized as such. We suggest students do so through dialogue with the interlocutor, understanding the specificity of intersecting axes of difference, connecting the difference to wider structural arrangements, and investigating the interlocutors' as well as their own viewpoints. Applying inclusive practices in education abroad necessitates moving away from binary thinking in favor of multiple and more flexible reasoning.

Project 2: Inclusive Practices in Multiple Linguistic Landscape Interpretations

The second project that can be adapted before, during, or after education abroad was conducted by Kumagai in a second-year, Japanese-as-a-foreign-language classroom in spring 2018 and 2019 at a women's college of 2,600 students in Massachusetts known for progressive education. The project, "Cities in Japan: Linguistic Landscapes" (LL Project hereafter), took advantage of linguistic landscapes as sociocultural "texts" for students of Japanese language to sharpen their "critical language awareness" (Fairclough, 2014), aimed at transforming society to become more inclusive by exploring actual language-in-space and thus permitting students to understand how language is integrated within broader social structures. The results included multiple interpretations of signage that one would see on a city street and illuminated the sociocultural assumptions of the sign readers, including both students and instructors. This is a kind of outcome useful for global education, as explored here.

Linguistic landscapes are defined by Landry and Bourhis (1997) as:

> The language of public road signs, advertising billboards, street names, place names, commercial shop signs, and public signs on government buildings combine to form the linguistic landscape of a given territory, region or urban agglomeration. (p. 25)

By applying the notion of linguistic landscapes to language education, Shohamy and Waksman (2009) argue that it provides a rich context for learning how language is employed to construct and manipulate meanings and how it is implicated in histories, cultural relations, and politics. There are further educational effects such as "symbolic competence" (Kramsch, 2011), multicompetence, critical language awareness, multimodal literacy skills, and multilingual communication. By walking down the street, taking pictures of various signs, categorizing these images, and analyzing the results, learners engaged in *linguistic landscape* projects become "language detectives" (Sayer, 2009) or "urban geographers" (Malinowski, 2010). This process imbues students with agency: They are no longer merely "learners" but also co-"investigators."

Cities in Japan: Linguistic Landscape Project

The LL Project aimed at providing students with an opportunity to analyze issues such as what languages and other semiotics are used on signs, what functions each of them play, what such signs suggest about the community, and what power relationships among the different languages can be extrapolated through a critical "reading" of signs in Japan. Although this project was conducted in a classroom, it would in fact fit better in an education abroad setting by allowing for a more contextually nuanced analysis of signs, with access to other semiotics: relationships to other signs, people, sounds, and smells in the given space. Without going abroad, nearby larger metropolitan areas may serve as an alternative by offering various languages as a part of the cityscape, especially in some streets/blocks with a concentration of stores targeting specific linguistic groups. However, if such a linguistic landscape is not accessible, as was the case here, Google Street View suffices.

A total of 16 (spring 2018) and 18 (spring 2019) students with diverse backgrounds participated in the LL Project. The professor (Kumagai) and the teaching assistant who co-taught the course were born and raised in Japan. In groups of two to three, students were instructed to choose a city and select 10 signs that capture their interest, including at least three that they deemed to be "incomprehensible." The signs were analyzed using a critical literacy framework of decoding and describing, meaning-making, evaluating, and critiquing, and transforming. Students presented their findings in class, wrote an analytical essay, and created a multimodal page on WordPress.

Being influenced by the (still) prevalent "native speaker" ideology in the field of foreign language education, teachers' and/or "native" language users' interpretations may be considered "correct." However, challenging such a premise is the very essence of critical pedagogy and critical literacy. Being inclusive of multiple interpretations and aware that these interpretations are shaped by sign-readers' background, thus, were essential aspects of the LL Project.

Various features of the project required students to negotiate different interpretations and to self-reflect on what led them to particular conclusions, including group discussions, multiple class presentations with feedback, and multiple check-in meetings with the instructors. Drawing on students' final multimodal essay on WordPress, post-project questionnaires, and individual interviews, the project provided both students and teachers with an opportunity to engage with diverse interpretations, leading all participants to recognize their own "blind spots" concerning socioculturally sanctioned norms. Such a recognition is essential for practicing inclusive practices in two ways: (1) having students learn from each other (Angela and So-Yun's case) and (2) having teachers learn from students (Sara's case) (see also Kumagai, 2018; Kumagai & Takahashi, 2018; Kumagai & Takahashi, forthcoming).

Students learning from each other: "If you see like a big fish, what does it mean?" (Angela & So-Yun)

The discussions about the sign for the "Pufferfish Restaurant" analyzed by Angela and So-Yun shows how students appreciated each other's diverging interpretations and learned from their peers. Angela identified herself as "European American" (as students were asked not to simply list "White") from Kentucky, while So-Yun identified herself as Korean, while noting that she had spent her kindergarten years in Japan and then lived in Korea until coming to the United States for college. With Google Street View, they explored streets in Shibuya, Tokyo, and selected the Pufferfish Restaurant sign that features a massive three-dimensional figure of a pufferfish head, jutting out of the building. There was no writing accompanying the sculpture (Figure 10.1).

In the final essay posted on the WordPress, they wrote the following in Japanese (translated by Kumagai):

> Angela, an American, saw this type of sign for the first time in her life. Because, in the West, there is no sign with a big figure of seafood like this, when she saw this pufferfish sign, she thought there would be foreigners who think the sign is for an aquarium or for a pet shop specialized with fish, rather than for a restaurant. However, other foreigners do have a different idea. So-Yun, who lived in Korea and Japan, has seen many signs like this. So, she understands immediately that it is for a restaurant. If you know Japanese dietary life, which includes much seafood, people may understand the sign easily.

Here, Angela and So-Yun wrote their differing interpretations of the sign and reasons why they came to the interpretations: past experiences ("has/has not seen") and knowledge about customs ("dietary life"). This highlights the importance of having knowledge of the sociocultural context in which a sign was situated in order to make sense of the sign: signs "with a big figure of seafood" are quite common in Japan (and in South Korea, according to So-Yun). During the interview, Angela stated:

Fig. 10.1 "Pufferfish Restaurant". © the author.

> It was a shock when I saw this; when I had no context for it, so I didn't know what to think. If you see like a big fish, what does it mean? [...] I have no idea what the cultural perspective on it was, 'cause I had never seen a sign like that before [...] I literally thought it was an aquarium or fish pet shop. Because first of all, food signs in America aren't realistically represented and this is like an upgraded sized version of a realistic animal. Like Red Lobster in America, it's like a silhouette of a lobster; it's just a red outline; it's not detailed or like 3D. Well, people who are cultured in America doesn't put that much effort into things like that... It looks like an exhibit, probably that's why I thought aquarium 'cause it's a realistic representation. It doesn't scream 'eat me!'

If Angela had been in Shibuya and encountered this sign within a larger semiotic landscape, she might have been able to realize that it was for a restaurant. Analyzing a sign uni-dimensionally on a computer screen poses more difficulty. Yet, her interpretation was based on her own socioculturally acquired logic and expectations. Indeed, if the same sign were placed in the United States, it could well be for an aquarium or for a pet shop selling fish.

Angela and So-Yun concluded their essay with the following statement:

> Exploring some signs in Shibuya, we have found both interesting and hard-to-understand signs. And we came to realize that even though we are looking at the same sign, we each think and feel differently. Because there are various cultures in the world, our ways of thinking are different depending on cultures that you are familiar with and fields that you are interested in.

Although it was Angela who misunderstood the intention of the sign without sufficient cultural knowledge, she was not the only one to learn from the exchange; So-Yun and their classmates and teachers who listened to their presentations also benefitted, teaching us the possibility of a wide spectrum of interpretations.

This suggests a benefit of inclusive classroom practice that allows for multiple interpretations. As one interpretation reflects a set of worldviews that made it possible, learning one interpretation leads one to learn a new worldview. Even if that interpretation does not match the intended meaning, it helps expand students' understanding of various worldviews.

Teachers learning from students: "Why is there a fish for earthquakes?" (Sara)

Sara and her two groupmates chose to explore streets of Ginza, Tokyo. Sara identified herself as a Latinx of Costa Rican descent. Her group selected the "emergency road" sign as one that captured their interest and was incomprehensible. The sign had been posted by the Tokyo Metropolitan Police Department to alert drivers that the road would be closed to public in case of an earthquake (Figure 10.2). The sign has three lines of Japanese text, the first two accompanied by English translations, and a large cartoon-like catfish illustration. The first line (both Japanese and English) reads "emergency road," indicating that the road is an emergency evacuation route for rescue vehicles. The second line in Japanese translates as: "In the Event of Earthquake, No Thoroughfare by the General Public" whereas the English version states that the road is "Closed in the Event of Major Earthquake." The discrepancy suggests that emergency vehicles are driven by Japanese-language users and thus, for non-Japanese users, the road is practically "closed." The red color is used to highlight the words "In the Event of Earthquake Disaster/Major Earthquake," both in Japanese and English. The third line at the bottom reads "Tokyo Metropolis – Police Department."

Through our discussions with Sara, it became clear that the sign's incomprehensibility derived from the use of a catfish illustration. For those familiar with the sociocultural meaning of a catfish in Japan, it is not a mystery: Japanese folklore has it that an earthquake occurs when a catfish behaves violently underground. The instructors, familiar with this particular type of sign in Japan, did not think twice about the connection. It was only through this exchange that the instructors realized the connection to be a sociocultural one. They thus recognized the problem of using such a culture-specific drawing on an official warning sign, which needs to be comprehensible for

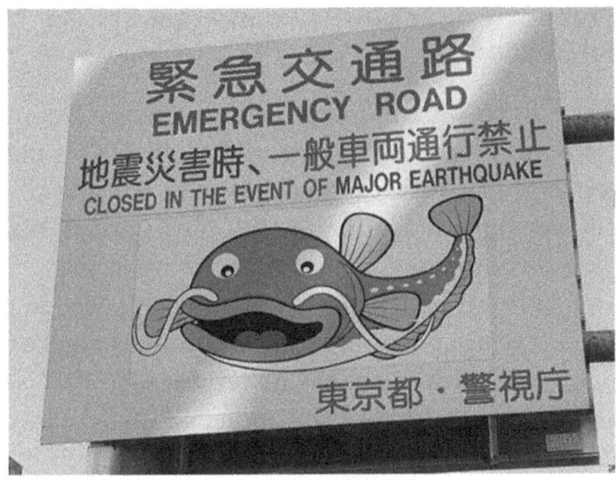

Fig. 10.2 "Emergency Road". © the author.

everyone in Japan. Clearly, the sign maker did not include "foreigners" as its audience despite the rough English translation. In fact, the English would be clearer if it stated "Emergency Route: Reserved for Emergency Vehicles in the Event of Major Earthquake."

A more fundamental issue that prevented students from understanding the sign soon became clear: the cultural practice of having a cartoon illustration on official signs. During the interview, Sara reported:

> I thought it was funny because this is like...a pretty serious sign, like you know emergency sign that everyone needs to see. And it's just like a fun little cartoon. [. . .] Lot of people would become confused: why is there a fish for earthquakes? [. . .] If you don't know the context of it, it wouldn't make sense because like in America, all the emergency signs are just text and no pictures.

Here, the source of incomprehensibility of the sign was due to the difference in cultural expectation for what "emergency" signs should look like in Japan and the United States. Similar thoughts were expressed by several other students during the class discussions. For them, it was unthinkable to have a cartoon-like illustration on official signs of such a serious nature.

Intrigued, the instructors conducted an online search of official signs in Japan to see if there are more with "cute" illustrations and found an abundance. Since having cute illustrations on official signs are a normalized practice in Japan, the instructors had never questioned their appropriateness or effectiveness on emergency signs, let alone whether they would undermine the urgency and seriousness of the warning and prevent the sign from communicating an important message to its target audience.

Inclusive Practice via Linguistic Landscape Project: Education Abroad and Beyond

The analysis of linguistic landscape affords diverse interpretations since the signs' "intentions" are not necessarily explicit. This puts teachers and students on a level playing field, allowing all to become collaborative partners and seek new knowledge from each other. Further, it destabilizes and transforms the dichotomous relationships between teachers versus learners, native versus non-native users, and the knowledge-provider versus knowledge-seeker. Through the process, we are able to make visible the invisible assumptions that each of us hold, remember that what is normal to some is not so for others, and recognize and appreciate diverse interpretations.

The sort of project described here would lend itself even better to an education abroad context, where instructors are able to provide a richer textual/semiotic environment. On-site instruction could also include people from the host society in discussions, learning diverse interpretations from them and allowing students, perhaps more importantly, to reflect critically and question their own socioculturally sanctioned assumptions behind their interpretations.

Inclusive Projects in Global Education

The projects described here are adaptable in that they can be offered both abroad and on the home campus. Reframing what counts as "difference" and where we can experience it—from those restricted to experience abroad to encounters with any kind of difference, abroad or home—the previous examples suggest not only concrete projects that can be done abroad or at home but also concrete ways of being inclusive about differences. Moreover, both projects are inclusive of diverse viewpoints—even ones considered "uncritical" or "incorrect"—in order to foster students' skills in negotiating and living with differences.

Theoretically also, in the spirit of inclusivity, we have advocated for moving away from conventional categories such as culture that tend to prioritize these differences in static ways. Instead, we have introduced the more fluid and situated concept of "flickers of difference," which allows students to investigate specific differences they encounter and which emerges at the overlapping and intersecting axes of differences—multiscalar networks—shaped by wider structural arrangements that then allow students to find commonality.

We have also encouraged students to engage in dialogue to investigate what has shaped their interlocutors' viewpoints, as well as their own. Starting with that concrete difference helps students avoid explaining things away as merely "cultural difference," which can stop the exploration and engagement with the complex ways people's views and actions are shaped. This addresses some goals of education abroad often listed under the notion of "intercultural competence," including understanding and empathy.

Students can build on the projects described earlier in layers, developing from virtual exploration in the predeparture stage (interviewing via emails or using Google Street View, respectively), and deepening and expanding the investigation once they are abroad. Alternatively, they might begin a project overseas and continue upon returning to the home campus, perhaps in a reentry course or as part of a senior seminar. These projects are a fruitful part of global education, both in and around education abroad.

Conclusion

In striving for inclusivity in higher education, merely including different students or viewpoints often is not productive and may even be harmful by negatively affecting marginalized students (see Doerr, 2020) or perpetuate rigid notions of difference without connecting them to wider structural arrangements that shaped them. We need to see difference as fluid and contextual, with potential to connect through commonality in other areas. We also need to carefully examine what we include and how we relate with what is included. This chapter suggests the importance of including what we often exclude—"uncritical" or "incorrect" viewpoints—and in engaging in dialogue with them by finding commonality with them in other areas so that we can work together to transform society for the better. This involved using old (i.e., cultural relativism) as well as new (i.e., multiscalar networks, flickers of difference) theoretical frameworks and prompts like reading linguistic landscapes. It also involved being inclusive at the disciplinary level, rethinking what global education is and where it can be done.

Understanding that there can be limits to travel for students and faculty, as we have learned all too well with the recent pandemic, our approach does not privilege physical movement and instead focuses on qualitative differences that can be experienced anywhere—in a domestic context or virtually—allowing for maximum flexibility. Our approach helps avoid treating education abroad as a discrete experience; instead, we believe that education abroad can and should start before a student leaves and continue upon their return. Difference exists everywhere, and it is ultimately the goal of both the practices described here and the broader endeavor of education abroad to help students learn to appreciate, understand, and negotiate new and varying ways of seeing and experiencing the world.

Acknowledgment

We thank all the students who participated in our research and the anonymous reviewer of the manuscript. The text's deficiencies are wholly our responsibility.

References

Anderson, V. (2000). Property rights: Exclusion as moral action in 'the battle of Texas.' *College English, 62*(4), 445–472.

Appadurai, A. (1990). Disjuncture and difference in the global cultural economy. *Public Culture, 2*(2), 1–24.

Baldwin, J. (1984, April). On being 'white' ... and other lies. *Essence*, 90–92.

Beelen, J., & Jones, E. (2015). Redefining internatinalization at home. In A. Curaj, L. Matei, R. Pricopie, J. Salmi & P. Scott (Eds.), *The European higher education area: Between critical reflections and future policies.* Springer.

Bourdieu, P., & Passeron, J. C. (1977). *Reproduction in education, society and culture.* Sage.

Çağlar, A., & Glick Schiller, N. (2017). Introduction. In A. Çağlar & N. Glick Schiller (Eds.), *Migrants and city-making: Multiscalar perspectives on dispossession* (pp. 1–46). Duke University Press.

Coates, Ta-Nehisi. (2020). The great fire. *Vanity Fair.* https://www.vanityfair.com/culture/2020/08/september-2020-issue-the-great-fire

D'Amato, J. (1993). Resistance and compliance in minority classrooms. In E. Jacob & C. Jordan (Eds.), *Minority education: Anthropological perspectives* (pp. 181–207). Ablex.

Doerr, N. M. (2012). Producing American citizens with 'global competence': Internationalization of higher education and the unique contribution of the community college through English-as-a-second-language education of adult immigrants. In A. W. Wiseman, A. Chase-Mayoral, T. Janis & A. Sachdev (Eds.), *Community colleges worldwide: Investigating the global phenomenon* (pp. 71–98). Emerald Group Publishing Inc.

Doerr, N. M. (2013). Damp rooms and saying "please": Mimesis and alterity in host family space in study-abroad experience. *Anthropological Forum, 23*(1), 58–78.

Doerr, N. M. (2017). Phantasmagoria of the global learner: Unlikely global learners and the hierarchy of learning. *Learning and teaching, 10*(2), 58–82.

Doerr, N. M. (2018). *Transforming study abroad: A handbook.* Berghahn Books.

Doerr, N. M. (2020). 'Global competence' of minority immigrant students: Hierarchy of experience and ideology of global competence in study abroad. *Discourse: Studies in the Cultural Politics of Education, 41*(1), 83–97.

Doerr, N. Modes of Study Abroad Learning: Toward Short-Term Study Abroad Program Designs Beyond the Study Abroad Effect. (2022) *Frontiers: The Interdisciplinary Journal of Study Abroad, 34*(2). Retrieved from https://frontiersjournal.org/index.php/Frontiers/article/view/526

Fairclough, N. (2014). *Critical language awareness.* Routledge.

Fendler, L. (1988). What is it impossible to think? A genealogy of the educated subject. In T. S. Popkewitz & M. Brennan (Eds.), *Foucault's challenge: Discourse, knowledge, and power in education* (pp. 39–63). Teachers College Press.

Frankenberg, R. (1997). Introduction: Local whiteness, localizing whiteness. In R. Frankenberg (Ed), *Displacing whiteness: Essays in social and cultural criticism* (pp. 1–34). Duke University Press.

Freire, P. (1970). *Pedagogy of the oppressed.* Continuum.

Giroux, H. A. (2007). Democracy, education, and the politics of critical pedagogy. In P. MacLaren & J. L. Kincheloe (Eds.), *Critical pedagogy: Where are we now?* (pp. 1–5). Peter Lang.

Glick Schiller, N., & Salazar, N. B. (2013). Regimes of mobility across the globe. *Journal of Ethnic and Migration Studies, 39*(2), 183–200.

Haigh, M. (2008). Internationalization, planetary citizenship and higher education, Inc. *Compare, 38*(4), 427–440.

Hooks, B. (1992). *Black looks: Race and representation.* South End Press.

Kincheloe, J. L., & Steinberg, S. R. (1997). *Changing multiculturalism.* Open University Press.

Kramsch, C. (2011). The symbolic dimensions of the intercultural. *Language Teaching, 44*(3), 354–367.

Kumagai, Y. (2018). Possibility of linguistic landscapes project for critical content-based language education. Paper presented at international symposium for critical language education. Musashino University, Tokyo, Japan.

Kumagai, Y., & Takahashi, Y. (2018). "Incompetence" as a productive force for making the invisible visible: "Translating" linguistic landscapes as practicing a dialogic space for knowledge creation for all. Paper presented at American Anthropological Association (AAA) Annual Meeting, Santa Cruz, CA.

Kumagai, Y., & Takahashi, Y. (forthcoming). "Of course just in Japanese! Why would the Government do anything else? This is Japan!": Recognizing language ideology through a linguistic landscape project in a Japanese language classroom. In S. Johnson et al. (Eds.), *How we take action: Social justice in K-16 language classrooms.* Information Age Publishing.

Landry, R., & Bourhis, R. Y. (1997). Linguistic landscape and ethnolinguistic vitality: An empirical study. *Journal of language and social psychology, 16*(1), 23–49.

Lassiter, L. E. (2006). *Invitation to anthropology.* Altamira Press.

Laubscher, M. R. (1994). *Encounters with difference: Student perceptions of the role of out-of-class experiences in education abroad.* Greenwood Press.

Luschmann, M. (2019). Discourses of "herbivore masculinity" in Japanese love advice books. *Vienna Journal of East Asian Studies, 11,* 125–154.

Malinowski, D. (2010). Showing seeing in the Korean linguistic cityscape. In E. G. Shohamy, E. B. Rafael & M. Barni (Eds.), *Linguistic landscape in the city* (pp. 199–215). Multilingual Matters.

McDermott, R., & Varenne, H. (1995). Culture as disability. *Anthropology and Education Quarterly, 26*(3), 324–348.

McIntyre, A. (1997). *Making meaning of whiteness: Exploring racial identity with white teachers.* State University of New York Press.

Olneck, M. (2000). Can multicultural education change what counts as cultural capital? *American Educational Research Journal, 37,* 317–348.

Ornstein, M., & Ornstein, N. (2016) *Accidental courtesy: Daryl Davis, race, and America.* Sound & Vision.

Pascoe, C. J. (2007). *Dude, you're a fag: Masculinity and sexuality in high school.* University of California Press.

Roediger, D. (1991). *The wages of whiteness: Race and the making of the American working class.* Verso.

Sayer, P. (2009). Using the linguistic landscape as a pedagogical resource. *ELT Journal, 64*(2), 143–154.

Shohamy, E., & Waksman, S. (2009). Linguistic landscape as an ecological arena: Modalities, meanings, negotiations, education. In E. Shohamy & D. Gorter (Eds.), *Linguistic landscape: Expanding the scenery* (pp. 313–330). Routledge.

Torres, C. A. (2015). 'Global citizenship education and global peace', address at the United Nations, 6 March.

Volosinov, V. N. (1973). *Marxism and the philosophy of language.* Harvard University Press.

11

Training "American" Identity: Engaging On-Site Staff in Diversity, Equity, and Inclusion Work

Martha Johnson, Bradley Titus and Mariarosa Mettifogo

The need to diversify education abroad, both from the perspective of the participants and the practitioners, has become apparent and urgent over the past decade. As stated by Contreras et al. in the Introduction to the *Special Issue on Diversity, Equity and Inclusion in Education Abroad,* there is "a need to for critical examination of education abroad practice in order to make significant strides toward equity" (2020, p. 1). The emphasis on practice is key in addressing equity and inclusion. There have been calls for the integration of frameworks such as inclusive excellence into study abroad support and programming.

Such efforts, however, have tended to focus on the recruitment and predeparture stages of study abroad. As Sweeney points out in her article, "Inclusive excellence and underrepresentation of students of color in study abroad" (which focuses on students originating in U.S. institutions of higher education to study abroad in other regions of the world): "the climate at the host university and/or in the host community may also have an impact both on the student abroad and future participants" (p. 7). It is widely agreed that local experiences of racism need to be assessed and acknowledged, yet there is little available guidance and few resources specific to navigating microaggressions or discrimination on-site. The responsibility is often put on the student to learn about race, gender, and sexuality norms and histories. While student responsibility is fair and appropriate, the call for partners to better understand U.S. racism and systems of discrimination, to understand how these systems might overlay or intersect with systems of racism and discrimination in the host country context, and to create strategies for helping students develop a sense of belonging and space for positive identity development, has not been a focus.

This chapter explores the steps taken by one institution attempting to fill this gap: the Learning Abroad Center (LAC) at the University of Minnesota (UMN), located in Minneapolis, Minnesota, when creating training for on-site faculty, staff, and partners. The academic perspectives used to develop the training and write this chapter include grounding in identity development theory, American studies, literary and cultural studies, and theatre, allowing for the incorporation of an interdisciplinary approach to the content. This effort has not been formally assessed, but rather reflects over 10 years of the intentional fostering of conversations with local staff and faculty designed to help them better understand the complexities of constructions of identity for U.S. undergraduate students.

While the strategy of training on identity risks promoting ethnocentrism, we have instead found that by providing better context as to *why* students respond so emotionally to incidents and microaggressions, international educators can better prepare the staff and faculty on programs to intervene and support students more effectively. While each overseas program will be different, the hope is that this case study provides strategies for successfully fostering and navigating simple yet oftentimes uncomfortable conversations with on-site staff and partners whose cultural contexts for racism, gender inequities, and discrimination are very different from the United States.

We begin by sharing the approach and training content highlights and later discuss the response and impact for some of the sites involved in the project.

To Intervene or Not to Intervene? The Role of On-Site Staff

There are differing opinions on the question of intervention. Historically, full immersion in the host community and language was believed to be the "gold standard" in study abroad, and programs offering facilitated learning were often considered less effective or rigorous. Intervention is often referenced in derogatory terms such as "hand-holding" (see also Gozik & Oguro, 2020). Studies by researchers such as Paige and Vande Berg's Georgetown Consortium Project in the early 2000s asserted the value of intervention in study abroad based on intercultural gains assessed with the Intercultural Development Inventory (IDI) (Vande Berg et al., 2009). The Georgetown Project and similar studies have supported the efficacy of facilitated culture-learning strategies in improving gains and helping students better make meaning of local culture. Intervention strategies have since become more pervasive and acknowledged as effective tools to foster learning in education abroad.

In his article "Beyond 'it was great'? Not so fast!: A response to the argument that study abroad results are disappointing and that intervention is necessary to promote students' intercultural competence," Wong (2015) directs criticism toward strategies for intervention, particularly their grounding in constructivism and myopic focus on intercultural development rather than broader student development gain. His arguments bring up important points; however, they do not incorporate reflection of negative experience, particularly for diverse students, but rather seem to take the perspective of a culturally dominant, or White, observer.

Anderson et al. (2016) found that, at least in the case of instructor-led programs, the efficacy of the instructor was, in fact, the most critical factor in the intercultural gains of students. Particularly in cultures that rely heavily on context to communicate and with diverse student cohorts, they found that IDI development was highly correlated to the aptitudes and proficiency of specific instructors, which regression interviews with students confirmed. They summarize by stating, "a key finding of our research is that frequent and spontaneous facilitation by instructors has a strong impact on achieving intercultural gains in students." In other words, intervention needs to be facilitated by practitioners with the experience, knowledge, and skill to do so effectively. This understanding of the critical role the staff or faculty play in intervention influenced the LAC plan or training.

The historical response from on-site faculty and staff to the suggestion of a training on U.S. identities and how to support them was met with resistance deriving from the belief that these discussions would lead to doing too much for students rather than having them do for themselves, could further promote ethnocentrism, or that students should navigate cultures on their own and independently. This may also derive from prevalent and well-meaning—if perhaps a bit misguided—hiring practices for education abroad tend to give preference to local and national staff and faculty deriving from the dominant or prototypical groups in the host society as a means to deepen students' immersion in the culture. As study abroad student identities diversifies, this tendency may, in fact, become even more problematic if we do not provide local partners with the training and tools or lived experiences to support U.S. students. Previous on-site training models, similarly, tended to assume a single U.S. identity and did not sufficiently address specific issues of race, gender, or sexual identity.

The paradox of fostering independence as a goal for education abroad participants has resulted in a resistance to and denial of need for more nuanced and specific support for students. The truth is educators cannot (perhaps should not) change host cultures or mitigate the potential for (negative) experiences related to a facet of a student's identity. They can change, however, student preparation and support. Incidents may or may not be a result of cultural norms or conceptions, and students may misunderstand, or have an extreme reaction based on their identity and their previous experience living with that identity in a potentially very different U.S. context. If this reality is accepted and anticipated, and appropriate intervention woven into practice, the imperative becomes to support the student. Otherwise, the student suffers in silence or their learning experience is impeded.

About the Context of Our Case

The UMN is one of the largest public universities in the United States, with more than 50,000 students, 5 campuses, and over 20,000 faculty and staff. As a public institution, and additionally as one of the few urban public state flagship institutions in the United States, the University has a commitment to serving a wide and diverse array of students. At the same time, UMN has a long history of international engagement and activity.

The LAC is the central education abroad office at the University and serves over 20,000 students annually. On average, over 4,000 students participate in experiences abroad each year and the office has been an innovator in developing methodologies such as "Curriculum Integration and Career Integration" models (LAC, n.d.). The LAC manages a global portfolio of University-sponsored programs in collaboration with University colleges and departments in 20 countries.

A Long and Winding Road

The conception and implementation of a comprehensive equity, diversity, and inclusion (EDI) plan might seem relatively simple or straightforward.

However, making a true difference takes time and requires allowance for trial and error. The LAC has had a long commitment to diversity and inclusion, beginning in the1990s when the LAC (then called The Global Campus) applied for and received a grant called "Access Abroad." With this grant, the office worked to identify programs abroad that could support students with disabilities. The commitment continued into the early 2000s when the LAC developed a system-wide committee called the Multicultural Study Abroad Group (MSAG). The membership of MSAG were staff and faculty from all five campuses of the UMN system working toward increasing the number of students of color studying abroad. The group included staff from the LAC but was never chaired by LAC staff by design. This group ended around 2010 and the diversity efforts were folded into the LAC.

During the intervening years, the LAC focused on four inclusive practices: program/course development, inclusion in advising, funding models, and orientations. In more recent years, attention has shifted to focus on trainings for LAC staff, trainings for on-site staff, site visits for student-facing diversity office staff, and resources for students. A video series and accompanying panel sessions for Asian Americans, Black students, Native Americans, Latinx, first-generation college students, and LGBTQIA students have been developed. There are new videos being developed for Veterans and students with disabilities. The "Parent Information" and "Financing Study Abroad" brochures have been translated into Hmong, Somali, and Spanish, the three most commonly spoken languages at home after English for UMN students. Marketing and communications now feature an inclusive avatar campaign called "Alex and Friends." Alex and their friends help UMN students understand how to navigate the study abroad process.

Important to these efforts, oversight of diversity and inclusion work was written into the position description for a full-time staff role in the LAC office. Initially, this work represented 10% of that position's time (in 2014). It was later increased to 25%. Shortly after 2014, the decision was made to include a particular focus on the development and delivery of a training (1–2 hours) as well as a workshop (4–6 hours) for on-site staff. The training has evolved to incorporate an in-depth discussion of the histories, complexities, and dynamics specific to American identity. In 2016, the UMN was designated an Asian American, Native American, Pacific Islander serving institution (AANAPISI), which furthered the work specifically with students of Southeast Asian descent. The LAC had already been developing programs (both semester and short-term) that focused on specific identities, but this designation invited even more focus on these identities.

The Development of Diversity, Equity, and Inclusion Focused On-Site Training

Starting in 2014, one of the goals of the LAC was to provide training for on-site staff. Early missteps in diversity efforts were troubling and exposed complicated specific cultural dynamics impacting the students' experiences. For example, Somali American students were successfully recruited (as Minnesota has the largest U.S. population of this particular immigrant group), but Moroccan homestay placements did not want to host the students because of widely held cultural attitudes toward Somalis. At about the same time, the institution's first disclosing nonbinary student studying in India struggled daily and did not feel understood or well supported by program structures. The student's assumptions about an Indian "third gender" had influenced their program choice, but the local reality in the conservative community in Jaipur did not match their expectations.

It was determined that a primary focus for the office going forward would be to provide the staff and faculty at LAC program sites with expanded training on the complexities of diverse identities, with a focus on highlighting strategies for better supporting the students. The goal was to engage on-site staff and faculty in the conversations, with the hope that programs could better anticipate and prepare students for likely situations or perceptions. In addition, a goal was to engage support structures including housing or homestays in exploration of identity-related needs well in advance of student arrival.

Various components were developed based on the self-assessment provided when the UMN participated in the pilot for Diversity Abroad's AID (Access, Inclusion, and Diversity) Road Map project, such as a diversity inventory U.S.-based staff could use to interview or survey local staff on perceptions or attitudes toward various identities within a given culture. Tools were created for a facilitated discussion, including a PowerPoint and script that could be delivered by various trained staff, as well as a more in-depth workshop that would be co-delivered by a team over the course of a day. Presentation preparation is designed to be minimal, drawing from information previously obtained through the survey and interview process or in student evaluation and feedback. In all cases, local personnel help facilitate and provide comparative context throughout the dialogue. Ideally, the presenters have some chance to interact with students on-site before the presentation to gather "real-time" feedback and experiences. In many cases, the presenters have personal experience in the country, and if not, presenters spend significant time researching and interviewing host nationals, past study abroad students, and staff that work with the country. In the case of the full-day workshop, preparation sometimes takes up to a year.

From the earliest version, the facilitated presentation began by asking participants to consider two questions: What is the U.S. context students bring with them? What are some of the unique considerations for historically underrepresented U.S. populations abroad? Early versions of our on-site training tended to focus on the second question, in particular acknowledging that the same body can elicit different responses and signify different meanings depending on the cultural context. As the training evolved, however, the need to provide even greater information and history concerning American identity became clear.

In preparation for one of the pilot sessions, the trainers engaged a group of students studying on a language intensive program in Mexico at a social event. Many within this group were Asian American—Hmong American or Vietnamese American—as these are the two largest populations of Asian Americans in Minnesota. Students were asked if they would mind sharing their experiences, and they were happy to agree, and opened by stating that they were doing "fine." When asked if they had experienced any challenges specific to their identity, they began to open up and shared frustration that they were called "*china*" or "*chino*" wherever they went. Given the complex histories that both Vietnamese and Hmong cultures have with China, this was upsetting to the students. When asked if they had spoken with any of the program staff, they said they had not because while everyone was very nice, they believed they would not understand. One student shared that she tried to explain her Hmong identity to a language instructor who subsequently referred to them as "Mongols" or "Mongolians."

This conversation stands out as a truly educative moment for several reasons. First, it demonstrates the reality that students are not likely to share experiences of racism or stereotyping if they do not believe local staff and faculty understand or are open to the conversation. Second, it highlights the need to prepare them for the realities of experiences that are likely to happen. It also led to consideration of what specific identities might need to be incorporated into the training. In all subsequent trainings, time is taken to explain to on-site staff the origins of the Hmong culture and diaspora, resulting in a large population in Minnesota. By actively addressing the reality that Asian Americans are referred to as Chinese in many languages and cultures, staff and faculty can help the students prepare for that experience and better support the student. Perhaps more importantly, this incident revealed the role American history and context played in explaining *why* it might be offensive to a Vietnamese American student to be called Chinese. The section of the training focusing on American constructions of identities and histories was expanded and became a much larger focus in order to help local partners understand the *why* as well as the *what.*

Many programs abroad have operated with the hope that racist or discriminatory actions will not occur and the assumption that students will say something when they do. Instead, by actively addressing what might happen and opening the door to the conversation, students may be far more likely to disclose when incidents take place. It may be presumed, due perhaps in part to the dominance of cultural production and news from and about the United States, that staff and faculty abroad understand American complexities more than they actually do. Many local staff have spent time in the United States for varying amounts of time, but they may not fully understand regional variations, may have only visited as a tourist, and/or may have an outdated knowledge of the United States if significant time has passed.

The training always begins by asking how many of the attendees have lived in or travelled to the United States, followed by a request to share their experiences. These participants are critical during the dialogue, as they often reinforce points made or make connections to experiences that they had—or had but did not understand the context of at the time the incident happened. In many of the trainings, however, almost none of the staff or faculty have been to the United States. In one training in Kenya, only one participant (the resident director) had lived in the United States and three of the other 12 participants had visited. All of those visits were for training provided by the LAC.

Content Focus on "American" Identity

The term "American" is inherently problematic. It is often conflated with citizenship or cultural upbringing in the United States, despite the rightful claim to American identities by residents of Canada, Mexico, and the many countries and cultures in Latin America. Apart from indigenous Americans, there is no ethnic grounding. In the LAC training, it is clarified that the focus is on the idea of American identity as part of the formation and establishment of the United States, and the consequences and impact of that legacy on contemporary notions of American identity. The "Founding Fathers" attempted to create an idea of "America" based on equality and freedom. In contrast to the European societies, the early colonists had fled or been evicted from, which were ruled by monarchies and divided by centuries old feudal systems, the cornerstone of the U.S. democracy was, and still is, the stated belief that "all men are created equal."

The fact that these aspirational ideals were written and ratified by a group of slave-owning men and that the equality they envisioned did not extend to women, enslaved people, or Native Americans tends to get lost in the pervasive rhetoric. The "American Dream" is the ideal that is still taught to schoolchildren in the United States. The underlying, intense belief—particularly for White, Christian, Americans—that anyone can succeed in the United States if they work hard enough, has evolved into an inability or refusal to see and acknowledge systemic inequities. Conversely, for people of color, and African Americans in particular, the fallacy of the myth of equality is a source of trauma and anger.

Any attempt to quickly summarize a subject as broad and complex as the history of, and discourse on, identity in American culture—or any national culture or identity, for that matter—risks being cursory at best. It is, nevertheless, useful to have an understanding of some of the overarching questions and controversies that remain to a large degree contested and unresolved. In addition, the global saturation of films and television produced in the United States has resulted in a disproportionate exposure to narratives mired in cliché and stereotype that come to represent U.S. culture for the rest of the world. From *Dynasty* to *Beverly Hills 90210* to *The Fresh Prince of Bel Air*, American culture has been simultaneously reduced and distorted as it has been consumed around the world. The result is that students need to be prepared to navigate stereotypes and assumptions as well as their own identities.

The following is a summary of the topics emphasized and discussed in the LAC training module in an attempt to better familiarize on-site partners with the dynamics at play.

Part I: With an introduction to the idea of American identity, a focus is placed on the fact that the conceptualization of the United States as a singular national identity is relatively new and does not rely on a single ethnic identity from a dominant group as it is a source of cultural identity and unity in the way observed in many other nations. In training with staff in very "old cultures" (cultures where the dominant cultures has been long-established and recognized, e.g., Italy, China, and Jordan), the distinction is a stark contrast. The idea that there is not necessarily consensus on dominant culture is counterintuitive. The myth of assimilation, immigration, and the legacy of slavery are discussed in depth. It is often a new insight that the United States is the only slave-trading country where descendants of enslaved people and descendants of slave traders still cohabitate without a political process having changed the power structure that supported chattel slavery, as is the case in postcolonial nations with large populations of slave descendants. European slave-trading nations may have descendants of enslaved people as immigrants, but that is far different than the case of the United States. Millions of African Americans are descended from enslaved peoples brought and later bred specifically as property for White American citizens.

Other groups who have suffered discrimination and racism in the United States are discussed. Attendees are shocked to hear about racist legislation such as the Chinese Exclusion Act of 1882, or that the majority of Chinese workers who built the railroads were kidnapped, worked under slave conditions, and died by the thousands for the sake of U.S. westward expansion. The internment of Japanese Americans during the Second World War, and the fact that there has still not been an acknowledgment or reparations for the basic and egregious violation of that this group's rights as U.S. citizens is shared.

The atrocities of the decimation of the indigenous populations of the United States and the ongoing systemic marginalization of their communities are discussed, as is the ongoing conflict over immigration policies and the exploitation of workers from Central and Latin America. Ongoing LGBTQIA legislation battles and the discriminatory laws in many states are addressed. On-site staff members are often befuddled that employees in the United States can be fired simply for identifying as LGBTQIA. These are tough histories to share and summarize. The reality, however, is that the information is often new for our colleagues abroad and helps them gain insight into the deep traumas many of our students carry within their personal and family histories.

U.S. regionalism is covered as well. Given the size and diversity of the United States, this is not necessarily surprising to colleagues abroad. The divide of the political North and South, as they relate to the Civil War, are often understood to a basic degree. Many countries have strong regional cultures that do not historically identify on the national level, but attendees are often surprised to hear how strongly students may identify as being from New England, the East Coast, or the West Coast.

It is helpful if program staff and faculty understand that some generalizations applied to Americans, such as extroversion and willingness to complain or speak up, may in fact be much more prominent in students from certain regions or cities. Minnesota culture tends toward the excessively polite, and students often do not report challenges because "they do not want to be a bother" to a degree that can be detrimental to the student experience abroad.

Part II: In the second section, trainers invite a dialogue with the on-site staff to consider and challenge some of the basic assumptions they may have about U.S. culture or race, or impressions they may have from their own experiences. The validity of various assumptions, or dimensions that may complicate them, are discussed. The negative perceptions are interrogated, that is, what outsiders often dismiss as U.S. culture being overly "politically correct" and discuss why it is critical to understand and respect the pain and trauma a word or phrase can carry for a student.

Particularly for our White European colleagues, it is important to help them understand that students of color are highly unlikely to share incidents of discrimination or discomfort with them unless they have addressed or demonstrated some understanding of racial identities. On a review of a European program in a location perceived as highly liberal and inclusive, several students of color agreed to share their experience. Their first response often was that it had been "fine," but when followed up with specific questions, they shared stories of microaggressions, jokes, and experiences that had clear racial dimensions. They had not shared these experiences with the staff. The program staff were shocked to hear that the students had not said anything but admitted they did not actively discuss race or cultural diversity in the on-site orientation. Sometimes the absence of saying something is perceived as an aversion to, or ignorance of, the topic.

LGBTQIA students may not openly share their sexual identities in many situations in the United States. Students may, in fact, go abroad to explore sexual identities they have not expressed at home. They are not likely to seek information or resources on LGBTQIA social life from program staff unless it has been proactively offered. The importance of addressing safety is critical for these students as they look to navigate social networks that are culturally different on multiple levels. This is even more important in cultures where homosexuality is illegal or persecuted.

Finally, in this section of the training, we address the assumptions that heritage students or identity seekers may bring and ultimately need help unpacking. African Americans may choose programs in Africa out of a desire for a homecoming or celebration of their heritage. During a workshop in Kenya, the female staff shared their struggles in supporting students from the United States who expected a great sense of kinship with Black Africans. The staff felt helpless because their experience of being lack had very little in common with that of the students. Similarly, Asian American students studying in Thailand are often shocked to find Thais may discriminate against them if they know they are of Hmong descent. In both these cases, it is critical that the staff understand the American identity informing the student's assumptions.

The final section of this part of the training focuses on the conflicts and complexities of the very notion of an agreed upon modern American identity, particularly for Gen Z. In an era of racialized violence and tension, the exploration and evolution of American identity offers an opportunity for intervention. While students will inevitably vary enormously in terms of their identity or even their awareness of an identity, white students will sometimes declare that they "don't have a culture," which is indicative of their lack of awareness as to the dominance of their culture.

This section discusses phenomena such as the "hyphenated identity" and nuanced historical difference in terminology such as African American versus Black. There is, most certainly, fluidity in these terms, but they are not synonymous and the nuances in identification for individuals are important to understand. Similarly, there is discussion of the term Asian American, used to cover descendants from over 40 countries with little in common historically other than some racial similarities. Hyphenated identities can be very important to students, and they may be resistant to being denied that part of their identity while abroad.

Hidden identities are those that are not apparent but may be an important part of the individual's self-perception. Students who, for instance, identify as LGBTQIA may view this facet of their identity as primary, but it will not be as obvious as racial identities. Other hidden identities include disabilities or religious affiliations that are important to the individual's identification.

Understanding intersectionality is important. The content addresses situations where a student may feel anxiety because they are not sure which identity triggered a reaction such as a "cat call" on the street. The notion of tribalism is also addressed, as sites are often surprised to find students from different institutions forming identity groups on-site based on those they perceive as understanding them on a cultural, or subcultural, basis.

As this chapter is being written in the early 2020s, the United States is immersed in a time of massive cultural change and activism on the part of Gen Z. From the establishment of the Black Lives Matter movement in 2013, to the Me Too and Time's Up watershed in 2017, and most recently the national protests in the wake of the murder of George Floyd in May 2020, American students are immersed in conversations and conflict related to identities and discrimination or abuse related to those identities. U.S. institutions should prioritize educating on-site partners as to the historical context and associations that inform why a student perceives an interaction as harassment or a microaggression. To try to minimize incidents as cultural and harmless will not be sufficient or acceptable.

Part III: The final section of the training involves successful strategies for preparing and supporting students. Again, it is important to reinforce the understanding that staff and partners cannot change their cultures, nor can they prevent incidents that may be related to a student's identity. That is not the goal. They can, however, prepare students for realities and increase the odds that the students will come and talk to someone. The philosophy being promoted is that while the student may experience microaggressions or harassment in the culture, they should not experience it in the education abroad center or their housing as these are the parts of the experience under the program's control.

It is important to normalize these difficult conversations during orientation and in classes. It is easy for members of a culture to become defensive or try to explain the cultural context. Postcolonial histories and patterns of migrations, discussions of marginalized groups, are all helpful in opening conversations later and providing context for experiences.

Preparing students for words, whether it be specific to the language or slang, is discussed. For instance, Asian American students need to know that they are likely to be referred to as some derivation of Chinese in many countries and languages. Being prepared can allow them to decide if they will correct people who use that term and explain their identity if they are not of Chinese descent, or if they will accept it. This gives the student the power in the situation and often mitigates the trauma somewhat because they are able to prepare.

In the end, the two pieces of advice the staff involved in the training have found most useful are simple yet take time and intentionality. The first recommendation is to ask proactively how students, particularly students of color, are doing, and then to ask again. Because the response "fine" usually does not mean fine. The second recommendation is to listen, affirm, and not always try to fix or explain a situation. In a field full of "doers" and "fixers," this can be very hard for staff, but there is great power in simply listening and saying, "that must have been really tough for you." In the moment of anxiety or fear, support and feeling heard are the most critical components.

This is a lot. Obviously, a relatively short training can only scratch the surface. In the LAC's experience, however, opening up the conversation and warning as to the complexities has gone a long way.

Implementation on the Ground: Florence

One lesson that LAC staff learned early on was that each workshop needed to be adapted to the circumstances of individual locations, given the unique aspects of local culture and level/experience of on-site staff. Even with a standard PowerPoint and lesson plan, it was necessary to work with resident staff to customize the training. As one example, the LAC collaborated with the Accent Study Center in Florence for staff and faculty working with its "Study & Intern" program. The LAC partners with Accent Global Learning, a program provider with multiple locations throughout Europe, including the Florence program for UMN and non-UMN study abroad students. This program is offered in the fall and spring semesters and typically enrolls approximately 120 students each year. It could be argued that popular study abroad destinations like Florence, which every year attracts a great number and wide range of students because of its perceived familiarity and approachability, are more likely to provide a representative snapshot of the campus population, and for this reason to serve as a microcosm where home and campus sociocultural dynamics, including those gravitating around diversity, can easily be transferred and replicated. According to Open Doors, Italy remains the second most popular destination for U.S. students abroad, after Great Britain. The Association of American College and University Programs in Italy (AACUPI) reports that about 80% of all U.S. students in Italy enroll in study abroad programs in Florence and Rome (Prebys, Ricciardelli, pp. vi–vii, Prebys, 2013, p. 121). About 50 U.S. study abroad programs are hosted in Florence (Prebys, Ricciardelli, p. 17).

Over the past 9 years, the program has consistently been expanding its curriculum and attracting a larger and more diverse number of students from all colleges and majors. Self-reported members of the LGBTQIA community have traditionally found in the city a welcoming environment and have consistently been well represented in the program. In addition, the number of students from other diverse groups and from ethnic minorities has also increased, due in large part to LAC initiatives on inclusion and diversity. Another feature of the program is the solid presence of students affiliated with campus social fraternities and sororities, which has made it increasingly important to face the unique challenge "Greek life" poses to study abroad. Based on our observations and conversations with students, the presence of Greek-life students, who tend to stay within their circle of friends and share with them housing, courses, and free time activities, can lead to less inclusive group dynamics, in some cases leaving students not affiliated with any fraternities and sororities to struggle harder to integrate in the group, socialize and adjust to their life abroad. This further motivates local staff to integrate diversity and inclusion into the curriculum as a value that should involve all students, including those that could potentially be less engaged in it.

Significant differences exist in the way diversity is defined and articulated in the United States as opposed to the Italian or even European context. Thus, when asked about their expectations in attending the workshop, the majority of resident faculty and administrators not surprisingly answered they hoped to receive specific information on how diversity is talked about in the United States and the actual language and terminology that frames the conversation there. They were also eager to engage in a reflection on the centrality of race in the U.S. discussion on diversity, with a goal of better understanding the context from which students were coming and how best to work with them. Such expectations reflect a general awareness on the part of local staff of a meaningful gap in the way that conversations around diversity can be approached in the Italian/European and U.S. contexts, a gap due to distinct histories of colonization and migration, to culturally specific forms of discrimination, as well as to different theories informing feminist and gender studies and civil rights activism in the two continents. The awareness of a substantial difference in how diversity is spoken about and addressed in various cultural contexts, not just at a cultural and sociological level, but also at a linguistic one, can indeed make study abroad professionals, who by definition operate across multiple cultures, more tentative in tackling questions of diversity and identity.

The workshop "Supporting Diverse U.S. Students Abroad" was offered over 2 days in April 2018 and was preceded by surveys and interviews on diversity in Italy compiled by study center staff and program faculty. It included several visits on the part of the workshop leaders in program courses and cultural activities, and individual meetings and interviews with staff members. It then culminated with a collective session. The invitation to attend the workshop was extended to all Accent staff, including the study center director; coordinators in charge of program planning, social media, housing, service-learning and internships; and all faculty with past or current teaching appointments with the program. Participation in the workshop was required of Study Center staff and optional for faculty, and the turnout in the final session was around 20 participants.

In announcing the workshop, it was anticipated that topics on the agenda fell under the larger rubric of diversity from a U.S. perspective, including racial identity and LGBTQIA identity theories, but included other points such as diversity from an Italian perspective and discussion of how the different approaches and frameworks of diversity may contradict, conflict, or complement each other for U.S. students abroad. Some of the questions to be discussed collectively during the final session were also announced, including strategies available to education abroad professionals to prepare students to the new context and to help them adjust more quickly, and the learning gains for students of a guided reflection on how they may be experiencing differences in the treatment of diversity abroad. Finally, real-life scenarios involving U.S. students from diverse backgrounds in Italy were to be discussed, prompted also by specific examples shared by workshop participants.

The workshop was preceded by interviews by workshop leaders with select local staff regarding diversity in the Italian/Florentine context, in particular on the impact of recent refugee flows in Italy, social perceptions of race, gender and race stereotypes, and social customs and policies addressing sexual identity. The information gathered allowed the workshop leaders to focus the discussion around topics of greater relevance to the local context. During the collective session, participants were then solicited to provide real-life examples of students reporting negative experiences in Florence, including instances of students feeling targeted and discriminated by locals, and these incidents were analyzed through the American lens that students inevitably carry with them. The exercise was enlightening in that it made staff more aware of the cultural friction that U.S. students can experience in Italy when it comes to diversity and gave them additional tools to address such challenges in advance. A discussion was engaged, for example, on how to select internship placements where diverse students would find a safe environment. Another point that was touched upon was how to prepare students to face with greater cultural perspective some possible scenarios where they could feel discriminated. Although the discussion could not be exhaustive, the most valuable gain for local staff was reinstating the importance of opening the conversation on diversity in Italy as early as possible with students arriving in Florence.

Another effective component of the workshop was the review of U.S. terminology around diversity, more specifically the explanation of respectful and politically correct terms in U.S. culture as opposed to others that are considered offensive and politically incorrect, even when they may bear a similarity with terms that in the Italian/European context do not carry a negative connotation. Faculty and staff agreed that this part of the workshop created greater awareness of how a lack of appropriate terminology can unintentionally lead to offensive and disrespectful communication with students. One language faculty member, for example, noted how through the workshop he had "discovered [English] terms [he] was not even aware of." A program coordinator working at the front desk also praised the part on politically correct/incorrect terminology as "extremely useful," adding how "for us non-native speakers, it can happen to inadvertently use inappropriate language and to involuntarily hurt the feelings of others." Indeed, the precise and exhaustive information provided in this section of the workshop on terms to be used and terms to be avoided turned out to be, according to the majority of participants, the most practical gain of the workshop as it immediately helped ease the fear some were experiencing of engaging in inappropriate communication with students.

The other aspect of the workshop that was greatly appreciated was the overview of the discourse on identity as multifaceted and the discussion of hyphenated identities as a peculiarly U.S. phenomenon. Staff found it useful to reflect collectively on how broadly diversity can be defined and, as one colleague noted, this helped us realize "just how different and unique each person is" and how, depending on context, people can assign more identity value to some categories instead of others. The conversation on identity made many staff "more aware of and interested in" the various forms of diversity that can be encountered among students in the Florence program but also among ourselves. Above all, most participants appreciated the fact that the workshop created more sensitivity around the subject and, the most valuable outcome, that it encouraged an ongoing discussion on diversity.

In practice, this has translated into different outcomes. In working with faculty on course content and activities, for example, the open conversation initiated during the workshop has led to shifting the frame for class discussion in courses as disparate as *Cross-Cultural Psychology, Modern Consumerism, Literature* and *Art History*. It has made staff and faculty more confident and intentional in managing potentially uncomfortable situations or conflictual moments in interactions with students in and out of class, for example, by addressing during orientation cultural, gender, and racial stereotypes in Italy. It has also encouraged staff to plan events and guest lectures and prepare courses and teaching materials that take diversity more explicitly into account. Instructors in the language courses, for instance, have been more upfront in discussing in class the lack of gender-neutral pronouns in the Italian language and how that could pose a challenge for gender transitioning students. They have also felt more confident addressing this aspect of learning Italian with individual students who had raised concerns. Another example is the addition in the *Cross-Cultural Psychology* course of a class on trauma and mental health in the refugee population in Italy that provides a new angle for reading diversity in Italy. The new class content creates a stronger frame also for the visit, during a weeklong study tour in Sicily, to an association operating for the integration of immigrants from different countries. Out of class, staff have been more intentional in introducing activities such as guest lectures and movie screenings that touch upon diversity in contemporary Italy, for example, on gender stereotypes and sexual identity, or on Italian laws and European Union policies regulating the refugee flows to the country. Attendance to these open events is in some cases recommended by faculty and integrated into selected courses (e.g., *Sociology of Crime: Mafia and the Media in Italy*, or *Cross-Cultural Psychology*), where students are then asked to deepen the reflection on the topics at hand through specific class content and readings. Finally, being more aware of different types of diversity within student groups, including their social background, has led to a greater effort to enhance the experience abroad for less privileged students, with several low-cost or free cultural activities offered regularly throughout the semester.

Ultimately, the diversity workshop has helped the Accent Florence staff and faculty to foster a culture of awareness around diversity that is being constantly reinforced through regular exchanges of experiences among colleagues and in mutual confrontation, during staff and faculty meetings, on new activities and initiatives, course content, and teaching materials that could enhance the experience of all students. After the input received during the workshop, staff are even more invested in putting inclusion into practice. To this purpose, several workshop participants have suggested, for future workshops, discussing more real-life scenarios as to make the format more interactive and relevant, and incorporating more practical hints and tools "to manage teaching materials without offending students." While this is a work in progress, staff are aware that on-site intervention is and will be crucial to any initiative aimed at supporting diverse students abroad and, most importantly, at embracing diversity as a core value and invaluable asset in global learning for the future.

Summary

The development and facilitation of training for on-site staff as described earlier has proven to be of high value and has opened up lines for inquiry and communication. There is no "shaming" and the training is designed to share and learn from missteps and errors. The question of positionality in reference to many of the identities presented and discussed is fair and necessary, and yet the fear of engaging in tough conversations is one of the factors that has undoubtedly hindered the development of necessary training. International education needs to diversify the practitioners and thought leaders engaged in the work, but to wait until that representation is realized and established is not sufficient. Educators must learn to engage in conversations beyond their own experiences and identities, not necessarily with authority, but with a true desire to learn and amplify.

By providing a foundation for understanding the complexity of the identities that students bring with them when travelling abroad, the staff and faculty abroad are better equipped to support students and successfully intervene. Opportunities for using technology and new modalities for learning are part of the plan moving forward, but always with the commitment to create spaces for questions, dialogue, and context. This work is never done, but the initial trainings have allowed for expanding the conversation and tailoring the content for individual sites. Continual dialogue normalizes these conversations in line with best global practices. If it is an expectation that sites can support diverse identities, then the responsibility lies with universities and organizations to provide the training and tools to our staff and faculty to do so effectively.

References

Anderson, C. L., Lorenz, K., & White, M. (2016). Instructor influence on student intercultural gains and learning during instructor-led, short-term study abroad. *Frontiers: The Interdisciplinary Journal of Study Abroad, 28*(1), 1–23. https://doi.org/10.36366/frontiers.v28i1.377

Contreras, E., López-McGee, L., Wick, D., & Willis, T. Y. (2020). Introduction: Special issue on diversity, equity, and inclusion in education abroad. *Frontiers: The Interdisciplinary Journal of Study Abroad, 32*(1), 1–11. https://doi.org/10.36366/frontiers.v32i1.431

Gozik, N., & Oguro, S. (2020). Beyond the gold standard: A review of program components in education abroad. In A. Ogden, B. Streitwieser & C. van Mol (Eds.), *Education abroad: Bridging scholarship and practice* (pp. 59–72). Routledge.

Hoff, J. G., & Paige, R. M. (2008). A strategies-based approach to culture and language learning in education abroad programming. *Frontiers: The Interdisciplinary Journal of Study Abroad, 17*(1), 89–106. https://doi.org/10.36366/frontiers.v17i1.246

Huntington, S. P. (2004). *Who are we?: The challenges to America's national identity.* Simon and Schuster.

Learning Abroad Center. (n.d.). *What is career integration?* Retrieved at https://umabroad.umn.edu/professionals/career-int/what-is-career-integration#:~{}:text=Career%20Integration%20is%20designed%20to,specific%20focus%20on%20career%20planning&text=Create%20program%20selection%20and%20advising,build%20skills%20in%20career%20interests

Sweeney, K. (2013). Inclusive excellence and underrepresentation of students of color in study abroad. *Frontiers: The Interdisciplinary Journal of Study Abroad, 23*(1), 1–21. https://doi.org/10.36366/frontiers.v23i1.326

Vande Berg, M., Connor-Linton, J., & Paige, R. M. (2009). The Georgetown Consortium Project: Interventions for student learning abroad. *Frontiers: The Interdisciplinary Journal of Study Abroad, 18*(1), 1–75. https://doi.org/10.36366/frontiers.v18i1.251

Wong, E. D. (2015). Beyond "it was great"? Not so fast!. *Frontiers: The Interdisciplinary Journal of Study Abroad, 26*(1), 121–135. https://doi.org/10.36366/frontiers.v26i1.362

12

Fulbright Noir: Race, Identity, and Empowerment in the Fulbright U.S. Student Program

LaNitra Berger, Lee Rivers and Erica Lutes

Postgraduate fellowships, such as the Fulbright U.S. Student Program, are an important aspect of education abroad that deserve more study. These fellowships serve students and alumni who have recently completed a bachelor's degree and may or may not be enrolled in graduate school. Participants often have the chance to live abroad for a more extended period (e.g., up to an academic year or longer for the Fulbright U.S. Student Program) to do research, internships, or teach English, which gives them more time to engage in their host country, travel, and deepen their academic study. Such an opportunity can be transformative academically, professionally, and personally for participants as it gives them the chance to think deeply about their interests, goals, and values, including their beliefs, identities, and relationship to a broader society.

For grantees of color, specifically those who identify as Black or African American grantees, the postgraduate experience abroad provides a unique opportunity to interrogate their own understanding of race, as well as how they understand the connection between their own racial identity and society. This process can fundamentally alter a participant's view of the world, unlocking new avenues of thought, social activism, and academic or professional pursuits. However, this process is not always straightforward or positive. Many Black students encounter racism or discrimination abroad. They can be stereotyped in public spaces, treated differently in the classroom, or excluded from social life and activities (Cole, 1991, pp. 4–5). In addition, fellow grantees may dismiss their experiences with discrimination, compounding the problem.

Although enriching, competitive, and usually life changing, postgraduate fellowships can also expose participants to racism and discrimination in their host countries. Because grantees already hold a bachelor's degree and may be viewed as more independent, participants may not have access to the same support services and resources that a traditional education abroad program might offer.

This chapter focuses specifically on the Fulbright U.S. Student Program and the work of formal and grassroot mechanisms leveraged by program alumni, to recruit, support and empower Black program participants to have a successful experience abroad and to serve as mentors to future applicants. Using the case study of the Fulbright Noir affinity group that was incubated by the Belgium Fulbright Commission, we examine how an awareness of the challenges Black participants face abroad can help commissions and other education abroad practitioners who work with Black participants identify strategies to assist students in facing discrimination abroad, while also cultivating strong relationships with other Black students around issues of race, identity, and social justice. In addition, we explore how the influence of peer-to-peer initiatives, like the Fulbright Alumni Ambassador Program, Fulbright Affinity Groups, and social media platforms, such as Instagram and the Fulbrighter App, are used to inspire participation in and navigation through one's Fulbright experience.

As one of the U.S. oldest and largest cultural exchange programs, Fulbright's expansive reach permits students, recent graduates, and young professionals to conduct research, study, teach English, and build cross-cultural relationships around the world. Program alumni often describe their Fulbright year abroad as pivotal in their development as professionals and leaders. Thus, it is important to understand how Fulbright engages with participants during and after the program. More broadly, the case described here offers examples for other areas of education abroad, and particularly the ways in which program leaders can more effectively foster a culture of inclusion, community engagement, and peer leadership.

It is important to note that we are practitioners, not scholars, in the field of international education, and we approached the writing of this chapter through that lens. We each work with students, alumni, faculty, and administrators to support Fulbright grantees during and after their participation in the program. Although we have attempted to ground our discussion in the current scholarship, this chapter draws from our observations and direct experiences as frontline advisors, program administrators, and social justice international educators (Berger, 2020).

The Fulbright Program: 75 Years of Cultural Exchange

The principles that led to the establishment of the Fulbright Program 75 years ago are still relevant today, including the desire to foster mutual understanding between the United States and partner nations, share knowledge across communities, and improve lives around the world. The Fulbright Program is the U.S. State Departments' (DOS) flagship educational and cultural exchange program and is sponsored by the Bureau of Educational and Cultural Affairs (ECA). In its long history, the program has had more than 400,000 participants worldwide. Each year, approximately 8,000 grants are awarded to study, teach, or conduct research, in most academic fields in over 160 countries.

The Fulbright Program has a strong track record of supporting grantees who go on to become leaders in their respective fields. For example, Fulbright alumni include 61 Nobel Prize recipients, 89 Pulitzer Prize winners, 16 U.S. Presidential Medal of Freedom recipients, and over 75 MacArthur Foundation Fellows (U.S. DOS, n.d.-b). The HBCU & HSI Institutional Leader Initiatives are recent efforts to support and recognize noteworthy Fulbright engagement at select institutions. With an increased focus on diversity and reaching out to underserved communities within the U.S. educational systems, Fulbright has proven itself an effective vehicle for supporting both individual and institutional growth.

The Fulbright Program is made up of a wide range of activities that include exchanges for U.S. and international students, scholars, and administrators. As one element within the Fulbright portfolio, the Fulbright U.S. Student Program offers grants for 1 academic year to U.S. graduating college seniors, graduate students, early-career professionals, and artists. Participants pursue graduate or professional study, advanced research, or English teaching in elementary and secondary schools or colleges and universities. Each year, over 2,200 Americans receive grants from the Fulbright U.S. Student Program to travel to more than 140 countries.

As an exchange between the United States and partnering host countries, the Fulbright U.S. Student Program operates through a network of 49 bilateral commissions that match funds from the U.S. government to develop programming, events, and in-country support to Fulbright grantees. These commissions also usually manage the finalist selection process for grantees. For countries that do not have a bilateral commission, grantee selection and support are conducted at the respective U.S. embassy. Each commission is led by an executive director, who can be a U.S. citizen or a citizen of that country. Commission directors report to the Director, Office of Academic Exchange Programs at the ECA who oversees the Fulbright Program at the DOS.

Fulbright Diversity and Inclusion Efforts

As with many organizations, achieving representational and demographic diversity in the Fulbright Program has not always been easy or straightforward. Early reports describe the low numbers of selected grantees in the program's early years. In 1950, for instance, a total of 10 out of 548 grantees were Black according to the Institute of International Education (IIE) report published in the same year (The Indiana Recorder, 1950).

At the same time, the Fulbright Program has had a longstanding commitment to engage students, scholars, professionals, and artists from all walks of life to play an active role in fostering mutual understanding and building lasting connections with people from other nations. For example, the Fulbright-Hays Act of 1961 states that the program "shall be balanced and representative of the diversity of American political, social, and cultural life." In addition, program-wide efforts have been guided by the ECA's diversity statement. Over time, this statement has been adapted to include wider audiences, but at its core the program "strives to ensure that it reflects the diversity of U.S. society and societies abroad" and the Bureau "seeks and encourages the involvement of people from traditionally underrepresented audiences in all its grants, programs, and other activities" (U.S. DOS, n.d.-a).

In the past 15 years, within the Fulbright U.S. Student Program, there has been a sharpening of focus on diversifying the types of students and institutions participating in the program. Outreach and training materials, for example, highlight the experiences of grantees from underrepresented backgrounds. As more diverse students have begun participating in the program, diversity initiatives have also stressed the importance of inclusion for all grantees. While this is a continuous effort, the program has directed resources to reaching diverse audiences and prioritized training of U.S. college and university-based Fulbright Program Advisers (FPAs). As a result, the program has had applicant pools, semi-finalists pools, and cohorts that have increased in terms of all aspects of diversity. Over the past 10 years, total participation from minority populations has increased 61.6% (Fulbright, n.d.). Although the program tracked and celebrated the incremental increases in the numbers of participants from minority populations, the in-country challenges faced by grantees from varied backgrounds and identities was not initially a central focus, thus creating a need for the type of programming explored in subsequent section.

Equally important to diversity is inclusion, in-country structured support and one's experience and sense of belonging while abroad. In response to participant feedback, Fulbright has shifted its approach to embrace the importance of inclusion. The program has taken steps to ensure that its diverse participants are heard and supported so they can have successful and rewarding exchange experiences. These diversity and inclusion efforts have not materialized out of thin air but have been a continuation of effort on behalf of ECA, the IIE, FPA's, commissions, embassies, and program alumni. These efforts include, but are not limited to:

- The development of a comprehensive outreach and recruitment unit, communications and social media team that are responsible for every aspect of outreach to the public.
- A priority placed on outreach and training to Minority Serving Institutions (MSIs). This consists of outreach, training, and support to new and previous Fulbright campus contacts.
- The creation of Fulbright Outreach Partners, which are strategic alliances with organizations that successfully support diverse populations in higher education and serve audiences that have been historically underrepresented in education abroad.
- The implementation of the FPA Development Initiative, which since 2004, has supported over 245 institutions that serve a diverse student population through in-depth in-person and virtual trainings.
- The expansion of online resources that are easily accessible to FPAs, including manuals, toolkits, and interactive training.
- Investments in infrastructure through Fulbright Accident and Sickness Program for Exchanges (ASPE) Assist that supports diverse participants' inclusion, safety, and security while on program.
- The hiring of in-country Regional Diversity and Inclusion Coordinators.
- Fulbright Commission-driven efforts, like those in Europe with the European Fulbright Diversity Initiative (EFDI).
- Funding in-country enrichment seminars, trainings, and orientations for program participants.

- An annual investment by the Trustees at the IIE to a special group of alumni, who are chosen by competition of recent alumni and represent in themselves the diverse centers of U.S. society and represent the greater diversity found within the Fulbright Program. These Fulbright Alumni Ambassadors are the faces and voices of the program that can speak to students on their own terms (Fulbright Alumni Ambassadors Program).

In addition to the efforts mentioned, ECA has staff dedicated to ensuring that the program stays true to its commitments to equity, diversity, and inclusion (EDI). One of these dedicated DOS employees is David Levin, who has served as a Senior Program Manager and Diversity Coordinator since 1999. Specifically, with the Fulbright Program, Levin plays a crucial role leading efforts to develop and maintain key partnerships with external organizations that serve diverse populations, as well as underrepresented colleges and universities.

Although these initiatives and efforts have yielded some progress toward diversifying the program demographically, they have not been able to address the issue of helping grantees feel supported and included in the host country. Inclusion concerns include (but are not limited to): (1) addressing racism and discrimination in the group dynamics in the grantee cohort, (2) confronting bias and discrimination in the host country, (3) training Fulbright Commission staff about unconscious bias in a cross-cultural context, (4) acknowledging mental health challenges that result from racism and discrimination, and (5) connecting grantees with a broader network of diverse Fulbrighters who can provide support, resources, and networking opportunities.

In this chapter, we are zooming in on the importance of giving agency to Black grantees and alumni, who can fill the voids and tackle the complexities that exist within the day-to-day operation of the program and ultimately help the program to rethink and rebuild the grantee and alumni experience around EDI. The sheer size and complexity of Fulbright presents challenges—challenges that cannot always be addressed by implementing initiatives or initiating sweeping structural, administrative, or policy changes. Serving over 2,200 U.S. Student Program participants each year while working in tandem with program stakeholders, administrative partners in the United States and in 140 countries, is no small undertaking. Due to the size and complexities of the program, married with the uniqueness of the individuals who participate (each bringing their unique history, interests, needs, experiences, and diversity of background to the table) and the varied interests of the stakeholders who support the program, not every need has been met—and this has created space for grantees and alumni to step in.

Challenging the Status Quo: A Grassroots Effort within Fulbright

Globally, EDI efforts in the Fulbright Program have evolved in various forms over several decades. Fulbright Commissions manage both inbound and outbound programs and several, including those in Belgium and Germany, have been examining EDI efforts for both types of grantee populations. The EFDI, led by the German-American Fulbright Commission, was created to facilitate the work of European Union (EU) Commissions regarding their EDI strategy for inbound and outbound grantees (Securius-Carr & Reiner Rohr, 2018). It is within this context that the Fulbright Commission in Brussels participated in events and task forces organized through EFDI, including the EFDI Conferences in Berlin (September 2018) and Sofia (February 2019).

Commissions are encouraged to develop strong academic, cultural, and professional programming activities for all grantees that give them the chance to strengthen their knowledge and understanding of the host country, as well as to network with fellow grantees who are often spread out around the country. They also work together, usually regionally, to develop enrichment seminars on special topics so that grantees can travel to other countries and meet other "Fulbrighters."

In 2018, the German Fulbright Commission sponsored an enrichment seminar in Berlin where a session called "Cultural Sensitivity" was organized to help U.S. Fulbright ETA grantees understand how to navigate interpersonal relationships in the classroom. During the seminar, many of the grantees expressed an interest in discussing the topic of race relations in the classroom and in their host communities and proposed a second discussion called "Cultural Sensitivity 2.0," which was subsequently supported. In the latter, grantees voiced the need for more support from commissions when these situations occur. For context, many of the grantees had been enrolled in an institution of higher education around the time of the mass student demonstrations beginning in 2014 against police murders of unarmed Black men in places such as Ferguson, Missouri, and Cleveland, Ohio, among other cities. Like their peers, they were outraged, horrified, and galvanized by racial violence, and they were inspired to examine their own immediate environments to root out racism and demand equal treatment. This renewed sense of purpose carried into the arena of international exchange, where students noticed that people of color were not well represented in study abroad programs and encountered additional hurdles in participating due to being discriminated against in the classroom, their cohorts, and the host community. A group of grantees from several EU countries met with the

German Commission leadership and asked to form a task force to study these issues further.

The Fulbright Belgium Commission and the Fulbright Noir Seminar

Around the same time that the German Fulbright Commission hosted its Cultural Sensitivity workshop in 2018, Fulbright grantees across Europe were expressing concerns about racism and asked the commissions for additional support. Several commission directors heard the concerns and began working with grantees in addressing the structural and interpersonal issues caused by racism. In response, the Belgian Fulbright Commission created a Fulbright Diversity Committee, adopted a statement on diversity and inclusion, and developed unconscious bias training for all its selection committees. Grantee leaders proposed to use the term "Fulbright Noir" to refer to the Belgian Commission's EDI initiatives.

As part of its participation in EFDI and in response to the aforementioned report and alumni feedback, the Fulbright Commission in Belgium incubated a Fulbright Noir grantee affinity group and hosted the first Inaugural Fulbright Noir seminar. Not necessarily a straightforward process, the way in which this initiative came about speaks not only to the openness of the commission leaders, yet also of the vision and tenacity of Fulbright grantees—a central theme in this chapter and the focus of our collective work. Grantees and alumni need to have the support and encouragement to develop their voice in education abroad programs. When they believe that their voice matters and their experiences are acknowledged and validated, they are placed in a stronger position to recommend structural and policy changes that support EDI.

After working at Fulbright Brussels for over a decade, Executive Director Erica Lutes observed several ways in which Fulbrighters approached their grant experience. Some grantees, for example, use the grant to complete their proposed projects, experience life in the host country, and make meaningful connections with their host communities. Others also arrive with these goals, but they have additional interests in fostering mutual exchange through broadening outreach and service to communities in the host country and at home. In 2018, Lutes connected with Chiamaka "Chi-Chi" Ukachukwu, a doctoral student who came to study bacteria in Brussels (see inset). During their mid-year meeting, Ukachukwu mentioned that she had started an Instagram profile "Fulbright Noir," which highlighted one Black Fulbrighter each month. This seemed like a terrific initiative that should be highlighted so Lutes asked her to submit something for a conference proposal. Ukachukwu proposed that the conference should focus on the Black student experience, a perspective that is often diluted in general discussions about diversity.

In Her Own Words: Chiamaka "Chi-Chi" Ukachukwu, Fulbright Research Grantee, Belgium and Founder, Fulbright Noir

When I discovered that I had been selected as a Fulbright finalist to Belgium, the first thing that I did was search for other Black Fulbright grantees in Europe. I hoped to learn about their experiences as Black cultural ambassadors and receive encouragement and support as I prepared to move abroad. Unsurprisingly, it proved extremely difficult to find Black Fulbright grantees, even when I expanded my search globally. By the time I started my Fulbright grant in Belgium, I was the only Black person in that space, an experience that I am all too familiar with as a Black woman in science.

Consequently, inspired by Travel Noire, I created Fulbright Noir with the goal of increasing representation in the Fulbright Program by supporting Black scholars through sharing their stories, amplifying their voices and experiences, and building a network and community. Higher education studies show that seeing oneself reflected in positions they aspire to be in has a major impact on their ability to do so. Furthermore, throughout my scientific training, I have had firsthand experience with the positive impact of affinity group programming. Thus, I immediately recognized the value and necessity for Fulbright Noir to be created.

As the platform continued to grow, I contacted the Fulbright Commission to Belgium to address the concerns of Black Fulbright grantees and solutions to improve their experience. They were eager to support and an instrumental resource in helping us develop programming to achieve this.

We also discussed the need for additional affinity groups to serve the unique needs of each marginalized community in the Fulbright program. Fulbright Noir was the inspiration and catalyst for the creation of these spaces. There are now a number of Fulbright affinity groups, including Fulbright Latinx and FulbrightPrismŮsupporting scholars that identify as Latinx or LGBTQIA+, respectivelyŮthat are working to create inclusive spaces so that all scholars feel welcomed and supported. This reiterates the fact that marginalized scholars require structured support to help navigate systemic barriers to ensure their success and livelihood in these programs.

In 2019, the first Fulbright Noir seminar was held in Brussels. The seminar activities included outreach to over 100 students from two high schools in Brussels to discuss racial and ethnic discrimination in Belgium, and study abroad opportunities within the realm of EducationUSA's mission; enrichment through presentations and networking opportunities with external partners; and a third day for internal reflection, discussion, and filming of grantee testimonials that described how they confronted and overcame discrimination abroad.

Outcomes of the seminar have since included 10 grantee testimonials, which aim to inspire diverse applicants to apply for the program, constructive conversation between program participants and Fulbright staff, and recommendations for posts to enhance their in-country orientations to include topics important to grantees of color, like:

- History of immigration and the politics of discrimination and racism
- A discussion about appropriate and inappropriate work conditions and expectations
- Emergency services
- For English teaching assistants, information about school and workplace culture

Additional takeaways cited by Fulbright staff included a recognition of the importance to:

- believe and not undermine grantees
- employ Black staff in the offices
- develop racial insensitivity training for staff at Fulbright Commissions and Posts
- convey a willingness to discuss racism and discrimination that grantees face
- develop formal discrimination reporting and recording of procedures

From the perspective of staff who were employed at the Belgian commission at the time, including Marie-Aimée Ntawukulityayo (see inset), the efforts started here were gratifying to see, both for the benefits of the Fulbrighters themselves and for those who identify as Black and were able to see progress in an organization that they had come to care for so much. At the same time, the takeaways from this program are not only relevant for the Fulbright U.S. Student Program or other postgraduate programs, they are also helpful for all practitioners in education abroad who are interested in strengthening their diversity initiatives and developing more inclusive support services where alumni are considered to be equal thought partners.

In Her Words: Marie-Aimée Ntawukulityayo, former EducationUSA advisor and Diversity, Equity, and Inclusion Officer for the Belgium Fulbright Commission

When I decided to study in the United States, one of my aunts asked me: "Why are you going to the United States, (a) it is expensive, (b) I am not sure of the quality of education, and (c) Belgium has one of the greatest education system in the world!"

In my private circle, not everyone was supportive of my dream to study abroad and certainly not in the United States. When I decided to pursue my dream, I wanted (a) to be fluent in English as I was understanding the language shift that was happening in Rwanda, (b) I was really inspired by the amount of support that my Rwandan friends were receiving at their U.S. universities, and (c) I had a feeling that although Black people had to work twice as hard to make it, the representation that I received from the United States is that there was a tiny of chance for Black people to succeed, if they worked very hard. The latter was reinforced as I grew up with many African American figures when looking at the business world, listening to music and watching TV.

And when Barack Obama was elected as the first Black President, many Afro-Europeans were very much inspired and had hope that a change could come.

On the contrary, in Belgium, we barely had any Afro-Belgians who were represented in the education system, political institutions, on TV or in the music industry. What I saw most of the time is that many Afro-Belgians had to figure out everything with no support from institutions let alone universities. I had a feeling that I could not really succeed in that country. Despite the fact that education is almost free in Belgium, it certainly does not create an inclusive atmosphere for Black students to succeed. From my own experience, in high school, to my high school math teacher and school counselors, my Black friends and I were not university material. Thus, while extolling equal opportunities in education and society in general, Afro-Belgians have in fact been excluded from fair competition in all spheres of the Belgian society. Looking back, today, I can now name exactly what I was trying to get away from: structural racism and lack of opportunity for Afro-Belgians. For many people, it is very difficult to understand but growing up in Belgium as an Afro-Belgian is truly a challenge.

When I arrived in Minneapolis, although sometimes challenging, I finally had a voice that could be heard and had a community that worked along with me to make sure that me and my Black friends were going to succeed. First, I was given an adviser from my department and we discussed my academic planning and what my goals were. I was really lucky to have had a white advisor who was culturally sensitive, a good listener and provided me with all the resources to study abroad. As the first Black woman going to university, they encouraged me to study abroad in the United Kingdom, and in Norway while simultaneously applying for the Nobel Peace Prize Scholarship. Surprisingly, I was selected as a 2013 Nobel Peace Scholar. Truly my experience in Minneapolis had a huge impact on my self-esteem, academic and career development, and I was quite certain that it would have been very challenging to have had these opportunities while studying in Belgium.

Second, I had a mentor who was a person of color who supported me in all my work and encouraged me to be involved on campus. One year later, I joined the Black Student Group on campus which facilitated my social integration on campus and exposed me to the politics of racism and how it impacted the Black community. I saw the creation of Student for Racial Justice, as a student-to-student facilitation group whose focus is to educate and dismantle racism and white supremacy within the context of my university.

It is only in Minneapolis and through my studies that I finally could speak to and name all the overt/covert racism that Afro-Belgians had undergone for decades. While growing up in Belgium, the expectation for Afro-Belgians when faced with racism then, was to be quiet and accept our circumstances. Studying abroad in Minneapolis where I had a support system and was involved in a Black Student Group allowed me to discover my voice and freely speak to the continuous barriers and challenges that Black people/students have to go through around the world.

When I started working at the Fulbright Commission in Belgium and began organizing the Inaugural Fulbright Noir Seminar, I realized that our commission barely had any students of African descents in their past and current cohort. Unfortunately, a lack of representation is pervasive in many societies. As scholar and postcolonial theorist Paul Gilroy (2002) notes, "We certainly get to see more Black people in the dreamscape of advertising, on television, and on the sports field, though not in Parliament, the police service, or the judge's bench" (p. xxxiv). The case of Belgium is very close to one of the United Kingdom. In

> *spite of Afro-descendants in Belgium being highly educated, they are still portrayed in the nation's imagination through the lens of the last Colonial Museum in Europe, the Africa Museum.*
>
> *In light of the global events, our commission [worked] to address some of these systemic issues. Some of the questions that guide our work include, how does the Fulbright Program participate in better recruiting and creating a different representation of all marginalized communities at the student and staff level? How can we participate in creating successful role-models of all marginalized communities? These are the questions that are crucial to answer in order to avoid designing One-Size-Fits strategies.*

Impact & Next Steps of Fulbright Noir

As a direct result of the Inaugural Fulbright Noir seminar, the Fulbright Commission in Brussels implemented new practices, policies, and programs, with the goal of promoting sustainable and systemic change. What had started as informal conversations with grantees led to a much greater shift in thinking and action. New initiatives included mandatory staff training on race, privilege and power facilitated by a trained professional; mandatory training on LGBTQ awareness and inclusion & considerations for higher education; and supporting students with visible and invisible disabilities. In addition, opportunities provided to grantees included the incorporation of diversity and inclusion as a key topic in the U.S. Fulbright Grantee Orientation and reentry resources, programming, and conferences, as well as the launch of diversity roundtable discussions.

At the same time the commission was implementing these changes, world events altered much of what was possible. In 2020, 1 year after hosting Fulbright Noir's inaugural event in Brussels, the COVID-19 global pandemic halted student mobility and all programs were forced to end early. In addition, a new series of murders of Black Americans at the hands of the police—including Atatiana Jefferson, Rayshard Brooks, Breonna Taylor, and George Floyd—led to the largest civil rights demonstrations in the history of the United States, with ripple effects and solidarity protests felt around the world (Buchanan et al., 2020). Many grantees were outspoken about the long-term realities of structural racism, racial injustice, white supremacy, and police brutality in the United States and globally.

This sort of awakening is not new within the United States. The concerns raised by grantees and alumni are part of a longer history of Black student activism in higher education that began in the late 1960s and resulted in the establishment of Black Studies programs at universities nationwide. In providing context for this movement, Black Studies scholar and historian Peniel Joseph also notes the role of travel abroad in galvanizing student activism, "through street-speaking, revolutionary journals, study groups, and overseas travel, radical black students anticipated and contributed to the institutionalization of the Black Studies Movement" (2003, p. 196). At the same time, the timing of these calls was valuable in moving forward the work of Fulbright Noir. Conversations about race, racism, and inequities brought about discomfort but were also crucial in breaking the silence. Grantee and alumni activism helped the Fulbright Commission to Belgium understand the need to expand its efforts to include two Black Lives Matter events, two LGBTQIA+ Trainings, and a book club with a focus on EDI. Importantly, these events and discussions empowered grantees to participate in critical discussions of world events and how they can use their privileges as Fulbrighters to amplify marginalized voices and serve their communities.

In response to the work occurring in the Belgian Fulbright Commission and in other regions, ECA created an EDI position and hired full-time diversity coordinators, in three of the six world areas, to support grantees.

Formal & Informal Mechanisms to Support EDI

As Belgium initiatives have taken root to address systemic racial equity, parallel actions have been taken by program stakeholders to address the broader landscape of the Fulbright U.S. Student Program. We have learned that gaps inevitably occur while long-term structural changes to policies and processes are taking place. We have likewise realized that progress can be expedited by leveraging the energy, creativity, and efforts of engaged program participants and alumni. As institutions begin to adapt structurally, there are movements, both formal and grassroots, taking place within alumni communities to provide supplementary support for EDI efforts. In this closing section, we explore some ways in which Fulbright, its grantees, and alumni have continued to develop initiatives around EDI, building on the formal and grassroots efforts started in places like the German and Belgian Fulbright commissions.

Empowered by the work they had done in their host countries, to raise awareness of how discrimination negatively impacts grantees, program alumni have created independent grassroot organizations. Formed out of Fulbright alumni networks, Fulbright Affinity Groups, like Fulbright Noir and Fulbright HBCU (see Brown-Grier et al., 2022 for more on this topic), have continued to be relatable role-models and use their collective influence to advocate for structural improvements in the Fulbright Program. In 2020, external societal events, like the dual crises of COVID-19 and anti-Black racism, played a role in expanding participation in peer-to-peer support and alumni activism. For example, in June 2020, a collective of affinity group leaders petitioned the DOS to respond to civil rights demonstrations with a renewed commitment to diversity, equity, inclusion, and student support in the Fulbright Program. In addition, several active members of these groups used their voices to bring attention to systemic barriers, mental health support needs, and safety concerns for program participants. These examples highlight the power of students to affect change and importance of institutions listening to and adapting policies and practices based on student input.

Building on earlier success, in June 2020, program alumni met with the Fulbright Program staff at IIE and ECA to discuss the program's response to systemic racism and tangible changes to the program that could improve its outreach to and support of diverse populations. Alumni discussed how their identity affects the grantee experience and how experiences with racism and discrimination abroad shaped their desire to create more opportunities to prepare grantees and support them abroad. They presented a plan for enhancing the role of affinity groups and other groups in participating in predeparture orientations, organizing virtual meetups and conversations, and one-on-one mentoring of new grantees. The meeting was considered successful by all parties involved and both groups left with the feeling that their questions and concerns were heard by the other side.

For its parts, Fulbright has responded actively and positively to requests for more support and action, helping to facilitate grassroots efforts by grantees and alumni. In 2019, for example, the U.K. Fulbright Commission developed the Fulbrighter App. This new tool acts as a bridge between formal and informal networks by simplifying the process of building peer-to-peer connections. From a visual and functional standpoint, the user experience with the app is a blend between two other social networking tools: Facebook and LinkedIn. The stated mission of the Fulbrighter App is to be a grassroot platform that allows alumni and grantees to connect and network with like-minded thinkers that one identifies with professionally and personally. The app seeks to "engage with Fulbrighters to discover and support their work and collaborate on initiatives to build cross-cultural understanding" (Fulbrighter, n.d.). To date, this exclusive platform has over 21,000 users and is available to all verified Fulbright alumni and grantees.

The app features a global space that allows Fulbrighters to engage with each other, interface with Commissions, and find and create events where users can share advice, best practices, and develop collaborative projects. Within the local space on the app, users can build a profile and connect with Fulbrighters locally and across the globe. It is within this local space that Fulbright Noir, Fulbright HBCU, and other identity-based affinity groups can be established as nurturing safe spaces and function as agents of action to address current issues, like EDI.

For decades, technology has connected us in various industries, cultures, and disciplines across the globe; it has made our vast world seem a bit smaller, bridging the gap for humanity and increasing our understanding of one another. To make a greater impact and enhance the student experience abroad, the work here demonstrates that practitioners should embrace technology's role in facilitating communication and dialogue between students and alumni.

Another aspect of empowerment has been in preparing Fulbright grantees and alumni to serve in their fields as thought leaders. In an effort to gather the Fulbright community and create a space where grantees and alumni could process and discuss the unique ways that international exchange contributes to social change, Fulbright added a special panel discussion in July 2020 called "Race, Justice, and the Global Civil Rights Struggle" as part of its Fulbright Impact in the Field virtual panel series (Fulbright, 2020). This special program, organized quickly to respond to the national moment, included Fulbright Program alumni from a variety of disciplines who discussed how their Fulbright experiences shaped their research on race, civil rights, and policing in the United States and abroad. Panelists not only discussed their personal experiences as Fulbright grantees, but they also reflected on how this opportunity shaped the intellectual questions they have pursued throughout their careers. With over 500 participants, this event was an example of how the Fulbright Program encourages grantees and alumni to be vocal "thought leaders" who are prepared to act and respond to global challenges. The event emphasized the importance of connection among Fulbright grantees and alumni to stimulate intellectual exchange, mentoring, and community engagement.

Conclusion

The Fulbright U.S. Student Program provides a powerful example of how education abroad helps students develop and hone community engagement and leadership skills that allow them to deepen their impact on social issues.

Through their experiences navigating identity and confronting racial bias and discrimination while abroad, Fulbright grantees have learned how to identify challenges, raise concerns with administrators in positions of power, and use their experiences and expertise to take meaningful actions that would benefit future program participants. This work has involved managing cross-cultural relationships, being persistent, growing as advocates and allies, and developing an understanding of how federally funded programs are structured.

Education abroad professionals, faculty, and administrators should closely examine their program structure and content to understand how it affects the student experience, particularly since these students eventually become alumni and program advocates. Alumni engagement and postgraduate professional development are becoming an important element in the field of education abroad. The Fulbright Alumni Ambassador Program and the Fulbright Affinity groups offer one approach to cultivating strong alumni connections to the education abroad experience while also working toward achieving EDI goals.

Acknowledgments

The authors would like to thank Mary Kirk, David Levin, Daniel Kramer, Lora Seery, Elisabeth Bloxam, and Rob Ellis for their helpful advice and guidance in completing this chapter. Thank you to Chiamaka "Chi-Chi" Ukachukwu and Marie-Aimée Ntawukulityayo for providing first-hand accounts. We would also like to thank Eliza Buckner for providing research assistance.

References

Berger, L. (Ed.). (2020). *Social justice in international education: Research, practice, and perspectives.* NAFSA: Association of International Educators.

Brown-Grier, A., Montgomery, M., & Daring, D. (2022). Social media and its impact on black student engagement in education abroad. In Stevenson, A. & Abraham, K. (Eds.), *The Half Not Yet Told: Study Abroad and HBCUs.* The Forum on Education Abroad.

Buchanan, L., Bui, Q., & Patel, J. (2020, July 3). Black lives matter may be the largest movement in U.S. history. *The New York Times.*

Cole, J. (1991). Opening address of the 43rd international conference on educational exchange. In *Black students and overseas programs: Broadening the base of participation.* Council on International Educational Exchange. Retrieved from https://files.eric.ed.gov/fulltext/ED340323.pdf

Fulbright U.S. Student Program. (n.d.). *Diversity and inclusion.* https://us.fulbrightonline.org/about/diversity-inclusion

Fulbright Alumni Ambassadors Program. (n.d.). https://us.fulbrightonline.org/alumni/alumni-ambassadors

Fulbright. (2020, July 1). *Fulbright impact in the field: Race, justice, and the global civil rights struggle* [YouTube]. Retrieved November 27, 2021, from https://youtu.be/HcPnEoNw9fQ

Fulbrighter. (n.d.). *Welcome to Fulbrighter.* https://fulbrighternetwork.com/page/welcome.

Gilroy, P. (2002). *There ain't no black in the Union Jack: The cultural politics of race and nation.* Routledge.

Joseph, P. E. (2003). Dashikis and democracy: Black studies, student activism, and the black power movement. *The Journal of African American History, 2*(88), 182–203. https://www.journals.uchicago.edu/doi/pdf/10.2307/3559065?casa_token=S2_T0y4BeXEAAAAA:6qxAOOIGqfTBeO-xpAIoaAlaDk15RVFlxKXGnhV1pbKvng6I7Hq0ZJY3zF0dyH4QsUyePCi7gIuh

Securius-Carr, C., & Rohr, R. (2018). Educating for inclusive diversity. In S. K. Gertz, B. Huang, & L. Cyr (Eds.), *Diversity and inclusion in higher education and societal contexts international and interdisciplinary approaches* (pp. 97–118). Palgrave-MacMillan.

The Indianapolis Recorder. (1950, June 10). *Graduate study aid granted ten under the Fulbright Act.*

U.S. Department of State. (n.d.-a.). *Bureau of cultural affairs diversity statement.* https://eca.state.gov/files/bureau/diversity.pdf

U.S. Department of State. (n.d.-b.). *Notable Fulbrighters.* https://eca.state.gov/fulbright/fulbright-alumni/notable-fulbrighters

13

Deepening Reentry Impact through Inclusive Practice in Education Abroad

Maraina Montgomery, Neal McKinney, Jane Nzomo, Angela Manginelli and Lily López-McGee

Introduction

Of the stages of the education abroad process, that is, from when students first consider going abroad to when they return, reentry programming is often the phase that receives comparatively less attention (Brubaker, 2017). Many international education practitioners lament how few opportunities there are to engage students once they return home and how few students participate. These reasons often include student's prioritizing immediate demands (e.g., classes, work, family), the timing of students' return (e.g., returning during holiday/seasonal break before returning to campus), a lack of prioritizing reflection in the reentry period, and the reliance on students to proactively seek out activities when they return home. These factors—valid and legitimate in their own right—place the burden of planning almost exclusively on the student. If education abroad practitioners take seriously the charge to develop more inclusive practices, reentry must be reimagined as a tool for reflection, goal alignment, and personal and professional growth for students. Education abroad practitioners must also consider how the nuance of each student's experience affects their reintegration into their home or campus community and develop advising and programming strategies that make it easier, not harder, to access reentry resources.

Prevailing research and inquiry on the reentry stage has tended to emphasize outcomes assessment rather than programming (Brubaker, 2017; Szkudlarek, 2010). This chapter aims to offer insight into the latter, thus filling an important gap in both scholarship and practice. Here, we offer strategies for reengaging students following international learning experiences and recommendations for how the field can provide more and inclusive opportunities to advance students' learning well beyond their time abroad. In reimagining reentry, this chapter proposes that the success of diverse students is best predicated on those actions taken before students board the plane, emphasized while they are abroad, and reiterated when they return home. The case studies that follow contribute to an underdeveloped area of literature that focuses on the programmatic features of inclusive reentry practices and not simply the evaluation of student gains and satisfaction by way of assessment.

It is important to acknowledge the moment in which this piece was written. The global pandemic caused by COVID-19 and the global movement to end police brutality and racism have consumed everyday activities. As practitioners in a field that prides itself on cooperation across difference, intercultural engagement, and the exchange of ideas, we endeavor to reflect on how international experiences have the potential to foster longer term learning and reflection that undergird students' transitions back home.

Reentry: Moving Beyond Assessment

It has largely been within the past two decades that international educators and education abroad practitioners have explored more deeply the implications and need for student reentry activities. As Szkudlarek (2010) outlines in her literature review, scholarship addressing the affective, cognitive, and behavioral aspects of returned students is broad and multidisciplinary. Scholars, for example, have documented the growth and skill development that may come from an education abroad experience including affective, behavioral, and cognitive learning such as intercultural competencies (e.g., Gray & Savicki, 2015; Hammer et al., 2003; Vande Berg et al., 2012), adaptability and tolerance to ambiguity (e.g., Kitsantas, 2004; Williams, 2005), language acquisition (e.g., Mohajeri Norris & Steinberg, 2008; Segalowitz et al., 2004), and global citizenship (e.g., Morais & Ogden, 2011; Tarrant et al., 2014). Notably, the scholarship in this domain emphasizes assessment of student learning as a way to make the case for reentry programming rather than evaluating reentry programming and activities directly.

Students ideally continue to learn and build on the skills they have developed when they return home, and for this reason, reentry programming offers many possibilities to integrate the core tenets of inclusive excellence where practitioners attend to students' intellectual and social development poststudy abroad; mobilize campus resources to ensure returned students have an opportunity to deepen their learning; integrate strategies that consider distinct cultural experiences students bring with them from their time abroad; and develop a welcoming climate where students' unique experiences are celebrated rather than minimized (Milem et al., 2005). Still, the theoretical understanding can sometimes be difficult to tie to the day-to-day practices of those supporting students in their return.

Reintegration and Advising

Scholars have shown that students returning from a study abroad experience may find it difficult to locate people with whom they can process their experience (e.g., Arouca, 2013; Wielkiewicz & Turkowski, 2010; Young, 2014). For students from minoritized communities, the experience of returning home may be particularly isolating as many may not have individuals in their network (i.e., family and friends) who have had international experiences (Salisbury et al., 2011). In addition to processing the common reentry challenges—reintegrating to home culture, missing the abroad experience—students from minoritized communities are also met with having to navigate being different from many people in their immediate social circles. Moreover, students from minoritized populations may have had experiences while abroad that their peers from majority populations did not that they want to discuss, such as different treatment from locals (e.g., the expectation of a heritage student to speak the local language, face harassment based on their appearance) and interactions with their peers who have had less exposure to diverse communities in the United States (e.g., microaggressions, tokenism).

In light of the recent global pandemic and protests against racism and police brutality, some students—students of color in particular—may be more comfortable discussing issues around diversity, equity, power, and privilege while their White peers may be less prepared to do so (Stallman, 2009). Providing space and different modalities for students to reflect (e.g., individual advising, group discussions, student ambassador programming) can in and of itself signal to students that the abroad experience does not have to end simply because they have returned home and that there are communities that can help students continue to make meaning of their experiences. Developing reentry programming and support allows practitioners to connect students to resources they may need, particularly as it relates to mental health services and counseling if appropriate.

Research has shown that students from minoritized backgrounds (e.g., racial/ethnic, gender/sexual identity) who have meaningful relationships with faculty and staff at their home institution are able to utilize their community in a way that mitigates the negative influence of bias and bigotry in their daily experiences on campus (Cress, 2008). However, institutions of higher education suffer "a lack of a clear definitive framework" for inclusive excellence that often undermines students' participation in and access to an inclusive campus and education environment (Chun & Evans, 2016, p. 7). For this reason, advising can provide a venue where practitioners are able to develop meaningful and direct relationships with students, which can help foster a sense of connection with staff and offer students a sense of community with which they are excited to reengage.

Program Design

Furthermore, when considering reentry efforts, we argue that practitioners should prepare for students' return at the time that programs are developed, well before the student leaves the country. Integrating reentry into the program design has the potential to extend student learning beyond their time abroad and deepen the learning. Embedding opportunities for reflection (e.g., Engle & Engle, 2003; Gross & Goh, 2017) into the structure of education abroad programs can be as important as outlining required readings for a course and determining which assignments will most appropriately develop students' understanding of a concept. Preparing in this way ensures that practitioners prioritize elements of reentry in developing syllabi, scheduling programming, and determining other interventions that can equip students to employ such skills long after the end of the program.

Research on reentry is interdisciplinary and helps inform practitioners' understanding of what students gain from going abroad. Nonetheless, more can be done to understand how to translate those findings into practical strategies that attend to students' cultural differences and experiences they have had while spending time away from their home or campus. The subsequent case studies highlight four institutional experiences in prioritizing reentry programming in the life cycle of education abroad.

Case Studies and Strategies

The following section details the reentry programming, engagement, and advising strategies of four distinct institutions. The case studies represent a diversity of institution types including an Historically Black College (HBCU) in the mid-Atlantic United States; a predominately White, liberal arts institution in the Midwest; a U.S.-based provider program based in Kenya; and a U.S.-based provider with its headquarters on the East Coast. In bringing together such unique experiences, this section endeavors to offer strategies and approaches that practitioners from different institutional and organizational ties may incorporate into their practice.

Howard University, Washington, DC

Howard University (HU) is a private, federally funded HBCU founded in 1867, located in Washington, DC. During the 2018 to 2019 academic year, the institution enrolled 6,243 undergraduate and 2,896 graduate-level students. An estimated 86% of HU's student population identifies as Black or African American, and 4% of the student body are from countries outside the United States. Of the undergraduate student body, approximately 8.9% studied abroad in 2018 to 2019 (Ralph Bunche Center Newsletter, 2019). HU students who study abroad for credit for a semester or academic year are generally high achievers, as they must meet a minimum 3.0 GPA requirement. HU's history of sending students abroad through third-party provider programs reaches back to 1983, and its 12 study abroad partners award students credit for participation in programs in over 85 countries. HU is distinct among its peer institutions for having the Ralph J. Bunche International Affairs Center (RBC), which is dedicated to creating an energy of enthusiasm and accessibility related to all things international on campus by promoting international affairs and study abroad.

In 2016, the RBC sought to reimagine and increase its promotion of study abroad to HU's largely Black student body and hired a new program manager to lead this initiative. Over a period of 5 years, and due to new energy and effort, student participation in study abroad nearly tripled. Today, the HU Bison Abroad Office (BAO) markets study abroad as an empowering life experience that is accessible and important for the holistic development of HU students. At the time this chapter was written, the BAO sent approximately 100 students abroad each semester.

Trust, Study Abroad, and the Role of Practitioners: Despite having motivated new staff members, building buy-in within the greater campus community, especially among students, has taken time, intentionality, and trust building. These efforts have been the cornerstone to the BAO's success in student engagement in programming efforts, but particularly after they return from being abroad. These efforts start early on with an extensive predeparture orientation process that brings students and staff closer together through intimate conversations related to Blackness (and other marginalized identities) within the global context, information for first-time travelers, and preparation for maximizing study abroad. An important part of the predeparture experience is a collective reading of the #StudyAbroadSoBlack manifesto that solidifies students' membership into a new community of global citizens and commitment to ensuring that they support other students in accessing global opportunities. This pledge undoubtedly draws students back to participate in reentry programs at a similar rate of predeparture programs as it ties their success to the success of a broader community.

HBCU Values & a Call-to-Service Leadership: HU and other HBCUs are seen as a beacon in the United States due to their commitment to uplifting the pan-African community, dedication to service, and encouragement to "pay-forward" what one has gained with the support of others. These values are what the BAO leadership team harnesses when marketing resources and support systems and ultimately compels students to reengage upon their return. By encouraging what Greenleaf calls "servant leadership" (1970)—a leadership philosophy in which the main goal of the leader is to serve—students are invited to lead with the goal of informing their peers as part of the *#StudyAbroadSoBlack* movement on campus. In effect, students become recognized as a leading source of information, guidance, and empathetic support for their peers who express interest in international opportunities. This approach to student leadership development begins during the predeparture phase and continues while students are abroad through the encouragement of the use of the *#StudyAbroadSoBlack* hashtag to make visible and own the narrative around their global experiences. These experiences crescendo upon their return to campus, especially following the "Welcome Back Mixer" each semester where students continue to invest in the community they have developed.

Bison Abroad returnees are welcomed back to a campus community by previous cohorts of study abroad participants and BAO staff. During and at events following the welcome back gathering, returnees are encouraged to become Bison Abroad Ambassadors, peer advisors, develop content for social media, facilitate classroom visits in their major department, produce short marketing films, participate in programming, and intern within the BAO. This cycle of servant leadership development, volunteerism, and campus engagement provides returnees with a platform to express their newly expanded selves and a community of peers who have shared the same growth process. The success in reentry engagement with returnees is largely predicated on a collectivist approach to study abroad that encourages students to create deep and meaningful connections with each other.

Outcomes: Students have fostered a community of support for each other, taken on leadership roles to increase study abroad operations and visibility on campus, and become advocates for change and improvements within the professional field through their active use of reentry resources. Using digital and physical space, returnees connect with one another through BAO tools—such as an ambassadors' GroupMe chat and regular (monthly, bimonthly) in-person and remote alumni meetings—a regular flow of returnees remain engaged with the office and each other. Student participation in reentry programming like the biannual "Night of Reflection," "Leveraging Study Abroad," "Teaching English Abroad," and "International Careers and Graduate Schools" has steadily increased. These programs offer students regular opportunities to plug back into their study abroad campus community while also gaining important skills and information for how to leverage their experience abroad for career and longer term professional and academic success. See event flyers in Figure 13.1.

In addition, the BAO staff and the HU globally minded community provide an important audience for returned students to process their individual abroad experiences. Many families and communities from which returning students come are unfamiliar with the study abroad process, the overseas experience, and the multitude of ways in which their Black scholars' experiences abroad can challenge them emotionally. Students find initial support and resources in the BAO and peer advisors, and this support frequently supplements the services (or lack thereof) offered in other campus offices such as careers services and the counseling center.

Recommendations: The lessons from the experience of BAO staff suggest that practitioners working with underrepresented students, especially Black students and/or students attending HBCUs, should do the work of engaging these student populations early and consistently. Developing programming for prospective participants that empowers study abroad alumni to reflect on and authentically share about their study abroad experience in a way that naturally informs listeners of the challenges and successes experienced is one way to gain the attention of returnees. Upon reentry, inviting returnees to become part of a campus community of global-minded peers and professionals offers students a much-desired space for belonging among peers during the resettling process. By investing in building a campus culture that empowers students, builds community, and encourages servant leadership

Fig. 13.1 Howard University Select Outreach Flyers for Returned Student Activities.

and role-modeling, practitioners can set the foundation from which useful reentry programming and student support can flourish.

DePauw University, Greencastle, Indiana

DePauw University is a baccalaureate-granting, private liberal arts institution that enrolls just under 2,000 students, with 19% of the population identifying as first-generation students, 20% domestic students of color, and

20% international students (DePauw University, 2020). DePauw ranks seventh in the nation for study abroad participation by institution type (Institute of International Education, 2019) with 20% of all DePauw students participating in semester-long study abroad (referred to internally as off-campus study) through the Hubbard Center for Student Engagement (Hubbard Center). In 2018 to 2019, the Hubbard Center tracked that 182 students participated in semester off-campus study, and within this group, 19% of participants are domestic students of color, 19% are first-generation students, and 19% are Pell eligible (DePauw University, n.d.).

DePauw is not immune to the challenge of low student participation with off-campus study reentry programming. The Hubbard Center's Off-Campus Study (OCS) team continuously offers a myriad of reentry opportunities for returned OCS students (e.g., reentry luncheon, participation in provider campus visits, peer advising); however, the participation results for the majority of returned students have remained low. At the same time, the OCS team began to realize that in spite of the low attendance, the highest participation in reentry programming came from minoritized students of diverse identities (e.g., race/ethnicity, first-generation, socioeconomic, +) and that has been a pivotal education opportunity for better supporting this student population at a Predominantly White Institution (PWI).

Over the past 5 years, the biggest lesson learned in reentry support for minoritized students at DePauw is that they take pride in guiding their own reentry process, and the best way to support them is to provide them with the space and opportunity to participate. In general, returned OCS students demonstrate a high level of independence, but the minoritized students in particular come back and indicate that their biggest motivation to process their abroad experiences is rooted in encouraging their peers to pursue OCS opportunities. Gilman scholarship recipients (who are required to carry out follow-on service projects that reach out to minoritized students after they return), as well as students who are selected to be ambassadors for their study abroad programs, have been particularly eager to work with the Hubbard Center to promote and produce their own outreach programs. Such programming has included panel discussions on what it is like to be a student of color while abroad, information sessions on scholarship resources, and one-on-one mentoring.

In response to this student initiative, the OCS team has prioritized supporting minoritized students in a number of tangible ways. First, logistical support is offered for every program students would like to host. In practice, this support is realized by an OCS team member either proactively reaching out to students or vice versa, and meeting to discuss their event, generate ideas for advertising/promotion (which includes sharing information via social media), and offering to book campus spaces on their behalf. See Figure 13.2 for examples of social media outreach.

Second, the office offers modest financial resources to subsidize program food costs, which is covered by a line item in the yearly budget. Through these mechanisms, the OCS team is able to serve as a partner to these students and witness how motivated and passionate they are about encouraging their peers to go abroad (which directly influence overall pre-OCS advising/engagement and OCS participation rates).

As one example of how office–student partnerships have worked, since 2015 the OCS team has taken particular attention to promoting the Gilman scholarship to eligible minoritized students. Upon reentry, many of the Gilman awardees have dedicated themselves to putting together projects to unpack their experiences abroad with their peers in mind. For their part, the OCS has made a concerted effort to partner with the Gilman awardees beyond the surface level of marketing by also offering financial, technical, and physical resources. Due to these efforts, DePauw has garnered 30 Gilman awardees since 2015, with 1 year resulting in 13 awardees (2017–2018), and minoritized DePauw students are participating at rates near parity with their enrollment demographics. In addition to helping recruit new students, the efforts have helped to give awardees greater confidence during and upon return from OCS.

Recommendation: As with the HU example, this case demonstrates the significant benefits of forming intentional relationships with students throughout the study abroad process, with the goal of not only increasing participation yet also in championing individual students' success. Minoritized students want to be assured of their choices, so offices/practitioners should act as an authentic source of empowerment to promote self-authored motivation, independence, and passion. Though minoritized students may experience hardships while abroad due to their identities, their resilience in processing these realities is best unpacked by practitioners in a support role, as has been described earlier in this case study. This supportive approach in reentry is noticed by prospective minoritized students, who become more willing to trust in building relationships with the study abroad office.

Minnesota Studies in International Development - Kenya Program, Nairobi

The Minnesota Studies in International Development (MSID) – Kenya program is an academic study abroad program with semester- and year-long

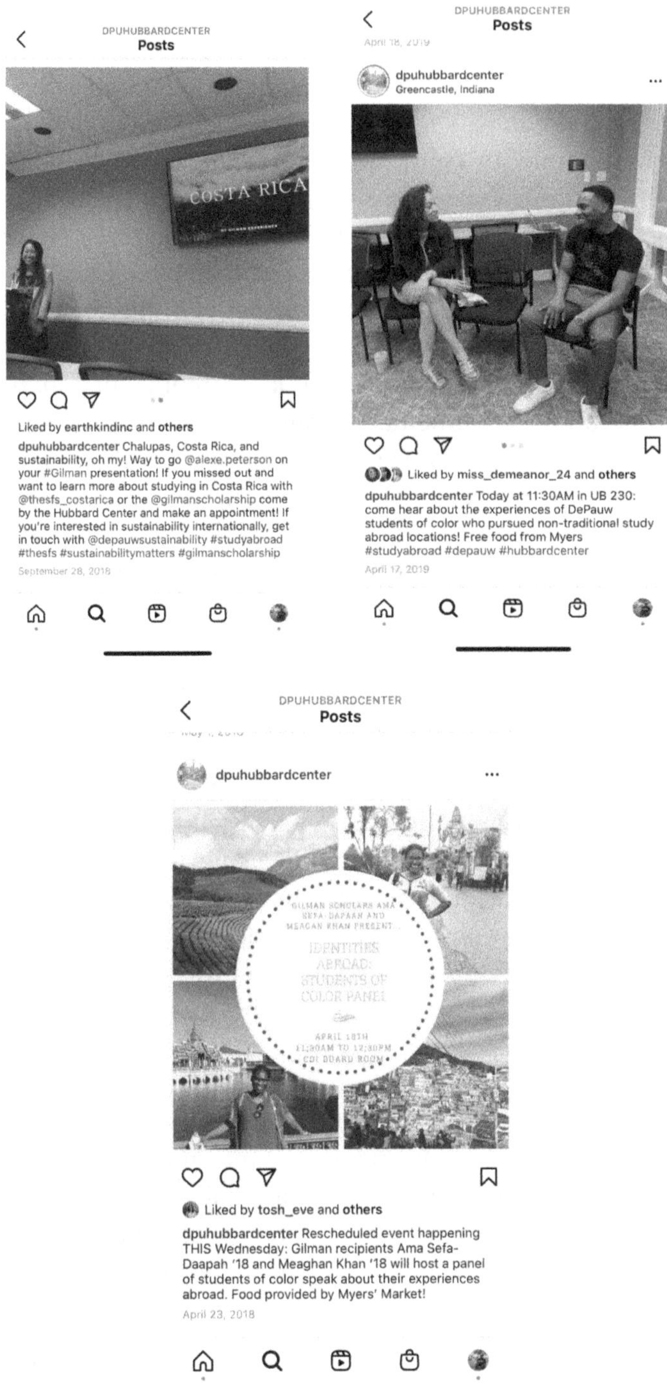

Fig. 13.2 DePauw University Select Social Media Outreach for Returned Student Activities.

options developed by the University of Minnesota. MSID Kenya is one of several programs operated by the Learning Abroad Center at the University of Minnesota open to any university-going student and offers an example of what a program do while students are still abroad to prepare for reentry. The program combines coursework with hands-on experience in a non-governmental or government institution working with local communities. It is designed for undergraduate and graduate university students who are interested in issues of development, sustainability, and social justice. The program puts the student into direct contact with the social and economic realities of Kenyan communities and affords participants opportunities to learn through experience in areas such as entrepreneurship, public health, social service, and environmental sustainability. Through classes, excursions, and an extended internship or research placement, the program strives to establish a continual dialogue that links experience with theory and critical analysis. While the majority of the participants are White, each cohort has some Africans, African Americans, and/or Asian American students, with an average of 12 students total each semester. All participants live with Kenyan host families and engage regularly with staff who are all Kenyans. MSID Kenya is an affiliate of Wildlife Clubs of Kenya, an education institution based in Nairobi.

In-Country Orientation: During the first week of orientation, staff and faculty are intentional about preparing students for cultural immersion in the host culture. Students with minimal or extended knowledge of the country engage in local excursions that require them to think about their home and host cultures. To track their own progress, participants are asked to reflect and write down their individual goals for the study abroad experience, initial impression of the host culture, what they think will be the most challenging and rewarding experiences, and personal aspirations. Each student writes a self-addressed letter prior to departure, reviews it mid-semester, and reads it again at the end. This activity achieves two seemingly separate goals that ultimately help prepare students for their return home: It offers students a model for how to take time to reflect intentionally on their experiences, while also helping them develop a deeper awareness of their perceived and actual understanding of cultural differences, where there is often a gap.

Students often find that the most challenging or rewarding experiences shift by the end of the semester, when it is time to reflect back on their time in Kenya. This experience helps students develop more self-awareness of what they know and practice reflection in an intentional way that gives them valuable strategies they can employ when they return home as they process their experience abroad and identify ways to articulate what they have experienced. Notably, MSID staff frequently receive correspondence from students months after they have returned home that demonstrates these continued reflections. Among many examples, one MSID alumnus wrote:

> There is no way I would have gotten my current position (working in Monitoring and Evaluation in Rwanda) without my time in MSID. The on-the-ground experience that the program gives you, really prepares you to work abroad in a developing country. I honestly credit this program 100% for landing me my dream job.

Workshops to Reflect on Student Learning: During the final week of the program, students participate in a session on preparing for their return home. Staff guide them through materials and activities that begin to encourage students to think about what it will be like to return and how they can integrate their experience adjusting to the Kenyan culture to their reintegration home. The session encourages students to continue to reflect on how to incorporate all of their cultural identities into their own perspective on the world. Students learn strategies for managing the emotional challenges of study abroad (e.g., homesickness, adapting to new cultural surroundings) and reentry (e.g., reverse culture shock and making career, academic, personal decisions). As with their initial arrival in Kenya, so too must students give themselves time to go readjust and adapt to their home culture. The workshop also offers students strategies for how to share with friends and family what they might be feeling (e.g., difficulty adjusting, sadness, loss) as a way to help them process their international experiences. Staying in contact with friends and contacts from the host culture, joining an international student group, and becoming active in events sponsored by their international studies/education abroad office offer students an outlet to share their concerns and experiences. Importantly, program staff urge students to apply what they have learned abroad in planning for their next phase of life.

This workshop plays a very important role in preparing students' expectations for their return. Some report that it was not until a couple of months after being home that they started to experience reverse culture shock and readjustment challenges. The activities MSID has employed to support student preparation for the reentry stage can be especially helpful for students who may be returning home to communities with less exposure to international travel. Being able to independently reflect and having had practice expressing their growth prior to departure helps students feel more comfortable articulating what they are processing and reengage with communities back home where they can share their experiences. One returnee wrote:

> The discussion we had at the end of the trip on what we might experience when re-entering the US was very helpful. There's much more of an emphasis on the changes you might notice and the feelings you may have upon entry of a new country but not as much focus on the reverse culture shock you may face when returning so for me, it was an eye-opening discussion. For many people including myself, being immersed in another country for a few months can change your perspective on life and even thoughts on your own culture. When you go back to your friends and family, you may feel as if they don't understand you or can't relate to your passion about what you discovered and experienced abroad. We discussed that although you may experience loneliness or frustration, patience is necessary when explaining your experience to others. The group discussed that you also need to give yourself some time and space to fully understand your feelings and emotions as you transition back into regular life.

Recommendation: From these experiences, it would be helpful for institutional partners to have a dedicated returnee support staff or team for returned study abroad students so that students can continue to use their skills in reflection they gained abroad to help returnees continue to process their experience. This could include facilitated group discussions, individual advising, and a seminar that focuses on reflective practices, among other possible activities staff could lead. Importantly, the MSID Kenya program experience suggests that more can be done while students are abroad to prepare them for the reentry process before they leave their study abroad location. This helps facilitate the transition for students back to their home campus and students create plans for how to navigate postprogram transitions.

AIFS Study Abroad, Stamford, Connecticut

AIFS Abroad is one of nine cultural exchange programs offered by the American Institute for Foreign Study (AIFS). AIFS is an education abroad provider organization that hosts students from a wide range of schools, and this case study offers an example of how providers can both prepare students for the reentry process while they are abroad and design reentry programs that keep them engaged after returning to their home campus. Since 1964, AIFS has been a leading provider of educational opportunities for more than 1.6 million people. More than 5,000 students participate in an AIFS study abroad program annually, choosing from more than 70 comprehensive programs spanning more than 35 host cities during the semester, academic year, summer, or January term. Many students who participate in the programs are going abroad for the first time and more than 50% of students receive scholarships or grants from AIFS (AIFS Study Abroad, 2020a). While applicants have been asked to provide optional demographic information, most have not done so, making it difficult to track participation rates. Beginning in spring 2021, recently adjustments have been made to encourage student self-reporting, as part of the AIFS Abroad Plan of Action for Access, Inclusion, Diversity, and Equity (AIFS Study Abroad, 2021).

As an international education organization, AIFS aims to build the best possible relationship with each of its partners, representing a variety of institutional types. This provides a unique responsibility to understand and meet the needs of individual campuses, something that is only possible through collaboration and trust. Since implementing these programs, there has been anecdotal evidence of increased interest and participation of students from minoritized backgrounds, including students of color, first-generation college attendees, students who identify as LGBTQIA+, and students with cognitive and mobility considerations. As noted earlier, more work is needed to collect demographic data, allowing for better tracking. This work is never finished, and the goal is to improve continuously as individuals and as an organization through research, education, assessment, and collaboration.

The experience abroad is approached comprehensively (before, during, and after) and, as such, programs and resources have been created that engage students early in their experience abroad and continue throughout their physical return to their home institution. This is exemplified through the AIFS Alumni Ambassador program.

AIFS Alumni Ambassador Program: Each year, AIFS collaborates with partner institutions to select 40 to 50 students for the Alumni Ambassador program. Students must apply and be approved by their home institution, respective AIFS resident director, admissions officer, and the alumni team. Accepted participants commit to providing 80 hours of outreach on their home campuses and online throughout the school year. A comprehensive training in August provides participants space to process the emotional side of their return, learn about the entire AIFS program portfolio, review outreach best practices and information on the current study abroad participation data, and discuss how to remove potential barriers for participation in education abroad.

Since 2017, Alumni Ambassadors have been asked to do intentional outreach to two underrepresented communities that have been historically underrepresented in education abroad on their home campus. They can choose the targeted populations, based on their campus' needs, yet are asked to pick one community they already have ties to and one that is outside their own lived experience. The latter invites all participants to engage with a new group and thus move out of their comfort zone as they did when abroad. This process provides opportunities for students from diverse backgrounds to connect in a meaningful way and helps to build increased empathy and awareness in student leaders. For example, McKenzy Kelley, an Alumni Ambassador at Lake Forest College in 2017 to 2018, offers the following observation:

> Participating in the AIFS Alumni Ambassador program allowed me to gain experience with a diverse group of people. To connect with other students I had to establish a genuine relationship that allowed me to get to know someone's motivation for desiring to study abroad.

Program marketing materials clearly articulate that ambassadors will be expected to contribute to access efforts that expand the scope of who has information about and access to resources for education abroad. Related questions appear in the application and interviews. In addition, ambassadors participate in monthly meetings with staff where they continue to engage in identity reflection in a cohort setting and report their progress in engaging with their selected communities throughout the year. First-year participants are paired up with a returning ambassador buddy who can provide personalized support and mentorship as new students find their footing in the program.

In a postprogram survey, 94.6% of the 2019 to 2020 AIFS Alumni Ambassador cohort (AIFS, 2020b) and 97.7% of 18 to 19 cohorts (AIFS, 2019) indicated they were able to connect with two communities on their home campus. Examples of programming have included tabling in academic departments and spaces for students that are underrepresented in study abroad; meetings with and office hours in the multicultural center, LGBTQIA+ office, financial aid office, diversity and inclusion office, and office for adult students; information sessions focused on social identities; alumni panels comprised of diverse students; open discussion events; meeting with underrepresented student groups on campus; and continued one-on-one outreach and conversations. Amie Knowles, an Alumni Ambassador at Emmanuel College in 2018 to 2019, reflected on the experience:

> My most successful activity and one I feel that I grew from the most was speaking at a conference that revolved around Diversity and Inclusion. It was a project that I had been working on all year. My presentation was called 'Cultural Immersion: How I Learned to Love Myself and the World Around Me.' I shared my thoughts about culture shock and identity. It was very interesting and I was able to make connections with a lot of people whom I had never talked to before. I felt that this was one of my most successful moments.

The ambassador program has provided opportunities for AIFS to continue collaborating with university partners and take an active role in expanding access and information for and with students from minoritized backgrounds—something that can be challenging for a provider organization that works with students from around the United States. The program also allows students from diverse backgrounds to serve as leaders to their peers and come together with a common goal. The programmatic intentionality encourages participants to continue to learn from each other after their experiences in-country have concluded, mirroring the experience they will have in the professional world when they work within diverse teams. Participants develop lifelong relationships that can have a positive impact on their career opportunities and social network. Career development is a large component and draw of the program, which includes advice on how to market international experience, interview etiquette, and how to navigate the transition from college student to professional. Individual resume and LinkedIn reviews are conducted with the alumni team, who provide mentorship long after the program end date.

Recommendation: At many organizations and institutions, efforts for continuing to work with and invest in alumni are seen as nonessential or a lower priority. However, the investment is time well spent as alumni are often the biggest cheerleaders/influencers among their peers, and institutions/organizations are likely to see near-term results in increased interest in study abroad.

AIFS also believes it is important to utilize alumni in outreach efforts with intentionality. Encouraging students to concentrate their outreach efforts on one or two underrepresented communities in study abroad not only provides students with a greater focus on how to tell their study abroad story, but it also allows them to build trust and deeper relationships with members of communities which they may not have had connections to before. The alumni program can serve as an example for both providers and individual campuses, looking to move DEI (diversity, equity, and inclusion) efforts forward in real and meaningful ways.

Key Takeaways

Each case study has presented its own set of strategies and approaches that education abroad practitioners can take with them into their daily practice. There are also several key themes that emerged from this collaborative process that warrant additional attention.

Invest Early and Often

While practitioners often lament the lack of time for strategy and planning, dedicating space to thinking through and documenting offices, institutions, and organizations' priorities is key to ensuring these priorities are reflected in daily operations and in the areas where time and resources are dedicated. Education abroad practitioners must commit to investing *time and energy* early with students. This work begins from the moment a student expresses interest in education abroad and continues through their time abroad to when they return. All four cases emphasized the importance of communicating with students early on in their experiences, that is, during predeparture advising for HU and DePauw, before the students arrive in-country with MSID, and while students are still abroad as with AIFS.

For universities, DePauw and Howard offer insight into the importance of leveraging *outside opportunities and resources* to help practitioners promote poststudy abroad engagement/support. Modeling after programs such as the Benjamin A. Gilman and AIFS' ambassador program, practitioners have built-in levers that encourage students to engage their peers and communities creatively upon their return. Institutions are positioned to utilize such programs to ensure students return to campus already thinking about how they will share their experiences with others. Similarly, providers (education abroad and scholarship/fellowship) are well positioned to incorporate elements of reentry programming and engagement that allow students to return ready to discuss their international experiences.

Collaboration Is Vital

Education abroad offices and international education organizations cannot and should not be seen as the sole providers of every service that students may need when they return to campus. The following are three particular groups with whom it is important to cultivate collaborative partnerships.

Campus Partners: U.S. institutions of higher education are structured in such a way that students have access to services that extend well beyond their academic interests. Many campuses have offices and units dedicated to career preparation and physical and mental health, and diversity and inclusion services, among others. Such services can be of particular importance to students upon their return. An education abroad practitioner's role should not be to replicate such services. Rather, education abroad professionals should identify ways to collaborate with colleagues in offices across campus and share the specific needs and concerns of returned students. Education abroad professionals can maximize partnerships by identifying key points of contact in other units and referring students to appropriate services upon their return.

Providers and Programs: In the same way practitioners can develop collaborative partnerships with campus units, practitioners on campus and at education abroad provider organizations are positioned to develop relationships with in-country teams and U.S.-based teams. Supporting students' reentry experience can and should be an ongoing and back and forth conversation between domestic and overseas staff. In-country teams can begin to prepare students for return, as MSID and AIFS have demonstrated, and share relevant information about students' experiences for their U.S.-based counterparts. Beyond information sharing, U.S.-based practitioners and in-country teams might collaborate to offer additional integrated resources (e.g., identity-based information relevant to the country) and activities (e.g., community building, navigating difficult dialogues) based on the students going abroad, which can be particularly relevant when working with students from populations underrepresented abroad. This can also provide a continuity of support for students returning from abroad. Organizations such as Diversity Abroad, The Forum on Education Abroad, and the NAFSA regularly publish resources for practitioners to explore such topics and hone skills to support their students (e.g., The Forum Standards of Good Practice, Diversity Abroad's Access, Inclusion, Diversity, and Equity Roadmap).

Alumni: Education abroad alumni are both recipients and prospective providers of reentry services. While practitioners support students upon their return, these same practitioners are also positioning students to support, create, and lead outreach efforts for populations underrepresented in education abroad. Institutions and organizations can develop reentry programming that continues student growth in several ways including leading outreach efforts to student populations underrepresented in education, serving as peer advisors to prospective education abroad students, and offering input on developing more inclusive services. Their involvement in such activities not only supports their growth but also helps engender systemic change in our institutions and organizations that can lead to a more diverse and inclusive education abroad ecosystem.

Technology: Although the case studies did not explicitly reference the use of technology, virtual spaces, social media, and other technological tools are important resources practitioners can use to connect and reengage students when they return from abroad. HU's use and expansion of the *#StudyAbroadSoBlack* hashtag has developed a unique space for Black students to celebrate and share their experiences abroad, demonstrating the possibility of developing online communities that invite minoritized communities to share and reflect on their experiences. Other initiatives such as Fulbright Noir (see Chapter 12 in this volume), Fulbright Latinx, and Fulbright Prism represent other primarily online spaces building virtual communities. These efforts also provide a unique way to leverage the idea of "paying it forward" as highlighted in nearly all of the case studies presented here. In a pandemic and postpandemic world, identifying technological tools that can bolster reentry efforts (e.g., virtual gatherings via Zoom, reflective workshops that leverage Google Jamboard, career development discussions done via Twitter) will be important for professionals entering the field.

Reentry Courses: The case studies also offer strategies focused on hiring or involving students in activities that are voluntary. However, developing a reentry course for credit for returned students may offer practitioners the opportunity to carve out space for students to continue honing their reflective skills (as noted in MSID) and share their experiences in an intentionally designed and facilitated way. To the extent that such courses are offered by instructors trained to navigate difficult conversations and help students build on their intercultural competencies, such courses may provide students a venue to discuss issues related to identity, challenging experiences from abroad, and more.

Concluding Thoughts

The case studies offer distinct strategies for how to approach the reentry phase of education abroad and have demonstrated that the field needs more examples, models, and research on the reentry process that help practitioners understand how to improve services and programming. These examples offer both insight into successful models and motivation for others to document and share their reentry efforts. They also contribute to the existing literature that goes beyond assessment and considers the programmatic implications for reentry, particularly for groups historically minoritized and underserved in the education abroad process. Having more voices and perspectives on reentry efforts offers the field a better understanding of effective programming and opportunities to incorporate these efforts into the full life cycle of the education abroad experience.

The case studies remind practitioners that in order to integrate inclusive practices that strive for excellence, the reentry stage is not one that can be omitted. Just as learning begins before students go abroad, learning continues well after the students have returned home. Practitioners must ensure that *all* students can continue to learn and grow after they return home, not only the students who are independently motivated to reengage. Practitioners can begin with small steps like scheduling one or two reflection activities a term and integrating alumni into outreach sessions. Smaller, sustained efforts lay the foundation for more robust efforts later.

This chapter is written at a time when these case studies offer important insight into what successful reentry has looked like in a pre–COVID-19 world. There are certainly lessons and strategies that will continue to be relevant in a postpandemic environment. It is conceivable that education abroad will look different from the field in which these cases were operating. As a result, the approaches to reentry explored here will require changes and modifications based on the new reality following the current health crisis that has already had an incredible impact on international education and exchange. Sustaining and advancing efforts to embed DEI is more important than ever and will require our continued attention and commitment.

References

AIFS Study Abroad. (2019). *Alumni ambassador survey results.* Internal AIFS report: unpublished.

AIFS Study Abroad. (2020a, April). *AIFS study abroad scholarships, grants & financial support.* Retrieved from https://www.aifsabroad.com/financial-aid/

AIFS Study Abroad. (2020b). *Alumni ambassador survey results.* Internal AIFS report: unpublished.

AIFS Study Abroad. (2020, November). *Navigating uncertainty: Resources for thoughtfully processing your time abroad and your return.* Retrieved from https://www.aifsabroad.com/alumni/pdf/navigating-uncertainty.pdf

AIFS Study Abroad. (2021). *Access, inclusion, diversity & equity.* Retrieved from https://www.aifsabroad.com/inclusion

Arouca, R. A. (2013). *A qualitative study of returning study abroad students: The critical role of reentry support programs.* Graduate Student Theses, Dissertations, and Professional Papers. 33. https://scholarworks.umt.edu/etd/33

Brubaker, C. (2017). Re-thinking re-entry: New approaches to supporting students after study abroad. *Die Unterrichtspraxis/Teaching German, 50*(2), 109–119.

Chun, E., & Evans, A. (2016). Rethinking cultural competence in higher education: An ecological framework for student development. *Ashe Higher Education Report, 42*(4), 7–162. https://doi.org/10.1002/aehe.20102

Cress, C. M. (2008). Creating inclusive learning communities: The role of student–faculty relationships in mitigating negative campus climate. *Learning Inquiry, 2*(2), 95–111. https://doi.org/10.1007/s11519-008-0028-2

Engle, L., & Engle, J. (2003). Study abroad levels: Toward a classification of program types. *Frontiers: The interdisciplinary journal of study abroad, 9*(1), 1–20.

Gray, K. M., & Savicki, V. (2015). Study abroad: Behavior, affect, and cultural distance. *Frontiers: The Interdisciplinary Journal of Study Abroad, XXVI*, 264–278.

Greenleaf, R. K. (1970). *The servant as leader.* Center for Applied Studies.

Gross, L. S., & Goh, M. (2017). Mindful reflection in intercultural learning. In B. Kappler Mikk & I. E. Steglitz (Eds.), *Learning across cultures: Locally and globally* (3rd ed., pp. 167–190). NAFSA Publications and Stylus Publishing.

Hammer, M. R., Bennett, M. J., & Wiseman, R. (2003). Measuring intercultural sensitivity: The intercultural development inventory. *International Journal of Intercultural Relations, 27,* 421–443.

HU Bison Abroad Updates. (2019, April/May). *Howard University's Ralph J. Bunche Center Newsletter.* Retrieved from https://myemail.constantcontact.com/Ralph-J--Bunche-Center-Newsletter---April-May-2019.html?soid=1123721102917&aid=10h7LJnUynU

Institute of International Education. (n.d.). *IIE generation study abroad initiative.* Retrieved June 24, 2020, from https://www.iie.org/programs/generation-study-abroad

Institute of International Education. (2019). *"Student profile" Open Doors report on international educational exchange.* Retrieved from http://www.iie.org/opendoors

Kitsantas, A. (2004). Studying abroad: The role of college students' goals on the development of cross-cultural skills and global understanding. *College Student Journal, 38*(3), 441–452.

Milem, J. F., Chang, M. J., & Antonio, A. L. (2005). *Making diversity work on campus: A research-based perspective.* Association of American Colleges and Universities.

Mohajeri Norris, E., & Steinberg, M. (2008). Does language matter? The impact of language of instruction on study abroad outcomes. *Frontiers: The Interdisciplinary Journal of Study Abroad, 17*(1), 107–131. https://doi.org/10.36366/frontiers.v17i1.247

Morais, D. B., & Ogden, A. C. (2011). Initial development and validation of the Global Citizenship Scale. *Journal of Studies in International Education, 15*(5), 445–466. https://doi.org/10.1177/1028315310375308

Sanford, N. (1966). *Self and society: Social change and individual development.* Transaction Publishers.

Segalowitz, N., Freed, B., Collentine, J., Lafford, B., Lazar, N., & Díaz-Campos, M. (2004). A comparison of Spanish second language acquisition in two different learning contexts: Study abroad and the domestic classroom. *Frontiers: The Interdisciplinary Journal of Study Abroad, 10*(1), 1–18. https://doi.org/10.36366/frontiers.v10i1.130

Stallman, E. M. (2009). *Intercultural competence and racial awareness in study abroad* (Doctoral dissertation). University of Minnesota. Retrieved from http://conservancy.umn.edu/handle/11299/56226

Szkudlarek, B. (2010). Reentry—A review of the literature. *International Journal of Intercultural Relations, 34,* 1–21. DOI: 10.1016/j.ijintrel.2009.06.006\

Tarrant, M. A., Rubin, D. L., & Stoner, L. (2014). The added value of study abroad: Fostering a global citizenry. *Journal of Studies in International Education, 18*(2), 141–161.

Vande Berg, M., Paige, R. M., & Lou, K. H. (2012). *Student learning abroad: What our students are learning, what they're not, and what we can do about it.* Stylus.

Wielkiewicz, R. M., & Turkowski, L. W. (2010). Issues upon returning from study abroad programs. *Journal of College Student Development, 51*(6), 649–664. Retrieved from https://search-proquest-com.proxyau.wrlc.org/docview/807531460?accountid=8285

Williams, T. R. (2005). Exploring the impact of study abroad on students' intercultural communication skills: Adaptability and sensitivity. *Journal of Studies in International Education, 9*(4), 356–371. https://doi.org/10.1177/1028315305277681

Young, G. (2014). Reentry: Supporting students in the final stage of study abroad. *New Directions for Student Services, 2014*(146), 59–67. https://doi.org/10.1002/ss.20091

14

Alignment, Belongingness, and Social Justice: Using Assessment to Advance Inclusive Excellence in Education Abroad

Katherine Yngve and Elizabeth Brewer

Introduction

Excellence in higher education has all too often been exclusionary. The history of educational assessment is rife with examples of both intentional (c.f. Crouse & Trusheim, 1988; Synnott, 1974) and unintentional exclusionary policies and practices (Artiles et al., 2005; Ryan, 2004) and with scholarly works that point out that assessment practice has often been biased (Arewa, 1977; Berlak, 2001; Inoue, 2015; Klenowski, 2009; Volante, 2008; Wall et al., 2014). The history of assessment of study abroad is closely tied to conceptualizations of academic rigor (Salisbury, 2015), arising from the need to prove that the off-campus endeavor is of worth to the individual student, the institution, and the national interest (Twombly et al., 2012). For various reasons, this reification of the paradigm called "rigor" is understandable. However, rigor is a nebulous and socially defined construct (D'Ignazio & Klein, 2020;

Johnson et al., 2018; Okun & Jones, 2001) and is, almost by definition, the antithesis of inclusive, as it seeks to demarcate that which is valued from that which is not.

Within this context, education abroad (EA)—including overseas study, research, internships, and volunteer activities—is no exception. In a field in which claims of transformation are uncritically accepted, and where overseas programming may be a cost center or revenue source, discussions of what constitutes excellence (or more tellingly, what constitutes inclusive excellence) can fail to occur, as can exploring how rigor in EA, if poorly defined, might be antithetical to equity. A more equitable approach can and should replace notions of rigor with a definition of excellence that values each student's unique and multiple intersectional identity characteristics (Broda et al., 2018; Clayton-Pedersen & Musil, 2009). These questions are critical if EA is to be inclusive of *all* students, faculty, staff, and local hosts of today and tomorrow.

When seeking to create transformative learning experiences, it is a best practice, as described in Chapter 5 of this volume on program design, to begin with the end in mind. In response, this chapter on inclusive excellence focuses on the notions of belonging (defined as feeling accepted, valued, included, and encouraged as an individual) and belongingness (group/campus/program climate), which we position as the desired outcome of inclusive excellence efforts. Belongingness is now recognized as critical to success in a wide range of contexts, including education, careers, and civic life (Baumeister & Leary, 1995; Den Hartog et al., 2007; Moallem, 2013). When institutions build structures that provide belongingness for minoritized or marginalized students, more equitable educational results occur (Broda et al., 2018; Good et al., 2000; Patton, 2010). Not surprisingly, therefore, the foundational calls-to-action for the creation of an inclusive excellence paradigm in higher education define a climate of belongingness as critical to such endeavors (Clayton-Pederson & Musil, 2009; Williams et al., 2005).

Belonging and belongingness are also frequent topics of research when the topic is adaptation and success of international students (c.f. Bender et al., 2019; Poteet & Gomez, 2015). However, belonging and belongingness have received little attention within the field of EA, despite the demonstrated potential of these concepts, and the community-building practices derived from them, to increase equity, diversity, and inclusion (EDI). In this chapter, we argue that belonging and belongingness are the keys to shifting from a paradigm of excellence that focuses almost exclusively on increasing an individual's global or intercultural competence, to one that is centered in a collective ability to foster inclusiveness. To that end, we provide concepts, tools, and suggestions from beyond the EA "bubble." Our guiding principle is that assessment is an evidence-based process of continuous improvement for teaching and learning and is a professional practice distinct in many important ways from both research and program evaluation. To date, the published EA literature and professional conference trends, in the authors' experience, suggest that the EA practice of analyzing learning outcomes has aligned more with the realm of research and program evaluation than with assessment as a tool for institutional change.

Good assessment practice begins with aligning learning outcomes with institutional mission. With EDI now widely understood as critical to the mission and delivery of both higher education and EA within the U.S. context, if not around the world, however, the focus of this chapter is how assessment can help advance inclusive excellence in EA. Readers interested in understanding the relationship among learning outcomes, assessment, and program/institutional mission are advised to consult the foundational volumes on EA assessment cited in this chapter. The National Institute for Learning Outcomes Assessment (NILOA, n.d.), a pioneer in providing resources for equity-minded assessment, also provides a "New to Assessment" section that is of use in this regard.

Positionality Statement

The authors of this chapter are both White, cisgender women with multiple degrees and long careers in higher education. Each has felt the stings of misogyny, the academic caste system, and (increasingly) ageism on our perceived value to society and academia, but we also know that we lead lives of privilege. In part because of this dual perspective, our life experiences have caused us to care deeply about all students' learning, social justice, and the world. Our privilege affords us the duty and the opportunity to act as allies in advancing equity and improving social justice in higher education (and the world). We understand assessment as being about learning, and we envision belonging(ness) as the key to improving both equity and learning in EA. Moreover, we believe it is insufficient for EA to entice students to advance their individual career goals through the acquisition of global competence skills and attitudes, without also equipping them with the agency, empathy, and desire to foster inclusiveness wherever they find themselves, including in their home campuses, social communities, and future workplaces.

Assessment as Continuous Process Improvement

Since the publication of the first comprehensive guide to outcomes assessment in EA (Bolen, 2006), practitioners have become much more comfortable with using instruments to define and demonstrate institutional or program "excellence" (Savicki & Brewer, 2015; Vande Berg et al., 2012). The EA field has also recognized and responded to the need to demonstrate mastery of the professional skills of research and of program evaluation. This work has been important and even groundbreaking. However, it is too often the case that what the average EA practitioner or faculty-member refers to as "assessment" often encompasses only a single facet of assessment. In contrast, university assessment professionals typically define assessment as a cyclical, intentional, multiphase, student-centered, change-oriented enterprise (Gozik, 2015; Salisbury, 2015; Suskie, 2018). As can be seen in Table 14.1, research and program evaluation, on the other hand, are distinct in significant ways from assessment, even if they often use the same instruments and methods (Levy, 2017; Lundquist, 2019). This distinction is critical for nurturing belongingness and inclusive excellence. Research and program evaluation alone are inadequate for the advancement and attainment of inclusive excellence in EA, as they seldom hold improvement of student learning as a core value.

The Forum on Education Abroad's *Standards of Good Practice* (The Standards) (2020) recommend that EDI be emphasized by every EA organization. Furthermore, they advocate adoption and dissemination of learning outcomes, regular assessment of the outcomes, and application of findings to improve student learning (p. 22). Thus, while it is important to know that implementation of a new EDI policy or scholarship diversified and/or increased participation in EA, such numbers alone reveal nothing about

Table 14.1 Distinguishing between research, program evaluation, and assessment.

Category	Description
Research	A rigorous truth-seeking inquiry that seeks to uncover generalizable knowledge.
Program evaluation	An inquiry that seeks to determine the worth or impact of a learning intervention, program, or set of programs; sometimes in comparison to a standard or benchmark.
Assessment	A cyclical and iterative process, using research methods, yet often theory driven, that seeks to improve student learning. At the institutional or system level, it may also focus on improving instructional effectiveness and/or climate for learning.

learning outcomes. Neither is it enough to tease out, as some universities have done, a correlation between participation in EA and timely graduation by members of marginalized groups (Malmgren & Galvin, 2008; Schneider & Thornes, 2019). The importance of this distinction cannot be overemphasized: Participation in an educational intervention, even getting good grades and being "retained" long enough to graduate, is not the same thing as learning, nor is it indicative of having the skills, either individually or in groups, to put inclusion (or other leadership and career skills) into practice after graduation. Failure to distinguish educational outputs from learning outcomes is a flaw that keeps many promising diversity efforts from being both inclusive and excellent.

The *Standards* further recommend that data be disaggregated to investigate whether equitable outcomes arise for *all* students and that structures and policies examine and address systemic biases (The Forum on Education Abroad, 2020, p. 25). The *Standards*, in short, embrace the aims and methods of inclusive excellence, including its assessment. All of this bodes well for an inclusively excellent future—but this future will not happen without greater intentionality and a willingness to reframe our definitions of both "excellence" and "assessment." To this end, NILOA offers two excellent case studies on intentional disaggregation of data for inclusive excellence, from San Diego State University (Montenegro, 2020, June) and Capital University (Lynner et al., 2020, June).

Belonging and Belongingness

Belonging is widely defined as "an individual's sense of being accepted, valued, included, and encouraged by others," while need to belong (belongingness) has been hypothesized to be basic to human functioning (Baumeister & Leary, 1995, p. 497). Belonging is closely associated with "academic and social engagement" (Thomas, 2012, p. 12) and can also be understood as "an affinity with a place or situation" such as a school (Korpershoek et al., 2019) or a study abroad locale. In this chapter, "belonging" refers to an individual and "belongingness" to a group of students or a campus climate, but usage varies in practice and the scholarly literature. The matrix in Table 14.2, adapted from Shore et al. (2011), expresses the connection between belonging(ness) and inclusion.

Using a matrix or checklist to codify the degrees of excellence is an assessment technique, which like many attempts to measure attainment, development, or "talent" may lead to educational *exclusion*. The matrix in Table 14.2, by contrast, is consciously used to allow readers to begin to define

Table 14.2 Matrix of belongingness and inclusion.

	Low Belongingness	High Belongingness
Low value in uniqueness	Exclusion: Student not treated as an insider.	Assimilation: Student treated as insider only when conforming to dominant cultural norms and values.
High value in uniqueness	Diversity: Student's unique characteristics are valued; but the student is not treated as an insider.	Inclusion: Student's unique characteristics are valued, as are the contributions of the student's home-culture norms and values; e.g., the student is treated as an insider.

and reframe inclusion as excellence. To apply the matrix to EA, think of movement from left to right along the top row as representing the aspirational path of the typical EA participant: for example, wanting to move from the status of being a transactional visitor (tourist) to being mistaken for a local based on language fluency or behavioral adaptability, or both. The bottom row of the inclusion matrix indicates, however, that assimilation—sometimes also known as "going along to get along"—is not the same as belongingness and is, therefore, incongruent with inclusive excellence.

Belongingness occurs when one's authentic self is valued. Expecting individuals of a marginalized identity to work toward assimilation into the dominant culture is damaging. Even if not racist, as that term is commonly understood, efforts to urge a student toward assimilation or immersion can still be, however unintentionally, discriminatory and inequitable. For example, a White, but neurologically atypical, student can be judged to be "too much trouble," and either not be selected for participation or, if accepted, experience fear of dismissal for "refusing" to be "more outgoing" or "normal" in behavior. While it is natural for students to want to learn to blend in to the host culture, this is only a first step toward attaining inclusion. True belongingness is a two-way street, arising from openness by (1) the host society or dominant culture individual, (2) the program provider staff or host institution, and (3) other members of the program cohort, where applicable—as well as from (some) adaptability on the part of the sojourner or member of a nondominant group.

Instructional interventions found to increase belongingness for minority or marginalized students include cohort programs, learning communities, and the use of constructivist learning frameworks in course design

(Dibartolo et al., 2016). Co-curricular interventions that increase belongingness for minority students include resiliency training (Broda et al., 2018), faculty mentoring (Glass et al., 2017), culture-specific support centers (Patton, 2010), peer mentorship (Good et al., 2000), and structural support for community service (Soria et al., 2003).

In contrast to the abovementioned studies, all of which focus on either domestic minority populations and/or international students, there has been very little research on belonging or belongingness in EA. Yet, important foundational work has been done. First, EA programs are full-to-bursting with exactly the type of curricular and co-curricular interventions that have been cited earlier as increasing belongingness. These programs and interventions are ripe for using assessment to measure their effectiveness across identity groups, thus allowing the program or institution to make strategic, measurable, time-bound, transparent, and context-specific plans for EDI improvement. Second, although they seldom specifically reference the belongingness or EDI literature, a few excellent EA studies do examine the role of gender identity as a barrier to feeling comfortable enough with locals to attain language-learning goals (Polanyi, 1995; Trentman, 2013). More work of this sort is needed and not just about language acquisition. Finally, today's EA practitioners understand research and program evaluation and are increasing their fluency with assessment methods. As suggested at the end of this chapter, those skills can be put to productive use in collaborations with campus EDI units to promote inclusive excellence on the home campus as well as abroad.

Backward Design for Social and Racial Justice

It is our firm belief, in concert with most educational assessment experts as cited earlier, that the purpose of educational assessment is to illuminate pathways toward structural or instructional improvements that more pervasively support student success. Yet, it cannot be denied that educational assessment has often served to preserve the power and privilege of White culture. This makes it difficult for marginalized groups to believe in the possibility of systemic change or of the power of institutional assessment to create it; this, it should hardly need to be said, impairs belongingness for individuals of these identities.

While EA has a rich history of applying critical theory to its own gendered and colonialist thought patterns (Adkins & Messerly, 2019; Gore, 2005; Hartman & Kieley, 2015; Ogden, 2007; Sharpe, 2015), it has in general failed to apply the backward-design and accountability techniques of assessment to ameliorate these conditions and turn theory into praxis. Nor has it owned up to the fact that, particularly when it comes to successfully crossing racial divides and/or job and disciplinary silos, it is possible that EA professionals are not, as a whole, quite as interculturally competent as one would like to think (El Ganzoury, 2012). Of the six steps toward equitable assessment practice that have been identified by the aforementioned NILOA experts, the first, and most vital, is to begin by examining one's own biases and assumptions, as well as those of relevant institutional settings (2021). EA professionals know that culture has a profound impact on many things. In the context of the purposes of both this volume and this specific chapter, it is, therefore, vital for EA professionals to reflect deeply and honestly upon the fact that culture profoundly impacts:

(a) what you chose to assess (Henning & Lundquist, 2018),
(b) how you collect and analyze data (D'Ignazio & Klein, 2020; Noble, 2018), and
(c) how you calibrate your response, as a critical embodiment of the assessment process, to your informants and/or your institution's assessment needs (Symonette, 2015).

EA prides itself on teaching students to be aware of their own biases and cultural influences, yet power and privilege can easily act as blinders to how our professional preconceptions and habits (even our hard-won research training and its requisite objectivity lenses) may be impairing the profession's ability to advance inclusive excellence. For example, belongingness is far less likely to occur in an environment in which some students consistently receive the message that they are deficient or aberrant in some way—which, unfortunately, often occurs in the mission statements, recruitment materials, and data-disaggregated outcome reports of minority-supporting programs. Numerous studies have shown that when marginalized students perceive that society expects them not to succeed, they quite often do not (Jussim & Harber, 2005). Some practical resources for "doffing one's blinders" are cataloged in the following paragraph.

As a first step, we suggest that before sitting down to craft learning outcomes, the equity-minded EA practitioner or team would do well to work through the reflective self-assessment questions in Symonnette's four-quadrant Integral Evaluator Model in her chapter on culturally responsive evaluation (2015). The "Practicing Equity-Centered Assessment Worksheet" (Anthology, 2020) is equally valuable, in this case for brainstorming practical ways to enact equitable assessment in one's own context. In addition, the

Equity by Design principles and infographic (University of Southern California, 2015) offer easy-to-grasp corrective examples that illustrate some ways to ensure that institutions align messaging and student outcome reporting to the inclusive excellence outcomes desired (e.g., belongingness). Another valuable tool is the Logic Model technique (Frechtling, 2015; LeCroy, 2018; Rogers, 2008). Although typically used to focus on outputs or throughputs of education rather than student learning, this backward-design method can be used to help leaders better align resources to, and assess outcomes of, the desired equity goals of a program or institution, including long-term societal impact (Cooper et al., 2020; Deardorff, 2005; Doerr, 2018).

Those who are eager to change the relationship between power, assessment, and equity, or who may have the need for a larger community of practice around equity and assessment, will want to become acquainted with the work of the Socially Just Assessment Project, an alliance of nine North American higher education professional associations, four of which are specialized in assessment and/or standards definition. In 2018, these organizations committed to intentionally working to reposition assessment in higher education as a tool to advance equity and social justice (Henning, 2018). One of the most thought-provoking outputs of the project to date is a five-stage Continuum of Socially Just Assessment, first described by Henning and Lundquist (2018), which is rapidly evolving from the purely theoretical into suggestions for theory-informed practice (Henning & Philippon, 2019). Socially just assessment practice is still somewhat rare, but case studies of application of these concepts to campus practice are beginning to accumulate in the public domain (see Assessment Institute, 2021; Association for the Advancement of Learning in Higher Education [AALHE], 2019; NILOA, 2021) and are ripe for replication by EA practitioners.

Each of these approaches and models can assist professionals in taking a critical look at the role of social justice in EA and spur them to identify institutional structures that perpetuate social inequality. Furthermore, the "bottom-up" approach they exemplify can help us consider how marginalized groups are affected by their relationships to power and privilege and develop processes that seek to analyze and interrogate individual and group biases (Berger, 2020, p. 3). Using backward-program design to engender an inclusive excellence structure will ensure that notions of belonging and belongingness are not simply tacked on as an after-thought in a compliance-with-regulations mode, but instead are intentionally and strategically threaded throughout office and program missions and learning outcomes. We turn to the latter next.

Alignment 101: Setting Belongingness as a Learning Outcome

> *Creating a culture of belonging depends on our ability to shift cultural perspectives and appropriately adapt behaviors to cultural differences and commonalities.*
>
> Center for Inclusion and Social Change, University of Colorado, Boulder

How can assessment help us define and nurture belongingness, that is, to create an environment inclusive of all students? There is no canonical definition or rubric of the constructs, attitudes, or skills of belongingness. Tracking gains in participation, retention, or graduation tells us nothing about how students learn to be open to and supportive of difference, let alone whether their persistence is relevant to their sense of belonging or individual determination to persist. Instead, we suggest that institutions need to assess with a focus on equity rather than equality. Creating an environment in which all students feel welcomed involves multiple stages, with significant preparation on the part of faculty and staff to align all aspects of programming.

As mentioned earlier, most contemporary introductions to the art of assessment suggest beginning with the end in mind (McTighe, 2018). In other words, start by defining what learners should be able to do (better) after the lesson, course, experience, or degree program in question. While instructional design purists might cavil that wholesale borrowing of others' learning outcomes statements or assessment framework is generally unwise, in our own practice we have found it to be instructive to review outcomes and frameworks set by others as models for adaptation to one's own context, particularly with faculty or staff who are new to educational assessment. To that end, some resources which merit discussion are discussed.

AAC&U's VALUE Rubrics and Learning Outcomes

Aligning rubrics with specific learning outcome goals and institutional objectives is both critical and surprisingly easy; it can also help build faculty and staff consensus, shared meaning, and purpose (Brewer, 2011; Yngve, 2019). The Association of American Colleges and Universities (AAC&U) valid assessment of learning in undergraduate education (VALUE) rubrics (AAC&U, n.d.) has been specifically designed by subject matter experts for this purpose. The four rubrics that focus on personal and social responsibility (intercultural competence, civic engagement, global learning, and ethical reasoning), as well as the critical thinking rubric, are particularly relevant to the intentional fostering of belongingness and inclusive excellence. Plausible belongingness competencies they identify and delineate include empathy, communication and openness, civic identity and commitment, personal and social responsibility, and ethical self-awareness.

The AAC&U encourages innovative, mix-and-match, adaptation of the rubrics, rather than rote adoption, in order to better ensure mission-specific alignment. For example, by selecting elements from several of the rubrics, an institution might come to a consensus that a combination of high levels of empathy, student positionality, civic commitment, ethical self-awareness, and social responsibility should compose its desired skill set for belongingness and inclusivity. Program-level goal setting can then proceed, as shown by this hypothetical example:

> Through participation in this two-week education abroad program, 80% of students will be able to recognize both intellectual and emotional aspects of the issue of racism from more than one worldview, as measured by use of the AAC&U intercultural competence rubric to assess individual capstone reflective essays.

A Behavioral Inventory Approach to Belongingness

Behavioral inventories are widely used to quantify and assess the outcomes of clinical treatment and wellness interventions but have not been much used in EA or inclusion work. Yet, they have the potential to help mentors recognize when students are actively walking the walk of inclusion, instead of just talking about embracing diversity. Ruben's Behavioral Inventory (1976), for example, is an observational instrument designed to help the instructor measure several behaviors of cross-difference effectiveness. Each page details four to five levels of competency using culture-general language for a given construct (e.g., respect, empathy), thus enabling the observer/instructor to systematically identify and quantify behaviors. The original tool is in the public domain and freely downloadable; so, too, is a related rubric, intended to facilitate the coaching of students toward respectful and empathetic behavior (Yngve, 2020). Behavioral assessment should be approached in a spirit of critical self-reflection: culturally influenced notions of what constitutes respectful classroom behavior have often been used to discriminatory effect (Kramarczuk-Voulgarides et al., 2017; Van Houtte, 2010). Nonetheless, this technique offers a fruitful assessment avenue for moving beyond declarative inclusivity toward habitually performed inclusivity, resulting in greater aggregate belongingness.

Consider this possible outcome statement as an example of how application of an element from one of these inventories can help EA students learn the art of not stigmatizing or responding unfavorably toward difference:

> Through participation in this two-week inclusion training program, which forms a part of your pre-departure preparation for living in Oman, we expect that all students

will gain the ability to consistently behave respectfully in the presence of cultural practices which differ from their own, as described by the level three explanation of "Respectfulness towards Others" on Yngve's Behavioral Rubric of Intercultural Competence Development.

Taxonomies Versus Indigenous Ways of Knowing-Being

Many introductions to generating learning outcomes advocate using Bloom's Taxonomy of learning. Some educational support services have even created learning outcome generators that require the taxonomy's use (e.g., Arizona State University, n.d.). Such step-by-step scaffolds for thinking about alignment are a good introduction to assessment best practice. However, a rigid focus on the cognitive domain may be detrimental to inclusive excellence. Taxonomies focused strictly on (so-called) objectivity, accountability, standardization, and measurability of learning outcomes are increasingly being interrogated as harmful to non-White populations and are seen by some as aligned with systemic racism (D'Ignazio & Klein, 2020; Inoue, 2015; Okun & Jones, 2001). Cultures differ in how they categorize knowledge and excellence; hierarchical and straight-line taxonomies may not apply. Thus, indigenous researchers and their allies have sought to define, operationalize, and disseminate a more holistic and supportive approach to student learning (Krakouer, 2015; Manning et al., 2020; O'Toole, 2014). For example, in Hawai'i, the entire general education curriculum of the K-12 public education system has been revised to focus upon the indigenous values of belonging, excellence, and well-being (Hawai'i State Department of Education, 2015).

Similarly, the Medicine Wheel approach[1] to education (LaFever, 2016) draws from the sacred practices of the First Nations of Turtle Island, North America, to integrate the four deeply intertwined quadrants of balanced knowing and well-being: physical, emotional, intellectual, and spiritual. Practicing the design and alignment of outcomes, learning interventions, and assessments around the Medicine Wheel or other models of indigenous ways of knowing and learning can help EA learning interventions and milieus feel

[1] This anti-taxonomy communicates that inclusive excellence, or even individualized personal excellence, cannot be achieved without acknowledging the holistic importance of all four learning quadrants for internalized, creative, analytical, and self-actualization. A simpler introduction to these can be found in LaFever's taxonomic table of sample verbs for the spiritual domain (ibid., p. 418), in a progression suitable for creating graduated learning outcome statements. LaFever's chapter on using the Medicine Wheel for curriculum design in intercultural and multicultural education contexts (LaFever, 2017) may be particularly helpful to education abroad practitioners and educators.

more welcoming to students from a wide variety of communities and learning styles. As yet, apart from one case study from Montana State University (Carjuzaa & Ruff, 2010), there appears to be less published guidance about using and assessing outcomes of indigenous frameworks. Amplifying and operationalizing indigenous frameworks in EA assessment, program evaluation, and research constitute a significant opportunity for the inclusively excellent future of the field.

Alignment 201: Deploying Formative Assessment to Facilitate Belonging and Equity

Rubrics and inventories make it easier, as indicated earlier, to align learning outcome goals and their assessment because they allow for alignment of both formative and summative assessments within the same tool. *Formative assessment* has been defined as a low-stake appraisal that helps students (and instructors) identify their strengths and weaknesses so that they can target areas that need work. *Summative assessment* is a higher stake evaluation, most typically done at the end of a learning intervention, intended to compare the student's state of mastery to an external standard or benchmark (Eberle Center, 2020). Formative assessment has been identified by a number of educator organizations as a foundational equity practice (Kalinec-Craig, 2017; National Council of Teachers of English, 2020). A close cousin to formative assessment is cultural mentoring (Paige & Goode, 2009), a process in which a knowledgeable and approachable person assists the study abroad participant in making sense of a confusing cultural encounter, hopefully leading to more effective and appropriate behavior on the part of the learner. In large-scale studies in Australia, formative assessment has been shown to advance inclusion and equity for students from minoritized cultures (Klenowski, 2014).

In line with a formative approach, individual reflection and guided group discussion can deepen learning among returned study abroad participants. This is assessment *as* learning (Dubec, 2019) and is also an example of focusing on inclusive co-creation of excellence as an outcome of EA, rather than on more individualistic outcomes, such as intercultural competence. When artifacts produced by students are used for assessment, this acknowledges and validates their importance and becomes an inclusive action (Stevens & Levi, 2013; Suskie, 2000). Although the reflections and other artifacts of learning could be measured against a rubric in order to satisfy grading or accreditation needs (e.g., for program evaluation), it is in fact the instructor and the fellow students who are the true calibration (e.g., assessment) instruments as they cocreate a community of belongingness around personal transformation and accountability.

As with any teaching tool or technique, formative assessment is not a panacea: For example, students accustomed to instructional paradigms that focus on summative assessment may interpret some types of formative assessment (quizzes, reflections, giving peer feedback, etc.) as busy work (Green, 2020). Furthermore, when used by instructors who, consciously or unconsciously, subscribe to "majoritarian assumptions" (Ravet, 2012, p. 948) about behavior and learning, formative assessment may result in a feedback loop that is damaging to the development of the student who is perceived as failing to assimilate to White or gendered norms.

While rubrics and inventories are beneficial to alignment and equity, surveys can also serve as both formative and summative instruments. In fact, two of the surveys commonly in use in EA, the Kolb Learning Style Inventory (Kolb, 2007) and the Intercultural Conflict Style Inventory (Hammer, 2005), measure personality-related behaviors that are unlikely to shift much after attaining adulthood; in other words, they work best as formative instruments. The wisest use of such instruments in a belongingness context is to help learners recognize that (1) a certain skill, trait, or set of skills exists along a predictable continuum and (b) difference and open discussion of difference are not to be feared. To that end, the Intercultural Learning Hub, a free resource developed by Purdue University (2018) for educators, contains a searchable digital toolbox that includes several open-source surveys designed to measure characteristics that may be conducive to belongingness, such as humility, empathy, communication style, or self-awareness. Alternatively, the Global Belonging Collaborative offers an open-source repository (2018) of validated belongingness surveys suitable for measuring the effectiveness of any belongingness initiative, grouped by audience.

Conclusion: Take Action

This chapter has drawn on a range of literature to make the case that (1) belongingness goes hand in hand with EDI and (2) assessment, done systematically and well, can both strengthen student learning outcomes and help institutions and organizations hold one another accountable. These principles apply to many contexts, including, broadly, higher education, and EA more narrowly. If as a reader you have accepted these principles or arguments, you likely now ask, "Where do I begin?" Anticipating this question, here we suggest several principles and practical steps to guide the work.

Align your belongingness work and its assessment with institutional EDI and belongingness goals and efforts. Assessment works best when (1) it addresses issues that people care about and (2) when representatives from across the many stakeholder identities of an educational community are involved (Astin et al., 1992; Hutchings et al., 2012). Aligning EA belongingness work and assessment with institutional goals and efforts can help take advantage of institutional expertise resources, align efforts with institutional priorities, and increase buy-in.

Collaborate With Stakeholders to inform your work and strengthen its impact. Banta and Blaich (2011) suggest doing so from the start in order to align assessment with stakeholder needs and interests and ensure stakeholder ownership of the process. Absent such collaboration, assessment findings will not lead to the changes in stakeholder practice needed to improve learning outcomes. Appendices 1 and 2 offer two case studies of collaboration. At Western Kentucky University (WKU; Appendix 1), collaborations spanning student affairs and academic affairs around intercultural learning and EDI promise to de-silo this work and make it a shared project. And at State University of New York (SUNY) Albany (Appendix 2), the Office of Student Affairs Assessment and Planning collaborated with the university's Gender and Sexuality Resource Center to amend the first-year belonging survey. In the process, they discovered that one of the main barriers to inclusiveness was their own discomfort with nontraditional ways of analyzing data and reporting on gender identity.

Define Belonging and Belongingness for you, your institution/organization, and your students. As seen in an earlier discussion in this chapter, definitions vary. It will be important, therefore, for you, together with stakeholders in your organization and institution, to use iterative processes to arrive at workable definitions. Follow up to develop a rubric that identifies characteristics or metrics of belonging and/or belongingness. Doing so will give you assessment criteria. The AAC&U LEAP rubrics offer good examples of rubric development. However, do not feel you must wait to begin your work until you have a fully developed rubric. You can begin with discrete steps; this makes assessment doable. Therefore, focus initially on measuring a small subset of belonging/belongingness metrics. At a later stage, you can identify and pay attention to additional metrics.

Disaggregate Data Collaboratively. Working with students, institutional data, and the scholarship on intersectionality all tell us that there is no one student nor one group of students; the scholarship on intersectionality, EDI, and international student belonging are all helpful here. Data must be disaggregated to understand who participates and why; who benefits, how and why; how power and privilege matter; and how belonging affects EA participation and learning outcomes.

Do Not Fear the Small Sample. The current allure of big data approaches to knowledge generation may sway researchers away from methods that amplify the voices and the needs of the small sample demographic group. Yet, the inclusive excellence paradigm tells us that excellence requires both inviting nonpowerful groups to the table and listening to them with respect. In that regard, the EA practitioner will find support for smaller data assessment approaches by consulting the scholarship on myths and misconceptions about using qualitative methods in institutional research and assessment (Harper & Kuh, 2007).

Invite Students In. Activities, assignments, and assessments that invite students in promote inclusion and belonging. Inviting in means designing opportunities for students to take ownership roles so that they truly care about the activity, assignment, assessment, or learning outcome because it is meaningful to them. This in turn aids in helping the EA instructor or practitioner better understand the students as individuals and as learners.

Keep It Simple. Experimenting with small stakes assessment will help you build confidence and gather evidence you can act on. Adding a query or two about aspects of belonging in a poststudy abroad evaluation is low stakes, but the responses can shed light on the student experience. Similarly, using nonbinary demographic options for gender and/or race when designing surveys or applications is a simple adjustment and helps often-marginalized populations feel valued from the get-go.

Lean Into a Mindset of Learning to Decenter Whiteness. Defining excellence as inclusion and becoming comfortable with anti-racism has now been recognized by NAFSA and other organizations as an articulated educational policy imperative for the postpandemic world (Contreras et al., 2021). Although this may sound daunting as a concept when writ large, it is easier to begin to put into EA assessment practice than one might think. Recently, examples of work to decenter traditional (e.g., White) notions of excellence in EA include eliminating grading—but not assessment—in a graduate-level study abroad program (Hardy & Totman, 2021), reducing higher-than-equitable GPA requirements as a standard for applying to participate in EA (Lochner-Atkinson, 2021), and using Black feminist empowerment theory as an alignment-and-assessment paradigm (Martin et al., 2021).

Practice Personal and Institutional Self-Reflection. Inclusive excellence and collaboration across campus silos and ethnic identity groups both require that EA professionals humbly own their own biases, power, and privilege. It is not enough to assume that cosmopolitan experiences have equipped us with the fortitude and the skills to dismantle systemic inequities, whether on our home turf or in the locales to which we send our students. Regularly using formative assessment and reflection techniques to address and improve our own competencies—and those of our working peer groups—is as important as using assessment to improve and make equitable the student learning outcomes of EA programs.

Report Your Assessment Findings using methods and language that are clear to nonspecialists. For suggestions, see Venaas' (2019) work. In addition, data analysts may need support to become comfortable applying nondominant perspectives to data gathering and analysis. To put it in the vernacular of feminist and Black scholars of evaluation, you will need to "show your work" (D'Ignazio & Klein, 2020; Symonette, 2014) to help the audiences for this work understand why it matters. This is particularly important for building trust and belongingness among less privileged stakeholder groups. In this regard, the Transparency Framework of the NILOA offers examples of excellence in the field; in particular, see the Framework in the Field (2021) examples illustrating work at a variety of campuses.

Education abroad as a field and practice has evolved considerably over the years, and it now also takes many forms. There is growing consensus, however, that it is imperative to take all measures needed to ensure that EA is inclusive and equitable of today and tomorrow's diversity of students. Furthermore, EA should result in robust student learning, and assessment is key to both understanding the learning outcomes being achieved (or not) and making changes to practice to strengthen outcomes. This chapter has made the case that assessing student belonging and belongingness can help advance exclusive excellence in EA. Practicable suggestions have been made for doing so. Much good and innovative work lies ahead, with promise to strengthen EA's contribution to students' lives, higher education, and society.

Appendix 1. Building the Foundation for Cross-Divisional Assessment

Caryn E. Lindsay, Western Kentucky University

The silos within universities are notoriously difficult to dismantle. Academic affairs' focus, in general, is on students' intellectual development, while students' personal and social development fall under student affairs. Budgetary sources and constraints and competing funding priorities contribute to the challenge of collaboration. Nonetheless, when key elements are in place, cross-divisional collaboration is possible, as suggested in a case study from WKU.

- **Relationships**
  Staff in the Study Abroad and Global Learning Office (SAGL), housed in academic affairs, share a strong commitment to providing access to an international experience (study, research, internship, or service learning) for all WKU students who wish to participate. Over the past 5 years, SAGL has successfully increased the number of underrepresented students studying abroad by developing cooperative relationships across WKU, including with the deans of five colleges and the dean of students. In particular, SAGL's annual training on study abroad opportunities includes student affairs advisors and mentors in the Cynthia and George Nichols III Intercultural Student Engagement Center and the Academic and Career Development Center.
- **Shared Values and Motivation**
  WKU values and promotes both equal access for students and high-impact practices (Kuh, 2008), including study abroad, throughout the curriculum and co-curriculum. A new university strategic plan focuses on improving retention and graduation rates; the campus units referenced here understand themselves as key contributors to the success of these goals. Data on the positive impact of study abroad on WKU student retention and graduation can be found in a study by Byrd (2018).
- **A Validated Tool**
  SAGL's director has encouraged the use of the IDI or Intercultural Development Inventory (n.d.) as one way to assess both cultural understanding in general at WKU and as a study abroad outcome. Thus, she introduced the idea to faculty program leaders; diversity, equity, and inclusion committee members; college deans; the undergraduate curriculum committee; and in a WKU research grant proposal. A qualified administrator of the IDI, she understood that as a rigorously tested tool with proven validity, it met the bar for acceptance within academia.

Against this backdrop, in fall 2019, a window of opportunity opened: WKU committed fully to focusing faculty and staff professional development efforts on enhancing diversity, equity, and inclusion. Subsequently, the dean of students proposed a joint effort to the associate provost of global learning and international affairs and the SAGL director to use the IDI with the 215 staff members reporting to them. Results would be used to help identify appropriate professional development opportunities and evaluate their outcomes, an approach that had proven successful within the Minneapolis Public Schools (DeJaeghere & Cao, 2009). The collaboration might also lead to adoption of the IDI more broadly at WKU.

Note: Within weeks of the IDI becoming available to target staff members in March 2020, WKU moved to remote work in response to the COVID-19 pandemic. Priority became a safe reopening in fall 2020. The IDI project team looks forward to resuming its work postpandemic: debriefings, group dissemination of the findings, and creation of a shared vision for future professional development.

Appendix 2: Collaborative and Self-Reflective Assessment Practices in Action

Emily Feuer and Doug Sweet, University at Albany, State University of New York (SUNY)

At the University at Albany, SUNY, first-year students are invited to participate in a survey about their experiences during the first 6 weeks of their first semester. The purpose of the survey is to measure whether students feel they belong to the university community as well as identify students who will benefit from an early alert outreach to improve their academic, social, and/or emotional experiences. Over the past 4 years, the Student Affairs Assessment and Planning (SAAP) group has worked to highlight the stories of the university's diverse student population by disaggregating data using demographic variables, that include gender identity and sexual identity. While this data-disaggregation work has proven to be invaluable, it has also come with challenges.

Key lessons include:

Collaboration—SAAP began working with the Gender and Sexuality Resource Center (GSRC) 4 years ago after realizing there was no reliable source of data to inform the university on the experience of LGBTQ+ students. To ensure the survey includes appropriate and inclusive LGBTQ+ options for students to self-identify, SAAP reviews the survey instrument with the (GSRC) each year. Furthermore, with suggestion from the coordinator of the GSRC, SAAP has piloted report templates and findings with students in the GSRC to ensure the analysis accurately reflects the community.

Flexibility—Members of SAAP discovered their own comfort was biased toward traditional, mutually exclusive categories. Thus, initially, mutually exclusive categories of Man, Woman, and Transgender/Non-Conforming

(TGNC) were used. After working with the GSRC, SAAP realized that these categories did not correctly categorize TGNC identifying students; the analysis needed to adapt to count students identifying as transgender within both the TGNC category and respective man/woman category.

Thorough Analysis—Data analysis revealed a surprise: more students than expected identified as Asexual. After pairing these data with race/ethnicity variables, the analysis discovered that many international students, especially international students identifying as Asian, selected Asexual as their sexual identity, possibly due to definitional differences based on their cultural norms and beliefs. Subsequently, SAAP modified the instrument to provide clearer definitions. As a result of this layered approach, data are now representative across ethnic and cultural demographics.

Note: A 2018 report about the survey contained information on both its findings and methodology.

References

Adkins, R., & Messerly, B. (2019). Toward decolonizing education abroad: Moving beyond the self/other dichotomy. In E. Brewer & A. Ogden (Eds.), *Education abroad and the undergraduate experience: Critical perspectives and approaches to integration with student learning and development.* Stylus.

Anthology. (2020). *Equity-centered assessment: Embedding equity throughout the assessment cycle.* https://anthology.com/material/practicing-equity-centered-assessment-worksheet

Arewa, O. (1977). Cultural bias in standardized testing: An anthropological view. *The Negro Educational Review, 28*(3), 153.

Arizona State University. (n.d.). *Learning objectives builder.* https://teachonline.asu.edu/objectives-builder/

Artiles, A. J., Rueda, R., Salazar, J. J., & Higareda, I. (2005). Within-group diversity in minority disproportionate representation: English language learners in urban school districts. *Exceptional Children, 71*(3), 283–300.

Assessment Institute. (2021). *2020 Assessment Institute session recordings.* www.assessmentinstitute.iupui.edu/program/recordings.html

Association of American Colleges and Universities. (n.d.). *VALUE rubrics.* www.aacu.org/value-rubrics

Astin, A. W., Banta, T. W., Cross, K. P., El-Khawas, E., Ewell, P. T., Hutchings, P., Marchese, T. J., McClenney, K. M., Mentkowski, M., Miller, M. A., Moran, E. T., & Wright, B. D. (1992). Principles of good practice for assessing student learning. *AAHE Bulletin, 45*(4), 1–20.

Banta, T. W., & Blaich, C. (2010). Closing the assessment loop. *Change: The Magazine of Higher Learning, 43*(1), 22–27. http://dx.doi.org/10.1080/00091383.2011.538642

Baumeister, R. F., & Leary, M. R. (1995). The need to belong: Desire for interpersonal attachments as a fundamental human motivation. *Psychological Bulletin,* 117(3), 497–529. https://doi.org/10.1037/0033-2909.117.3.497

Bender, M., van Osch, Y., Sleegers, W., & Ye, M. (2019). Social support benefits psychological adjustment of international students: Evidence from a meta-analysis. *Journal of Cross-Cultural Psychology, 50*(7), 827–847.

Berlak, H. (2001). Academic achievement, race, and reform: Six essays on understanding assessment policy, standardized achievement tests, and anti-racist alternatives. https://files.eric.ed.gov/fulltext/ED464973.pdf

Berger, L. M. (2020). Introduction. In L. M. Berger (Ed.). *Social justice and international education: Research, practice, and perspectives* (pp. 1–7). NAFSA.

Bolen, M. C. (Ed.). (2006). *A guide to outcomes assessment in education abroad.* The Forum on Education Abroad.

Brewer, E. (2011, October). *Developing and assessing student agency: The process at Beloit College.* Presentation given as part of the culminating conference of ACM Faculty Career Enhancement Project, held at Colorado College, Colorado Springs, Colorado. https://serc.carleton.edu/acm_face/student_agency/beloitoverview

Broda, M., Yun, J., Schneider, B., Yeager, D. S., Walton, G. M., & Diemer, M. (2018). Reducing inequality in academic success for incoming college students: A randomized trial of growth mindset and belonging interventions. *Journal of Research on Educational Effectiveness, 11*(3), 317–338.

Byrd, A. (2018). *Effects of study abroad on graduation and retention rates.* (WKU Institutional Research No. 86823). Western Kentucky University. https://www.wku.edu/instres/documents/wku_ir_study_abroad_retention_grad_rates.pdf

Carjuzaa, J., & Ruff, W. G. (2010). When Western epistemology and an Indigenous worldview meet: Culturally responsive assessment in practice. *Journal of Scholarship of Teaching and Learning, 10*(1), 68–79.

Center for Inclusion and Social Change. (n.d.). *Intercultural development inventory.* Office of Diversity, Equity and Community Engagement, University of Colorado. https://www.colorado.edu/cisc/intercultural-development-inventory-idi

Center for Urban Education. (2015). *Five principles for creating equity by design.* American Association of Colleges and Universities. https://www.aacu.org/node/12604

Clayton-Pedersen, A. R., & Musil, C. M. (2009). *Making excellence inclusive: A framework for embedding diversity and inclusion into colleges and universities' academic excellence mission.* American Association of Colleges and Universities. https://www.aacu.org/sites/default/files/files/mei/MakingExcellenceInclusive2017.pdf

Contreras, E., Montgomery, M., & Sevilla-Garcia, H. (2021, January 5). An anti-racist framework for education abroad [blog]. *NAFSA Education Abroad Practice Area Column.* https://www.nafsa.org/ie-magazine/2021/1/5/antiracist-framework-education-abroad

Crouse, J., & Trusheim, D. (1988). *The case against the SAT.* University of Chicago Press.

Cooper, C. R., Rocha-Ruiz, M., & Herzon, C. (2020). Using integrated logic models to build equity in students' pathways and systemic change. *Equity & Excellence in Education, 53*(1–2), 105–120.

Deardorff, D. K. (2005). A matter of logic?. *International Educator, 14*(3), 26.

DeJaeghere, J. G., & Cao, Y. (2009). Developing U.S. teachers' intercultural competence: Does professional development matter? *International Journal of Intercultural Relations, 33*(5), 437–447. https://doi.org/10.1016/j.ijintrel.2009.06.004

Den Hartog, D. N., De Hoogh, A. H., & Keegan, A. E. (2007). The interactive effects of belongingness and charisma on helping and compliance. *Journal of Applied Psychology, 92*(4), 1131.

DiBartolo, P. M., Gregg-Jolly, L., Gross, D., Manduca, C. A., Iverson, E., Cooke III, D. B., Davis, G. K., Davidson, C., Hertz, P. E., Hibbard, L., Ireland, S. K., Mader, C., Pai, A., Raps, S., Siwicki, K., Swartz, J. E., & Marsteller, P. (2016). Principles and practices fostering inclusive excellence: Lessons from the Howard Hughes Medical Institute's Capstone Institutions. *CBE—Life Sciences Education, 15*(3), ar44.

D'Ignazio, C., & Klein, L. F. (2020). *Data feminism.* MIT Press.

Doerr, D. (2018, November 15). Logic models and "big" assessment questions [blog]. *Student Affairs Assessment Leaders.* http://studentaffairsassessment.org/entries/blog/logic-models

Dubec, R. (2019, December 18). *Assessment for, as and of learning [blog post].* Teaching Commons. https://teachingcommons.lakeheadu.ca/assessment-and-learning

Eberle Center. (2020). *What is the difference between formative and summative assessment?* Carnegie Mellon University. https://www.cmu.edu/teaching/assessment/basics/formative-summative.html

El Ganzoury, H. A. (2012). *Assessing intercultural competence for educational leaders: An empirical investigation.* [Unpublished doctoral dissertation]. University of Minnesota. https://conservancy.umn.edu/bitstream/handle/11299/127965/ElGanzoury_umn_0130E_12671.p?sequence=1

Fantini, A. (2007). *Exploring and assessing intercultural competence.* CSD research report. Center for Social Development, Washington University of St. Louis. https://openscholarship.wustl.edu/cgi/viewcontent.cgi?article=1815&context=csd_research

Frechtling, J. A. (2015). Logic models. *International Encyclopedia of the Social & Behavioral Sciences* (pp. 299–305). Elsevier. doi: 10.1016/b978-0-08-097086-8.10549-5. ISBN 978-0-08-097087-5.

Glass, C. R., Gesing, P., Hales, A., & Cong, C. (2017). Faculty as bridges to co-curricular engagement and community for first-generation international students. *Studies in Higher Education, 42*(5), 895–910.

Global Belonging Collaborative. (2018). *Repository.* www.globalbelonging.org/repository

Good, J. M., Halpin, G., & Halpin, G. (2000). A promising prospect for minority retention: Students becoming peer mentors. *Journal of Negro Education,* 375–383.

Gore, J. E. (2005). *Dominant beliefs and alternative voices: Discourse, belief, and gender in American study abroad.* Routledge.

Gozik, N. (2015). Closing the loop: Linking stages of the assessment cycle. In V. Savicki & E. Brewer (Eds.), *Assessing study abroad: Theory, tools, and practice* (pp. 57–82). Stylus Publishing.

Green, J. (2020, December 13). The Strange case of the exploding student workload. Just visiting blog, *Inside Higher Education.* https://www.insidehighered.com/blogs/just-visiting/guest-post-strange-case-exploding-student-workload

Hammer, M. R. (2005). The intercultural conflict style inventory: A conceptual framework and measure of intercultural conflict resolution approaches. *International Journal of Intercultural Relations, 29*(6), 675–695.

Hardy, M., & Totman, S. (2021). Taking a pass on grades for a career-focused tour of the Middle East. *Frontiers: The Interdisciplinary Journal of Study Abroad, 33*(1).

Harper, S. R., & Kuh, G. D. (2007). Myths and misconceptions about using qualitative methods in assessment. *New Directions for Institutional Research, 2007*(136), 5–14.

Hartman, E., & Kiely, R. (2014). A critical global citizenship. *Crossing boundaries: Tensions and transformation in international service-learning,* 215–242.

Hawai'i State Department of Education. (2015). *Na Haopena Ao (H?).* Hawai'i Public Schools. http://www.hawaiipublicschools.org/TeachingAndLearning/StudentLearning/HawaiianEducation/Pages/HA.aspx

Henning, G. (2018). *The assessment for social justice project.* Council for the Advancement of Standards in Higher Education. https://www.cas.edu/blog_home.asp?Display=82

Henning, G., & Lundquist, A. E. (2018, August). *Moving towards socially just assessment (Equity Response).* University of Illinois and Indiana University, National Institute for Learning Outcomes Assessment (NILOA). https://www.learningoutcomesassessment.org/wp-content/uploads/2019/08/EquityResponse-HenningLundquist.pdf

Henning, G., & Philippon, R. G. (2019, December 11). *Socially just assessment: Theories and examples of practice.* NECHE Annual Conference, Boston, MA. https://www.neche.org/wp-content/uploads/2020/01/145pm-Socially-Just-Assessment.pdf

Hutchings, P., Ewell, P., & Banta, T. (2012, May). *AAHE principles of good practice: Aging nicely.* University of Illinois and Indiana University, National Institute for Learning Outcomes Assessment (NILOA).

Intercultural Development Inventory. (n.d.). https://idiinventory.com/

Inoue, A. B. (2015). *Antiracist writing assessment ecologies: Teaching and assessing writing for a socially just future.* WAC Clearinghouse.

Johnson, J. E., Weidner, T. G., Jones, J. A., & Manwell, A. K. (2018). Evaluating academic course rigor, part 1: Defining a nebulous construct. *Journal of Assessment and Institutional Effectiveness, 8*(1–2), 86–121.

Jussim, L., & Harber, K. D. (2005). Teacher expectations and self-fulfilling prophecies: Knowns and unknowns, resolved and unresolved controversies. *Personality and Social Psychology Review, 9*(2), 131–155.

Kalinec-Craig, C. A. (2017). The rights of the learner: A framework for promoting equity through formative assessment in mathematics education. *Democracy and Education, 25*(2), 5.

Klenowski, V. (2009). Australian Indigenous students: Addressing equity issues in assessment. *Teaching Education, 20*(1), 77–93.

Klenowski, V. (2014). Towards fairer assessment. *The Australian Educational Researcher, 41*(4), 445–470.

Kolb, D. A. (2007). *The Kolb learning style inventory.* Hay Resources Direct.

Korpershoek, H., Canrinus, E. T., Fokkens-Bruinsma, M., & de Boer, H. (2019). The relationships between school belonging and students' motivational, social-emotional, behavioural, and academic outcomes in secondary education: A meta-analytic review. *Research Papers in Education.* https://doi.org/10.1080/02671522.2019.1615116

Krakouer, J. (2015). Literature review relating to the current context and discourse on Indigenous cultural awareness in the teaching space: Critical pedagogies and improving Indigenous learning outcomes through cultural responsiveness. *Australian Council for Educational Research (ACER).* https://research.acer.edu.au/indigenous_education/42

Kramarczuk Voulgarides, C., Fergus, E., & King Thorius, K. A. (2017). Pursuing equity: Disproportionality in special education and the reframing of technical solutions to address systemic inequities. *Review of Research in Education, 41*(1), 61–87.

LeCroy, C. W. (2018, June 25). Logic models. *Encyclopedia of Social Work.* DOI: 10.1093/acrefore/9780199975839.013.1273

LaFever, M. (2016). Switching from Bloom to the medicine wheel: Creating learning outcomes that support Indigenous ways of knowing in post-secondary education. *Intercultural Education,* 27(5), 409–424.

LaFever, M. (2017). Using the medicine wheel for curriculum design in intercultural communication: Rethinking learning outcomes. In G. Garcia-Perez & C. Rojas-Primus (Eds.), *Promoting intercultural communication competencies in higher education* (pp. 168–199). IGI Global.

Levy, J. (2017, February 14). *How to differentiate assessment, evaluation and research* [Web log message]. https://www.presence.io/blog/how-to-differentiate-assessment-evaluation-research/

Lochner Atkinson, S. (2021, February 9). *Re: Minimum GPA requirements for study abroad (best practices)?* [Online forum post]. NAFSA Education Abroad Knowledge Community Network Digest. https://network.nafsa.org/communities/community-home/digestviewer/viewthread?MessageKey=4d71eabc-a57e-4dd3-aa31-91a9ebe840e2&CommunityKey=ea8645bb-ab94-4172-8e07-0dc26c1bde66&tab=digestviewer

Lundquist, A. (2019). *Assessment, evaluation and research: Relationships and definitions in the field of student affairs.* ACPA Students Affairs Assessment Institute. https://baselinesupport.campuslabs.com/hc/en-us/article_attachments/115017881466/AER-Definitions-Handout-Module-1.pdf

Lynner, B., Ho, W., Narui, M., & Smith, J. (2020, July). *Capital University: Pilot campus climate assessment through critical race theory.* National Institute for Learning Outcomes Assessment, Council for the Advancement of Standards in Higher Education, and Campus Labs.

Malmgren, J., & Galvin, J. (2008). Effects of study abroad participation on student graduation rates: A study of three incoming freshman cohorts at the University of Minnesota, Twin Cities. *NACADA Journal, 28*(1), 29–42.

Manning, R., Martin, J., Reyhner, J., Steeves, L., & Macfarlane, A. (2020). Research regarding Indigenous student learning outcomes in New Zealand, Canada, and the USA: Recurring themes. *Handbook on Promoting Social Justice in Education,* 2021–2039.

Martin, J., Moore, C., Foley, A., & McDermid, K. (2021). Culturally conscious assessment as pedagogy in study abroad: A case study of the Higher Education in the Ghanaian Context program. *Frontiers: The Interdisciplinary Journal of Study Abroad, 33*(1).

McTighe, J. (2018, August 10). Three lessons for teachers from Grant Wiggins. *Eduplanet21 blog.* https://eduplanet21.com/2018/08/10/three-lessons-grant-wiggins/

Moallem, I. (2013). *A meta-analysis of school belonging and academic success and persistence.* [Doctoral dissertation]. Loyola University Chicago.

Montenegro, E. (2020, June). *San Diego State University: Supporting commuter students through equity-driven and student-focused assessment.* University of Illinois and Indiana University, National Institute for Learning Outcomes Assessment, Council for the Advancement of Standards in Higher Education, and Anthology.

National Council of Teachers of English. (2020, November 11). *Position statement: Expanding formative assessment for equity and agency.* https://ncte.org/statement/expanding-formative-assessment/

National Institute on Learning Outcomes Assessment. (n.d.). *New to assessment?* https://www.learningoutcomesassessment.org/browse-by/new-to-assessment/

National Institute on Learning Outcomes Assessment. (2021). *Equity in assessment.* https://www.learningoutcomesassessment.org/equity/

Noble, S. U. (2018). *Algorithms of oppression: How search engines reinforce racism.* NYU Press.

Ogden, A. (2007). The view from the veranda: Understanding today's colonial student. *Frontiers: The Interdisciplinary Journal of Study Abroad, 15*(1), 35–56.

Okun, T., & Jones, K. (2001). Characteristics of white supremacy culture. *Dismantling racism: A workbook for social change groups.* dRworks. https://www.dismantlingracism.org/

O'Toole, S. (2014). Indigenous learning styles – Common themes from around the world. *Training & Development, 41*(2), 8.

Paige, R. M., & Goode, M. L. (2009). Intercultural competence in international education administration: Cultural mentoring: International education professionals and the development of intercultural competence. In D. Deardorff (Ed.), *The SAGE handbook of intercultural competence* (pp. 333–349). Sage Publishing. https://us.sagepub.com/en-us/nam/the-sage-handbook-of-intercultural-competence/book232239#contents

Palomba, C., & Banta, T. W. (1999) *Assessment essentials: Planning, implementing, and improving assessment in higher education.* Jossey-Bass, Inc.

Patton, L. D. (2010). *Culture centers in higher education: Perspectives on identity, theory, and practice.* Stylus.

Polanyi, L. (1995). Language learning and living abroad. *Second Language Acquisition in a Study Abroad Context, 9,* 271.

Poteet, M., & Gomez, B. (2015). "It's both ways": How international students negotiate belonging in local and global contexts. *Journal of New Brunswick Studies/Revue d'études sur le Nouveau-Brunswick, 6*(1).

Purdue University, Center for Intercultural Learning, Mentorship, Assessment and Research. (2018). *Welcome to the intercultural learning hub (HubICL)!* hppts://hubicl.org/gettingstarted

Ravet, J. (2013). Delving deeper into the black box: Formative assessment, inclusion and learners on the autism spectrum. *International Journal of Inclusive Education, 17*(9), 948–964.

Rogers, P. J. (2008). Using programme theory to evaluate complicated and complex aspects of interventions. *Evaluation, 14*(1), 29–48. DOI: 10.1177/1356389007084674

Ruben, B. D. (1976). Assessing communication competency for intercultural adaptation. *Group & Organization Studies, 1*(3), 334–354. https://journals.sagepub.com/doi/pdf/10.1177/105960117600100308

Ryan, J. E. (2004). The perverse incentives of the no child left behind act. *NYUL Review, 79,* 932.

Salisbury, M. (2015). How we got to where we are (and aren't) in assessing study abroad learning. In V. Savicki & E. Brewer (Eds.), *Assessing study abroad: Theory, tools and practice* (pp. 15–33). Stylus Publishing.

Savicki, V. & Brewer, E. (Eds.). (2015). *Assessing study abroad: Theory, tools, and practice.* Stylus Publishing.

Schneider, J., & Thornes, L. (2019, April 26). *Education abroad participation influences graduate rates.* NAFSA Research Symposium, Chicago, IL.

Sharpe, E. K. (2015). Colonialist tendencies in education abroad. *International Journal of Teaching and Learning in Higher Education, 27*(2), 227–234.

Sinicrope, C., Norris, J., & Watanabe, Y. (2007). Understanding and assessing intercultural competence: A summary of theory, research, and practice (Technical report for the foreign language program evaluation project). *University of Hawai'i Second Language Studies Paper, 26*(1).

Shore, L. M., Randel, A. E., Chung, B. G., Dean, M. A., Holcombe Ehrhart, K., & Singh, G. (2011). Inclusion and diversity in work groups: A review and model for future research. *Journal of Management, 37*(4), 1262–1289.

Soria, K. M., Troisi, J. N., & Stebleton, M. J. (2003). Reaching out, connecting within: Community service and sense of belonging among college students. *Higher Education in Review, 9,* 65–68.

Stevens, D. D., & Levi, A. J. (2013). *Introduction to rubrics: An assessment tool to save grading time, convey effective feedback, and promote student learning.* Stylus Publishing, LLC.

Suskie, L. (2018). *Assessing student learning: A common sense guide* (3rd. ed.). Jossey-Bass.

Suskie, L. (2000). Fair assessment practices: Giving students equitable opportunities to demonstrate learning. *AAHE Bulletin, 52*(9), 7–9.

Symonette, H. (2014). Culturally responsive evaluation as a resource for helpful help. *Continuing the Journey to Reposition Culture and Cultural Context in Evaluation Theory and Practice,* 109–129.

Synnott, M. G. (1974). *A social history of admissions policies at Harvard, Yale, and Princeton, 1900-1930.* [Doctoral dissertation]. University of Massachusetts, Amherst. https://scholarworks.umass.edu/dissertations_1/575

The Forum on Education Abroad. (2020). *Standards of good practice for education abroad* (6th ed.). The Forum on Education Abroad.

Thomas, L. (2012). *Building student engagement and belonging in higher education at a time of change: Final report from the What Works? Student Retention & Success Programme.*

Paul Hamlyn Foundation. www.heacademy.ac.uk/system/files/what_works_final_report_0.pdf

Trentman, E. (2013). Imagined communities and language learning during study abroad: Arabic learners in Egypt. *Foreign Language Annals, 46*(4), 545–564.

Twombly, S. B., Salisbury, M. H., Tumanut, S. D., & Klute, P. (2012). Study abroad in a new global century: Renewing the promise, refining the purpose. *ASHE Higher Education Report, 38*(4), 1–152.

University of Southern California Center for Urban Research. (2015). *Five principles for creating equity by design.* www.aacu.org/sites/devault/files/CUE_equity_design_principles.pdf

Van Houtte, M. (2010). So where's the teacher in school effects research? The impact of teachers' beliefs, culture, and behavior on equity and excellence in education. In *Equity and excellence in education* (pp. 87–107). Routledge.

Vande Berg, M., Paige, R. M., & Lou, K. H. (2012). *Student learning abroad: What our students are learning, what they're not, and what we can do about it.* Stylus.

Venaas, M. (2019). Five ways to improve your data visuals today [blog]. *ACPA College Student Educators International.* https://www.myacpa.org/entity/commission-assessment-and-evaluation/blog/five-ways-improve-your-approach-data-visuals-today

Volante, L. (2008). Equity in multicultural student assessment. *The Journal of Educational Thought (JET)/Revue de la Pensée Educative,* 11–26.

Wall, A. F., Hursh, D., & Rodgers III, J. W. (2014). Assessment for whom: Repositioning higher education assessment as an ethical and value-focused social practice. *Research & Practice in Assessment, 9,* 5–17.

Williams, D. A., Berger, J. B., & McClendon, S. A. (2005). *Toward a model of inclusive excellence and change in postsecondary institutions.* Association of American Colleges and Universities.

Yngve, K. N. (2019). Using assessment to align and interweave core curriculum objectives and education abroad learning outcomes. In E. Brewer & A. Ogden (Eds.), *Education abroad and the undergraduate experience: Critical perspectives and approaches to integration with student learning and development* (pp. 149–164). Stylus.

Yngve, K. N. (2020). *Behavioral rubric for intercultural competence.* (Faculty Development Workshop handout). Center for Intercultural Learning, Mentorship, Assessment and Research (CILMAR), Purdue University, West Lafayette, IN. https://hubicl.org/toolbox

Next Steps

15

Acting with Courage: Charting a Path Forward for Education Abroad

Nick J. Gozik and Heather Barclay Hamir

> *Hope is not blind optimism. It's not ignoring the enormity of the task ahead or the roadblocks that stand in our path. It's not sitting on the sidelines or shirking from a fight. Hope is that thing inside us that insists, despite all evidence to the contrary, that something better awaits us if we have the courage to reach for it, and to work for it, and to fight for it.*—U.S. President Barack Obama

A House Where All Belong: Redesigning Education Abroad for Inclusive Excellence began as a way of answering the calls for change within the field of education abroad (EA) around the need to provide greater access and inclusion for students of all identities and backgrounds. In our previous edited volume, *Promoting Inclusion in Education Abroad: A Handbook of Research and Practice* (Barclay Hamir & Gozik, 2018), we explored the ways that practitioners and policymakers can work to increase participation among students who have historically been underrepresented in EA including, but not limited to, Students of Color, first-generation college students, students with disabilities, certain fields of study (e.g., STEM fields), males, and community college students. Although we continue to believe that targeted outreach is beneficial and necessary, the work cannot stop there. Simply getting students through the door (and then abroad) does not mean that we have completed our task: from an inclusive excellence approach (Milem et al., 2005), it is equally vital to ensure that every participant is valued and given the tools, resources, and support they need to succeed, both on the home campus and on abroad.

Despite much good work around the promotion of equity, diversity, and inclusion (EDI) in EA, in this book, we aim to help the field advance further. To truly achieve equity—and go beyond diversity and inclusion alone—we argue that a radically different path needs to be charted, and that the process begins with ourselves as individuals, professionals, and the gatekeepers to the EA experience. This involves looking inward, to challenge our own biases and assumptions, for example, in asking what we mean by concepts such as "fairness" within application processes (Chapter 8) and "rigor" within course content and outcomes assessment (Chapter 14). While we have focused on EDI as the guiding framework for change, the approach proposed through much of the volume and here speaks to the criticality of a social justice lens when engaging in this work.

Seeking equity also means acknowledging the ongoing influence of the historical roots of the profession, which serve as the foundation of what we "know" about how EA works, including how to recruit, screen, and prepare students, and what their most frequent challenges are likely to be abroad, among many other embedded assumptions. Those roots are founded in privilege. For decades, the majority of participants in the United States were White, predominantly female, and affluent or enrolled in an affluent institution that covered the cost of EA. Who went abroad and why stems from societal, economic, and systemic factors. As an example, U.S. federal educational policy did not explicitly identify study abroad as a legitimate educational expense until the 1992 expansion of the Higher Education Act (NAFSA, n.d.), a turning point that undeniably has influenced the growth in EA over the past decades. Other countries will have followed different pathways, yet it is difficult to imagine any place where EA has not historically been reserved for a select group, with broader mobility happening relatively recently, as with the expansion of the ERASMUS program in Europe.

As a profession, our greatest source of learning is often each other through on-the-job training, conferences, publications, and informal peer-to-peer consulting and mentoring. While sharing is usually a positive practice, it is also by these means that we unintentionally perpetuate biases and assumptions within the profession, missing critical opportunities to assess our systems and processes. Often, we do not see those foundational assumptions for what they are; we have worked with and within our existing structures for so long, it is difficult to diagnose the beliefs that set us down a path of inequity. As an example, Barclay Hamir (2019) has written about an advising experience early in her career when a student continually failed to purchase an airline ticket, despite multiple reminders. When at last the student came into the office, it suddenly became clear that she was not being forgetful or irresponsible; instead, she did not have a credit card. The student was a Latinx, first-generation college student. While a first-generation student herself, Barclay Hamir had never encountered that specific problem nor had she questioned that the task could not be done as expected. Despite our best efforts, assumptions, and gaps in our own lived experience mean that, even with all good intentions, we sometimes completely miss what is really going on for our students.

In this book, we have sought to accomplish two primary tasks with the goal of achieving a "house where all belong." The first is to outline the current state of higher education and specifically EA from an inclusive excellence perspective. The second, and where we have devoted most of the space, is to follow the student journey through the EA process, from the moment one starts to learn about EA, through to advising, applying, being oriented, going abroad, and returning. We fundamentally believe that it is necessary to look critically at the entire process, borrowing from work on backward design (Chapter 5) to ensure that inclusive practices are intentionally woven throughout a student's experience. We have also noted areas such as organizational culture and hiring (Chapter 4), pedagogical practices (Chapter 9), and outcomes assessment (Chapter 14) where improved policies and procedures are needed to support students better through the EA experience. We contend that such a systematic, process-driven approach is critical, and one that requires adoption of a mindset that tenaciously interrogates policies, practices, and programs with the goal of supporting EDI.

The work described here supports The Forum on Education Abroad's ("The Forum") *Standards of Good Practice, 6th Edition* (2020), which embraces EDI as one of four guiding principles. As the Standards Development Organization (SDO) for the field recognized by the U.S. Department of Justice and the Federal Trade Commission, The Forum's *Standards* are designed to guide all institutions serving U.S. students engaged in EA, in the United States and abroad. The *Standards* are not designed to be prescriptive; they offer streamlined guidelines that can be applied to a wide variety of settings. Accordingly, the authors in this volume offer resources, concrete examples, and theoretical approaches for how institutions might apply the *Standards* to their unique contexts.

In this concluding chapter, we begin by summarizing key insights from preceding chapters to advance EDI in EA, along with recurrent themes that begin to inform the holistic mindset necessary to replicate and expand this work. Recognizing that it is often harder to solve problems than to identify them, we discuss the successes, and their underpinnings, of several organizations that are unrelated to EA as exemplars of the thinking and action that brings about real change. Finally, we offer suggestions for further research and investigation.

Key Themes

The chapters in this volume provide a wealth of insights and recommended practice to advance inclusion in all aspects of EA, from engagement with students, to systems and programmatic structures, to our own institutions and organizations. While the full volume approaches the discrete building blocks that comprise the EA experience, overall themes reinforce the recommendations across many chapters. Collectively, these themes suggest how we can build a mindset that creates a virtuous cycle of action, assessment, and continuous improvement in the direction of EDI.

The First Step: Moving to Equity-Mindedness

The authors identify the internal work we must do as practitioners in moving to an equity mindset, the foundation of our ability to implement inclusive practices for all students. In the United States, at least, we operate within an established profession that has largely been constructed over the past 70 years by the experiences and perspectives of predominantly White professionals and participants, within a system of higher education with the same historical antecedents. Particularly within higher education, the processes and policies governing admissions through to graduation are positioned as unbiased, intended to serve all equally. Belief that processes and policies are fair, yet inequities in outcomes exist, transfers responsibility for those inequities to the individuals who are excluded and underserved.

To advance inclusive excellence within EA, the authors in this volume note that the first step is an individual journey to critically examine our beliefs, biases, and assumptions about ourselves, others, and society. There are many good resources for exploration of privilege, power, and oppression in the U.S. context referenced throughout this book, including in Contreras et al. (Chapter 3), Serrano et al. (Chapter 5), and Castiello-Gutiérrez and Gozik (Chapter 9), all of whom identify equity-mindedness as a goal. Others, such as Doerr and Kumagai (Chapter 10), note the need to help students (and the instructors leading courses) to understand the relativity of cultural differences, as well as to learn how to communicate with people who are different from ourselves. Likewise, Woodman et al. (Chapter 8) and Yngve and Brewer (Chapter 14) point to an equally important construct: the need to decenter Whiteness and other privileged identities.

Decentering Privileged Identities

While this book is not about race and ethnicity exclusively, it is nearly impossible to talk about equity-mindedness without considering these identities. Moreover, exploring one set of identities can help us think about others related to promoting inclusion in EA. From the introduction and threaded throughout the subsequent chapters is the acknowledgment that the majority White culture in the United States has significantly shaped what EA is and how it operates. This is an extension of the larger society in the United States, which is centered on Whiteness, a social construct that is largely unacknowledged in common discourse or specifically by White U.S. Americans (Hitchcock & Flint, 2015). In their update of *Decentering Whiteness* (2015), Hitchcock and Flint argue that the U.S. "mainstream"—the center of U.S. culture—remains predominantly White and male-dominated in terms of power and roles associated with power. In addition, the center is also heterosexual, cis-gendered, able bodied, and Christian in the United States. For those with power through these aspects of identity, it remains largely invisible if unexamined—it is the unquestioned "background" to everything else, unspoken and unacknowledged. Accordingly, attention is focused instead on how individuals of other racial, religious, ability, and gender identity groups differ from the "norm."

As educators, we see evidence of this centering on White culture when some students, if asked about their culture, indicate that they do not have one. Clearly, they must, as all people do, yet the sheer numbers of White individuals in the United States who interact predominantly with other people who identify similarly allows this gap in self-awareness to persist. This broader lack of recognition shapes our practice on multiple levels, from the building blocks of the EA process, to the way we approach student learning and engagement while abroad. For those seeking further insights to inform work in this space, Serrano et al. (Chapter 5) recommend cultural humility (Hook et al., 2013) as a framework that allows us to decenter the norm by seeking aspects of others' cultural identities that are most valued to them, with the added benefit that it also illuminates the biases that prevented us from seeing others' self-placed value. The hidden curriculum is also a useful framework for examining the unintended messages and impact of our work, as Woodman et al. demonstrate in their analysis of embedded bias in standard application processes (Chapter 8).

Certainly, the reality of specific identities with power and privilege is not unique to the United States. Due to colonization, one would be hard pressed to find a society that has not been shaped by the beliefs embedded in notions of racial superiority, with Whiteness being viewed as an ideal—among other views tied to European culture and the dominance of Christianity. Today, such beliefs persist within virtually all aspects of life, and in all regions of the world, including those that were not colonized or that colonized others. Among far too many examples to mention here, a few include marketing (e.g., billboards and advertisements of White models, including in countries without White majorities), entertainment (e.g., the predominance of Hollywood films and television, which have been slow to diversify), and beauty ideals and products (e.g., whitening creams and hair products). Whiteness, then, goes beyond skin color or hair type; it also serves a proxy for power and privilege, which link to other inequities that persist—something that becomes essential for EA students to understand as they go out into the world, as Castiello-Gutiérrez and Gozik (Chapter 9) outline in their chapter on the decolonization of EA.

Definitions and perceptions of race and ethnicity also vary greatly by language and culture, and so Whiteness as a construct cannot be viewed in purely monolithic terms. Berger et al. (Chapter 12) share, for example, their experiences with Fulbright Noir, an initiative started by Fulbright scholars studying in Belgium, and which included staff originating from the United States, Europe, and Sub-Saharan Africa; not all came to this work with the same understanding of what it means to be Black. Similarly, Johnson et al. (Chapter 11) acknowledge the initial differences that they needed to bridge in training around EDI with local staff in Italy, requiring a two-way dialogue between U.S.- and Europe-based faculty and staff. By offering a case study from the University of Auckland, Berquist et al. (Chapter 6) provide a helpful example of how race and culture play out differently in New Zealand compared with other settings, illustrating the distinctive histories and cultures that inform EDI work globally.

Moving Beyond Dualities

As multiple chapters highlight, decentering privileged identities aligns with the need for a more nuanced approach to our collective construct of inclusion and equity in action. We often describe issues in EA participation in terms of who is underrepresented, using "racial and ethnic minority" as an aggregate term. Yet within various identity groups—race, ethnicity, religion, and gender—there are many individual subgroups that, on reflection, we know embody different histories and levels of marginalization or acceptance.

With race and ethnicity, we tend to focus on the broad strokes of being nonmajority versus each distinct identity group and their experience abroad. While it is common not to have differentiated guidance for Black or Latinx students going abroad, we would typically not aggregate students who are Orthodox Jews or Catholic into a parallel category called "religious" and then offer the same information to all. We would approach these individuals through the identity they share with us, seeking to support them around their specific needs and interests.

The need for more complex engagement with student identity, and intersectional identities, manifests as both the need for EA staff and faculty to learn and the parallel need to help students learn. As noted earlier, Johnson et al. (Chapter 12) map out a thoughtful approach to elevating professional practice. For example, they are mindful of the distinct histories and cultures of Hmong American and Somali American students, two are significant populations at the University of Minnesota and in the local community, which importantly cannot simply be lumped neatly into "Asian" or "African" categories. Elevating awareness and understanding of U.S. identities and their historical contexts, which inform the interpretation and response of students while in a new culture, is a critical component of creating a sense of belonging for all students on-site.

Beyond the awareness and mindset of staff, we have the opportunity to integrate intersectionality into practice. In course and program design, moving beyond Eurocentrism to integrate culturally relevant frameworks and curricula for all students can contribute to a sense of belonging for all. Simultaneously, we can help students see the cultural nuances all around them and learn to engage with people different from themselves in respectful and constructive ways. Doerr and Kumagai's concept of "flickers of difference" (Chapter 10) describes a unique way to foster student thinking beyond dualities by surfacing the subtleties and similarities around individual and cultural preferences with exploration of the cultural context that gives rise to both. This reflective exploration serves a dual purpose in EA by deepening cultural learning in situ, with the further potential to engage that learning and reflection within the dynamics of the student group. In this way, approaches that advance cultural learning can simultaneously advance inclusive excellence.

Stakeholder Engagement

The importance of stakeholder feedback and engagement surfaces repeatedly as a critical component of inclusive excellence-oriented work in EA. The goals of this work are to gain critical perspectives on the EA office itself and how EA is perceived; ensure alignment with institutional goals and the goals, needs, and interests of departmental counterparts that also value EDI; and use this knowledge to inform changes that advance EDI in EA, with appropriate input and involvement from key stakeholders.

Campus climate surveys or similar assessment approaches are recommended across multiple chapters for gaining critical perspectives on the work of the EA office and the campus itself (see Chapters 2, 3, and 4). Whether the campus or organization has access to this specific resource, every department or organization can survey key stakeholders to gather anonymous, honest feedback on how they are perceived in terms of inclusivity and equity-mindedness. Similarly, it is necessary to consider the perspective of alumni (Chapters 12 and 13), applicants who do not pursue EA, and students who do not consider EA in the first place. Nonparticipant feedback is particularly useful in confirming or putting to rest assumptions about student populations that are not well served, so as to redirect critical resources and support strategies. As an example, one of us had the benefit of feedback from a student focus group on why they had not studied abroad. A first-generation Latinx engineering major shared that he was fully aware of study abroad, but everyone he knew who went just spoke about "fun." Fun was not his motivator; graduating with a good education and securing a good job was, and every peer message negated EA's value for him. Feedback from program participants will shed light on gaps in preparation or support before, during, and after the program, with suggestions throughout this volume to address identified gaps.

Any adjustments in policy, practice, or programs suggested by this feedback will benefit from alignment between the department's goals; institutional goals related to EDI, student well-being, and student success; and the goals of other departments that are also invested in these outcomes. Alignment will strengthen the work that is undertaken within and external to the EA office, allowing disparate offices to collaborate for mutual benefit to students and mission. Yngve and Brewer (Chapter 14) also note that stakeholder engagement as part of assessment development sheds light on what is valued, allowing for a discussion and ideally consensus around key principles such as cultural humility and the decentering of privileged identities. Similarly, Howard University's approach to reentry programming (Chapter 13), which engages students as members of a community that is obligated to "pay it forward" to future students, serves as an example of student stakeholder engagement and the different strategies and outcomes it can generate.

As with much of the work needed to advance EDI within EA, one may feel vulnerable in asking for and receiving this type of input. As a community of lifelong learners, framing the resulting insights as a road map to overcome known and unknown factors that impede EDI progress makes this feel less personal, and more about shared purpose. There may be feedback that suggests further self- and workgroup-reflection is needed, or that financial aid policies, program offerings, advising structures, or other factors contribute to gaps in participation and belongingness while abroad. Regardless of what is reflected through this process, once we begin down the path of engaging others, we have an opportunity to deepen and build critical relationships in how we respond to that feedback, what we share, and the actions we take.

Begin With the End in Mind

With the preceding work to inform how we advance EDI, practitioners will have the mindset, contextual awareness, and stakeholder feedback and engagement to enact change. To transform this knowledge into action, several chapters point to backward design to ensure that changes serve the purpose for which they are intended. Backward design is simple in concept within this context: Program development should begin with the desired goal or learning outcomes in mind, an understanding of what evidence of that learning looks like, and then development the curriculum and experience so that each component builds toward achievement of the desired understanding and transferability of learning (Bowen, 2017). The process itself consists of three stages—identify desired results, determine assessment evidence, and plan learning experiences and instruction—each of which has a plethora of approaches and templates to support effective implementation (Wiggins & McTighe, 2005; see also Bowen, 2017). As with any purposeful change initiative, integrating and improving EDI-related outcomes is a process. Backward design in conjunction with continuous improvement aligns the planning and delivery building blocks of EA programming with an emphasis on outcomes assessment, thereby providing the data needed to continue refining aspects of the student experience.

Chapters 5 and 14, on program design and assessment, respectively, complement each other in suggesting strategies to implement EDI-enhancing programmatic changes and continuously improve through the assessment feedback loop. At the programmatic level, learning goals should integrate an emphasis on EDI. Ideally, EDI-derived learning goals point to learning about the local host community; and larger global themes related to power, privilege, and oppression; and opportunities for students to reflect on their own place and agency within such structures. As Castiello-Gutiérrez and Gozik (Chapter 9) argue, integrating decolonizing educational approaches alongside inclusive excellence present(s) the possibility of acknowledging and addressing the social and historical context of individual EA programs, as well as the unbalanced nature of the power relationships between and within "home" and "host" actors. During and following the program, informal and formal assessment measures allow educators to understand the impact of program design—what works, and what requires improvement. An emphasis on belonging as a key assessment metric, as suggested by Yngve and Brewer (Chapter 14), ensures that in addition to learning about EDI-related constructs in an academic way, we are collectively focused on the individual experience of students and whether we are effective in our efforts to create learning environments where all students feel welcomed, supported, and valued.

The foregoing recommendations lay the foundation EA needs to redesign a house where all belong. As with (re)designing an actual building, the final structure should be understood before construction starts, yet EA—and higher education, for that matter—does not have an existing, proven design to ensure the outcomes we seek. Differences between student populations, campus cultures, local and regional communities, governance structures, and funding, among other factors, mean that each institution is asked to design and build an equitable, inclusive EA ecosystem that values diversity, shaped by the multiple factors that promote or inhibit achievement. What does success look like for EA as a whole or on a given campus? What models already exist that suggest transferrable approaches? Chapters in this volume provide examples from campuses and third-party program providers with potential transferability to other institutions. In addition, it is worthwhile to look beyond the profession, where organizations have been advancing EDI for decades with demonstrated success.

Inspiration From Outside the Field

While attention on equitable participation in EA can be traced back to the 1970s (Shorrock, 1979) as a broad priority of the profession, the real focus began in the 2000s, the period when the Institute for International Education first added race and ethnicity to its annual, national *Open Doors* report. In the 1999 to 2000 academic year, the first year of reporting, minoritized students represented 15.7% of all EA participants (Institute of International Education [IIE], 2020), compared to 29.2% of postsecondary enrollment (National Center for Education Statistics, 2019), a disparity of 13.5%. Over the intervening two decades, the disparity between higher education and EA participation has fluctuated, with a low of 12.8% and high of 16.1%. The gap remains stubbornly constant even as higher education enrollments become more diverse, suggesting that new approaches are necessary on a broad scale to make meaningful progress on participation, with the understanding that it is no longer sufficient to focus on access alone in this work.

New outcomes require new ideas that help close the gaps in mindset and practice suggested throughout this volume. Beyond EA, a significant number of student- and practitioner-focused programs exist that demonstrate success in student outcomes, EDI education, or broader EDI work. To extend our collective learning, authors in this volume were invited to recommend organizations doing work in the EDI space that they viewed as having the potential to help EA advance inclusive excellence. These resources fell into two broad categories focused on effective EDI programming and educator resources to advance knowledge and practice.

Student Programs: Purposeful Design for Impact

A number of student programs focus on disrupting historic inequities in educational achievement. Common aspects of these programs include a cohort model, mentoring, leadership development, and/or financial support. Here, we look at two programs to understand their achievements and approaches that suggest practices transferrable to EA: the Posse Foundation and the Puente Project.

Of the two programs, the Posse Foundation is likely the best known in the United States. Initiated in 1989, the program aims to expand and diversify the pool of talent applying to 4-year institutions, assisting institutions in building more welcoming campus communities, and supporting Posse students' retention and graduation as a pathway to future leadership in the workforce through full-tuition scholarships and mentorship. The Posse model was formed as a result of the insight a single student provided: "I never would've dropped out of college if I'd had my posse with me" (The Posse Foundation, n.d.-a), thus leading to the program name and structure. Groups of high school students are nominated to belong to a cohort of 10 individuals, all from the same city, who are admitted together to one of 64 partner institutions—thereby forming a "posse," or group of students to support and encourage each other forward in an unfamiliar environment. Posse's outcomes are impressive: 90% of the program's 10,000 scholars graduated from an institution of higher education (The Posse Foundation, n.d.-b). A significant majority of scholars are from minoritized populations, lower and lower-middle income families, and 60% are the first in their families to attend college (The Posse Foundation, n.d.-c), all groups with national graduation rates well below the average for the program.

As we work toward EDI and belongingness in EA, Posse offers inspiration for approaches EA might adapt. The cohort model clearly serves as an important resource to students, supporting their sense of belonging because they unquestionably *do* belong. As with the appreciative advising approach described in Chapter 7, cohorts reinforce the assets and strengths group members possess, minimizing the impact of stereotype threat and facets of campus culture that may negate students' sense of belonging. Within EA, this could manifest as signature programming designed in partnership with success programs or programs that support Students of Color, LGBTQI+ students, or first-generation college students. Within established programs, students can be invited to opt in to affinity groups locally or globally, or to ongoing programming in partnership with host campus offices that explore identity, or allow space for reflection and decompression with other students who have similarly rich intersectional identities that may not be fully engaged or supported through existing structures.

The Puente Project takes a different approach to address a related problem: underrepresentation of specific groups, particularly Latinx, among college attendees and graduates. To address this issue, the program focuses on targeted interventions that address a suite of factors identified at the program's inception as characteristic of at-risk students: would be the first in the family to attend college, avoidance of college-level writing courses, and low engagement with academic advisors/counselors (The Puente Project, 2019). The three components of the program structure align to these needs beginning early in the college readiness pipeline by engaging with students in middle school, high school, and community college as they prepare for enrollment in 4-year institutions. Now celebrating 40 years of operation with hundreds of thousands of students touched by programming, the Puente Project shows notable results: Participants significantly outperform the state average on the California High School Exit Examination and transfer rates from community colleges to four-year institutions are similarly high (The Puente Project, 2021). Unlike Posse, where student funding is such a critical component of support and limiter of broad implementation, Puente has been implemented on a large scale in specific communities through engagement with teachers at all levels, community members, and students.

The Puente Project at first glance may seem less relatable to the structures and practices of EA; however, there are several key lessons to be learned from their proven approach. Puente began through an assessment of the factors that predicted a specific outcome—in this case, attrition from community college and low educational attainment. Had the program been designed based on assumptions or aggregate data on college attainment, it likely would not have achieved the successes it is known for, a reminder that to address any perceived problem relative to different groups requires specific investigation and knowledge of that group's needs, interests, and challenges. Through an integration of Latinx and multicultural authors into the mandated high school English curriculum, students see their own identities valued alongside the White, Eurocentric canon that is commonly taught, making content more relatable. This element offers insights into program design and student support that integrates "cultural relevance and intentionally facilitate[s] ... belonging and inclusion before, during, and after experiences" (D. Wick, personal communication, August 19, 2021), while also reminding us to consider the full range of factors that need to be addressed to instill a sense of belongingness.

Educator Resources: Advancing Knowledge and Practice

As with any mindset, equity-mindedness is learned, and perspectives on EDI are constantly evolving. Looking to existing resources and examples of effective practice allows us to benefit from the knowledge of practitioners specializing in EDI work within and external to higher education. Those presented here represent a range of organizations and learning modes, from on-demand resources to self-paced learning to in-person workshops on social justice.

An excellent starting point is Learning for Justice (n.d.), which provides a broad range of resources and thought-provoking content to aid educators. While their emphasis is on K-12 educators and communities, they offer a variety of resources and example activities with transferrable value to EA, along with resources for professional growth in EDI and beyond, including content on religious diversity, ability, gender and sexual identity, and socioeconomic class. Another resource, Racial Equity Tools (RET) offers "tools, research, tips, curricula and ideas for people who want to increase their own understanding and to help those working for racial justice at every level" (n.d.). RET has produced a succinct glossary and over 3,000 resources to advance EDI work and practice.

For individuals interested in doing the deeply personal work of unpacking biases and working toward an equity mindset, the Center for Organizational Responsibility and Advancement (CORA), similarly hosts programs and courses, some free of charge, to help educators "advance racial equity through an intentional focus on issues facing Black, Indigenous, and People of Color" (n.d.). Showing Up for Racial Justice (SURJ) delivers free, reflection-based "House Meetings" for and led by White individuals to understand, identify, and act against White privilege, racism, and structural inequities. House Meetings are offered across the United States by local chapters and online in some areas. For those who seek an opportunity for deeper engagement, the Social Justice Training Institute (SJTI) also "provides a forum for the professional and personal development of social justice educators and practitioners to enhance and refine their skills and competencies to create greater inclusion for all members of the community" (n.d.). The SJTI offers workshops for students as well as professionals.

In addition, two recommendations focus on specific areas of administrative practice: strategic leadership and hiring practices. The National Association of Diversity Officers in Higher Education (NADOHE) is a membership organization focused on advancing inclusive excellence in higher education. NADOHE focuses on institutional transformation to realize inclusive excellence on campuses, creating an active space for the exploration of strategy, promising practices, and current issues (n.d.). A second critical opportunity provides workshops for inclusive hiring: The Oregon State University Search Advocate Program (n.d.) offers a workshop series open to nonuniversity employees, along with regular updates. Given the complexity and criticality of hiring, the four-part series offers an investment in creating the inclusive professional communities that EA hiring managers aspire to realize.

These resources complement others that have been developed specifically to address EDI in EA, as will be explored in the next section. In addition, most employers will offer some sort of related training, either developed entirely in-house or in coordination with outside organizations. While participating in these and other events does not always necessitate verbalizing what may be uncomfortable reflections, actively listening is a good foundation to ensure that we are truly hearing what others have to say, allowing us to learn from their views and experiences.

Taking Action

As a collection, the chapters in this volume provide a roadmap for how we might move forward as individuals, organizations, and a field. There is no one way to engage in EDI work, and so the suggestions presented here are not meant to be prescriptive. Any strategy will require adaptation to the needs of individual campuses and locations, including for colleagues who are based in other countries, where the very definitions of terms such as "diversity" will mean something different than in the United States (Gozik, 2018). Accordingly, here we provide a loose framework for helping us advance the work around EDI from a systematic and holistic approach, and one that can be customized for the students, faculty, and staff we are serving.

Campuses and Organizations

It is easy for individuals, especially for those who are not in a senior leadership position, to feel powerless to effect change in EDI efforts. The challenges are great and complex. At the same time, change cannot happen without the courage and vision of individuals who are willing to do the heavy lifting. This work, as noted earlier, begins with a critical self-assessment, in which each person recognizes their own underlying assumptions and biases. Once we have begun to understand ourselves and those whom we serve better, it is time to update our practices. Individuals may not have control over how an organization or office is administered, though each advisor, mentor, and/or instructor usually does have agency in their own interactions with students.

For advisors, it may be that an appreciative advising approach (Chapter 7; also Bloom et al., 2008) can provide the necessary lens for shifting individual work toward EDI. The appreciative advising model approaches each student as an individual, exploring their interests and goals while emphasizing the assets they bring to their education and the campus community. In an EDI context, appreciative advising dovetails with the scholarship on Community Cultural Wealth (Yosso, 2005), which challenges traditional notions of cultural capital à la Bourdieu (1986) and offers a strengths-based approach, rooted in the belief that each student has certain assets, even if they have not historically been valued within higher education. For example, a first-generation, bilingual student will likely excel in skills that make her better prepared than her peers for an overseas experience, including perseverance, adaptability, cross-cultural awareness, and the ability to code switch. Focusing on students' assets rather than perceived weaknesses reframes how we perceive student eligibility and readiness for global experiences by contravening dominant narratives that influence how applicants are viewed.

For faculty who teach overseas, for example, on a faculty-led or in-residence program, there too are strategies for promoting an inclusive classroom environment. This can begin by taking advantage of on-campus resources such as through a center for teaching excellence or diversity and inclusion office. This professional development often stems from the scholarship on inclusive pedagogy and practices (e.g., Chapters 5, 9, and 10), addressing both what and how we teach. Including readings and case studies from non-Western countries can send a powerful signal to students, while also helping them to gain other cultural perspectives—a common learning outcome in EA. Similarly, it is helpful to reconsider one's pedagogical practices, to allow students with different needs and abilities to excel. A nonnative speaker of the language of instruction or *lingua franca* of a program, for example, may feel less comfortable contributing to a large group conversation and instead prefer small group projects or online discussion sites. This sort of shift will additionally benefit different types of learners, as well as make class sessions more dynamic.

Within the broader context of the EA office, conducting an audit is an important step that ensures action aligns to observed gaps or needs, setting a baseline for improvement. Several frameworks and assessment tools are available for this purpose. Karyn Sweeney's (2013) adaptation of the AAC&U's inclusive excellence scorecard (Williams et al., 2005) provides sample questions for assessing access and equity, campus climate, diversity in the formal and informal curriculum, and learning and development. EA-specific content allows for a full inventory of the factors that may influence a students' decision to go abroad, going beyond an individual international office to consider the campus environment. Many of the data [e.g., What is the race/ethnicity of staff, including student workers, in the study abroad office? (p. 20) or "Do advising materials/resources address race and ethnicity?" (p. 21)] can be pulled from existing data sets, information posted on websites, and prior surveys. In other cases, it may be necessary to create new surveys or hold focus groups or interviews, to understand students' perspectives—particularly if we want to go beyond numbers and learn whether and where (or where not) students feel a sense of belonging within the EA process.

Additional resources that similarly guide and offer self-directed assessment frameworks include Diversity Abroad's *Global Equity and Inclusion Guidelines* (2019) and companion scorecard assessment service and The Forum on Education Abroad *Standards of Good Practice* (2020) with companion self-assessment prompts. Stakeholder engagement and feedback provides important insights into this process and paves the way for collaborative planning and implementation aligned to the many elements of the EA process as described throughout this volume.

The Field of Education Abroad

Inclusion in EA is a priority for the profession as a whole, as well as for higher education, the larger context within which equity of educational opportunity resides. Associations, institutions, and organizations have long conducted research and created spaces and materials for addressing aspects of this issue. Over the past several decades, larger, coordinated efforts have included the Benjamin A. Gilman International Scholarship Program in 2001; the Abraham Lincoln Study Abroad Commission in 2005, which proposed a framework to send one million U.S. college students to study abroad every year by 2017; and IIE's Generation Study Abroad initiative, which started in 2014 with a goal of increasing and diversifying participation rates over a 5-year span. The latter involved more than 800 members, in the United States and abroad, representing a total of 37 countries (Calvert & Sanger, 2021). Although U.S. based, the goal of reaching beyond national borders has helped to expand and complement the work of professional organizations and higher education institutions elsewhere in the world.

In a similar vein, we have seen a shift in standards for the field. As mentioned previously, The Forum on Education Abroad produced the 6th edition of the *Standards of Good Practice* (2020) through significant stakeholder engagement, which surfaced the need for the Standards to serve a wider community, including colleagues outside the United States, and to incorporate EDI more explicitly and holistically throughout. The new edition has led to revised workshops, certification exercises, and the *Standards in Action* book series, of which the current volume is a part.

This abbreviated and incomplete historical overview reminds us of how much has been done in the field. People care and want to "do right" by students, and this shows in the volume of work and consistent emphasis on EDI within the profession. Our argument in this volume is not a lack of effort, or indicators of progress for that matter; it is simply that we must think more holistically about the root causes of inequities within our space and work systematically to address them. This requires us, in part, to consider the entire EA process from the perspective of students, taking into consideration their lived experiences, perspectives, and what they value.

Given the limited research and assessment on the efficacy of EDI efforts in EA specifically, there is significant room for the field to contribute. At the level of the profession, we can contribute to advances overall by reframing dialogues, events, and publications to take on this more holistic approach, while also focusing on concrete outcomes and recommendations in these fora, versus descriptions of the work alone. Most conferences include sessions on marketing or outreach efforts, yet these stages are separated out, without the framework of the entire EA process. Encouraging speakers to contextualize more fully can help. Just as importantly, the solicitation for proposals that address seemingly "neutral" and impartial stages of the EA process, such as applications and participant selection, contributes to a broader awareness of the many points of influence existing policy and practice have on who goes abroad and whether they feel a sense of belonging at every stage of the process.

While individuals and organizations/institutions can embrace the sorts of changes noted here, for true impact, we look to the field as a whole, and particularly the role of professional organizations, which have the ability to shift thinking through conference themes, publications, training, and advocacy efforts. There may be reticence from some, though it is just as likely that most colleagues will embrace a new way of looking at long-standing issues, especially if there is a feeling that real progress can be made. At the same time, the conversations cannot rest at the theoretical level. Practitioners need concrete examples of how their work can be altered, and especially in ways that are actionable. Strategic planning and reforms are often put on a back burner, displaced by the daily work that needs to happen for students to go abroad. Acknowledging that we are all accountable for EDI elevates the conversation, while demonstrating practical ways of taking on this work makes it more likely that the work gets done, alongside and embedded within other strategic and operational priorities.

Having the Courage to Make Difficult Decisions

This book has ultimately been about courage, as the opening quote defines it: the courage to fight for what we believe in, making decisions that advance equity over equality, even when it makes others uncomfortable. Those of us in higher education generally embrace progressive ideals, yet we can also be slow to act. There is a belief in a greater good that propels us to want to make a difference in students' lives, including those who have long been underserved by activities such as EA. However, we are often tethered to what we know and what is comfortable, which can be at odds with the foundational change needed to advance EDI and inclusive excellence within the profession.

Each of us will eventually find ourselves in a position where we may need to make decisions that may not be popular or well understood as we challenge the status quo. This could involve changing how we hire new employees, recruit, and select students, or how we educate all students to advance belongingness within global programs. It will mean reconsidering advising strategies and accepting that we need to design overseas programming in very different ways, thus enlisting the support of faculty, staff, and students on the home campus and in the countries where students live and learn abroad.

While change can be difficult, it is also invigorating—and, we would argue, urgently needed. The risk of not changing now will mean that we leave behind even more students who would benefit from EA. It may also mean that EA itself is left behind, as campus decision makers perceive that such programming is not a scalable avenue for global learning if it cannot meet the needs of a full student body. And, more importantly, if we are not acting with courage, what does it say about why we entered the field in the first place? Many of us benefitted from a cross-cultural experience as EA participants, international students, and/or through some other sort of exposure to individuals from different cultural backgrounds. If we are truly committed to making sure that students have access to the same life-changing experiences we enjoyed, we need to rethink and redesign our programs and processes.

We hope that *A House Where All Belong* serves as a starting place for individuals at all levels and in a variety of capacities to move forward with courage. If there was ever a time to engage in this collective work, it is now.

Acknowledgment

We are grateful for the thoughtful feedback of Carla Fullwood, Lily López-McGee, and Amelia Dietrich on earlier drafts of this chapter.

References

Barclay Hamir, H. (2019). *The importance of swim fins.* https://ifsa-butler.org/ifsa-story/the-importance-of-swim-fins

Barclay Hamir, H., & Gozik, N. J. (Eds.). (2018). *Promoting inclusion in education abroad: A handbook of research and practice.* Stylus and NAFSA: Association of International Educators.

Bloom, J. L., Hutson, B. L., & He, Y. (2008). *The appreciative advising revolution.* Stipes Publishing.

Bourdieu, P. (1986). The forms of capital. In J. Richardson (Ed.), *Handbook of theory and research for the sociology of education* (pp. 241–258). Greenwood.

Bowen, R. S. (2017). *Understanding by design.* Vanderbilt University Center for Teaching. https://cft.vanderbilt.edu/understanding-by-design

Calvert, L., & Sanger, J. (2021). *A Commitment to building a global generation: The five-year impact of IIE's generation study abroad initiative.* https://iie.widen.net/s/kgfrxsjvwc/iie-gsa-report-2021_final

Center for Organizational Responsibility and Advancement. (n.d.). *About CORA.* Retrieved January 10, 2021, from https://coralearning.org/about

Diversity Abroad. (2019). *Global equity & inclusion guidelines for education abroad* (2nd ed.). https://cdn.ymaws.com/www.diversitynetwork.org/resource/resmgr/documents/2020_geiguidlines.pdf

Gozik, N. J. (2018, Winter). Diversity in an age of nationalism: Education abroad and the role of terminology. *The Global Impact Exchange, 201,* 13–15. https://www.diversitynetwork.org/page/GlobalImpactExchange

Hitchcock, J., & Flint, C. (2015). *Decentering whiteness* (Issue September). http://www.euroamerican.org/public/DecenteringWhiteness.pdf

Hook, J. N., Davis, D. E., Owen, J., Worthington, E. L., & Utsey, S. O. (2013). Cultural humility: Measuring openness to culturally diverse clients. *Journal of Counseling Psychology, 60*(3), 353–366.

Institute of International Education. (2020). *OpenDoors.*

Learning for Justice. (n.d.). *About learning for justice.* Retrieved January 10, 2021, from https://www.learningforjustice.org/about

Milem, J. F., Chang, M. J., & Antonio, A. L. (2005). *Making Diversity work on campus: A research-based perspective.* https://www.aacu.org/sites/default/files/files/mei/MakingDiversityWork.pdf

NAFSA. (n.d.). *Financial aid for study abroad: An undergraduate student's resource.* https://www.nafsa.org/about/about-international-education/financial-aid-study-abroad-undergraduate-students-resource

National Association of Diversity Officers in Higher Education. (n.d.). *About us: Vision & mission statements.* Retrieved January 10, 2021, from www.nadohe.org/vision-a-mission-statements

National Center for Education Statistics. (2019). *Table 326.10: Graduation rate from first institution attended for first-time, full-time bachelor's degree-seeking students at 4-year postsecondary institutions, by race/ethnicity, time to completion, sex, control of institution, and percentage of applicat.* https://nces.ed.gov/programs/digest/d19/tables/dt19_326.10.asp

Oregon State University. (n.d.). *OSU Search Advocate Program.*

Racial Equity Tools. (n.d.). *Racial equity tools.* Retrieved January 10, 2021, from https://www.racialequitytools.org

Shorrock, H. (1979). *Report on the University of California Education Abroad Program's project: To stimulate enrollment and provide orientation for minority and disadvantaged students.*

Showing Up for Racial Justice. (n.d.). *About showing up for racial justice.* Retrieved January 10, 2021, from Justice,

Sweeney, K. (2013). Inclusive excellence and underrepresentation of students of color in study abroad. *Frontiers: The Interdisciplinary Journal of Study Abroad, XXIII*(1), 1–21. http://frontiersjournal.org/past-volumes/

The Forum on Education Abroad. (2020). *Standards of Good Practice for Education Abroad* (6th ed.). https://doi.org/10.36366/S.978-1-952376-04-7

The Posse Foundation. (n.d.-a). *Mission & history.* Retrieved January 10, 2021, from www.possefoundation.org/shaping-the-future/mission-history

The Posse Foundation. (n.d.-b). *Posse facts & figures.* Retrieved January 10, 2021, from www.possefoundation.org/posse-facts

The Posse Foundation. (n.d.-c). *The Posse alumni report: The next generation of leaders.* Retrieved January 10, 2021, from https://www.possefoundation.org/posse-facts

The Puente Project. (2019). *About Puente.* www.thepuenteproject.org/about

The Puente Project. (2021). *Puente success data.* www.puente.berkeley.edu/content/puente-success-data

Wiggins, G., & McTighe, J. (2005). *Understanding by design* (2nd ed.). ASCD.

Williams, D. A., Berger, J. B., & McClendon, S. A. (2005). *Toward a model of inclusive excellence and change in postsecondary institutions | Presidential Task Force on Inclusion and Belonging.* https://inclusionandbelongingtaskforce.harvard.edu/publications/toward-model-inclusive-excellence-and-change-postsecondary-institutions

Yosso, T. J. (2005). Whose culture has capital? A critical race theory discussion of community cultural wealth. *Race, Ethnicity and Education, 8*(1), 69–91.

Author Biographies

LaNitra M. Berger is associate professor of art history and director of the African and African American Studies Program at George Mason University. For 12 years, she was the Fulbright Program Advisor and helped over 60 students win Fulbright grants. She has served in a consulting role as Diversity Coordinator for the Fulbright Program. She is the editor of *Social Justice and International Education: Research, Practice, and Perspectives* and the author of *Irma Stern and the Racial Paradox of South African Modern Art: Audacities of Color.*

Brett Berquist is Amokapua | Assistant Vice-Chancellor Engagement, University of Canterbury, Christchurch, New Zealand. As Amokapua |Assistant Vice Chancellor Engagement, Brett Berquist leads the University of Canterbury's engagement, institutional advancement, and strategic partnerships. Previously, he led the international portfolio at the University of Auckland after leading education abroad at Michigan State University. He has experience across the breadth of international education, as faculty and administrator in Europe, the US, and Australasia. Recent research has focused on employability, internships, and community engagement.

Elizabeth Brewer is Director Emerita of International Education at Beloit College. Charged with leading campus internationalization, initiatives she led included increasing access to study abroad and strengthening its learning outcomes. She has edited four volumes on aspects of education abroad, including its assessment and curricular integration, and has also written on comprehensive internationalization, partnerships, curriculum internationalization, and conducting internationalization reviews. She has also been responsible for area studies programs and international student advising.

Nikki Bruckmann, MA, is Senior Global Operations Manager at Cultural Experiences Abroad (CEA). Nikki has worked in higher education for over 12 years, including education abroad four years experience and as an adjunct professor of Cultural Anthropology. Prior to CEA, Nikki spent over nine years at the Institute for Study Abroad (IFSA) as Director of Student Engagement. At IFSA, she developed a passion for curating the student experience. Her professional work focuses on building academic enrichment, intercultural learning, inclusive excellence, and process improvement.

Aileen Bumphus, Ph.D., is an award-winning educational leader who effectively guides organizations and institutions in creating and implementing innovative and progressive student success programs for diverse students from PreK-PhD. In her professional experience as Assistant Professor of Practice and Associate Vice President of Diversity at the University of Texas at Austin, Dr. Bumphus has demonstrated success in community/stakeholder/institutional relationships. She holds a Ph.D. in Educational Leadership and Research and a Master of Science and Bachelor of Science in Speech Pathology.

Jennifer Calvert Hall is the former Executive Director at the Fund for Education Abroad (FEA), a non-profit that increases access to education abroad for U.S. first-generation college students and students of color through the provision of scholarships. Currently, she works to advance diversity, equity, accessibility, and inclusion (DEAI) in museum practices and standards as senior director at the American Alliance of Museums.

Santiago Castiello-Gutiérrez is Assistant Professor of higher education at Seton Hall University in the Department of Education Leadership, Management and Policy. Dr. Castiello-Gutiérrez is a scholar-practitioner whose work is centered on the intersection of organizational theory around higher education institutions, their global interconnectedness, and current global policies and practices of internationalization of higher education. As a practitioner he has 15 years of experience serving as administrator of international programs for institutions in Mexico and the United States.

Alma R. Clayton-Pedersen, Ph.D., is CEO of Emeritus Consulting Group, LLC, which uses organizational development principles to assist education and public nonprofits in enhancing their efficacy for public good. She was briefly a senior scholar and then vice president for Education and Institutional Renewal at AAC&U (2000–2010) and is currently serving as a distinguished fellow. She led AAC&U's team in crafting the initial Inclusive Excellence concept and leading the Making Excellence Inclusive initiatives.

Eduardo Contreras: Eduardo Contreras is the inaugural Associate Provost for International Education, Diversity, and Inclusion at the University of Portland, where he also teaches graduate and undergraduate courses. Dr. Contreras has a long-term commitment to equity, inclusion, and international education. He has written and presented extensively in peer-reviewed journals, book chapters, and conferences. Dr. Contreras has a B.A. and M.A. from the University of Texas at Austin, and a master's and doctorate of education from Harvard.

Thandi Dinani, Ph.D., is Director of Global Education at Belmont University. Thandi has worked in higher education for over 15 years, including ten years in education abroad and six years in DEI roles. Thandi maintains an active presence in numerous international education organizations, consults with various institutions to strengthen the effectiveness of their programming efforts, and particularly enjoys working with faculty to further develop inclusive global education programming.

Neriko Musha Doerr received a Ph.D. in cultural anthropology from Cornell University. Her research interests include politics of difference, language and power, civic engagement, and education in Japan, Aotearoa/New Zealand, and the United States, as well as on study abroad experiences. Her publications include *Transforming Study Abroad: A Handbook, The Global Education Effect and Japan* (the editor), and articles in various peer-reviewed journals. She currently teaches at Ramapo College in New Jersey, U.S.A.

Michelle Foley serves as Associate Director of Network Services and Communications at NASPA. Her graduate studies at the Harvard Graduate School of

Education focused on federal, state, and institutional policy interventions to support student access and success in college. Originally from Istanbul, she is an advocate for the potential of higher education to advance economic, racial, and gender equity.

Jeremy Gombin-Sperling, (he, him) is a Ph.D. Candidate in the International Education Policy program at University of Maryland-College Park, and works as the Diversity and Inclusion Liaison for Fulbright Western Hemisphere Programs. His research and teaching focus on the integration of social justice pedagogies into international education programs. He holds an M.A. in International Education Policy from University of Maryland-College Park, and a B.A. in Religious Studies and Psychology from New York University.

Nick J. Gozik is Dean of Global Education and Assistant Professor at Elon University. Previously he held positions in education abroad at Boston College, the University of Richmond, New York University, and Duke University. He has also served as a Visiting Assistant Professor at New York University, and as a Research Consultant for the Social Science Research Council. Gozik is co-editor of *Promoting Inclusion in Education Abroad: A Handbook of Research and Practice* (2018, Stylus & NAFSA). Gozik holds an MA in French Language and Civilization and PhD in International Education from New York University.

Heather Barclay Hamir, PhD, is President and CEO of the Institute for Study Abroad. Her passion for impactful, equitable, and inclusive education abroad for all students infuses her leadership at IFSA and in past roles. While at UT Austin, the institution received awards from NAFSA and Diversity Abroad for initiatives that increased participation among underrepresented groups. She currently serves as Secretary and Member-At-Large on the NAFSA Board of Directors. Barclay Hamir is co-editor of *Promoting Inclusion in Education Abroad: A Handbook of Research and Practice* (2018, Stylus & NAFSA).

Kevin Hovland worked at AAC&U for two decades to make global learning a central theme of curricular design, faculty development, and assessment. He was program director for AAC&U's annual meeting and executive editor of *Diversity & Democracy: Civic Learning for Shared Futures*, a periodical that supported academic leaders as they designed diversity programs, civic engagement initiatives, and global learning opportunities. From 2014 to 2017 he led similar efforts at NAFSA.

Patricia Izek is the Equity, Diversity, and Inclusion Consultant in the Office of Human Resources at the University of Minnesota. She is a member of the Equity Lens Policy Review Committee, the Bias Response and Resource Network, the Diverse Community of Practice, and the Twin Cities Equity, Diversity & Inclusion Roundtable executive team member. Patricia Izek holds a bachelor's in history, Loyola University of Chicago and a Master of Education in Human Resource Development, University of Minnesota.

Shelley Jessee is Senior Marketing Director at CET Academic Programs. Shelley Jessee has extensive experience in communications, digital marketing, brand management, events management, and strategy. Building on her experience in education abroad and an MBA from UNC, she leads an inclusive marketing approach at CET.

Martha Johnson is the Executive Vice President and Provost for CAPA: The Global Education Network and CEA Study Abroad. She has worked in education abroad since 1991 and previously served as the Assistant Dean for Learning Abroad at the University of Minnesota. Martha holds a PhD in American Studies from the University of East Anglia in England. Martha has presented widely and authored numerous articles and chapters for publications including Frontiers and NAFSA resources.

Yuri Kumagai, Ed.D., is a Senior Lecturer at Smith College. Her specializations are critical literacy and multiliteracies in world language education. Her most recent publications include *"For Living together: Welfare linguistics and an ecological approach to language education"* (co-edited, *Shunpu-sha, 2021*), "'*Ekkyō-bungaku*' as crossing the border of language" (in *Global Education Effect*, Routledge, 2020), "Translingual Practices in a Monolingual Society: Language Learners' Subjectivities and Translanguaging" (co-authored, *Journal of Bilingual Education and Bilingualism*, 2020).

Opal Leeman Bartzis, Ed.D., is the Executive Director of Education Abroad at Michigan State University and Interim Director of the Global Youth Advancement Network (GYAN). She spent 20 years at the Institute for Study Abroad, Butler University, including as Vice President for Academic Affairs and Resident Director in Ireland. Her doctorate in adult, higher and community education focused on the development of culturally sensitive instructional practices through student teaching abroad. Her current research areas are inclusive pedagogy, academic ethics across cultures, advancing sustainability goals through education abroad, and appreciative advising.

Lily López-McGee has dedicated more than a decade to capacity building, EDI within global education, and U.S. national security and foreign policy. Dr. López-McGee is Executive Director of Diversity Abroad and previously supported federal grants at Howard University and UNCFSP. She is a practitioner, researcher, and speaker and has published in industry and academic outlets. She holds degrees from the University of Washington and George Mason University and is an ICAP and IIPP Fellow.

Erica Lutes is Executive Director of the Commission for Educational Exchange Between the United States and Belgium. She is also a lecturer at Odisee, the University College of Brussels and Thomas More University College in Mechelen. Erica received a degree from Mount Holyoke College in international relations and spent her junior year at Yale. She holds three master's degrees from the University of Leuven (Belgium) in political economy, conflict and peace studies, and international business.

Angela Manginelli, MA, is the former Vice President of Alumni and Inclusion Initiatives for AIFS Study Abroad and is currently the Talent Acquisition Manager for Funraise. She graduated from Ball State University with a BS in photojournalism and an MA in student affairs administration in higher education. She coauthored Making Meaning of Education Abroad: A Journal for the Returnee Experience (NAFSA, 2018) and received NAFSA's Lily von Klemperer award in 2019.

Ana M. Martínez Alemán: Ana M. Martínez Alemán, Ed.D., is Professor and Associate Dean of Faculty at the Lynch School of Education and Human Development at Boston College. Her books include *Critical Approaches to the Study of Higher Education; Accountability, Pragmatic Aims, and the American University,* and *#MeToo Matters: Bridging Student Activism and Institutional Practice.* She is President-elect of the Association for the Study of Higher Education, and has held leadership positions in the American Educational Researchers Association.

Neal McKinney previously served as the Associate Director of Off-Campus Programs at DePauw University, and is currently a doctoral student at The Ohio State University. His doctoral research focuses on using critical race theory to name and dismantle racist policies/practices that impact students' of color educational success, and studies education abroad practitioners' unconscious employment of racialized deficit narratives, and subsequently how students of color perceive these narratives, potentially contributing to decreased participation in education abroad.

Mariarosa Mettifogo serves as Academic Coordinator for the University of Minnesota *Study & Intern* program at the Accent Global Learning Center in Florence, where she also coordinates the UCEAP programs in Florence, leads workshops on intercultural learning and teaches a course on Florence in Literature. She holds a Ph.D. in Comparative Literature from the University of California, Davis, and has been working in the field of international education for 15+ years.

Maraina Montgomery has worked for the past seven years to leverage social media, ecotherapy, spirituality, and mindfulness as tools for advancing Justice, Access, Inclusion, Diversity, and Equity (JAIDE) within the field of Education Abroad. Formerly the Program Manager for Study Abroad at Howard University, she currently serves as the Director for Study Abroad at the University of Portland. She holds a BA from Howard University and a MA. Ed from Rutgers University and her perspective can be read in publications by NAFSA, the Forum on Education Abroad, Diversity Abroad, and the PIE. Maraina is a Forum on Education Abroad and International Career Advancement (ICAP) Fellow.

Qimmah Najeeullah is an International Educator committed to diversifying the narrative and image of America abroad and lives in Malawi as the Peace Corps' Director of Programming & Training. She is an RPCV, an alumna of the Critical Language Scholarship and Fulbright Fellowships, and continues to serve on selection committees for U.S. Dept. of State fellowships. She is the former Director of International Education & Services at two Maryland universities and received a Masters from American University and is currently finishing a Ph.D. in International Education Policy at the University of Maryland, College Park.

Jane Nzomo is an international development expert and currently manages relationships for the Thomson Reuters Foundation in Sub-Saharan Africa. Jane previously worked at the Minnesota Studies in International Development in Kenya and the World Wide Fund for Nature. She was awarded the prestigious Al Balkcum Award for excellence in and commitment to serving students abroad. Jane holds a degree in Environmental Science from Kenyatta University and a Diploma in Project Management from Kenya Institute of Management.

Asabe Poloma is the Associate Provost for Global Engagement and Director of the Mellon Mays Undergraduate Fellowship at Brown University, where she is responsible for pioneering Brown's diversity and inclusion plan for internationalization. Before joining Brown, she held roles at Phillips Academy Andover and The Andrew W. Mellon Foundation. She has a bachelor's from Hampton University, master's from Old Dominion University, a master's from Columbia University, and a Ph.D. from the University of Massachusetts-Boston.

Lee A. Rivers is an Outreach and Recruitment Specialist for the Fulbright U.S. Student Program. Since 2008, Lee has worked at IIE promoting federally funded exchanges such as Gilman International Scholarship, Boren Awards, and the Fulbright Program. Lee studied in Australia as a Gilman Scholar and participated in a Fulbright-Hays Group Project Abroad in Tanzania. As an advocate for educational opportunities abroad, Lee is passionate about increasing access for historically excluded populations.

Malaika Marable Serrano is the VP for Diversity, Equity, and Inclusion at Guild and leads the integration of DEI principles and best practices across the organization. Living abroad in Latin America and Australia greatly shaped her ability to foster culturally responsive learning environments. Previous positions include Head of DEI at WorldStrides, study abroad administration, and service-learning teaching positions. Malaika holds a M.A. in higher education administration from the University of Maryland and is currently pursuing a Ph.D. at the Università Cattolica del Sacro Cuore.

Betty Jeanne Taylor, Ph.D., is an educational leader with over twenty years of experience in higher education as an administrator and instructor. She currently serves as assistant vice president in the Division of Diversity and Community Engagement at The University of Texas at Austin, where she is also a faculty member in the Department of Educational Leadership and Policy. She holds a Ph.D. in higher education administration from The University of Texas at Austin and received a B.S. in communication and an M.S. in higher education from Florida State University. Her research interests focus on inclusive climates and recruitment/retention of underrepresented faculty.

Bradley Titus is the Director of Institutional Relations, Diversity and Inclusion in the Learning Abroad Center at the University of Minnesota where he spends a portion of his time coordinating and implementing diversity trainings for the staff in Minnesota as well as staff abroad. He holds a Masters degree in Comparative and International Development Education with a focus in Identity Development. He has published works within NAFSA and the International Educator Magazine.

Christopher Van Velzer, Ph.D., has worked for more than two decades in higher education roles spanning university advancement, student affairs, and study away. He has spent the past 15 years directing study away programs in China for multiple institutions and study away providers. His deepest joy in work and research utilizes the dialogue between theory and practice to study, build, and develop programs that meaningfully embody and advance global learning outcomes. He currently serves as the Director of Global Education for Duke Kunshan University.

Devin Walker directs DDCE Global at The University of Texas at Austin where he facilitates education abroad experiences to Cape Town, South Africa, Dubai & Abu Dhabi in the UAE and Beijing, China. Each fall, Dr. Walker teaches a course to 500 first year students entitled, *Cultural Intelligence in a Global Economy*. His research interests include 1) the intersection of race and sport, 2) Cultural awareness and intelligence, and 3) African-American students and education abroad.

Dawn Michele Whitehead is the Vice President of the Office of Global Citizenship for Campus, Community, and Careers at the American Association of Colleges and Universities. Whitehead has written and presented nationally and internationally on global learning, community-based learning, and curricular change. Named an inaugural member of the Institute for International Education's National Academy for International Education, she serves on the board of The Forum on Education Abroad, having earned her Ph.D. from Indiana University, Bloomington.

David Wick is associate professor and program chair of international education management at the Middlebury Institute in Monterey, California. Previously, Wick led study abroad at Arkansas State, San Francisco State, and Santa Clara Universities. Dr. Wick teaches graduate courses in education and social justice, program design, assessment, and student development. Wick leads study abroad programs, facilitates professional workshops, and conducts research on international education equity and inclusion in the US and around the world.

Taylor Woodman is an Assistant Clinical Professor of International Education Policy in the College of Education and Assocaite Director for Faculty Global Engagement in the Office of International Affairs at the University of Maryland, College Park. He teaches and researches on academic mobility, academic diplomacy, technology in international education and, issues in international higher education. He holds a B.A. from Virginia Tech and a M.A. and Ph.D. from the University of Maryland, College Park.

Katherine Yngve is an anti-racist educational measurement professional, specializing in identifying & measuring the competencies and constructs (also known as "soft" skills) of intercultural, inclusive, multicultural and interpersonal excellence. In short, she teaches people how to teach people to be effective and appropriate across difference. A "recovering" Senior International Officer, she currently works in Purdue's office of Institutional Data Analytics and Assessment, supporting the provost's strategic initiatives entitled Transformative Education 2.0 and Equity and Belongingness.

Index